PROGRAMMING IN
C

PROGRAMMING IN

C

Revised Edition

Stephen G. Kochan

HAYDEN BOOKS

A Division of Macmillan Computer Publishing

11711 North College. Carmel. Indiana 46032 USA

International Standard Book Number: 0-672-48420-X
Library of Congress Catalog Card Number: 87-63480

Acquisitions Editor: *Jim Hill*
Cover Art: *Visual Graphic Services, Indianapolis*
Typesetting: *Stephen Kochan*

This entire text was edited and processed under UNIX. The text was formatted
using `troff`, with the assistance of `tbl` for the tables. The figures were
created with MacDraw on an Apple Macintosh and then merged with the
`troff` input. The `troff` output was converted to PostScript using `devps`.
The camera ready copy was printed on an Apple LaserWriter Plus, with no
pasteup required.

Printed in the United States of America

Trademark Acknowledgements

Hayden Books
C
Library

The C Library is an integrated series of books covering basic to advanced topics related to C programming. The books are written under the direction of Stephen G. Kochan and Patrick H. Wood, who worked for several years teaching introductory and advanced courses at Bell Laboratories, and who themselves have written many books on C programming and the UNIX system.

The first book in the series, *Programming in C*, teaches the fundamentals of C programming. All aspects of the language are covered in this text, and over 90 *complete* program examples are shown with their output.

Topics in C Programming takes up where *Programming in C* leaves off. In this advanced-level book you'll learn more about the subtleties of working with structures and pointers in C. The book also covers the functions provided in the Standard C and Standard I/O Libraries. Of special interest to UNIX programmers are the chapters on the UNIX System Interface Library and on the curses routines for writing terminal-independent programs. The make program is also covered in the text, and the book describes in detail how to debug programs using tools like lint, the preprocessor, ctrace, and sdb.

Advanced C: Tips and Techniques is an in-depth book on advanced C programming, with special emphasis on portability, execution efficiency, and application techniques. Among the things you'll learn about are: C's run-time environment, debugging techniques, fast array transfers, multidimensional arrays, and dynamic memory allocation. Practical examples are given to demonstrate these techniques.

Programming in ANSI C is for people who want to learn how to write programs in the new ANSI standard C. Using the same approach as *Programming in C*, the book covers all of the features of ANSI C. Over 90 program examples are presented with step-by-step explanations of all the procedures involved.

Reviews of *Programming in C*

"If you are in search of an answer about almost any aspect of C, you will find it in this book . . . the book truly is 'for the novice and experienced programmer alike' . . . can serve as an excellent reference on the C language as well as a tutorial for learning C."

— Dr. Dobb's Journal, Nov/84

"At last a book . . . that supplements . . . without bogging the reader down. Kochan's book is well sequenced . . . provides over 90 program examples, with clear explanations for each one."

— Academic Technology

" . . . he explains each element of C so clearly, and takes them up in such a well-considered sequence, that the reader learns programming simply from seeing C used as an example."

— Hardcopy, August/84

" . . . a pleasant contrast to many of the recent books on UNIX and C. The approach of teaching by example is undeniably immediate, rich, and effective. Kochan's code is followed by program output which reassures the reader that what is seen really works . . . a very impressive package. This is, simply, the BEST introduction to C published to date."

— UNIX Review, June/84

" . . . an excellent job of anticipating strange things that may happen to you and explains them before you're frustrated . . . taking enough space to make it readable but concise . . . in English . . . not syntax diagrams. The appendix on common programming mistakes . . . is one of those things that should be on the wall."

— Microcomputing, August/84

" . . . a straight-forward comprehensive tutorial guide to using the C language that meets the needs of both novice and experienced programmers . . . provides excellent teaching tools while guiding the reader through the finer points of the language. The exercises are unusually well-designed . . . highly recommended for anyone learning C on their own . . . a comfortable book for people new to programming . . . a comprehensive and clear tutorial . . . an excellent book for the reader who wants to learn C to write application programs . . . the combination of Kochan's clear, easy writing style and well-designed examples made this one my choice for a primary reference."

— UNIX World, Feb/86

C O N T E N T S

٠ Acknowledgements ٠

I wish to thank the following people for their help in the preparation of this book: Doug McCormick and Maureen Connelly of Hayden Book Company, Jim Scharf, Henry Tabickman, and, above all, Ken Brown. Ken and I spent many hours discussing various approaches and ideas, and he was also kind enough to edit the entire text. For this I am sincerely grateful.

I also wish to thank Henry Mullish of New York University for teaching me so much about writing and for getting me started in the publishing business.

Undertaking a project such as this places an equal if not greater burden on the people closest to you. My wife, Leela, provided her patience and understanding. But above all she provided her love.

P R E F A C E

to the Revised Edition

When considering writing a revised edition of *Programming in C*, I was faced with the dilemma of how to deal with ANSI C. One choice was to try to teach ANSI C and the "older" C in the same text. Another was to leave the basic text alone and include some reference material about ANSI C in an appendix. I decided on the second approach. Because there are some significant differences between "old" C and ANSI C (most notably function *prototypes*), I thought that trying to teach both in a tutorial text would be confusing. The correct way to teach ANSI C from the "ground up" is with a separate text. Therefore, expect to see *Programming in ANSI C* in the near future. In the mean-time, the appendix on ANSI C (Appendix B) will give you a good overview of the features of ANSI C.

Besides the new appendix, most of the changes to the second edition are cosmetic. I typed and formatted the original manuscript for the first edition on my TRS-80 computer. The program examples and output that I submitted to the publisher were (to my dismay) cut out and pasted into the final book. This time around, I had full control over the production end. So you'll find that program examples are intelligently split across pages when necessary and that they're clearer and easier to read.

The figures have all been redone, and some additional ones were added to help clarify some complex issues. I softened my feelings about the `break` and-`continue` statements and the descriptions for them are no longer relegated to the back of the book. Other changes made include beefed up discussions on command line arguments and on dynamic memory allocation.

I would like to thank Dick Fritz for suggesting changes for this revised edition and also the many kind people who have offered thier unsolicited compliments on the first edition. From SAMS, I'd like to thank Jim Hill, Jennifer Ackley, Wendy Ford, and Frank Speights for their professionalism and support.

This revised edition is also dedicated to the memory of Maureen Connelly, my former production editor from Hayden Book Company. Maureen contributed so much to all of the books in the Hayden Books UNIX System Library. Not only did she care about her work, but she also cared about the people she worked with. She was a great person and I will miss her.

STEPHEN G. KOCHAN

To my mother

Introduction

The "C" programming language evolved from a succession of programming languages developed at Bell Laboratories in the early 1970s. It was not until the late 1970s, however, that this programming language began to gain widespread popularity and support. This was because until that time C compilers were not readily available for commercial use outside of Bell Laboratories. Furthermore, C's growth in popularity has been spurred on in part by the equal, if not faster, growth in popularity of the UNIX operating system. This operating system, which was also developed at Bell Labortatories, has C as its "standard" programming language. In fact, well over 90% of the operating system itself is written in the C language!

C is a so-called "higher-level language," yet it provides capabilities that enable the user to "get in close" with the hardware and deal with the computer on a much lower level. This is because, while the C language is a general-purpose structured programming language, it was designed with systems programming applications in mind and, as such, provides the user with an enormous amount of power and flexibility. In fact, programming applications exist that could be easily handled by the C language but that would be difficult, if not impossible, to develop in other languages, such as Pascal, FORTRAN, or BASIC.

This book proposes to teach you how to program in C. It assumes no previous exposure to the language whatsoever and was designed to appeal to both the novice and experienced programmer alike. If you have previous programming experience, you will find that C has a unique way of doing things that will probably differ significantly from any language you have used. Even if you are coming from a Pascal background—a language that C superficially resembles—you will quickly discover that there are many features that are unique to this language, such as pointers, character strings, and bit operations.

Every feature of the C language is treated in this text. As each new feature is presented, a small *complete* program example is usually provided to illustrate the feature. This reflects the overriding philosophy that has been used in writing this book: to teach by example. Just as a picture is worth a thousand words, so is a properly chosen program example. If you have access to a computer facility that supports the C programming language, then you are strongly encouraged to enter and run each program that is presented in this book, and to compare the results obtained on your system to those shown in the text. By doing so, not only will you learn the language and its syntax, but you will also become familiar with the process of typing in, compiling, and running C programs.

The style that is used for teaching the C language is one of posing a particular problem for solution on a computer and then proceeding to develop a program in C to solve the problem. In this manner, new language constructs are introduced as they are needed to solve a particular problem.

You will find that program readability has been stressed throughout the book. This is because I strongly believe that programs should be written so that they may be easily read—either by the author himself or by somebody else. Through experience and common sense, you will find that such programs are almost always easier to write, debug, and modify. Furthermore, developing programs that are readable is a natural result of a true adherence to a structured programming discipline.

Because this book was written as a tutorial, the material covered in each chapter is based on previously presented material. Therefore, maximum benefit will be derived from this book by reading each chapter in succession, and you are highly discouraged from "skipping around." You should also work through the exercises that are presented at the end of each chapter before proceeding on to the next chapter.

Chapter 2, which covers some fundamental terminology about higher-level programming languages and the process of compiling programs, has been included to make sure that we are speaking the same language throughout the remainder of the text. From Chapter 3 on, you will be slowly introduced to the C language. By the time Chapter 16 rolls around, all of the essential features of the language will have been covered. Chapter 16 goes into more depth about I/O operations in C. Finally, Chapter 17 includes those features of the language that are of a more advanced or esoteric nature.

Appendix A provides a summary of the syntax of the language, among other things, and is provided for reference purposes. Appendix B summarizes the major differences between the C language described in this text and the American National Standards Institute (ANSI) version of C. In Appendix C you'll find a list of the common programming mistakes. A comprehensive index is also provided so that you may quickly find explanations and program examples of particular C language features.

This book makes no assumptions about a particular computer system or operating system on which the C language is implemented. However, some special attention is given to using C under UNIX. The text describes how to compile and execute programs under UNIX, and Appendixes D through F provide a summary of many of the UNIX library routines, a description of the cc command, and an overview of the lint program. The library routines described in Appendix D are available on most non-UNIX systems as well.

Once you have mastered the material presented in this book, you may wish to continue your studies with *Topics in C Programming* (Kochan & Wood, Hayden Books, 1987). In that book you will find more detailed coverage of pointers and structures, and in-depth details on how to use the various C libraries. Other chapters in the book describe how to write terminal-independent programs with the UNIX system's `curses` package, how to use the `make` facility, and how to debug C programs. Admittedly, the book is slightly UNIX-oriented, but non-UNIX users should still find much of the material useful.

2

Some Fundamentals

This chapter describes some fundamental terms that you must understand before you can learn how to program in C. A general overview of the nature of programming in a higher-level language is provided, as is a discussion of the process of compiling a program developed in such a language.

◆ Programming ◆

Computers are really very dumb machines indeed, since they do only what they are told to do. Most computer systems perform their operations on a very primitive level. For example, most computers know how to add 1 to a number, or how to test if a number is equal to zero or not. The sophistication of these basic operations usually does not go much further than that. The basic operations of a computer system form what is known as the computer's *instruction set*. Some computers have very limited instruction sets. For example, the DEC PDP-8 computer has a very limited instruction set, while the DEC VAX machines contain instruction sets consisting of hundreds of basic operations.

In order to solve a problem using a computer, we must express the solution to the problem in terms of the instructions of the particular computer. A computer *program* is actually just a collection of the instructions necessary to solve a specific problem. The approach or method that is used to solve the problem is known as an *algorithm*. For example, if we wish to develop a program that tests if a number is odd or even, then the set of statements which solves the problem becomes the program. The method that is used to test if the number is even or odd is the algorithm. Normally, to develop a program to solve a particular problem, we first express the solution to the problem in terms of an algorithm and then develop a program which implements that algorithm. So the algorithm for solving the even/odd problem might be expressed as follows: "First divide the number by two. If the remainder of the division is zero, then the number is even; otherwise, the number is odd." With the algorithm in hand, we can then proceed

4

to write the instructions necessary to implement the algorithm on a particular computer system. These instructions would be expressed in the statements of a particular computer language, such as BASIC, Pascal, or C.

♦ Higher-Level Languages ♦

When computers were first developed, the only way they could be programmed was in terms of binary numbers which corresponded directly to specific machine instructions and locations in the computer's memory. The next technological software advance occurred in the development of *assembly languages*, which enabled the programmer to work with the machine on a slightly higher level. Instead of having to specify sequences of binary numbers to carry out particular tasks, the assembly language permits the programmer to use symbolic names to perform various operations and to refer to specific memory locations. A special program, known as an *assembler*, translates the assembly language program from its symbolic format into the specific machine instructions of the computer system.

Because there still exists a one-to-one correspondence between each assembly language statement and a specific machine instruction, assembly languages are regarded as low-level languages. The programmer must still learn the instruction set of the particular computer system in order to write a program in assembly language, and the resulting program is not *portable*; that is, the program will not run on a different computer model without being rewritten. This is because different computer systems have different instruction sets, and since assembly language programs are written in terms of these instructions sets, they are machine dependent.

Then, along came the so-called higher-level languages, of which the FORTRAN language was one of the first. Programmers developing programs in FORTRAN no longer had to concern themselves with the architecture of the particular computer, and operations performed in FORTRAN were of a much more sophisticated or "higher level," far removed from the instruction set of the particular machine. One FORTRAN instruction or *statement* would result in many different machine instructions being executed, unlike the one-to-one correspondence found between assembly language statements and machine instructions.

Standardization of the syntax of a higher-level language meant that a program could be written in the language to be machine independent. That is, a program could be run on any machine that supported the language with little or no changes.

In order to support a higher-level language, a special computer program must be developed that translates the statements of the program developed in the higher-level language into a form that the computer can understand—in other words, into the particular instructions of the computer. Such a program is known as a *compiler*.

◆ Operating Systems ◆

Before we proceed with our discussion of compilers, it is worthwhile discussing the role that is played by a computer program known as an *operating system*.

An operating system is a program that controls the entire operation of a computer system. All I/O operations that are performed on a computer system are channeled through the operating system. The operating system must also manage the computer system's resources, and must handle the execution of programs.

One of the most popular operating systems today is the UNIX operating system, which was developed at Bell Laboratories. UNIX is a rather unique operating system in that it can be found on many different types of computer systems. Historically, operating systems were typically associated with only one type of computer system. But because UNIX is written primarily in the C language and makes very few assumptions about the architecture of the computer, it has been successfully ported to many different computer systems with a relatively small amount of effort.

Miscrosoft's MS-DOS is another example of a popular operating system. That system is found primarily on the IBM-PC computer and its look-alikes.

◆ Compiling Programs ◆

A compiler is a software program that is in principle no different from the ones you will be seeing in this book, although it is certainly much more complex. A compiler analyzes a program developed in a particular computer language and then translates it into a form which is suitable for execution on your particular computer system.

Figure 2-1 shows the steps that are involved in entering, compiling, and executing a computer program developed in the C programming language.

The program that is to be compiled is first typed into a *file* on the computer system. Computer installations have various conventions that are used for naming files, but in general, the choice of the name is up to you. Under UNIX, C programs can be given any name provided the last two characters are '.c'. So the name `prog1.c` would be a valid file name for a C program running under UNIX.

In order to enter the C program into a file, the use of a text editor is usually required. `ed` and `vi` are two popular text editors used under UNIX. In order to be able to try the programs presented in this book, you will first have to learn how to use such an editor. Check with someone at your installation for getting help and the appropriate documentation for using the locally available text editor.

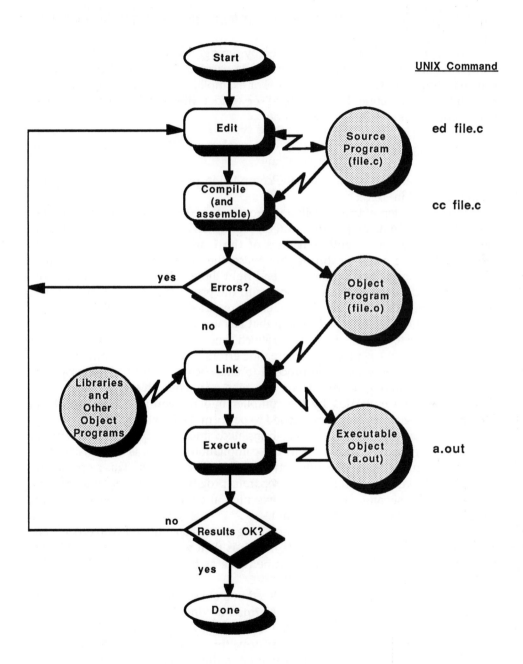

UNIX Command

Start

Edit   Source
                        Program   ed file.c
                        (file.c)

Compile
(and
assemble)   cc file.c

yes   Errors?   Object
                        Program
no   (file.o)

Link   Executable
Libraries   Object   a.out
and   (a.out)
Other
Object
Programs

Execute

no   Results OK?

yes

Done

Fig. 2-1. Entering, compiling, and executing C programs under UNIX

The program that is entered into the file is known as the *source program*, since it represents the original form of the program expressed in the C language. Once the source program has been entered into a file, we can then proceed to have it compiled.

The compilation process is initiated by typing in a special command on the system. When this command is entered, the name of the file that contains the source program must also be specified. For example, under UNIX, the command to initiate program compilation is called cc (under MS-DOS, Microsoft's C compiler command is msc). Typing the line

```
cc prog1.c
```

would have the effect of initiating the compilation process with the source program contained in prog1.c.

In the first step of the compilation process, the compiler examines each program statement contained in the source program and checks it to ensure that it conforms to the syntax and semantics of the language. If any mistakes are discovered by the compiler during this phase, then they will be reported to the user and the compilation process will end right there. The errors will then have to be corrected in the source program (with the use of the text editor), and the compilation process restarted. Typical errors reported during this phase of compilation might be due to an expression that has unbalanced parentheses (syntactic error) or due to the use of a variable which is not "defined" (semantic error).

When all of the syntactic and semantic errors have been removed from the program, the compiler will then proceed to take each statement of the program and translate it into a "lower" form. On most machines, this means that each statement will be translated by the compiler into the equivalent statement or statements in assembly language needed to perform the identical task.

After the program has been translated into an equivalent assembly language program, the next step in the compilation process is to translate the assembly language statements into actual machine instructions. This step may or may not involve the execution of a separate program known as an *assembler*. Under UNIX, a separate assembler is executed automatically whenever the cc command is used to compile a program.

The assembler takes each assembly language statement and converts it into a binary format known as *object code*, which is then written into another file on the system. This file will have the same name as the source file under UNIX, with the last letter an 'o' instead of a 'c'.

After the program has been translated into object code, it is then ready to be *linked*. This process is once again performed automatically whenever the cc command is issued under UNIX. Other operating systems may require issuance of another command needed to perform this task (e.g., under MS-DOS, Microsoft's C compiler requires that you issue the link command). The purpose of the linking phase is to get the program into a final form for execution on the computer. If the program uses other programs that were previously processed by the compiler, then during this phase the programs are "linked" together. Programs that are used from the system's program "library" are also searched and linked together with the object program during this phase.

The final linked file, which is in an *executable object* code format, is stored in another file on the system, ready to be run or *executed*. Under UNIX, this file is called a.out by default (under MS-DOS, the executable file usually has the same name as the source file, with the c extension replaced by an exe extension). To subsequently execute the program, all that we have to do is to type in the name of the executable object file. So the command

```
a.out
```

would have the effect of *loading* the program called a.out into the computer's memory and initiating its execution.

When the program is executed, each of the statements of the program is sequentially executed in turn. If the program requests any data from the user, known as *input*, the program will temporarily suspend its execution so that the input may be entered. Results that are displayed by the program, known as *output*, will normally appear at the terminal from which the program was executed.

If all goes well (and it probably won't the first time the program is executed), the program will perform its intended functions. If the program does not produce the desired results, then it will be necessary to go back and reanalyze the program's logic. This is known as the *debugging phase*, during which an attempt is made to remove all of the known problems or *bugs* from the program. In order to do so, it will most likely be necessary to make changes to the original source program. In that case, the entire process of compiling, linking, and executing the program must be repeated until the desired results are obtained.

Before leaving this discussion of the compilation process, we should point out that there is another method used for analyzing and executing programs developed in a higher-level language. With this method, programs are not compiled but are *interpreted*. An interpreter analyzes and executes the statements of a program at the same time. The BASIC programming language is the primary example of a language in which programs are interpreted and not compiled.

Several vendors are currently marketing interpreters for the C programming language, with the relative merits of this approach as cited above.

Writing a Program in C

In this chapter you will be introduced to the C language so that you can get a feeling as to what programming in C is all about. But what better way to gain an appreciation for this language than by taking a look at an actual program written in C?

To begin with, let's pick a rather simple example—a program that displays the phrase "Programming is fun." at the terminal. Without further ado, then, here is a C program to accomplish this task.

Program 3-1

```
main ()
{
      printf ("Programming is fun.\n");
}
```

In the C programming language, lowercase and uppercase letters are distinct. In most other programming languages, such as FORTRAN, COBOL, PL/I or BASIC, uppercase letters are used exclusively. If you are used to programming in any of these languages, the use of lowercase letters may take some getting used to.

Also, unlike many other programming languages, C does not particularly care where on the line you begin typing. Some languages, such as FORTRAN and COBOL, are very fussy about such things, but in C you may begin typing your statement at any position on the line. This fact can be used to advantage in developing programs that are easier to read.

Returning to our first C program, if we were to type this program into the computer, issue the proper commands to the system to have it compiled, and then execute it, we could expect the following results or output to appear at the terminal (minus the "Program 3-1 Output," of course):

Program 3-1 Output

```
Programming is fun.
```

Let's take a closer look at our first program. The first line of the program informs the system that the name of the program is `main`. `main` is a special name used by the C system that indicates precisely *where* the program is to begin execution.

The open and closed parentheses immediately following `main` specify that no "arguments" or parameters are expected by this routine. (This concept will be explained in more detail in Chapter 8 when we discuss functions.)

Now that we have told the system that the name of our program is `main`, we are ready to specify precisely what function this routine is to perform. This is done by enclosing all program statements of the routine within a pair of braces. (For those readers who are familiar with the Pascal programming language, the braces in C are somewhat analagous to the `BEGIN` and `END` block declarators of that language). All program statements included between the braces will be taken as part of the `main` routine by the system. In Program 3-1, we have only one such statement. This statement specifies that a routine named `printf` is to be invoked or *called*. The parameter or *argument* to be passed or handed to the `printf` routine is the string of characters

```
"Programming is fun.\n"
```

The `printf` routine is a function in the C system that simply prints or displays its argument (or arguments as you will see shortly) at the terminal or on the video screen. The last two characters in the string, namely the backslash (\) and the letter n, are known collectively as the *newline* character. A newline character tells the C system to do precisely what its name implies—that is, go to a new line. Any characters to be printed after the newline character will then appear on the next line of the terminal or display. In fact, the newline character is really very similar in concept to the carriage return key on a typewriter.

All program statements in C *must* be terminated by a semicolon. This is the reason for the semicolon that appears immediately following the closed parenthesis of the `printf` call.

Now that we have finished discussing our first program, why don't we modify it to also display the phrase "And programming in C is even more fun." This can be done by the simple addition of another call to the `printf` routine, as shown below. Remember that each and every C program statement must be terminated by a semicolon.

Program 3-2

```
main ()
{
    printf ("Programming is fun.\n");
    printf ("And programming in C is even more fun.\n");
}
```

If we type in Program 3-2 and then compile and execute it, we can expect the following output at our terminal.

Program 3-2 Output

```
Programming is fun.
And programming in C is even more fun.
```

As you will see from the next program example, it is not necessary to make a separate call to the printf routine for each line of output. Study the program listed below and try to predict the results before examining the output (no cheating now!).

Program 3-3

```
main ()
{
    printf ("Testing...\n..1\n...2\n....3\n");
}
```

Program 3-3 Output

```
Testing...
..1
...2
....3
```

The printf routine is the most commonly used routine in this book. This is because it provides an easy and convenient means to display program results. Not only can simple phrases be displayed, but the values of *variables* and the results of computations as well. In fact, the next program uses the printf routine to display the results of adding two numbers, namely 50 and 25.

Program 3-4

```
main ()
{
    int sum;

    sum = 50 + 25;
    printf ("The sum of 50 and 25 is %d\n", sum);
}
```

Program 3-4 Output

```
The sum of 50 and 25 is 75
```

A bit of explanation is in order with respect to the above program. The first C program statement *declares* the *variable* sum to be of type *integer*. C, like Pascal—and unlike FORTRAN or BASIC—requires that *all* program variables be declared before they are used in a program. The declaration of a variable specifies to the C compiler how a particular variable will be used by the program. This information is needed by the compiler in order to generate the correct instructions to store and retrieve values into and out of the variable. A variable declared as type *int* can only be used to hold integral values; that is, values without decimal places. Examples of integral values are 3, 5, -20, and 0. Numbers with decimal places, such as 3.14, 2.455, and 27.0, for example, are known as *floating point* numbers.

The integer variable sum will be used to store the result of the addition of the two integers 50 and 25. We have intentionally left a blank line following the declaration of this variable. This is done to visually separate the variable declarations of the routine from the program statements, and is strictly a matter of style. Sometimes the addition of a single blank line in a program can help to make the program more readable.

The program statement

```
sum = 50 + 25;
```

reads as it would in most other programming languages: the number 50 is added (as indicated by the plus sign) to the number 25 and the result is stored (as indicated by the *assignment operator*, the equals sign) into the variable sum.

The printf routine call in Program 3-4 now has two items or *arguments* enclosed within the parentheses. These arguments are separated by a comma. The first argument to the printf routine is always the character string to be displayed. However, along with the display of the character string, we may frequently wish to have the value of certain program variables displayed as well. In our case, we would like to have the value of the variable sum displayed at the terminal after the characters

```
The sum of 50 and 25 is
```

are displayed. The percent character inside the first argument is a special character recognized by the `printf` function. The character that immediately follows
the percent sign specifies what *type* of value is to be displayed at that point. In
the above program, the letter "d" is recognized by the system as signifying that
an integer value is to be displayed.

Whenever the `printf` routine finds the `%d` characters inside a character
string, it will automatically display the value of the next argument to the
`printf` routine. Since `sum` is the next argument to `printf`, its value is
automatically displayed after the characters "The sum of 50 and 25 is" are
displayed.

Now try to predict the output from the following program.

Program 3-5

```
main ()
{
    int   value1, value2, sum;

    value1 = 50;
    value2 = 25;
    sum = value1 + value2;
    printf ("The sum of %d and %d is %d\n", value1, value2, sum);
}
```

Program 3-5 Output

```
The sum of 50 and 25 is 75
```

The first program statement declares three variables called `value1`,
`value2,` and `sum` all to be of type `int`. This statement could have equivalently
been expressed using three separate declaratory statements as follows:

```
        int value1;
        int value2;
        int sum;
```

After the three variables have been declared, the program assigns the value
50 to the variable `value1` and then the value 25 to `value2`. The sum of these
two variables is then computed and the result assigned to the variable `sum`.

The call to the `printf` routine now contains four arguments. Once again,
the first argument, commonly called the *format string*, describes to the system
how the remaining arguments are to be displayed. The value of `value1` is to be
displayed immediately following the display of the characters "The sum of " are

displayed. Similarly, the values of value2 and sum are to be printed at the appropriate points as indicated by the next two occurrences of the %d characters in the format string.

The last program in this chapter introduces the concept of the *comment*. A comment statement is used in a program to document a program and to enhance its readability. As you will see from the following example, comments serve to tell the reader of the program—be it the programmer himself or someone else whose responsibility it is to maintain the program—just what the programmer had in mind when he or she wrote a particular program or a particular sequence of statements.

Program 3-6

```
/* This program adds two integer values and displays
   the results                                        */

main ()
{
    /* Declare variables */
    int  value1, value2, sum;

    /* Assign values and compute the result */
    value1 = 50;
    value2 = 25;
    sum = value1 + value2;

    /* Display the result */
    printf ("The sum of %d and %d is %d\n", value1, value2, sum);
}
```

Program 3-6 Output

```
    The sum of 50 and 25 is 75
```

A comment statement is initiated by the two characters / and *. These two characters must be written without any intervening spaces. To end a comment statement, the characters * and / are used, once again without any embedded spaces. All characters included between the opening /* and the closing */ are treated as part of the comment statement and are ignored by the C system. In Program 3-6, four separate comment statements were used. This program is otherwise identical to Program 3-5. Admittedly, this is a contrived example, since only the first comment at the head of the program is useful. (Yes, it is possible to insert so many comments into a program that the readability of the program is actually degraded instead of improved!)

The intelligent use of comment statements inside a program cannot be overemphasized. Many times a programmer will return to a program that he coded perhaps only six months ago, only to discover to his dismay that he can not for the life of him remember the purpose of a particular routine or of a particular group of statements. A simple comment statement judiciously inserted at that particular point in the program might have saved a significant amount of time otherwise wasted on rethinking the logic of the particular routine or set of statements.

It is a good idea to get into the habit of inserting comment statements into the program as the program is being written or typed into the computer. There are three good reasons for this. First, it is far easier to document the program while the particular program logic is still fresh in one's mind than it is to go back and rethink the logic after the program has been completed. Second, by inserting comments into the program at such an early stage of the game, the programmer gets to reap the benefits of the comments during the debug phase, when program logic errors are being isolated and debugged. A comment can not only help the programmer read through the program, but it can also help to point the way to the source of the logic mistake. Finally, it has yet to be my experience to discover a programmer who actually enjoyed documenting a program. In fact, once you have finished debugging your program, you will probably not relish the idea of going back to the program to insert comments. Inserting comments while developing the program will make this sometimes tedious task a bit easier to swallow.

This discussion concludes this introductory chapter on developing programs in C. By now you should have a good feel as to what is involved in writing a program in C and you should be able to develop a small program on your own. In the next chapter, we will begin to examine some of the finer intricacies of this wonderfully powerful and flexible programming language. But first, try your hand at the exercises which follow to make sure that you understand the concepts presented in this chapter.

♦ Exercises ♦

1. If you have access to a computer facility that supports the C programming language, type in and run the six programs presented in this chapter. Compare the output produced by each program with the output presented after each program.

2. Write a program which prints the following text at the terminal.
   1. In C, lowercase letters are significant.
   2. main is where program execution begins.
   3. Open and closed braces enclose program statements in a routine.
   4. All program statements must be terminated by a semicolon.

3. What output would you expect from the following program?

```
main ()
{
    printf ("Testing...");
    printf ("....1");
    printf ("...2");
    printf ("..3");
    printf ("\n");
}
```

4. Write a program which subtracts the value 15 from 87 and displays the result, together with an appropriate message, at the terminal.

5. Identify five syntactic errors in the following program. Then type in and run the corrected program to make sure that you have correctly identified all of the mistakes.

```
main ()
(
    INT   sum;

    /* COMPUTE RESULT
    sum = 25 + 37 - 19

    /* DISPLAY RESULTS */
    printf ("The answer is %d\n" sum);
}
```

6. What output might you expect from the following program?

```
main ()
{
    int answer, result;

    answer = 100;
    result = answer - 10;
    printf ("The result is %d\n", result + 5);
}
```

4

Variables, Data Types, and Arithmetic Expressions

In this chapter, we will discuss the formation of variable names and constants, take a look at the basic data types, and describe some fundamental rules for forming arithmetic expressions in C.

◆ Variables ◆

Early computer programmers had the onerous task of having to write their programs in the binary language of the machine they were programming. This meant that computer instructions had to be hand-encoded into binary numbers by the programmer before they could be entered into the machine. Furthermore, the programmer had to explicitly assign and reference any storage locations inside the computer's memory by a specific number or memory address.

Modern day programming languages allow the programmer to concentrate more on solving the particular problem at hand than on worrying about specific machine codes or memory locations. They enable us to assign symbolic names, known as *variable names*, for storing program computations and results. A variable name can be chosen by the programmer in a meaningful way so as to reflect the type of value that is to be stored in that variable.

In Chapter 3, we used several variables to store integer values. For example, we used the variable sum in Program 3-4 to store the result of the addition of the two integers 50 and 25.

The C language allows data types other than just integers to be stored in variables as well, provided the proper declaration for the variable is made *before* it is used in the program. Variables can be used to store floating point numbers, characters, and even *pointers* to locations inside the computer's memory.

The rules for forming variable names are quite simple: they must begin with a letter or underscore (_), and may be followed by any combination of letters (upper- or lowercase), underscores, or the digits 0-9. The following is a list of valid variable names.

```
sum
piece_flag
i
J5x7
Number_of_moves
_sysflag
```

On the other hand, the following variable names are not valid:

```
sum$value
piece flag
3Spencer
int
```

The name `sum$value` is not valid because the dollar sign is not a valid variable name character. In the second case, embedded blank spaces are not permitted. The name `3Spencer` is not valid since the name does not begin with a letter or underscore. Finally, `int` cannot be used as a variable name since its use has a special meaning to the C compiler. This use is known as a *reserved name*. In general, any name that has special significance to the C compiler cannot be used as a variable name. Appendix A provides a complete list of such reserved names.

You should always remember that upper- and lowercase letters are distinct in C. Therefore, the variable names `sum`, `Sum`, and `SUM` each refer to a different variable.

While there is no real restriction on the total number of characters that can be used in a variable name, on some systems only the first eight characters are significant. This means, for example, that the two variables `category1` and `category2` would not be distinguishable on such a system since the first eight characters are the same. With the DEC VAX-11 VMS compiler, variable name length rarely becomes a problem, as this compiler distinguishes names up to 31 characters long. As of UNIX System V Release 2, variable names can be as long as desired.

When deciding on the choice of a variable name, keep one recommendation in mind—don't be lazy. Pick names that reflect the intended use of the variable. The reasons are obvious. Just as with the comment statement, meaningful variable names can dramatically increase the readability of a program and will pay off in the debug and documentation phases. In fact, the documentation task will probably be greatly reduced since the program will be more self-explanatory. Just remember the point discussed above: only the first eight characters may be significant on your system. So, for example, if you have two variables, one which you would like to call `average_temperature`, and another which you would like to call `average_time`, then you might have to change the variable names to something else like `avg_temperature` and `avg_time` or `temperature_average` and `time_average` to avoid the eight-character name conflict.

◆ Data Types and Constants ◆

You have already been exposed to the C basic data type `int`. As you will recall, a variable declared to be of type `int` can be used to contain integral values only—that is, values that do not contain decimal places.

The C programming language provides the user with three other basic data types: `float`, `double`, and `char`. A variable declared to be of type `float` can be used for storing floating point numbers (values containing decimal places). The `double` type is the same as type `float` only with roughly twice the accuracy. Finally, the `char` data type can be used to store a single character, such as the letter 'a', the digit character '6', or a semicolon; more on this later.

In C, any literal number, single character, or character string is known as a *constant*. For example, the number 58 represents a constant integer value. The character string `"Programming in C is fun.\n"` is an example of a constant character string. Expressions consisting entirely of constant values are called *constant expressions*. So the expression

```
128 + 7 - 17
```

is a constant expression because each of the terms of the expression is a constant value. But if `i` were declared to be an integer variable, then the expression

```
128 + 7 - i
```

would not represent a constant expression.

It is important to understand the concept of constants in order to fully understand data types and operations in C.

Type `int`

In C, an integer constant consists of a sequence of one or more digits. A minus sign preceding the sequence indicates that the value is negative. The values 158, -10, and 0 are all valid examples of integer constants. No embedded spaces are permitted between the digits, and values larger than 999 cannot be expressed using commas. (So the value 12,000 is not a valid integer constant, and must be written as 12000.)

There are two special formats in C that enable integer constants to be expressed in a base other than decimal (base 10). If the first digit of the integer value is a zero, then the integer is taken as expressed in *octal* notation, that is in base 8. In that case, the remaining digits of the value must be valid base-8 digits and therefore must be from 0 through 7. So, for example, to express the value octal 50 in C, the notation 050 is used. Similarly, the C octal constant 0177 represents the decimal value 127 (1 x 64 + 7 x 8 + 7). An integer value can be displayed at the terminal in octal notation by using the format characters %o in the format string of a printf statement. In such a case, it is noted that the value will be displayed in octal *without* a leading zero.

If an integer constant is preceded by a 0 and the letter x (either lowercase or uppercase), then the value is taken as being expressed in hexadecimal (base 16) notation. Immediately following the letter x are the digits of the hexadecimal value, which can be composed of the digits 0 through 9 and the letters a through f (or A through F). The letters represent the values 10 through 15, respectively. So, to assign the hexadecimal value 5EB (= 16^2 x 5 + 16 x 14 + 11 = 1,515 decimal) to an integer variable called type_mask, the statement

```
type_mask = 0x5EB;
```

can be used. To display an integer value in hexadecimal format at the terminal, use the format characters %x. So the statement

```
printf ("Value = %x\n", type_mask);
```

would display the value of type_mask in hexadecimal format, *without* the leading 0x.

Octal and hexadecimal constants frequently find their way into systems programs and more advanced programming applications. As such, this notation will not be used again until much later in this book.

Type float

A variable declared to be of type float can be used for storing values containing decimal places. A floating point constant is distinguished by the presence of a decimal point. It is permissible to omit digits before the decimal point, or digits after the decimal point, but obviously not permissible to omit both. The values 3., 125.8, and -.0001 are all valid examples of floating point constants. To display a floating point value at the terminal, the printf conversion characters %f are used.

Floating point constants can also be expressed in so-called *scientific notation*. The value 1.7e4 is a floating point value expressed in this notation, and represents the value 1.7 x 10^4. The value before the letter e, is known as the *mantissa*, while the value that follows is called the *exponent*. This exponent, which may be preceded by an optional plus or minus sign, represents the power of 10 that the mantissa is to be multiplied by. So, in the constant 2.25e-3, the 2.25 is the value of the mantissa and -3 is the value of the exponent. This constant represents the value 2.25 x 10^{-3} or 0.00225. Incidentally, the letter e which separates the mantissa from the exponent can be written in either lower or uppercase.

In order to display a value in scientific notation, the format characters `%e` should be specified in the `printf` format string.

Type `double`

The type `double` is very similar to type `float`. It is used whenever the accuracy provided by a `float` variable is not sufficient. Variables declared to be of type `double` can store roughly twice as many significant digits as can a variable of type `float`. The precise number of digits that can be stored in either a `float` or `double` variable depends upon the particular computer system you are using. On the DEC VAX machines, a `float` variable can contain approximately seven decimal digits, while a variable of type `double` has a precision of approximately 16 decimal digits.

There is no special distinction made between a constant of type `float` or one of type `double`. In fact, *all* floating point constants are taken as `double` values by the C compiler. To display a `double` value at the terminal, the format characters `%f` or `%e`, which are the same format characters used to display a `float` value, can be used.

Type `char`

A `char` variable can be used to store a single character. A character constant is formed by enclosing the character within a pair of *single* quote marks. So `'a'`, `';'`, and `'0'` are all valid examples of character constants. The first constant represents the letter a, the second a semicolon, and the third the *character* zero—which is not the same as the *number* zero. Do not confuse a character constant, which is a single character enclosed in single quotes, with a character string, which is any number of characters enclosed in *double* quotes. We will learn more about this distinction in the chapter on character strings.

The character constant `'\n'`—the newline character—is a valid character constant even though it seems to contradict the rule cited above. The reason for this is that the backslash character is a special character in the C system and does not actually count as a character. In other words, the C compiler treats the character `'\n'` as a single character, even though it is actually formed by two characters. In Chapter 10, you will find that the backslash character can be used for purposes other than just for advancing to the next line.

The format characters `%c` can be used in a `printf` call to display the value of a `char` variable at the terminal.

In Program 4-1 that follows, the basic C data types are used. Notice how a value can be assigned to a variable at the time that the variable is declared.

Program 4-1

```
main ()
{
    int     integer_var = 100;
    float   floating_var = 331.79;
    double  double_var =  8.44e+11;
    char    char_var = 'W';

    printf ("integer_var = %d\n", integer_var);
    printf ("floating_var = %f\n", floating_var);
    printf ("double_var = %e\n", double_var);
    printf ("char_var = %c\n", char_var);
}
```

Program 4-1 Output

```
integer_var = 100
floating_var = 331.789978
double_var = 8.440000E+11
char_var = W
```

The first statement of Program 4-1 declares the variable `integer_var` to be an integer variable and also assigns to it an initial value of 100, as if the following two statements had been used instead:

```
int  integer_var;
integer_var = 100;
```

In the second line of the program's output, you will notice that the value of 331.79 that we assigned to `floating_var` is actually displayed as 331.789978. In fact, the actual value that is displayed is quite dependent on the particular computer system you are using. (The reason for this inaccuracy is due to the particular way that numbers are internally represented inside the computer system. You have probably come across the same type of inaccuracy when dealing with numbers on your pocket calculator. If you divide 1 by 3 on your calculator, you will get the result .33333333—with perhaps some additional 3s tacked on at the end. The string of 3s is the calculator's approximation to one-third. Theoretically, there should be an infinite number of threes. But the calculator can only hold so many digits, thus the inherent inaccuracy of the machine. The same type of inaccuracy applies to your computer system. Certain floating point values cannot be exactly represented inside the computer's memory.)

When displaying the values of `float` or `double` variables, you have the choice of two different formats. The `%f` characters are used to display values in a standard manner. Unless told otherwise, `printf` will always display a `float` or `double` value to six decimal places. We will see later in this chapter how to select the number of decimal places that are displayed.

The `%e` characters are used to display the value of a `float` or `double` variable in scientific notation. Once again, six decimal places are automatically displayed by the system.

In the last `printf` statement, the `%c` characters are used to display the single character `'W'` that we assigned to `char_var` when the variable was declared. Remember that while a character string (such as the first argument to `printf`) is enclosed within a pair of double quotes, a character constant must always be enclosed within a pair of *single* quotes.

Qualifiers `long`, `short`, and `unsigned`

Just as it is possible to extend the accuracy of a variable containing a floating point number by declaring it to be of type `double`, so is it possible to extend the accuracy of an integer variable. If the qualifier `long` is placed directly before the `int` declaration, then the declared integer variable will be of extended accuracy on many computer systems. An example of a `long int` declaration might be

```
long int  factorial;
```

which would declare the variable `factorial` to be a `long` integer variable. As with `floats` and `doubles`, the particular accuracy of a `long` variable depends upon the particular computer system. On the IBM-PC for example, the maximum positive value that can be stored inside a variable of type `int` is 32,767. Declaring a variable to be of type `long int` permits values up to 2^{31}-1 or 2,147,483,647 to be stored in the variable. On the VAX-11, an `int` and a `long int` both have the same accuracy (which is the same as that for a `long int` on the IBM-PC) and can therefore both be used to store integer values up to 2,147,483,647.

A constant value of type `long int` is formed by optionally appending the letter `L` (upper- or lowercase) onto the end of an integer constant. No spaces are permitted between the number and the `L`. So, the declaration

```
long int  memory_address = 131071L;
```

declares the variable `memory_address` to be of type `long int` with an initial value of 131,071. If the letter `L` is not specified, the compiler will treat any constant larger than the largest allowable integer constant as a `long` integer constant.

To display the value of a `long int` at the terminal, the letter `l` is used as a modifier before the integer format characters d, o, or x. This means that the format characters `%ld` can be used to display the value of a `long int` in decimal format, the characters `%lo` to display the value in octal format, and the characters `%lx` to display the value in hexadecimal format.

The qualifier short, when placed in front of the int declaration, tells the C system that the particular variable being declared will be used to store fairly small integer values. The motivation for using short variables is primarily one of conserving the computer's memory space, which may be an issue in cases where the program needs a lot of memory and the amount of memory available is limited. On many machines, a short int will take up half the amount of storage as a regular int variable will. On the VAX-11, a short int can be used to store integer values in the range -32,768 to 32,767.

The final qualifier that may be placed in front of an int variable is used when an integer variable will be used only to store positive numbers. The declaration

```
unsigned int  counter;
```

declares to the C system that the variable counter will be used only to contain positive values. By restricting the use of an integer variable to the exclusive storage of positive integers, the accuracy of the integer variable is extended. On the IBM-PC for example, a normal int variable can assume values from -32,768 through 32,767. The same variable declared to be of type unsigned int can assume values from 0 through 65,535.

When declaring variables to be of type long int, short int, or unsigned int, it is permissable to omit the keyword int. So the unsigned variable counter could have been equivalently declared as

```
unsigned  counter;
```

Don't worry if the discussions of the types long int, short int, and unsigned int seem a bit esoteric to you at this point. The discussion was included here mainly for the sake of completeness. In later sections of this book, we will illustrate the use of many of these different types with actual program examples.

◆ Arithmetic Expressions ◆

In C, just as in virtually all programming languages, the plus sign (+) is used to add two values; the minus sign (–) to subtract two values; the asterisk (*) to multiply two values; and the slash (/) to divide two values. These operators are known as *binary* arithmetic operators, since they operate on *two* values or terms.

We have seen how a simple operation like addition can be performed in C. The following program further illustrates the operations of subtraction, multiplication and division. The last two operations performed in the program introduce the notion that one operator can have a higher priority or *precedence* over another operator. In fact, each operator in C has a precedence associated with it. This precedence is used to determine how an expression that has more than one operator is evaluated: The operator with the higher precedence is evaluated first. Expressions containing operators of the same precedence are either evaluated from left to right or from right to left, depending upon the operator. This is known as the *associative* property of an operator. Appendix A provides a complete list of operator precedences and their rules of association.

Program 4-2

```
/* Illustrate the use of various arithmetic operators */

main ()
{
    int   a = 100;
    int   b = 2;
    int   c = 25;
    int   d = 4;
    int   result;

    result = a - b;          /* subtraction */
    printf ("a - b = %d\n", result);

    result = b * c;          /* multiplication */
    printf ("b * c = %d\n", result);

    result = a / c;          /* division */
    printf ("a / c = %d\n", result);

    result = a + b * c;      /* precedence */
    printf ("a + b * c = %d\n", result);

    printf ("a * b + c * d =  %d\n", a * b + c * d);
}
```

Program 4-2 Output

```
a - b = 98
b * c = 50
a / c = 4
a + b * c = 150
a * b + c * d = 300
```

After declaring the integer variables a, b, c, d, and result, the program assigns the result of subtracting b from a to result and then proceeds to display its value with an appropriate printf call.

The next statement

```
result = b * c;
```

has the effect of multiplying the value of b by the value of c and storing the product in result. The result of the multiplication is then displayed using a printf call that should be very familiar to you by now.

The next program statement introduces the division operator—the slash. The result of 4 as obtained by dividing 100 by 25 is displayed by the printf statement immediately following the division of a by c.

In mathematics, the result of dividing any number by zero is infinity (∞). On most computer systems, attempting to divide a number by zero will result in abnormal termination of the program. Even if the program does not terminate abnormally, the results obtained by such a division will be meaningless. In Chapter 6, we will see how we can check for division by zero before the division operation is performed. If it is determined that the divisor is zero, then an appropriate action (such as displaying a message at the terminal) can be taken and the division operation averted.

The expression

```
a + b * c
```

does not produce the result of 2550 (102 * 25) as might be expected; rather, the result as displayed by the corresponding printf statement is shown as 150. This is because C, like most other programming languages, has rules for the order of evaluating multiple operations or terms in an expression. Evaluation of an expression generally proceeds from left to right. However, the operations of multiplication and division are given higher precedence over the operations of addition and subtraction. Therefore, the expression

```
a + b * c
```

is evaluated as

```
a + (b * c)
```

by the C system. (This is the same way that this expression would be evaluated if we were to apply the basic rules of algebra.)

If we wish to alter the order of evaluation of terms inside an expression, then parentheses can be used. In fact, the last expression listed above is a perfectly valid C expression. Thus the statement

```
result = a + (b * c);
```

could have been substituted in Program 4-2 to achieve identical results; but if the expression

```
result = (a + b) * c;
```

were used instead, then the value assigned to result would be 2550 since the value of a (100) would be added to the value of b (2) *before* multiplication by the value of c (25) would take place. Parentheses may be nested, and evaluation of the expression will proceed outward from the innermost set of parentheses. Just be sure to have as many closed parentheses as there are open ones.

You will notice from the last statement in Program 4-2 that it is perfectly valid to give an expression as an argument to printf without having to first assign the result of the expression evaluation to a variable. The expression

```
a * b + c * d
```

is evaluated according to the rules stated above as

```
(a * b) + (c * d)
```

or

```
(100 * 2) + (25 * 4)
```

and the result of 300 "handed" to the printf routine.

Integer Arithmetic and the Unary Minus Operator

The next program reinforces what we have just discussed and introduces the concept of integer arithmetic.

Program 4-3

```
/* More arithmetic expressions */

main ()
{
      int     a = 25;
      int     b = 2;
      int     result;
      float   c = 25.0;
      float   d = 2.0;

      printf ("6 + a / 5 * b = %d\n", 6 + a / 5 * b);
      printf ("a / b * b = %d\n", a / b * b);
      printf ("c / d * d = %f\n", c / d * d);
      printf ("-a = %d\n", -a);
}
```

Program 4-3 Output

```
6 + a / 5 * b = 16
a / b * b = 24
c / d * d = 25.000000
-a = -25
```

We inserted extra blank spaces between int and the declaration of a, b, and result in the first three statements to align the declaration of each variable. This helps to make the program more readable. You also may have noticed in each program presented thus far that a blank space was placed around each operator. This too is not required and is done solely for aesthetic reasons. In general, you may add extra blank spaces just about anywhere that a single blank space is allowed. A few extra presses of the space bar will prove worthwhile if the resulting program is easier to read.

The expression in the first printf call of Program 4-3 reinforces the notion of operator precedence. Evaluation of this expression proceeds as follows:

1. Since division has higher precedence than addition, the value of a (25) is divided by 5 first. This gives the intermediate result of 5.

2. Since multiplication also has higher precedence than addition, the intermediate result of 5 is next multiplied by 2, the value of b, giving a new intermediate result of 10.

3. Finally, the addition of 6 and 10 is performed, giving a final result of 16.

The second printf statement introduces a new twist. We would expect that dividing a by b and then multiplying by b would return to us the value of a, which we have set to 25. But this does not seem to be the case, as shown by the output display of 24. Did the computer lose a bit somewhere along the way? Very unlikely. The fact of the matter is that this expression was evaluated using *integer arithmetic*.

If you glance back at the declarations for the variables a and b, you will recall that they were both declared to be of type int. Now, whenever a term to be evaluated in an expression consists of *two* integers, the C system performs the operation using integer arithmetic. In such a case, all decimal portions of numbers are lost. Therefore, when the value of a is divided by the value of b, or 25 is divided by 2, we get an intermediate result of 12 and *not* 12.5 as you might expect. Multiplying this intermediate result by 2 gives us the final result of 24, thus explaining the "lost" digit.

As can be seen from the next-to-last printf statement in Program 4-3, if we perform the same operation using floating point values instead of integers, we obtain the expected result.

The decision of whether to use a `float` variable or an `int` variable should be made based upon the variable's intended use. If you don't need any decimal places, then use an integer variable. The resulting program will be more *efficient*—that is, it will execute faster on most computers. On the other hand, if you need the decimal place accuracy, then the choice is clear. The only question that you then must decide is whether to use a `float` or `double`. The answer to this question will depend upon the desired accuracy of the numbers you are dealing with, as well as their magnitude.

In the last `printf` statement, the value of the variable a is *negated* by use of the *unary minus* operator. A unary operator is one which operates on a single value, as opposed to a binary operator, which operates on two values. The minus sign actually has a dual role: as a binary operator it is used for subtracting two values. As a unary operator, it is used to negate a value.

The unary minus operator has higher precedence than all other arithmetic operators, so the expression

```
c = -a * b;
```

will result in the multiplication of -a by b. Once again, in Appendix A you will find a table summarizing the various operators and their precedences.

The Modulus Operator

The last operator to be presented in this chapter is the *modulus* operator, which is symbolized by the percent sign (`%`). Try to determine how this operator works by analyzing the output from the following program.

Program 4-4

```
/* The modulus operator */

main ()
{
    int   a = 25, b = 5, c = 10, d = 7;

    printf ("a %% b = %d\n", a % b);
    printf ("a %% c = %d\n", a % c);
    printf ("a %% d = %d\n", a % d);
    printf ("a / d * d + a %% d = %d\n",
              a / d * d + a % d);
}
```

Program 4-4 Output

```
a % b = 0
a % c = 5
a % d = 4
a / d * d + a % d = 25
```

The first statement inside main declares and intiailzes the variables a, b, c, and d in a single statement.

In the first printf call, you will notice that we used *two* percent signs in the format string; yet, if you examine the program's output, you will notice that only a single percent sign was printed. The reason for this is due to the special significance of the % sign to the printf routine. As you know, printf uses the character that immediately follows the percent sign to determine how to print the next argument. However, if it is another percent sign that follows, then the printf routine takes this as an indication that you really intend to display a percent sign, and inserts one at the appropriate place in the program's output.

You are correct if you concluded that the function of the modulus operator % is to give the remainder of the first value divided by the second value. In the first example, the remainder after 25 is divided by 5 is displayed as 0. If we divide 25 by 10, we get a remainder of 5, as verified by the second line of output. Dividing 25 by 7 gives a remainder of 4, as shown in the third output line.

The last line of output in Program 4-4 requires a bit of explanation. First, you will notice that the program statement has been written on two lines. This is perfectly valid in C. In fact, a program statement may be continued onto the next line at any point where a blank space could be used. (An exception to this is when dealing with character strings—a topic to be discussed in Chapter 10.) At times it may not only be desirable, but perhaps even necessary to continue a program statement onto the next line. The continuation of the printf call in Program 4-4 was indented to visually show that it is a continuation of the preceding program statement.

Let us now turn our attention to the expression that is evaluated in this last statement. You will recall that any operations between two integer values in C are performed with integer arithmetic. Therefore, any remainder resulting from the division of two integer values will simply be discarded. Dividing 25 by 7, as indicated by the expression a / d, gives an intermediate result of 3. Multiplying this value by the value of d, which is 7, produces the intermediate result of 21. Finally, adding in the remainder of dividing a by d, as indicated by the expression a % d, leads to the final result of 25. It is no coincidence that this value is the same as the value of the variable a. In general, the expression

```
a / b * b + a % b
```

will always equal the value of a, assuming of course that a and b are both integer values. In fact, the modulus operator % is defined to work only with integer values.

As far as precedence is concerned, the modulus operator has equal precedence to the multiplication and division operators. This implies, of course, that an expression such as

```
table + value % TABLE_SIZE
```

will be evaluated as

```
table + (value % TABLE_SIZE)
```

Integer and Floating Point Conversions

In order to effectively develop C programs, it will be necessary for you to understand the rules that are used for the implicit conversion of floating point and integer values in C. In Chapter 14, the rules that are followed for conversion between other data types are described in detail.

Program 4-5

```c
/* Basic conversions in C */

main ()
{
    float  f1 = 123.125, f2;
    int    i1, i2 = -150;
    char   c = 'a';

    i1 = f1;            /* floating to integer conversion */
    printf ("%f assigned to an int produces %d\n", f1, i1);

    f1 = i2;            /* integer to floating conversion */
    printf ("%d assigned to a float produces %f\n", i2, f1);

    f1 = i2 / 100;     /* integer divided by integer */
    printf ("%d divided by 100 produces %f\n", i2, f1);

    f2 = i2 / 100.0;   /* integer divided by a float */
    printf ("%d divided by 100.0 produces %f\n", i2, f2);
}
```

Program 4-5 Output

```
123.125000 assigned to an int produces 123
-150 assigned to a float produces -150.000000
-150 divided by 100 produces -1.000000
-150 divided by 100.0 produces -1.500000
```

Whenever a floating point value is assigned to an integer variable in C, the decimal portion of the number gets *truncated*. So when the value of f1 is assigned to i1 in the above program, the number 123.125 gets truncated, which means that only its integer portion, or 123, is stored into i1. The first line of the program's output verifies that this is the case.

Assigning an integer variable to a floating variable does not cause any change in the value of the number. The value is simply converted by the system and stored into the floating variable. The second line of the program's output verifies that the value of i2, -150, was correctly converted and stored into the float variable f1.

The next two lines of the program's output illustrate two points that must be remembered when forming arithmetic expressions. The first has to do with integer arithmetic, which we have already discussed in this chapter. Whenever two operands in an expression are integers (and this applies to short, unsigned, and long integers as well), the operation is carried out under the rules of integer arithmetic. Therefore, any decimal portion resulting from a division operation will be discarded, even if the result is assigned to a floating variable (as we did in the program). So when the integer variable i2 is divided by the integer constant 100, the system performs the division as an integer division. The result of dividing -150 by 100, which is -1, is therefore the value that is stored into the float variable f1.

The next division that is performed in the above program involves an integer variable and a floating point constant. Any operation between two values in C will be performed as a floating point operation if *either* value is a floating point variable or constant. Therefore, when the value of i2 is divided by 100.0, the system treats the division as a floating point division and produces the result of -1.5, which is assigned to the float variable f1.

We have reached the end of discussion on variables, data types, and expressions. If you are familiar with other programming languages, you may have noticed that there is no operator for raising a number to a power (exponentiation). Many computer systems provide a function in the program library for performing exponentiation, or you can always compute the value yourself (for raising a number to an integer power by simply multiplying the number by itself the required number of times).

Try your hand at the exercises presented on the following pages before proceeding to the next chapter, which introduces the concept of program looping.

♦ Exercises ♦

1. If you have access to a computer facility that supports the C programming language, type in and run the five programs presented in this chapter. Compare the output produced by each program with the output presented after each program.

2. Which of the following are invalid variable names? Why?

```
Int              char            6_05
_calloc          Xx              alpha_beta_routine
floating         _1312           z
ReInitialize     _               A$
```

3. Which of the following are invalid constants. Why?

```
123.456          0x10.5          0X0G1
0001             0xFFFF          123L
0Xab05           0L              -597.25
123.5e2          .0001           +12.5
0996             -12E-12         07777
```

4. Write a program that converts 27° from degrees Fahrenheit (F) to degrees Celsius (C) using the formula

$$C = (F - 32)/1.8$$

5. What output would you expect from the following program?

```c
main ()
{
    char   c, d;

    c = 'd';
    d = c;
    printf ("d = %c\n", d);
}
```

6. Write a program to evaluate the polynomial

$$3x^3 - 5x^2 + 6$$

for $x = 2.55$

7. Write a program that evaluates the following expression and displays the results. (Remember to use exponential format to display the result.)

$$(3.31 \times 10^{-8} + 2.10 \times 10^{-7}) / (7.16 \times 10^{6} + 2.01 \times 10^{8})$$

8. To round off an integer i to the next largest even multiple of another integer j, the following formula can be used:

Next_multiple = i + j - i % j

For example, to round off 256 days to the next largest number of days evenly divisible by a week, values of $i = 256$ and $j = 7$ can be substituted into the above formula as follows.

Next_multiple   = 256 + 7 - 256 % 7
= 256 + 7 - 4
= 259

Write a program to find the next largest even multiple for the following values of i and j.

i	j
365	7
12,258	23
996	4

5

Program Looping

I f we were to arrange 15 dots into the shape of a triangle, we would end up
with an arrangement that might look something like this:

The first row of the triangle contains one dot, the second row two dots, and so
on. In general, the number of dots it would take to form a triangle containing *n*
rows would be the sum of the integers from 1 through *n*. This sum is known as a
triangular number. If we start at 1, then the fourth triangular number would be
the sum of the consecutive integers 1 through 4 (1 + 2 + 3 + 4), or 10.

Suppose we wished to write a program that calculated and displayed the
value of the eighth triangular number at the terminal. Obviously, we could
easily calculate this number in our heads, but for the sake of argument, let us
assume that we wanted to write a program in C to perform this task. Such a program is shown in Program 5-1.

The technique of Program 5-1 works fine for calculating relatively small triangular numbers. But what would happen if we needed to find the value of the
200th triangular number, for example? It certainly would be a bit tedious to have
to modify Program 5-1 to explicitly add up all of the integers from 1 to 200.
Luckily, there is an easier way.

Program 5-1

```
/* Program to calculate the eighth triangular number */

main ()
{
    int  triangular_number;

    triangular_number = 1 + 2 + 3 + 4 + 5 + 6 + 7 + 8;

    printf ("The eighth triangular number is %d\n",
                triangular_number);
}
```

Program 5-1 Output

```
The eighth triangular number is 36
```

One of the fundamental properties of a computer is its ability to repetitively execute a set of statements. These *looping* capabilities enable programmers to develop concise programs containing repetitive processes that could otherwise require thousands or even millions of program statements to perform. The C programming language contains three different program statements for program looping. They are known as the for statement, the while statement, and the do statement. Each of these statements will be described in detail in this chapter.

◆ The for Statement ◆

Why don't we dive right in and take a look at a program that uses the for statement. The purpose of Program 5-2 is to calculate the 200th triangular number. See if you can determine how the for statement works.

Some explanation is owed for Program 5-2. The method employed to calculate the 200th triangular number is really the same as that used to calculate the 8th triangular number in the previous program—the integers from 1 up to 200 are summed. The for statement provides the mechanism that enables us to avoid having to explicitly write out each integer from 1 to 200. In a sense, this statement is used to "generate" these numbers for us.

Program 5-2

```
/* Program to calculate the 200th triangular number */
/* Introduction of the for statement                */

main ()
{
    int   n, triangular_number;

    triangular_number = 0;

    for ( n = 1;  n <= 200;  n = n + 1 )
       triangular_number = triangular_number + n;

    printf ("The 200th triangular number is %d\n",
               triangular_number);
}
```

Program 5-2 Output

```
The 200th triangular number is 20100
```

The general format of the for statement is as follows:

```
for ( init_expression;  loop_condition;  loop_expression )
      program statement
```

The three expressions that are enclosed within the parentheses—*init_expression*, *loop_condition*, and *loop_expression*—set up the environment for the program loop. The program statement that immediately follows (which is of course terminated by a semicolon) can be any valid C program statement and constitutes the *body of the loop*. This statement will be executed as many times as specified by the parameters set up in the for statement.

The first component of the for, labeled *init_expression*, is used to set the initial values *before* the loop begins. In Program 5-2, this portion of the for statement is used to set the initial value of n to 1. As you can see, an assignment is a valid form of an expression.

The second component of the for statement specifies the condition or conditions that are necessary *in order for the loop to continue*. In other words, looping continues *as long as* this condition is satisfied. Once again referring to Program 5-2, we find that the *loop_condition* of the for is specified by the *relational expression*

```
n <= 200
```

This expression can be read as "n less than or equal to 200." The "less than or equal to" operator (which is the less than character < followed immediately by the equals sign =) is only one of several relational operators provided in the C programming language. These operators are used to test specific conditions. The answer to the test will be "yes" or, more commonly, TRUE if the condition is satisfied and "no" or FALSE if the condition is not satisfied.

Table 5-1 lists all of the relational operators that are available in C.

TABLE 5-1. Relational operators

Operator	Meaning	Example
==	Equal to	count == 10
!=	Not equal to	flag != DONE
<	Less than	a < b
<=	Less than or equal to	low <= high
>	Greater than	pointer > end_of_list
>=	Greater than or equal to	j >= 0

The relational operators have lower precedence than all arithmetic operators. This means, for example, that an expression such as

```
a < b + c
```

will be evaluated as

```
a < (b + c)
```

as you would expect, and would be TRUE if the value of a were less than the value of b + c, and FALSE otherwise.

Pay particular attention to the "is equal to" operator == and do not confuse its use with the assignment operator =. The expression

```
a == 2
```

tests if the value of a is equal to 2, whereas the expression

```
a = 2
```

assigns the value 2 to the variable a.

The choice of which relational operator to use will obviously depend on the particular test being made and in some instances on your particular preferences. For example, the relational expression

```
n <= 200
```

can be equivalently expressed as

```
n < 201
```

Returning to our example, the program statement which forms the body of the `for` loop:

```
triangular_number = triangular_number + n;
```

will be repetitively executed *as long as the result of the relational test is TRUE*, or in this case, as long as the value of n is less than or equal to 200. This program statement has the effect of adding the value of `triangular_number` to the value of n and storing the result back into the value of `triangular_number`.

When the *loop_condition* is no longer satisfied, execution of the program will continue with the program statement immediately following the `for` loop. In our program, execution will continue with the `printf` statement once the loop has terminated.

The final component of the `for` statement contains an expression that is evaluated each time *after* the body of the loop is executed. In Program 5-2, this *loop_expression* adds 1 to the value of n. Therefore, the value of n will be incremented by 1 each time after its value has been added into the value of `triangular_number`, and will range in value from 1 through 201.

It is worth noting that the last value that n attains, namely 201, is *not* added into the value of `triangular_number` since the loop is terminated *as soon as* the looping condition is no longer satisfied, or as soon as n equals 201.

In summary then, execution of the `for` statement proceeds as follows:

1. The initial expression is evaluated first. This expression usually sets a variable that will be used inside the loop, generally referred to as an *index* variable, to some initial value such as 0 or 1.

2. The looping condition is evaluated. If the condition is not satisfied (the expression is FALSE), then the loop is immediately terminated. Execution continues with the program statement that immediately follows the loop.

3. The program statement which constitutes the body of the loop is executed.

4. The looping expression is evaluated. This expression is generally used to change the value of the index variable, frequently by adding 1 to it or subtracting 1 from it.

5. Return to Step 2.

Since Program 5-2 actually generates all of the first 200 triangular numbers on its way to its final goal, it might be nice to generate a table of these numbers. To save space, however, we will assume that we just want to print a table of the first 10 triangular numbers. Program 5-3 below performs precisely this task!

Program 5-3

```
/* Program to generate a table of triangular numbers */

main ()
{
    int   n, triangular_number;

    printf ("TABLE OF TRIANGULAR NUMBERS\n\n");
    printf (" n     Sum from 1 to n\n");
    printf ("---     ----------------\n");

    triangular_number = 0;

    for ( n = 1;  n <= 10;   ++n )
    {
        triangular_number = triangular_number + n;
        printf (" %d             %d\n", n, triangular_number);
    }
}
```

Program 5-3 Output

```
TABLE OF TRIANGULAR NUMBERS

 n     Sum from 1 to n
---     ----------------
 1            1
 2            3
 3            6
 4            10
 5            15
 6            21
 7            28
 8            36
 9            45
10            55
```

It is always a good idea to add some extra `printf` statements to a program in order to provide more meaning to the output. In Program 5-3, the purpose of the first three `printf` statements is simply to provide a general heading and to label the columns of the output. You will notice that the first `printf` statement contains two newline characters. As you would expect, this has the effect of not only advancing to the next line but also inserting an extra blank line into the display.

After the appropriate headings have been displayed, the program proceeds to calculate the first 10 triangular numbers. The variable n is used to count the current number whose "sum from 1 to n" we are computing, while the variable triangular_number is used to store the value of triangular number n.

Execution of the for statement commences by setting the value of the variable n to 1. You will recall that we mentioned earlier that the program statement immediately following the for statement constitutes the body of the program loop. But what happens if we wish to repetitively execute not just a single program statement but a group of program statements? This can be accomplished by enclosing all such program statements within a pair of braces. The system will then treat this group or *block* of statements as a single entity. In general, any place in a C program that a single statement is permitted, a block of statements can be used, provided that you remember to enclose the block within a pair of braces.

Therefore, in the program above, both the expression that adds n into the value of triangular_number and the printf statement that immediately follows constitute the body of the program loop. Pay particular attention to the way the program statements are indented. At a quick glance, it is easy to determine which statements form part of the for loop. You should also note that programmers use different coding styles. Some prefer to type the loop this way:

```
for ( n = 1;  n <= 10;  ++n ) {
    triangular_number = triangular_number + n;
    printf (" %d               %d\n", n, triangular_number);
}
```

Here the opening brace is placed on the same line as the for. This is strictly a matter of taste and has no effect on the program.

The next triangular number is calculated by simply adding the value of n to the previous triangular number. The first time through the for loop, the "previous" triangular number is zero, so the new value of triangular_number when n is equal to 1 is simply the value of n, or 1. The values of n and triangular_number are then displayed, with an appropriate number of blank spaces inserted in the format string to ensure that the values of the two variables line up under the appropriate column headings.

Since the body of the loop has now been executed, the looping expression is evaluated next. The expression in this for statement appears a bit strange, however. Surely we must have made a typographical mistake and meant to insert the expression

```
n = n + 1
```

instead of the funny-looking expression

```
++n
```

The fact of the matter is that ++n is actually a perfectly valid C expression. It introduces us to a new (and rather unique) operator in the C programming language—the *increment operator*. The function of the double plus sign—or the increment operator—is to add 1 to its operand. Since addition by 1 is such a common operation in programs, a special operator was created solely for this purpose. Therefore, the expression ++n is equivalent to the expression n = n + 1. While at first glance it might appear that n = n + 1 is more readable, you will very soon get used to the function of this operator and will even learn to appreciate its succinctness.

Of course, no programming language that offered an increment operator to add 1 would be complete without a corresponding operator to subtract 1. And as you would guess, the name of this operator is the *decrement operator*, and is symbolized by the double minus sign. So, an expression in C that reads

```
bean_counter = bean_counter - 1
```

can be equivalently expressed using the decrement operator as

```
--bean_counter
```

One slightly disturbing thing that you may have noticed in Program 5-3's output is the fact that the 10th triangular number does not quite line up under the previous triangular numbers. This is because the number 10 takes up two print positions, whereas the previous values of n, 1 through 9, took up only one print position. Therefore, the value 55 is effectively "pushed over" one extra position in the display.

This minor annoyance can be corrected if we substitute the following printf statement in place of the corresponding statement from Program 5-3.

```
printf ("%2d          %d\n", n, triangular_number);
```

To verify that this change will do the trick, here is the output from the modified program (we'll call it Program 5-3A).

Program 5-3A Output

n	Sum from 1 to n
---	----------------
1	1
2	3
3	6
4	10
5	15
6	21
7	28
8	36
9	45
10	55

The primary change made to the `printf` statement was the inclusion of a *field width specification*. The characters `%2d` tell the `printf` routine that not only do we wish to display the value of an integer at that particular point, but also that the size of the integer to be displayed should take up 2 columns in the display. Any integer which would normally take up less than 2 columns (that is, the integers 0 through 9) will be displayed with a *leading* space. This is known as *right justification*.

Thus, by using a field width specification of `%2d` we guarantee that at least two columns will be used for displaying the value of n, and therefore ensure that the values of `triangular_number` will be lined up.

If the value that is to be displayed requires more columns than are specified by the field width, `printf` simply ignores the field width specification and uses as many columns as are necessary to display the value.

Field width specifications can be used for displaying values other than integers as well. We will see some examples of this in programs that will be coming up shortly.

Program Input

Program 5-2 calculates the 200th triangular number—and nothing more. What if we wanted to calculate the 50th or the 100th triangular number instead? Well, if that were the case, then we would have to go back and change the program so that the `for` loop would be executed the correct number of times. We would also have to change the `printf` statement to display the correct message.

An easier solution might be if we could somehow have the program ask us which triangular number we wished to calculate. Then, once we had given our answer, the program could calculate the desired triangular number for us. Such a solution can be effected in C by use of a routine called `scanf`. The `scanf` routine is very similar in concept to the `printf` routine. Whereas the latter routine is used to display values at the terminal, the function of the former routine is to enable the programmer to type values *into* the program. Program 5-4 below asks the user which triangular number he would like to have calculated, proceeds to calculate that number, and then displays the results.

Program 5-4

```
main ()
{
    int   n, number, triangular_number;

    printf ("What triangular number do you want? ");
    scanf  ("%d", &number);

    triangular_number = 0;

    for ( n = 1;  n <= number;  ++n )
      triangular_number = triangular_number + n;

    printf ("Triangular number %d is %d\n", number,
              triangular_number);
}
```

In the program output that follows, the number typed in by the user (100) is set in bolder type to distinguish it from the output displayed by the program.

Program 5-4 Output

```
What triangular number do you want? 100
Triangular number 100 is 5050
```

According to the output, the number 100 was typed in by the user. The program then proceeded to calculate the 100th triangular number and displayed the result of 5050 at the terminal. The user could have just as easily typed in the number 10, or 30, if it were desired to calculate those particular triangular numbers.

The first printf statement in Program 5-4 is used to prompt the user to type in a number. Of course, it is always nice to remind the user what it is you want entered. After the message is printed, the scanf routine is called. The first argument to scanf is the format string and is very similar to the format string used by printf. In this case, the format string doesn't tell the system what types of values are to be displayed but rather what types of values are to be read in from the terminal. Like printf, the %d characters are used to specify an integer value.

The second argument to the scanf routine specifies *where* the value that is typed in by the user is to be stored. The & character before the variable number is necessary in this case. Don't worry about its function here, though. We will discuss this character, which is actually an operator, in great detail in the chapter on pointers. Just remember for now that it *must* be placed before the variable name in the call to the scanf routine.

Given the preceding discussion, we can now see that the scanf call from Program 5-4 specifies that an integer value is to be read from the terminal and stored into the variable number. This value represents the particular triangular number that the user wishes to have calculated.

Once this number has been typed in (and the "Return" key on the keyboard pressed to signal that typing of the number is completed), the program then proceeds to calculate the requested triangular number. This is done the same way as in Program 5-2, with the only difference being that instead of using 200 as the limit, number is used as the limit instead.

After the desired triangular number has been calculated, the results are displayed and execution of the program is then complete.

Nested for Loops

Program 5-4 gives the user the flexibility to have the program calculate any triangular number that is desired. But suppose the user had a list of five triangular numbers to be calculated? Well, in such a case, the user could simply execute the program five times, each time typing in the next triangular number from the list to be calculated.

Another way to accomplish the same goals, and a far more interesting method as far as learning about C is concerned, is to have the program handle the situation. This can best be accomplished by inserting a loop into the program to simply repeat the entire series of calculations five times. We know by now that the for statement can be used to set up such a loop. The following program and its associated output illustrates this technique.

Program 5-5

```
main ()
{
    int   n, number, triangular_number, counter;

    for ( counter = 1;   counter <= 5;   ++counter )
    {
        printf ("What triangular number do you want? ");
        scanf   ("%d", &number);

        triangular_number = 0;

        for ( n = 1;   n <= number;   ++n )
           triangular_number = triangular_number + n;

        printf ("Triangular number %d is %d\n\n", number,
                  triangular_number);

    }
}
```

Program 5-5 Output

```
What triangular number do you want? 12
Triangular number 12 is 78

What triangular number do you want? 25
Triangular number 25 is 325

What triangular number do you want? 50
Triangular number 50 is 1275

What triangular number do you want? 75
Triangular number 75 is 2850

What triangular number do you want? 83
Triangular number 83 is 3486
```

The program consists of two levels of for statements. The outermost for statement

```
for ( counter = 1;  counter <= 5;  ++counter )
```

specifies that the program loop is to be executed precisely five times. This can be seen because the value of counter will be initially set to 1 and will be incremented by 1 *until* it is no longer less than or equal to 5 (in other words, until it reaches 6).

Unlike the previous program examples, the variable counter is not used anywhere else within the program. Its function is solely as a loop counter in the for statement. Nevertheless, since it *is* a variable, it must be declared in the program.

The program loop actually consists of all of the remaining program statements, as indicated by the braces. It might be easier for you to comprehend the way this program operates if you conceptualize it as follows:

For 5 times
{
  Get the number from the user.

  Calculate the requested triangular number.

  Display the results.
}

The portion of the loop referred to in the preceding as *Calculate the requested triangular number* actually consists of setting the value of the variable triangular_number to 0 *plus the* for *loop that calculates the triangular number.*

Thus we see that we have a `for` statement that is actually contained *within* another `for` statement. This is perfectly valid in C, and nesting may continue even further to any desired level.

The proper use of indentation becomes even more critical when dealing with more sophisticated program constructs, such as nested `for` statements. At a quick glance you can easily determine which statements are contained within each `for` statement. (To see how unreadable a program can be if correct attention isn't paid to formatting, see Exercise 5 at the end of this chapter.)

`for` Loop Variants

Before leaving this discussion of the `for` loop, we should mention some of the syntactic variations that are permitted in forming this loop. It may very well be that when writing a `for` loop that you will discover that you have more than one variable that you would like to initialize before the loop begins, or perhaps more than one expression that you would like evaluated each time through the loop. We can include multiple expressions in any of the fields of the `for` loop, provided that we separate such expressions by commas. For example, in the `for` statement that begins

```
for ( i = 0, j = 0;  i < 10;  ++i )
    . . .
```

the value of `i` is set to zero *and* the value of `j` is set to zero before the loop begins. The two expressions `i = 0` and `j = 0` are separated from each other by a comma, and both expressions are considered part of the *init_expression* field of the loop. As another example, the `for` loop that starts

```
for  ( i = 0, j = 100;  i < 10;  ++i, j = j - 10 )
    . . .
```

sets up two index variables, `i` and `j`; the former initialized to 0 and the latter to 100 before the loop begins. Each time after the body of the loop is executed, the value of `i` will be incremented by 1, while the value of `j` will be decremented by 10.

Just as the need may arise to include more than one expression in a particular field of the `for` statement, so too may the need arise to *omit* one or more fields from the statement. This can be done simply by omitting the desired field, but by marking its place with a semicolon. The most common application for the omission of a field in the `for` statement occurs when there is no initial expression that needs to be evaluated. The *init_expression* field can simply be "left blank" in such a case, as long as the semicolon is still included:

```
for  ( ;  j != 100;  ++j )
    . . .
```

The above statement might be used if j were already set to some initial value before the loop was entered.

A for loop that has its *looping_condition* field omitted effectively sets up an infinite loop, that is, a loop that theoretically will be executed forever. Such a loop can be used provided there is some other means used to exit from the loop (such as executing a return, break, or goto statement as discussed later in this book).

♦ The while Statement ♦

The while statement further extends the C language's repertoire of looping capabilities. The syntax of this frequently used construct is simply

```
while ( expression )
    program statement
```

The *expression* specified inside the parentheses is evaluated. If the result of *expression* evaluation is TRUE, then *program statement* that immediately follows is executed. After execution of this statement (or statements if enclosed in braces), *expression* is once again evaluated. If the result of the evaluation is TRUE, then *program statement* is once again executed. This process continues until *expression* finally evaluates FALSE, at which point the loop is terminated. Execution of the program then continues with the statement that follows *program statement*.

As an example of its use, the following program sets up a while loop which merely counts from 1 to 5.

Program 5-6

```
/* This program introduces the while statement */

main ()
{
    int  count = 1;

    while ( count <= 5 )
    {
        printf ("%d\n", count);
        ++count;
    }
}
```

Program 5-6 Output

```
1
2
3
4
5
```

The program initially sets the value of count to 1. Execution of the while loop then begins. Since the value of count is less than or equal to 5, the statement that immediately follows is executed. The braces serve to define both the printf statement and the statement that increments count as the body of the while loop. From the output of the program, we can readily observe that this loop is executed precisely 5 times, or until the value of count reaches 6.

You may have realized from this program that we could have readily accomplished the same task by using a for statement. In fact, a for statement can always be translated into an equivalent while statement, and vice versa. For example, the general for statement

    for (*init_expression; loop_condition; loop_expression*)
        program statement

can be equivalently expressed in the form of a while statement as

    init_expression;

    while (*loop_condition*)
    {
        program statement
        loop_expression;
    }

Once you become familiar with the use of the while statement, you will gain a better feel as to when it seems more logical to use a while and when to use a for. In general, a loop which is executed a predetermined number of times is a prime candidate for implementation as a for statement. Also, if the initial expression, looping expression, and looping condition all involve the same variable, then the for statement is probably the right choice.

The next program provides another example of the use of the while statement. The program computes the *greatest common divisor* of two integer values. The greatest common divisor (we'll abbreviate it hereafter as *gcd*) of two integers is the largest integer value that evenly divides the two integers. For example, the *gcd* of 10 and 15 is 5 since 5 is the largest integer that evenly divides both 10 and 15.

There is a procedure or *algorithm* that can be followed to arrive at the *gcd* of two arbitrary integers. This algorithm is based on a procedure originally developed by Euclid around 300 B.C., and can be stated as follows:

Problem: Find the Greatest Common Divisor of two nonnegative integers *u* and *v*.

Step 1: If *v* equals 0, then we are done and the *gcd* is equal to *u*.

Step 2: Calculate *temp* = *u* % *v*, *u* = *v*, *v* = *temp* and go back to Step 1.

Don't concern yourself with the details of how the above algorithm works—simply take it at faith. We are more concerned here with developing the program to find the greatest common divisor than in performing an analysis of how the algorithm works.

Once the solution to the problem of finding the greatest common divisor has been expressed in terms of an algorithm, it becomes a much simpler task to develop the computer program. An analysis of the steps of the algorithm reveals that Step 2 is repetitively executed as long as the value of *v* is not equal to 0. This realization leads to the natural implementation of this algorithm in C with the use of a while statement.

The following program will find the *gcd* of two nonnegative integer values typed in by the user.

Program 5-7

```
/* This program finds the Greatest Common Divisor
        of two nonnegative integer values           */

main ()
{
    int u, v, temp;

    printf ("Please type in two nonnegative integers.\n");
    scanf ("%d%d", &u, &v);

    while ( v != 0 )
    {
        temp = u % v;
        u = v;
        v = temp;
    }

    printf ("Their Greatest Common Divisor is %d\n", u);
}
```

Program 5-7 Output

```
Please type in two nonnegative integers.
150 35
Their Greatest Common Divisor is 5
```

Program 5-7 Output (Re-run)

```
Please type in two nonnegative integers.
1026 405
Their Greatest Common Divisor is 27
```

The double %d characters in the scanf call indicate that two integer values are to be entered from the keyboard. The first value that is entered will be stored into the integer variable u, while the second will be stored into the variable v. When the values are actually entered from the terminal, they can be separated from each other by one or more blank spaces or by a carriage return. However, they cannot be separated by a comma (BASIC programmers beware).

After the values have been entered from the keyboard and stored into the variables u and v, the program enters a while loop to calculate their greatest common divisor. After the while loop is exited, the value of u, which represents the *gcd* of v and of the original value of u, is displayed at the terminal, together with an appropriate message.

For our next program to illustrate the use of the while statement, let us consider the task of reversing the digits of an integer that is entered from the terminal. For example, if the user types in the number 1234 then we would like to have the program reverse the digits of this number and display the result of 4321.

To write such a program, we first must come up with an algorithm which accomplishes the stated task. Frequently, an analysis of one's own method for solving the problem will lead to the development of an algorithm. For the task of reversing the digits of a number, the method of solution can be simply stated as "successively read the digits of the number from right to left." We can have a computer program "successively read" the digits of the number by developing a procedure to successively isolate or "extract" each digit of the number, beginning with the rightmost digit. The extracted digit can be subsequently displayed at the terminal as the next digit of the reversed number.

We can extract the rightmost digit from an integer number by taking the remainder of the integer after it is divided by 10. For example, 1234 % 10 will give the value 4, which is the rightmost digit of 1234, and is also the first digit of the reversed number. (Remember the modulus operator, which gives the remainder of one integer divided by another.) We can get the next digit of the number by using the same process if we first divide the number by 10, bearing in mind the way integer division works. Thus, 1234 / 10 gives a result of 123, and 123 % 10 gives us 3, which is the next digit of our reversed number.

The procedure described above can be continued until the last digit has been extracted. In the general case, we know that the last digit of the number has been extracted when the result of the last integer division by 10 is zero.

Program 5-8

```
/* Program to reverse the digits of a number */

main ()
{
    int  number, right_digit;

    printf ("Enter your number.\n");
    scanf ("%d", &number);

    while ( number != 0 )
    {
        right_digit = number % 10;
        printf ("%d", right_digit);
        number = number / 10;
    }

    printf ("\n");
}
```

Program 5-8 Output

```
Enter your number.
13579
97531
```

Each digit is displayed as it is extracted by the program. Notice that we did not include a newline character inside the `printf` statement contained in the `while` loop. This forces each successive digit to be displayed on the same line. The final `printf` call at the end of the program contains just a newline character which causes the cursor to advance to the start of the next line.

◆ The do Statement ◆

The two looping constructs that we have discussed thus far in this chapter both make a test of the conditions *before* the loop is executed. Therefore, the body of the loop may never be executed at all if the conditions are not satisfied. When developing programs, it sometimes becomes desirable to have the test made at the *end* of the loop rather than at the beginning. Naturally, the C language provides a special language construct to handle such a situation. This looping statement is known as the do statement. The syntax of this statement is

```
do
        program statement
while ( expression );
```

Execution of the do statement proceeds as follows: *program statement* is executed first. Next, the *expression* inside the parentheses is evaluated. If the result of evaluating *expression* is TRUE, the loop continues and *program statement* is once again executed. As long as evaluation of *expression* continues to be TRUE, *program statement* is repeatedly executed. When evaluation of the expression proves FALSE, the loop is terminated and the next statement in the program is executed in the normal sequential manner.

The do statement is simply a transposition of the while statement, with the looping conditions placed at the end of the loop rather than at the beginning. As mentioned, this statement is most often used when it is desirable to execute a loop at least one time.

In Program 5-8, we used a while statement to reverse the digits of a number. Go back to that program and try to determine what would happen if the user had typed in the number 0 instead of 13579. The fact of the matter is that the loop of the while statement would never be executed and we would simply end up with a blank line in our display (as a result of the display of the newline character from the second printf statement). If we were to use a do statement instead of a while, then we would be assured that the program loop would be executed at least once, thus guaranteeing the display of at least one digit in all cases.

Program 5-9

```
/* Program to reverse the digits of a number */

main ()
{
    int   number, right_digit;

    printf ("Enter your number.\n");
    scanf ("%d", &number);

    do
    {
        right_digit = number % 10;
        printf ("%d", right_digit);
        number = number / 10;
    }
    while ( number != 0 );

    printf ("\n");
}
```

Program 5-9 Output

```
Enter your number.
13579
97531
```

Program 5-9 Output (Re-run)

```
Enter your number.
0
0
```

As you can see from the program's output, when 0 is keyed into the program, the program correctly displays the digit 0.

The break Statement

Sometimes when executing a loop it becomes desirable to leave the loop as soon as a certain condition occurs (for instance, maybe you detect an error condition, or you reach the end of your data prematurley). The break statement can be used for this purpose. Execution of the break statement causes the program to immediately exit from the loop it is executing, whether it's a for, while, or do. Subsequent statements in the loop are skipped, and execution of the loop is terminated. Execution continues with whatever statement follows the loop.

If a break is executed from within a set of nested loops, only the innermost loop in which the break is executed is terminated.

The format of the break statement is simply the keyword break followed by a semicolon:

```
break;
```

The continue Statement

The continue statement is similar to the break statement except it doesn't cause the loop to terminate. Rather, as its name implies, this statement causes the loop in which it is executed to be continued. At the point that the continue statement is executed, any statements in the loop that appear *after* the continue statement are automatically skipped. Execution of the loop otherwise continues as normal.

The continue statement is most often used to bypass a group of statements inside a loop based upon some condition, but to otherwise continue execution of the loop. The format of the continue statement is simply

```
continue;
```

Now that you are familiar with all of the basic looping constructs provided by the C language, we are ready to discuss another class of language statements that enable you to make decisions during the execution of a program. These decision making capabilities are described in detail in the next chapter.

♦ Exercises ♦

1. If you have access to a computer facility that supports the C programming language, type in and run the nine programs presented in this chapter. Compare the output produced by each program with the output presented after each program.

2. Write a program to generate and display a table of n and n^2, for integer values of n ranging from 1 through 10. Be sure to print appropriate column headings.

3. A triangular number can also be generated by the formula

   Triangular number = n (n + 1) / 2

   for any integer value of n. For example, the tenth triangular number, 55, can be generated by substituting the 10 as the value for n into the above formula. Write a program which generates a table of triangular numbers using the above formula. Have the program generate every fifth triangular number between 5 and 50 (that is, 5, 10, 15, ..., 50).

4. The factorial of an integer n, written $n!$, is the product of the consecutive integers 1 through n. For example, 5 factorial is calculated as

   5! = 5 x 4 x 3 x 2 x 1 = 120

   Write a program to generate and print a table of the first 10 factorials.

5. The following perfectly valid C program was written without much attention paid to its format. As you will observe, the program is not very readable. (And believe it or not, it is even possible to make this program significantly more unreadable!). Using the programs presented in this chapter as examples, re-format the program so that it is more readable. Then type the program into the computer and run it.

```
main () {
int n,two_to_the_n;
printf("TABLE OF POWERS OF TWO\n\n");
printf("n      2 to the n\n");
printf("-      ----------\n");
two_to_the_n=1;
for(n=0;n<=10;++n) {
printf("%d              %d\n",n,two_to_the_n);
two_to_the_n=two_to_the_n*2;}
 }
```

6. A minus sign placed in front of a field width specification causes the field to be displayed *left-justified*. Substitute the following `printf` statement for the corresponding statement in Program 5-2, run the program, and compare the outputs produced by both programs.

```
printf ("%-2d                 %d\n", n, triangular_number);
```

7. A decimal point before the field width specification in a `printf` statement has a special purpose. Try to determine its purpose by typing in and running the following program. Experiment by typing in different values each time you are prompted.

```
main ()
{
    int  dollars, cents, count;

    for ( count = 1;  count <= 10;  ++count )
    {
        printf ("Enter dollars\n");
        scanf ("%d", &dollars);
        printf ("Enter cents\n");
        scanf ("%d", &cents);
        printf ("$%d.%.2d\n\n", dollars, cents);
    }
}
```

If your system doesn't support the characters `%.2d`, try `%02d` instead.

8. Program 5-5 allows the user to type in only five different numbers. Modify that program so that the user can type in the number of triangular numbers to be calculated.

9. Rewrite Programs 5-2 through 5-5, replacing all uses of the `for` statement by equivalent `while` statements. Run each program to verify that both versions are identical.

10. What would happen if you typed a negative number into Program 5-8? Try it and see.

11. Write a program that calculates the sum of the digits of an integer. For example, the sum of the digits of the number 2155 is $2 + 1 + 5 + 5$ or 13. The program should accept any arbitrary integer typed in by the user.

6

Making Decisions

I n the previous chapter, we noted that one of the fundamental properties of a computer is its ability to repetitively execute a sequence of instructions. But another fundamental property lies in its ability to make decisions. We saw how these decision-making powers were used in the execution of the various looping statements to determine when to terminate the program loop. Without such capabilities, we would never be able to "get out" of a program loop and would end up executing the same sequence of statements over and over again, theoretically forever (which is why such a program loop is called an *infinite* loop).

♦ The `if` Statement ♦

The C programming language also provides a general decision-making capability in the form of a language construct known as the `if` statement. The general format of this statement is

```
if ( expression )
    program statement
```

Imagine if you will that we could translate a statement such as "If it is not raining then I will go swimming" into the C language. Using the above format for the if statement, this might be "written" in C as follows:

```
if ( it is not raining )
    I will go swimming
```

The `if` statement is used to stipulate execution of a program statement (or statements if enclosed in braces) *based upon specified conditions*. I will go swimming if it is not raining. Similarly, in the program statement

```
if ( count > COUNT_LIMIT )
   printf ("Count limit exceeded\n");
```

printf statement will be executed *only* if the value of count is greater than the value of COUNT_LIMIT; otherwise, it will be ignored.

An actual program example will help drive the point home. Suppose we wish to write a program which accepts an integer typed in from the terminal and then displays the absolute value of that integer. A straightforward way to calculate the absolute value of an integer is to simply negate the number if it is less than zero. The use of the phrase "if it is less than zero" in the previous sentence signals that a decision must be made by the program. This decision can be effected by the use of an if statement as shown in the program that follows.

Program 6-1

```
/* Calculate the absolute value of an integer */

main ()
{
    int  number;

    printf ("Type in your number: ");
    scanf ("%d", &number);

    if ( number < 0 )
        number = -number;

    printf ("The absolute value is %d\n", number);
}
```

Program 6-1 Output

```
Type in your number: -100
The absolute value is 100
```

Program 6-1 Output (Re-run)

```
Type in your number: 2000
The absolute value is 2000
```

The program was run twice to verify that it is functioning properly. Of course, it might be desirable to run the program several more times to get a higher level of confidence that it is indeed working correctly, but at least we know that we have checked both possible outcomes of the decision made by the program.

After a message is displayed to the user and the integer value that is entered is stored into number, the program tests the value of number to see if it is less than zero. If it is, then the following program statement, which negates the value of number, is executed. If the value of number is not less than zero, then this program statement is automatically skipped (if it is already positive, we don't want to negate it). The absolute value of number is then displayed by the program, and program execution ends.

Let us now look at another program that uses the if statement. Imagine that we had a list of grades whose average we wished to compute. But in addition to computing the average, suppose that we also needed a count of the number of failing grades in the list. For purposes of this problem, we can assume that a grade less than 65 is to be considered a failing grade.

The notion of keeping count of the number of failing grades indicates to us that we must make a decision as to whether a grade qualifies as a failing grade or not. Once again the if statement comes to the rescue.

Program 6-2

```
/* Program to calculate the average of a set of grades
     and to count the number of failing test grades       */

main ()
{
    int     number_of_grades, i, grade;
    int     grade_total = 0;
    int     failure_count = 0;
    float   average;

    printf ("How many grades will you be entering? ");
    scanf ("%d", &number_of_grades);

    for ( i = 1;  i <= number_of_grades;  ++i )
    {
        printf ("Enter grade #%d: ", i);
        scanf ("%d", &grade);

        grade_total = grade_total + grade;

        if ( grade < 65 )
            ++failure_count;
    }

    average = (float) grade_total / number_of_grades;

    printf ("\nGrade average = %.2f\n", average);
    printf ("Number of failures = %d\n", failure_count);
}
```

Program 6-2 Output

```
How many grades will you be entering? 7
Enter grade #1: 93
Enter grade #2: 63
Enter grade #3: 87
Enter grade #4: 65
Enter grade #5: 62
Enter grade #6: 88
Enter grade #7: 76

Grade average = 76.29
Number of failures = 2
```

The variable grade_total, which is used to keep a cumulative total of the grades as they are typed in at the terminal, is initially set to 0. The number of failing test grades will be stored in the variable failure_count whose value is also initially set to 0. The variable **average** is declared to be of type float, since the average of a set of integers is not necessarily an integer itself.

The program then proceeds to ask the user to enter the number of grades that will be keyed in and stores the value that is entered into the variable number_of_grades. A loop is then set up that will be executed for each grade. The first part of the loop prompts the user to enter in the grade. The value that is entered is stored into the variable called, appropriately enough, grade.

The value of grade is then added into grade_total, after which a test is made to see if it is a failing test grade. If it is, then the value of failure_count is incremented by 1. The entire loop is then repeated for the next grade in the list.

When all of the grades have been entered and totaled, the program then proceeds to calculate the grade average. On impulse, it would seem that a statement such as

```
average = grade_total / number_of_grades;
```

would do the trick. However, you will recall that if the above statement were used, then the decimal portion of the result of the division would be lost. This would be due to the fact that an integer division would be performed, since *both* the numerator and the denominator of the division operation are integers.

There are really two different solutions to this problem. One would be to declare either number_of_grades or grade_total to be of type float. This would then guarantee that the division would be carried out without the loss of the decimal places. The only problem with this approach is that the variables number_of_grades and grade_total are used by the program to store only integer values. Declaring either of them to be of type float would only obscure their use in the program and is generally not a very clean way of doing things.

The other solution, as used by the program, is to actually *convert* the value of one of the variables to a floating point value for the purposes of the calculation. The *type cast* operator (float) has the effect of converting the value of the variable grade_total to type float for purposes of evaluation of the expression. In no way does this operator permanently affect the value of the variable grade_total; it is a unary operator that behaves like other unary operators. And as the expression -a has no permanent effect on the value of a, neither does the expression (float) a.

The type cast operator has a higher precedence than all the arithmetic operators but the unary minus. Of course, if necessary, parentheses can always be used in an expression to force the terms to be evaluated in any desired order.

As another example of the use of the type cast operator, the expression

```
(int) 29.55 + (int) 21.99
```

will be evaluated in C as

```
29 + 21
```

since the effect of casting a floating value to an integer is one of truncating the floating point value. The expression

```
(float) 6 / (float) 4
```

will produce a result of 1.5 as will the expression

```
(float) 6 / 4
```

Returning to our program, since the value of grade_total is cast into a floating point value *before* the division takes place, the C system will treat the operation as the division of a floating value by an integer. Since one of the operands is now a floating point value, the division operation will be carried out as a floating point operation. This means, of course, that we will get those decimal places that we want in the average.

Once the average has been calculated, it is displayed at the terminal to two decimal places of accuracy. If a decimal point followed by a number (known collectively as a *precision modifier*) is placed directly before the format character f (or e) in a printf format string, the corresponding value will be displayed to the specified number of decimal places, rounded. So in Program 6-2, the precision modifier .2 is used to cause the value of average to be displayed to two decimal places.

After the program has displayed the number of failing grades, execution of the program is complete.

The `if-else` Construct

If someone asks you whether a particular number is even or odd, you will most likely make the determination by examining the last digit of the number. If this digit is either 0, 2, 4, 6, or 8, then you will readily state that the number is even. Otherwise, you will claim that the number is odd.

An easier way for a computer to determine whether a particular number is even or odd is effected not by examining the last digit of the number to see if it is 0, 2, 4, 6, or 8, but by simply determining if the number is evenly divisible by 2 or not. If it is, then the number is even, else it is odd.

We have already seen how the modulus operator `%` is used to compute the remainder of one integer divided by another. This makes it the perfect operator to use in determining if an integer is evenly divisible by 2 or not. If the remainder after division by 2 is zero, then it is even, else it is odd.

Let us now write a program which determines whether an `integer` value typed in by the user is even or odd, and then displays an appropriate message at the terminal.

Program 6-3

```
/* Program to determine if a number is even or odd */

main ()
{
    int  number_to_test, remainder;

    printf ("Enter your number to be tested.: ");
    scanf ("%d", &number_to_test);

    remainder = number_to_test % 2;

    if ( remainder == 0 )
       printf ("The number is even.\n");

    if ( remainder != 0 )
       printf ("The number is odd.\n");
}
```

Program 6-3 Output

```
Enter your number to be tested: 2455
The number is odd.
```

Program 6-3 Output (Re-run)

```
Enter your number to be tested: 1210
The number is even.
```

After the number is typed in by the user, the remainder after division by 2 is calculated. The first if statement tests the value of this remainder to see if it is equal to 0. If it is, then the message "The number is even." is displayed.

The second if statement tests the value of remainder to see if it is *not* equal to zero. If it is not, then a message is displayed to inform the user that the number is odd.

The fact of the matter is that whenever the first if statement succeeds, the second one must fail, and vice versa. If you recall from our discussions of even/odd numbers at the beginning of this section, we said that if the number is evenly divisible by 2 then it is even; *else* it is odd.

When writing programs, this "else" concept is so frequently required that almost all modern programming languages provide a special construct to handle this situation. In C, this is known as the if-else construct and the general format is as follows:

```
if    ( expression )
      program statement 1
else
      program statement 2
```

The if-else is actually just an extension of the general format of the if statement. If the result of the evaluation of the expression is TRUE, then *program statement 1*, which immediately follows, is executed; otherwise, *program statement 2* is executed. In either case, either *program statement 1 or program statement 2* will be executed, but *not both*.

We can incorporate the if-else statement into the program above, replacing the two if statements by a single if-else statement. You will see how the use of this new program construct actually helps to somewhat reduce the program's complexity and also improves its readability.

Program 6-4

```
/* Program to determine if a number is even or odd
                     (Version 2)                          */

main ()
{
    int   number_to_test, remainder;

    printf ("Enter your number to be tested: ");
    scanf ("%d", &number_to_test);

    remainder = number_to_test % 2;

    if ( remainder == 0 )
       printf ("The number is even.\n");
    else
       printf ("The number is odd.\n");
}
```

Program 6-4 Output

```
Enter your number to be tested: 1234
The number is even.
```

Program 6-4 Output (Re-run)

```
Enter your number to be tested: 551
The number is odd.
```

Compound Relational Tests

The if statements that we have used so far in this chapter set up simple relational tests between two numbers. In Program 6-1, we compared the value of number against 0, while in Program 6-2, we compared the value of grade against 65. Sometimes it becomes desirable, if not necessary, to set up more sophisticated tests. Suppose, for example, that in Program 6-2 we wished to count not the number of failing grades, but instead the number of grades that were between 70 and 79, inclusive. In such a case, we would not merely wish to compare the value of grade against one limit, but against the two limits 70 and 79 to make sure that it fell within the specified range.

The C language provides the mechanisms necessary to perform these types of *compound relational* tests. A compound relational test is simply one or more simple relational tests joined by either the *logical AND* or the *logical OR* operator. These operators are represented by the character pairs && and || (two vertical bar characters), respectively. As an example, the C statement

```
if   ( grade >= 70   &&   grade <= 79 )
   ++grades_70_to_79;
```

will increment the value of grades_70_to_79 only if the value of grade is greater than or equal to 70 *and* less than or equal to 79. In a like manner, the statement

```
if   ( index < 0   ||   index > 99 )
   printf ("Error - index out of range\n");
```

will cause execution of the printf statement if index is less than 0 *or* greater than 99.

The compound operators can be used to form extremely complex expressions in C. Two words of advice are in order. First, when forming compound relational expressions, use parentheses to aid readability of the expression and to avoid getting into trouble because of a mistaken assumption about the precedence of the various operators in the expression. (The && operator has *lower* precedence than any arithmetic or relational operator but *higher* precedence than the | | operator.) Blank spaces should also be used to aid in the expression's readability. An extra blank space around the && and | | operators will visually set these operators apart from the expressions that are being joined by these operators.

The second word of advice is to not make expressions overly complex. C gives the programmer ultimate flexibilty in forming expressions. This flexibility is a capability that is often abused. Simpler expressions are almost always easier to read and debug.

To illustrate the use of a compound relational test in an actual program example, let us write a program which tests to see if a year is a leap year or not. We all know that a year is a leap year if it is evenly divisible by 4. What you may not realize, however, is that a year that is divisible by 100 is *not* a leap year, unless it is also divisible by 400.

Let us try to think how we would go about setting up a test for such a condition. First, we could compute the remainders of the year after division by 4, 100 and 400, and assign these values to appropriately named variables, such as rem_4, rem_100, and rem_400, respectively. Then we could proceed to test these remainders to determine if the desired criteria for a leap year were met.

If we rephrase our definition of a leap year from above, we can say that a year is a leap year if it is evenly divisible by 4 and not by 100, or if it is evenly divisible by 400. Stop for a moment to reflect on this last sentence and to verify to yourself that it is equivalent to our previously stated definition. Now that we have reformulated our definition in these terms, it becomes a relatively straightforward task to translate it into a program statement as shown

```
if ( (rem_4 == 0  &&  rem_100 != 0) ||  rem_400 == 0 )
    printf ("It's a leap year.\n");
```

The parentheses around the sub-expression

```
rem_4 == 0  &&  rem_100 != 0
```

are not required since that is how the expression will be evaluated anyway, remembering that && has higher precedence than | |. (In fact, in this particular example, the test

```
if ( rem_4 == 0  &&  ( rem_100 != 0 ||  rem_400 == 0 ) )
```

would work just as well.)

If we add a few statements in front of our test to declare our variables and to enable the user to key in the year from the terminal, then we end up with a program that determines if a year is a leap year, as shown below.

Program 6-5

```
/* This program determines if a year is a leap year */

main ()
{
    int  year, rem_4, rem_100, rem_400;

    printf ("Enter the year to be tested: ");
    scanf ("%d", &year);

    rem_4 = year % 4;
    rem_100 = year % 100;
    rem_400 = year % 400;

    if ( (rem_4 == 0  &&  rem_100 != 0)  ||  rem_400 == 0 )
        printf ("It's a leap year.\n");
    else
        printf ("Nope, it's not a leap year.\n");
}
```

Program 6-5 Output

```
    Enter the year to be tested: 1955
    Nope, it's not a leap year.
```

Program 6-5 Output (Re-run)

```
    Enter the year to be tested: 2000
    It's a leap year.
```

Program 6-5 Output (Re-run)

```
    Enter the year to be tested: 1800
    Nope, it's not a leap year.
```

In the above examples, we used a year that was not a leap year because it wasn't evenly divisible by 4 (1955), a year that was a leap year because it was evenly divisble by 400 (2000), and a year that wasn't a leap year because it was evenly divisible by 100 but not by 400 (1800). To complete the run of test cases, we should also try a year that is evenly divisible by 4 and not by 100. This is left as an exercise for you.

We mentioned that C gives the programmer a tremendous amount of flexiblity in forming expressions. For instance, in the above program, we did not have to calculate the intermediate results rem_4, rem_100, and rem_400— we could have performed the calculation directly inside the if statement as follows:

```
if ( ( year % 4 == 0  &&  year % 100 != 0 )  ||
          year % 400 == 0 )
```

The use of blank spaces to set off the various operators still makes the above expression readable. If we decided to ignore adding blanks, and removed the unnecessary set of parentheses, we could end up with an expression that looked like this:

```
if(year%4==0&&year%100!=0)||year%400==0)
```

This expression is perfectly valid and would (believe it or not) execute identically to the expression shown immediately above it. Obviously, those extra blanks go a long way towards aiding our understanding of complex expressions.

Nested if Statements

In discussions of the general format of the if statement, we indicated that if the result of evaluating the expression inside the parentheses were TRUE, then the statement that immediately followed would be executed. It is perfectly valid that this program statement be another if statement, as in the statement

```
if ( game_is_over == 0 )
    if ( player_to_move == YOU )
        printf ("Your Move\n");
```

If the value of game_is_over is zero, then the following statement will be executed, which is in turn another if statement. This if statement will compare the value of player_to_move against YOU. If the two values are equal, then the message "Your Move" will be displayed at the terminal. Therefore, the printf statement will be executed only if game_is_over equals 0 *and* player_to_move equals YOU. In fact, this statement could have been equivalently formulated using compound relationals as

```
if ( game_is_over == 0  &&  player_to_move == YOU )
    printf ("Your Move\n");
```

A more practical example of "nested" if statements would be if we added an else clause to the above example, as shown in the following:

```
if ( game_is_over == 0 )
    if ( player_to_move == YOU )
        printf ("Your Move\n");
    else
        printf ("My Move\n");
```

Execution of this statement proceeds as described above. However, if game_is_over equals 0 and the value of player_to_move is not equal to YOU, then the else clause will be executed. This will display the message "My Move" at the terminal. If game_is_over does not equal 0, the entire if statement which follows, including its associated else clause, will be skipped.

Notice how the else clause is associated with the if statement that tests the value of player_to_move, and not with the if statement that tests the value of game_is_over. The general rule is that an else clause is always associated with the last if statement that does not contain an else.

We can go one step further and can add an else clause to the outermost if statement in the preceding example. This else clause would be executed if the value of game_is_over is not 0.

```
if ( game_is_over == 0 )
    if ( player_to_move == YOU )
        printf ("Your Move\n");
    else
        printf ("My Move\n");
else
    printf ("The game is over\n");
```

Obviously, the proper use of indentation in the above example goes a long way towards aiding our understanding of the logic of this complex statement. Of course, even if we use indentation to indicate the way we think a statement will be interpreted in the C language, it may not always coincide with the way that the system will actually interpret the statement. For instance, removing the first else clause from the above example

```
if ( game_is_over == 0 )
    if ( player_to_move == YOU )
        printf ("Your Move\n");
else
    printf ("The game is over\n");
```

will *not* result in the statement being interpreted as indicated by its format. Instead, this statement will be interpreted as

```
if ( game_is_over == 0 )
    if ( player_to_move == YOU )
        printf ("Your Move\n");
    else
        printf ("The game is over\n");
```

since the else clause is associated with the last un-elsed if. We could force a different association in those cases where an innermost if does not contain an else but an outer if does by the use of braces. The braces have the effect of "closing off" the if statement. Thus,

```
if ( game_is_over == 0 )
{
    if ( player_to_move == YOU )
        printf ("Your Move\n");
}
else
    printf ("The game is over\n");
```

will achieve the desired effect, with the message "The game is over" being displayed if the value of game_is_over is not 0.

The else if Construct

We have seen how the else statement comes into play when we have a test against two possible conditions—either the number is even, else it is odd; either the year is a leap year, else it is not. However, programming decisions that we have to make are not always so black and white. Consider the task of writing a program that displayed -1 if a number typed in by a user were less than zero, 0 if the number typed in were equal to zero, and 1 if the number were greater than zero. (This is actually an implementation of what is commonly called the *sign* function.) Obviously, we must make three tests in this case—to determine if the number that is keyed in is negative, if it is zero, or if it is positive. Our simple if-else construct will not work. Of course, in this case, we could always resort to three separate if statements, but this solution will not always work in general—especially if the tests that are made are not mutually exclusive.

We can handle the situation just described by adding an if statement to our else clause. We mentioned that the statement that followed an else could be any valid C program statement, so why not another if? Thus, in the general case, we could write

```
if ( expression 1 )
    program statement 1
else
    if ( expression 2 )
        program statement 2
    else
        program statement 3
```

which effectively extends the if statement from a two-valued logic decision to a three-valued logic decision. We can continue to add if statements to the else clauses, in the manner just shown, to effectively extend the decision to an *n*-valued logic decision.

The preceding construct is so frequently used that it is generally referred to as an else if construct, and is usually formatted differently from that shown previously as

```
if ( expression 1 )
    program statement 1
else if ( expression 2 )
    program statement 2
else
    program statement 3
```

This latter method of formatting improves the readability of the statement and makes it clearer that a three-way decision is being made.

The next program illustrates the use of the `else if` construct by implementing the sign function discussed earlier.

Program 6-6

```
/* Program to implement the sign function */

main ()
{
    int  number, sign;

    printf ("Please type in a number: ");
    scanf ("%d", &number);

    if ( number < 0 )
        sign = -1;
    else if ( number == 0 )
        sign = 0;
    else                    /* Must be positive */
        sign = 1;

    printf ("Sign = %d\n", sign);
}
```

Program 6-6 Output

```
Please type in a number: 1121
Sign = 1
```

Program 6-6 Output (Re-run)

```
Please type in a number: -158
Sign = -1
```

Program 6-6 Output (Re-run)

```
Please type in a number: 0
Sign = 0
```

If the number that is entered is less than zero, sign is assigned the value -1; if the number is equal to zero, sign is assigned the value 0; otherwise, the number must be greater than zero, so sign is assigned the value 1.

The next program analyzes a character that is typed in from the terminal and classifies it as either an alphabetic character (*a-z* or *A-Z*), a digit (*0-9*), or a special character (anything else). In order to read a single character from the terminal, the format characters %c are used in the scanf call.

Program 6-7

```
/* This program categorizes a single character
        that is entered at the terminal          */

main ()
{
    char   c;

    printf ("Enter a single character:\n");
    scanf ("%c", &c);

    if ( (c >= 'a'  &&  c <= 'z') || (c >= 'A'  &&  c <= 'Z') )
        printf ("It's an alphabetic character.\n");
    else if  ( c >= '0'  &&  c <= '9' )
        printf ("It's a digit.\n");
    else
        printf ("It's a special character.\n");
}
```

Program 6-7 Output

```
Enter a single character:
&
It's a special character.
```

Program 6-7 Output (Re-run)

```
Enter a single character:
8
It's a digit.
```

Program 6-7 Output (Re-run)

```
Enter a single character:
B
It's an alphabetic character.
```

The first test that is made after the character is read in determines if the char variable c is an alphabetic character or not. This is done by testing if the character is either a lowercase letter or an uppercase letter. The former test is made by the expression

```
( c >= 'a'   &&   c <= 'z' )
```

which will be TRUE if c is within the range of characters 'a' through 'z'; that is, if c is a lowercase letter. The latter test is made by the expression

```
( c >= 'A'   &&   c <= 'Z' )
```

which will be TRUE if c is within the range of characters 'A' through 'Z', that is, if c is an uppercase letter. These tests work on all computer systems that store characters inside the machine in a format known as ASCII format. However, they do not work correctly on machines which use the EBCDIC format, since there are characters other than letters which fall within the tested ranges.

If the variable c is an alphabetic character, then the first if test will succeed and the message "It's an alphabetic character." will be displayed. If the test fails, then the else if clause will be executed. This clause determines if the character is a digit. Note that this test compares the character c against the *characters* '0' and '9' and *not* the *integers* 0 and 9. This is because a character was read in from the terminal, and the characters '0' to '9' are not the same as the numbers 0-9. In fact, on a computer system that uses the ASCII format mentioned above, the character '0' is actually represented internally as the number 48, the character '1' as the number 49, and so on.

If c is a digit character, then the phrase "It's a digit." will be displayed. Otherwise, if c is not alphabetic and is not a digit, then the final else clause will be executed, and will display the phrase "It's a special character" at the terminal. Execution of the program will then be complete.

You should note that even though scanf is used here to read just a single character, the Return key must still be pressed after the character is typed to send the input to the program. In general, whenever you're reading data from the terminal, the program doesn't see any of the data typed on the line until the Return key is pressed.

Let us suppose for our next example that we wished to write a program that allowed the user to type in simple expressions of the form

number   operator   number

The program will evaluate the expression and display the results at the terminal, to two decimal places of accuracy. The operators that we want to have recognized are the normal operators for addition, subtraction, multiplication, and division. The following program makes use of a large if statement with many else if clauses to determine which operation is to be performed.

Program 6-8

```
/* Program to evaluate simple expressions of the form
                number   operator   number                  */

main ()
{
    float   value1, value2;
    char    operator;

    printf ("Type in your expression.\n");
    scanf ("%f %c %f", &value1, &operator, &value2);

    if ( operator == '+' )
        printf ("%.2f\n", value1 + value2);
    else if ( operator == '-' )
        printf ("%.2f\n", value1 - value2);
    else if ( operator == '*' )
        printf ("%.2f\n", value1 * value2);
    else if ( operator == '/' )
        printf ("%.2f\n", value1 / value2);
}
```

Program 6-8 Output

```
Type in your expression.
123.5 + 59.3
182.80
```

Program 6-8 Output (Re-run)

```
Type in your expression.
198.7 / 26
7.64
```

Program 6-8 Output (Re-run)

```
Type in your expression.
89.3 * 2.5
223.25
```

The scanf call specifies that three values are to be read into the variables value1, operator, and value2. A floating value can be read in with the %f format characters, the same characters used for the output of floating values. This is the format used to read in the value of the variable value1, which is the first operand of our expression.

Next, we wish to read in the operator. Since the operator is a character (`'+'`, `'-'`, `'*'`, or `'/'`) and not a number, we read it into the character variable operator. The `%c` format characters tell the system to read in the next character from the terminal. The blank spaces inside the format string indicate that an arbitrary number of blank spaces are to be permitted on the input. This enables us to separate the operands from the operator with blank spaces when we type in these values. If we had specified the format string `"%f%c%f"` instead, then no spaces would have been permitted after typing in the first number and before typing in the operator. This is because when the `scanf` function is reading a character with the `%c` format characters, the next character on the input, *even if it is a blank space*, is the character that is read. However, it should be noted that, in general, the `scanf` function will *always* ignore leading spaces when it is reading in either a decimal or floating point number. Therefore, the format string `"%f %c%f"` would have worked just as well in the preceding program.

After the second operand has been keyed in and stored in the variable value2, the program proceeds to test the value of operator against the four permissible operators. When a correct match is made, the corresponding `printf` statement is executed to display the results of the calculation. Execution of the program is then complete.

A few words about program thoroughness are in order at this point. While the preceding program does accomplish the task that we set out to perform, the program is not really complete since it does not account for mistakes made on the part of the user. For example, what would happen if the user were to type in a `?` for the operator by mistake. The program would simply "fall through" the `if` statement and no messages would ever appear at the terminal to alert the user to the fact that he had incorrectly typed in his expression.

Another case that is overlooked is when the user types in a division operation with zero as the divisor. We know by now that we should never attempt to divide a number by zero in C. The program should check for this case.

Trying to predict the ways that a program can fail or produce unwanted results and then taking preventative measures to account for such situations is a necessary part of producing good, reliable programs. Running a sufficient number of test cases against a program will often point the finger to portions of the program that do not account for certain cases. But it goes further than that. It must become a matter of self discipline while coding a program to always say "What would happen if ..." and to insert the necessary program statements to handle the situation properly.

Program 6-8A, a modified version of Program 6-8, accounts for division by zero and the keying in of an unknown operator.

Program 6-8A

```
/* Program to evaluate simple expressions of the form
            value    operator    value                    */

main ()
{
    float    value1, value2;
    char    operator;

    printf ("Type in your expression.\n");
    scanf ("%f %c %f", &value1, &operator, &value2);

    if ( operator == '+' )
        printf ("%.2f\n", value1 + value2);
    else if ( operator == '-' )
        printf ("%.2f\n", value1 - value2);
    else if ( operator == '*' )
        printf ("%.2f\n", value1 * value2);
    else if ( operator == '/' )
        if ( value2 == 0 )
            printf ("Division by zero.\n");
        else
            printf ("%.2f\n", value1 / value2);
    else
        printf ("Unknown operator.\n");
}
```

Program 6-8A Output

```
Type in your expression.
123.5 + 59.3
182.80
```

Program 6-8A Output (Re-run)

```
Type in your expression.
198.7 / 0
Division by zero.
```

Program 6-8A Output (Re-run)

```
Type in your expression.
125 $ 28
Unknown operator.
```

When the operator that is typed in is the slash, for division, another test is made to determine if `value2` is 0. If it is, an appropriate message is displayed at the terminal. Otherwise, the division operation is carried out and the results displayed. Pay careful attention to the nesting of the `if` statements and the associated `else` clauses in this case.

The `else` clause at the end of the program catches any "fall throughs." Therefore, any value of `operator` that does not match any of the four characters tested will cause this `else` clause to be executed, resulting in the display of "Unknown operator." at the terminal.

◆ The `switch` Statement ◆

The type of `if-else` statement chain that we encountered in the last program example—where the value of a variable is successively compared against different values—is so commonly used when developing programs that a special program statement exists in the C language for performing precisely this function. The name of the statement is the `switch` statement, and its general format is:

```
switch ( expression )
{
    case value1:
        program statement
        program statement
          . . .
        break;
    case value2:
        program statement
        program statement
          . . .
        break;
      . . .
    case valuen:
        program statement
        program statement
          . . .
        break;
    default:
        program statement
        program statement
          . . .
        break;
}
```

The *expression* enclosed within parentheses is successively compared against the values *value1*, *value2*, ..., *valuen*, which must be simple constants or constant expressions. If a case is found whose value is equal to the value of *expression*, then the program statements that follow the case are executed. You will note that when more than one such program statement is included, that they do *not* have to be enclosed within braces.

The break statement signals the end of a particular case and causes execution of the switch statement to be terminated. You must remember to include the break statement at the end of every case. Forgetting to do so for a particular case will cause program execution to continue into the next case whenever that case gets executed.

The special optional case called default is executed if the value of *expression* does not match any of the case values. This is conceptually equivalent to the "fall through" else that we used in the previous example. In fact, the general form of the switch statement can be equivalently expressed as an if statement as follows:

```
if    ( expression == value1 )
{
      program statement
      program statement
         . . .
}
else if ( expression == value2 )
{
      program statement
      program statement
         . . .
}
   . . .
else if ( expression == valuen )
{
      program statement
      program statement
         . . .
}
else
{
      program statement
      program statement
         . . .
}
```

Bearing the above in mind, we can translate the big if statement from Program 6-8A into an equivalent switch statement. We will call this new program Program 6-9.

Program 6-9

```
/* Program to evaluate simple expressions of the form
           value    operator    value                */

main ()
{
    float   value1, value2;
    char    operator;

    printf ("Type in your expression.\n");
    scanf ("%f %c %f", &value1, &operator, &value2);

    switch ( operator )
    {
        case '+':
            printf ("%.2f\n", value1 + value2);
            break;
        case '-':
            printf ("%.2f\n", value1 - value2);
            break;
        case '*':
            printf ("%.2f\n", value1 * value2);
            break;
        case '/':
            if ( value2 == 0 )
                printf ("Division by zero.\n");
            else
                printf ("%.2f\n", value1 / value2);
            break;
        default:
            printf ("Unknown operator.\n");
            break;
    }
}
```

Program 6-9 Output

```
Type in your expression.
178.99 - 326.8
-147.81
```

After the expression has been read in, the value of `operator` is successively compared against the values as specified by each case. When a match is
found, the statements contained inside the case will be executed. The `break`

statement will then send execution out of the switch statement, where execution of the program will be complete. If none of the cases match the value of operator, the default case, which displays "Unknown operator." will be executed.

The break statement in the default case is actually unnecessary in the preceding program since no statements follow this case inside the switch. Nevertheless, it is a good programming habit to remember to include the break at the end of every case.

When writing a switch statement, you should bear in mind that no two case values may be the same. However, we can associate more than one case value with a particular set of program statements. This is done simply by listing the mutiple case values (with the keyword case before the value and the colon after the value in each case) before the common statements that are to be executed. As an example, in the switch statement

```
switch  ( operator )
{
    . . .
   case '*':
   case 'x':
       printf ("%.2f\n", value1 * value2);
       break;
    . . .
}
```

the printf statement which multiplies value1 by value2 will be executed if operator is equal to an asterisk or to the lowercase letter x.

◆ Flags ◆

Just about anyone learning to program soon finds him or herself with the task of having to write a program to generate a table of *prime numbers*. To refresh your memory, a positive integer p is a prime number if it not evenly divisble by any other integers, other than 1 and itself. The first prime integer is defined to be 2. The next prime is 3, since it is not evenly divisible by any integers other than 1 and 3; and 4 is *not* prime because it *is* evenly divisible by 2.

There are several approaches that we could take in order to generate a table of prime numbers. If we had the task to generate all prime numbers up to 50, for example, then the most straightforward (and simplest) algorithm to generate such a table would simply test each integer p for divisibility by all integers from 2 through p-1. If any such integer evenly divided p, then p would not be prime; otherwise, it would be a prime number.

Program 6-10

```
/* Program to generate a table of prime numbers */

main ()
{
    int  p, is_prime, d;

    for ( p = 2;  p <= 50;  ++p )
    {
        is_prime = 1;

        for ( d = 2;  d < p;  ++d )
          if ( p % d  ==  0 )
            is_prime = 0;

        if ( is_prime != 0 )
          printf ("%d  ", p);
    }

    printf ("\n");
}
```

Program 6-10 Output

```
2  3  5  7  11  13  17  19  23  29  31  37  41  43  47
```

Several points are worth noting about the above program. The outermost for statement sets up a loop to cycle through the integers 2 through 50. The loop variable p represents the value we are currently testing to see if it is prime. The first statement in the loop assigns the value 1 to the variable is_prime. The use of this variable will become apparent shortly.

A second loop is set up to divide p by the integers from 2 through p-1. Inside the loop, a test is made to see if the remainder of p divided by d is 0. If it is, then we know that p cannot be prime since there exists an integer other than 1 and itself that evenly divides it. To "signal" that p is no longer a candidate as a prime number, the value of the variable is_prime is set equal to 0.

When the innermost loop finishes execution, the value of is_prime is tested. If its value is not equal to zero, no integer was found that evenly divided p; therefore p must be a prime number and its value is displayed.

You may have noticed that the variable is_prime takes on either the value 0 or 1, and no other values. Its value is 1 as long as p still qualifies as a prime number. But as soon as a single even divisor is found, it's value is set to 0 to indicate that p no longer satisifies the criteria for being prime. Variables that are used in such a manner are generally referred to as Boolean variables, or more simply, as *flags*. A flag will typically assume only one of two different values.

Furthermore, the value of a flag will usually be tested at least once in the program to see if it is "on" (TRUE) or "off" (FALSE) and some particular action taken based upon the results of the test.

In C the notion of a flag being TRUE or FALSE is most naturally translated into the values 1 and 0, respectively. So in the above program, when we set the value of is_prime to 1 inside the loop, we are effectively setting it TRUE to indicate that p "is prime." If during the course of execution of the inner for loop, an even divisor is found, the value of is_prime is set FALSE to indicate that p no longer "is prime."

It is no coincidence that the value 1 is typically used to represent the TRUE or "on" state and 0 to represent the FALSE or "off" state. This representation corresponds to the notion of a single bit inside a computer. When the bit is "on", its value is 1; when it is "off", its value is 0. But in C, there is an even more convincing argument in favor of these logic values. It has to do with the way the C language treats the concept of TRUE and FALSE.

When we began our discussions in this chapter, we noted that if the conditions specified inside the if statement were "satisfied," then the program statement that immediately followed would be executed. But what exactly does "satisfied" mean? In the C language, satisfied means nonzero, and nothing more. So the statement

```
if ( 100 )
    printf ("This will always be printed.\n");
```

will result in execution of the printf statement because the condition in the if statement (in this case simply the value 100) is nonzero and therefore is satisfied.

In each of the programs in this chapter, the notions of "nonzero means satisfied" and "zero means not satisfied" were used. This is because whenever a relational expression is evaluated in C, it is given the value 1 if the expression is satisfied and 0 if the expression is not statisfied. So evaluation of the statement

```
if   ( number < 0 )
    number = -number;
```

actually proceeds as follows:

1. The relational expression number < 0 is evaluated. If the condition is satisfied, that is, if number is less than 0, then the value of the expression is 1; otherwise, its value is 0.

2. The if statement tests the result of the expression evaluation. If the result is nonzero, then the statement that immediately follows is executed; otherwise the statement is skipped.

The preceding discussion also applies to evaluation of conditions inside the for, while, and do statements. Evaluation of compound relational expressions such as in the statement

```
while  ( char != 'e'  &&  count != 80 )
```

also proceeds as outlined above. If both specified conditions are valid, then the result will be 1; but if either condition is not valid, then the result of the evaluation will be 0. The results of the evaluation will then be checked. If the result is 0, then the while loop will terminate; otherwise it will continue.

Returning to Program 6-10 and the notion of flags, it is perfectly valid in C—and even clearer—to test if the value of a flag is TRUE by an expression such as

```
if ( is_prime )
```

rather than with the equivalent expression

```
if ( is_prime != 0 )
```

To easily test if the value of a flag is FALSE, we bring into play the *logical negation* operator, !. In the expression

```
if ( ! is_prime )
```

the logical negation operator is used test if the value of is_prime is FALSE (read this statement as "if not is_prime"). In general, an expression such as

```
! expression
```

negates the logical value of *expression*. So if *expression* is 0, the logical negation operator produces a 1. And if the result of the evaluation of *expression* is nonzero, the negation operator yields a 0.

The logical negation operator can be used to easily "flip" the value of a flag, such as in the expression

```
my_move = ! my_move;
```

As you might expect, this operator has the same precedence as the unary minus operator, which means that it has higher precedence than all binary arithmetic operators and all relational operators. So to test if the value of a variable x is not less than the value of a variable y, such as in

```
! ( x < y )
```

the parentheses are required to ensure proper evaluation of the expression. Of course, we could have equivalently expressed the above as

```
x >= y
```

◆ The Conditional Expression Operator ◆

Perhaps the most unusual operator in the C language is one called the conditional expression operator. Unlike all other operators in C—which are either unary or binary operators—the conditional expression operator is a *ternary* operator; that is, it takes three operands. The two symbols that are used to denote this operator are the question mark (?) and the colon (:). The first operand is placed before the ?, the second between the ? and the :, and the third after the :.

The general format of the conditional expression operator is:

condition ? *expression1* : *expression2*

where *condition* is an expression, usually a relational expression, that is evaluated by the C system first whenever the conditonal expression operator is encountered. If the result of the evaluation of *condition* is TRUE (that is, nonzero), then *expression1* is evaluated and the result of the evaluation becomes the result of the operation. If *condition* evaluates FALSE (that is, zero), then *expression2* is evaluated and its result becomes the result of the operation.

The conditional expression operator is most often used to assign one of two values to a variable depending upon some condition. For example, suppose we have an integer variable x and another integer variable s. If we wished to assign -1 to s if x were less than 0, and the value of x^2 to s otherwise, the following statement could be written:

```
s = ( x < 0 ) ? -1 : x * x;
```

The condition x < 0 is first tested when the above statement is executed. Parentheses are generally placed around the condition expression to aid in the statement's readability. This is usually not required, since the precedence of the conditional expression operator is very low—lower in fact then all other operators but the assignment operators and the comma operator.

If the value of x is less than zero, then the expression immediately following the ? will be evaluated. This expression is simply the constant integer value -1, which will be assigned to the variable s if x is less than zero.

If the value of x is not less than zero, then the expression immediately following the : will be evaluated and assigned to s. So if x is greater than or equal to zero, the value of x * x, or x^2, will be assigned to s.

As another example of the use of the conditional expression operator, the following statement assigns to the variable `max_value` the maximum of a and b.

```
max_value = ( a > b ) ? a : b;
```

If the expression that is used after the : (the "else" part) consists of another conditional expression operator, then we can achieve the effects of an "else if" clause. For example, the *sign* function that was implemented in Program 6-6 can be written in one program line using two conditional expression operators as follows:

```
sign = ( number < 0 ) ? -1 : (( number == 0 ) ? 0 : 1);
```

If `number` is less than zero, then `sign` is assigned the value -1; else if `number` is equal to zero, then `sign` is assigned the value 0; else it is assigned the value 1. The parentheses around the "else" part of the above expression are actually unnecessary. This is because the conditional expression operator associates from right to left, meaning that multiple uses of this operator in a single expression, such as in

e1 ? *e2* : *e3* ? *e4* : *e5*

will group from right to left and therefore will be evaluated as

e1 ? *e2* : (*e3* ? *e4* : *e5*)

It is not necessary that the conditional expression operator be used on the right-hand side of an assignment—it can be used in any situation where an expression could be used. This means that we could display the sign of the variable `number`, without first assigning it to a variable, using a `printf` statement as shown:

```
printf ("Sign = %d\n", ( number < 0 ) ? -1
                     : ( number == 0 ) ? 0 : 1);
```

This concludes our discussions on making decisions. In the next chapter you will get your first look at more sophisticated data types. The *array* is a powerful concept that will find its way into many programs that you will develop in C.

♦ Exercises ♦

1. If you have access to a computer facility that supports the C programming language, type in and run the 10 programs presented in this chapter. Compare the output produced by each program with the output presented after each program. Try experimenting with each program by keying in values other than those shown.

2. Write a program that asks the user to type in two integer values at the terminal. Test these two numbers to determine if the first is evenly divisible by the second, and then display an appropriate message at the terminal.

3. Write a program that accepts two integer values typed in by the user. Display the result of dividing the first integer by the second, to three decimal place accuracy. Remember to have the program check for division by zero.

4. We developed Program 5-9 to reverse the digits of an integer typed in from the terminal. However, this program does not function too well if we type in a negative number. Find out what happens in such a case and then modify the program so that negative numbers are correctly handled. By correctly handled, we mean that if the number -8645 were typed in, for example, then the output of the program should be 5468-.

5. Write a program that acts as a simple "printing" calculator. The program should allow the user to type in expressions of the form

    number   operator

    The following operators should be recognized by the program:

    +   –   *   /   S   E

    The S operator tells the program to set the "accumulator" to the typed-in number. The E operator tells the program that execution is to end. The arithmetic operations are performed on the contents of the accumulator with the number that was keyed in acting as the second operand. The following is a "sample run" showing how the program should operate.

`Begin Calculations`	
`10 S`	*Set Accumulator to 10*
`= 10.000000`	*Contents of Accumulator*
`2 /`	*Divide by 2*
`= 5.000000`	*Contents of Accumulator*
`55 -`	*Subtract 55*
`= -50.000000`	
`100.25 S`	*Set Accumulator to 100.25*

```
= 100.250000
4 *                          Multiply by 4
= 401.000000
0 E                          End of program
= 401.000000
End of Calculations.
```

Make sure that the program detects division by zero and also checks for unknown operators.

6. Write a program that takes an integer keyed in from the terminal and extracts and displays each digit of the integer in English. So, if the user types in 932, then the program should display

```
nine three two
```

(Remember to display "zero" if the user types in just a 0.) Note: This exercise is a hard one!

7. Program 6-10 has several inefficiencies. One inefficiency results from checking even numbers. Since it is obvious that any even number greater than 2 cannot be prime, the program could simply "skip" all even numbers as possible primes *and* as possible divisors. The inner for loop is also inefficient because the value of p is *always* divided by all values of d from 2 through p-1. This inefficiency could be avoided if we added a test for the value of is_prime in the conditions of the for loop. In this manner, the for loop could be set up to continue as long as no divisor was found and the value of d was less than p. Modify Program 6-10 to incorporate these two changes. Then run the program to verify its operation. (Note: In the next chapter, we will find even more efficient ways of generating prime numbers.)

Arrays

The C language provides a capability that enables the user to define a set of ordered data items known as an *array*. This chapter describes how arrays can be defined and manipulated in C. In later chapters, we will include further discussions on arrays to illustrate how well they work together with program functions, structures, character strings, and pointers.

Suppose we had a set of grades that we wished to read into the computer, and suppose that we wished to perform some operations on these grades, such as rank them in ascending order, compute their average, or find their median. In Program 6-2, we were able to calculate the average of a set of grades by simply adding each grade into a cumulative total as each grade was keyed in. However, if we wanted to rank the grades into ascending order, for example, then we would have to do something further. If you think about the process of ranking a set of grades, you will quickly realize that we cannot perform such an operation until each and every grade has been entered. Therefore, using the techniques we have already described, we would read in each grade and store it into a unique variable, perhaps with a sequence of statements such as:

```
printf ("Enter grade 1\n");
scanf ("%d", &grade1);
printf ("Enter grade 2\n");
scanf ("%d", &grade2);
        . . .
```

Once all of the grades had been entered, we could then proceed to rank them. This could be done by setting up a series of if statements to compare each of the values to determine the smallest grade, the next smallest grade, and so on, until the maximum grade had been determined. If you sit down and try to write a program to perform precisely this task, you will soon realize that for any reasonably sized list of grades (where reasonably sized is probably only about 10), the resulting program will be quite large and quite complex. All is not lost, however, as this is one instance where the array comes to the rescue.

In C, we can define a variable called `grades`, which represents not a *single* value of a grade, but an entire *set of grades*. Each element of the set can then be referenced by means of a number called an *index* number or *subscript*. Where in mathematics a subscripted variable, x_i, refers to the *i*th element x in a set, in C the equivalent notation is

```
x[i]
```

So the expression

```
grades[5]
```

(read as "grades sub 5") refers to element number 5 in the array called `grades`. In C, array elements begin with number 0, so

```
grades[0]
```

actually refers to the first element of the array. (For this reason, it is easier to think of it as referring to element number zero, rather than as referring to the first element.)

An individual array element can be used anywhere that a normal variable could be. For example, we can assign an array value to another variable with a statement such as

```
g = grades[50];
```

This statement takes the value contained in `grades[50]` and assigns it to `g`. More generally, if `i` is declared to be an integer variable, then the statement

```
g = grades[i];
```

will take the value contained in element number `i` of the `grades` array and assign it to `g`. So if `i` were equal to 7 when the above statement were executed, then the value of `grades[7]` would get assigned to `g`.

A value can be stored into an element of an array simply by specifying the array element on the left-hand side of an equals sign. In the statement

```
grades[100] = 95;
```

the value 95 is stored into element number 100 of the `grades` array. The statement

```
    grades[i] = g;
```

will have the effect of storing the value of g into grades[i].

The ability to represent a collection of related data items by a single array enables us to develop concise and efficient programs. For example, we can very easily sequence through the elements in the array by varying the value of a variable that is used as a subscript into the array. So the for loop

```
    for ( i = 0;   i < 100;   ++i )
       sum = sum + grades[i];
```

will sequence through the first 100 elements of the array grades (elements 0 through 99) and will add the value of each grade into sum. When the for loop is finished, the variable sum will then contain the total of the first 100 values of the grades array (assuming sum were set to 0 before the loop was entered).

In addition to integer constants, integer-valued expressions can also be used inside the brackets to reference a particular element of an array. So if low and high were defined as integer variables, then the statement

```
    next_value = sorted_data[(low + high) / 2];
```

would assign to the variable next_value the value indexed by evaluating the expression (low + high) / 2. If low were equal to 1 and high were equal to 9, then the value of sorted_data[5] would be assigned to next_value. And if low were equal to 1 and high were equal to 10 then the value of sorted_data[5] would also be referenced, since we know that an integer division of 11 by 2 gives the result of 5.

Just as with variables, arrays must also be declared before they are used. The declaration of an array involves declaring the type of element that will be contained in the array—such as int, float, or char—as well as the maximum number of elements that will be stored inside the array. (The C system needs this latter information in order to determine how much of its memory space to reserve for the particular array.)

As an example, the declaration

```
    int   grades[100];
```

declares grades to be an array containing 100 integer elements. Valid references to this array may be made by using subscripts from 0 through 99. (But be careful to make sure that valid subscripts are used, since C does not do any checking of array bounds for you. So a reference to element number 150 of array grades, as previously declared, would not necessarily cause an error but would most likely cause unwanted, if not unpredictable, program results.)

To declare an array called averages that contained 200 floating point elements, the declaration

```
float   averages[200];
```

would be used. This declaration would cause enough space inside the computer's memory to be reserved to contain two hundred floating point numbers. Similarly, the declaration

```
int   values[10];
```

would reserve enough space for an array called `values` that could hold up to 10 integer numbers. We could better conceptualize this reserved storage space by referring to Fig. 7-1.

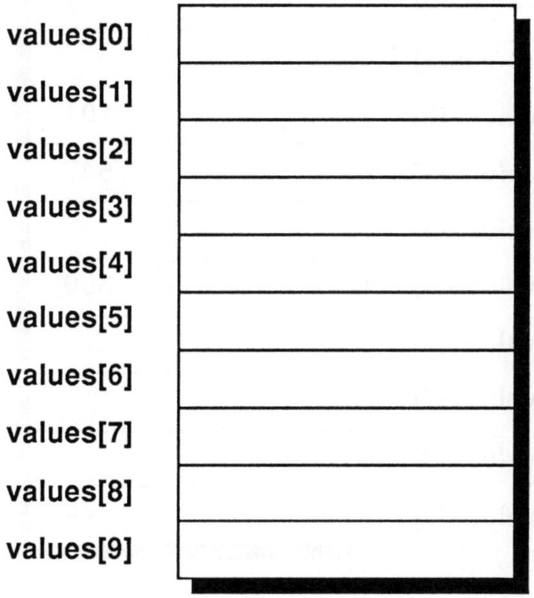

values[0]	
values[1]	
values[2]	
values[3]	
values[4]	
values[5]	
values[6]	
values[7]	
values[8]	
values[9]	

Fig. 7-1. The array `values` in memory

The elements of arrays declared to be of type `int`, `float`, or `char` may be manipulated in the same fashion as can ordinary variables: we can assign `values` to them, display their `values`, add to them, subtract from them, and so on. So if the following statements were to appear in a program

```
int   values[10];

values[0] = 197;
values[2] = -100;
values[5] = 350;
values[3] = values[0] + values[5];
values[9] = values[5] / 10;
--values[2];
```

then the array values would contain the numbers as shown in Fig. 7-2.

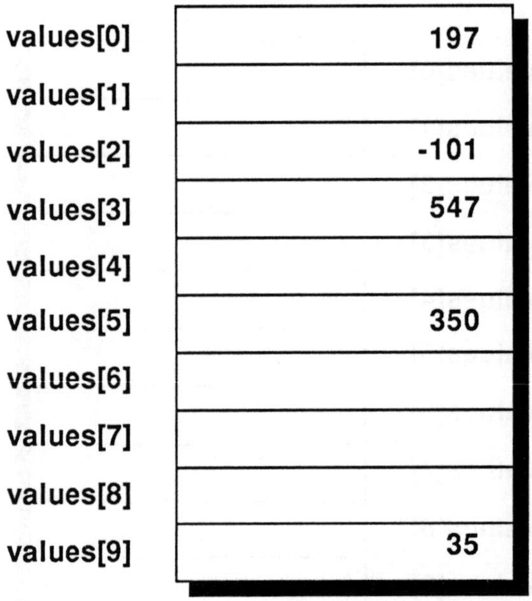

values[0]	197
values[1]	
values[2]	-101
values[3]	547
values[4]	
values[5]	350
values[6]	
values[7]	
values[8]	
values[9]	35

Fig. 7-2. values with some initialized elements

The first assignment statement has the effect of storing the value of 197 into values[0]. In a similar fashion, the second and third assignment statements store -100 and 350 into values[2] and values[5], respectively. The next statement adds the contents of values[0] (which is 197) to the contents of values[5] (which is 350) and stores the result of 547 in values[3]. In the following program statement, 350—the value contained in values[5]—is divided by 10 and the result stored into values[9]. The last statement decrements the contents of values[2], which has the effect of changing its value from -100 to -101.

The preceding program statements were incorporated into the following program (Program 7-1). The `for` loop sequences through each element of the array, displaying its value at the terminal in turn.

Program 7-1

```
main ()
{
     int   values[10];
     int   index;

     values[0] = 197;
     values[2] = -100;
     values[5] = 350;
     values[3] = values[0] + values[5];
     values[9] = values[5] / 10;
     --values[2];

     for ( index = 0;  index < 10;  ++index )
         printf ("values[%d] = %d\n", index, values[index]);
}
```

Program 7-1 Output

```
values[0] = 197
values[1] = 0
values[2] = -101
values[3] = 547
values[4] = 0
values[5] = 350
values[6] = 0
values[7] = 0
values[8] = 0
values[9] = 35
```

The variable `index` assumes the values 0 through 9, as the last valid subscript of an array is always one less than the number of elements (due to that zeroth element). Since we never assigned `values` to five of the elements in the array—elements 1, 4, and 6 through 8—the `values` that are displayed for them are meaningless. Even though the program's output shows these values as zero, the value of any uninitialized variable or array element is simply the value that happens to be sitting around inside the computer's memory at the time that the program is executed. For this reason, no assumption should ever be made as to the value of an uninitialized variable or array element.

It is now time to consider a slightly more practical example. Suppose we took a telephone survey to discover how people felt about a particular television show and we asked each respondent to rate the show on a scale from 1 to 10, inclusive. After interviewing 5,000 people we accumulated a list of 5,000 numbers. Now we would like to analyze the results. One of the first pieces of data we would like to gather is a table showing the distribution of the ratings. In other words, we would like to know how many people rated the show a 1, how many a 2, and so on up to 10.

Although not an impossible chore, it would be a bit tedious to go through each response and manually count the number of responses in each rating category. And if we had a response which could be answered in more than 10 ways (consider the task of categorizing the age of the respondent), this approach would be even more unreasonable. So we would like to develop a program to count the number of responses for each rating. The first impulse might be to set up ten different counters, called perhaps `rating_1` through `rating_10`, and then to increment the appropriate counter each time the corresponding rating were keyed in. But once again, if we considered the case where we were dealing with more than 10 possible choices, this approach could become a bit tedious. And besides, an approach that uses an array provides the vehicle for implementing a much cleaner solution, even in this case.

We can set up an array of counters called `rating_counters`, for example, and then we can increment the corresponding counter as each response is keyed in. Since we don't wish to take up 100 pages in this book for the 5,000 responses to the survey, in the program that follows we assume that we are dealing with only 20 responses. Anyway, it's always good practice to get a program working on a smaller test case first before proceeding with the full set of data, since problems that are discovered in the program will be much easier to isolate and debug if the amount of test data is small.

Program 7-2

```
main ()
{
    int  rating_counters[11], i, response;

    for ( i = 1;  i <= 10;  ++i )
        rating_counters[i] = 0;

    printf ("Enter your responses\n");

    for ( i = 1;  i <= 20;  ++i )
    {
        scanf ("%d", &response);

        if ( response < 1 || response > 10 )
            printf ("Bad response: %d\n", response);
        else
            ++rating_counters[response];
    }
```

```
        printf ("\n\nRating    Number of Responses\n");
        printf ("------    -------------------\n");

        for ( i = 1;   i <= 10;   ++i )
            printf ("%4d%14d\n", i, rating_counters[i]);
    }
```

Program 7-2 Output

```
Enter your responses
6
5
8
3
9
6
5
7
15
Bad response: 15
5
5
1
7
4
10
5
5
6
8
9
6

Rating    Number of Responses
------    -------------------
    1                1
    2                0
    3                1
    4                1
    5                6
    6                4
    7                2
    8                2
    9                2
   10                1
```

The array `rating_counters` is defined to contain 11 elements. A valid question you might ask is "If there are only 10 possible responses to the survey, why then is the array defined to contain 11 elements rather than 10?" The answer lies in the strategy for counting the responses in each particular rating category. Since each response can be a number from 1 to 10, the program keeps track of the responses for any one particular rating by simply incrementing the corresponding array element (after first checking to make sure that the user entered a valid response between 1 and 10). For example, if a rating of 5 is typed in, the value of `rating_counters[5]` is incremented by one. By employing this technique, the total number of respondents that rated the TV show a 5 will be contained in `rating_counters[5]`.

Getting back to the reason for 11 elements versus 10, the reason should now be clear. Since the highest rating number is a 10, we must set up our array to contain 11 elements in order to index `rating_counters[10]`, remembering that due to that zeroth element, the number of elements in an array is always one more than the highest index number. Since no response can have a value of zero, `rating_counters[0]` is never used. In fact, in the `for` loops that initialize and display the contents of the array, you will note that the variable `i` starts at 1, and thereby bypasses the initialization and display of `rating_counters[0]`.

As a point of discussion, it is mentioned that we could have developed our program to use an array containing precisely 10 elements. Then, when each response was keyed in by the user, we could have instead incremented `rating_counters[response - 1]`. This way, `rating_counters[0]` would have contained the number of respondents that rated the show a 1, `rating_counters[1]` the number that rated the show a 2, and so on. This is a perfectly fine approach. The only reason it was not used was because storing the number of responses of value n inside `rating_counters[n]` is a slightly more straightforward approach.

Study Program 7-3, which generates a table of the first 15 *Fibonacci* numbers, and try to predict its output. What relationship exists between each number in the table?

Program 7-3

```
/* Program to generate the first 15 Fibonacci numbers */

main ()
{
    int  Fibonacci[15], i;

    Fibonacci[0] = 0;     /* by definition */
    Fibonacci[1] = 1;     /*     ditto     */

    for ( i = 2;  i < 15;  ++i )
        Fibonacci[i] = Fibonacci[i-2] + Fibonacci[i-1];

    for ( i = 0;  i < 15;  ++i )
        printf ("%d\n", Fibonacci[i]);
}
```

Program 7-3 Output

```
0
1
1
2
3
5
8
13
21
34
55
89
144
233
377
```

The first two Fibonacci numbers, which we will call F_0 and F_1 are defined to be 0 and 1, respectively. Thereafter, each successive Fibonacci number F_i is defined to be the sum of the two preceding Fibonacci numbers F_{i-2} and F_{i-1}. So F_2 is calculated by adding together the values of F_0 and F_1. In the preceding program, this corresponds directly to calculating Fibonacci[2] by adding together the values Fibonacci[0] and Fibonacci[1]. This calculation is performed inside the for loop, which calculates the values of F_2 through F_{14} (or, equivalently, Fibonacci[2] through Fibonacci[14]).

Fibonacci numbers actually have many applications in the field of mathematics and in the study of computer algorithms. The sequence of Fibonacci numbers historically originated from the "rabbits problem": If we start with a pair of rabbits and assume that each pair of rabbits produces a new pair of rabbits each month, that each newly born pair of rabbits can produce offspring by the end of their second month, and that rabbits never die, how many pairs of rabbits will there be after the end of a year? The answer to this problem rests in the fact that at the end of the nth month, there will be a total of F_{n+2} rabbits. Therefore, according to the table from Program 7-3's output, at the end of the twelfth month, there will be a total of 377 pairs of rabbits.

Now it's time to return to the prime number program that we developed in Chapter 6 and see how the use of an array can help us to develop a more efficient program. In Program 6-10, the criteria that we used for determining if a number was prime was to divide the prime candidate by all successive integers from 2 up to the number minus one. In Exercise 7 in Chapter 6, we noted two inefficiencies with this approach that could easily be corrected. But even with these changes, the approach used is still not terribly efficient. And while such questions of efficiency may not be important when dealing with a table of prime numbers up to 50, these questions do become important, for example, when we start thinking about generating a table of prime numbers up to 100,000.

One method for generating prime numbers that is an improvement over the previous approach involves the notion that a number is prime if it is not evenly divisible by any other prime number. This stems from the fact that any non-prime integer can be expressed as a multiple of prime factors. (For example, 20 has the prime factors 2, 2, and 5.) We can use this added insight to help us to develop a more efficient prime number program. The program can test if a given integer is prime by determining if it is evenly divisible by any other previously generated prime. By now the term "previously generated" should trigger off in your mind the idea that an array must be involved here. We can use an array to store each prime number as it is generated.

As a further optimization of the prime number generator program, it can be readily demonstrated that any non-prime integer n must have as one of its factors an integer that is less than or equal to the square root of n. What this means is that it is only necessary to determine if a given integer is prime by testing it for even divisibility against all prime factors up to the square root of the integer.

Program 7-4 incorporates the above discussions into a program to generate all prime numbers up to 50. The expression

```
p / primes[i] >= primes[i]
```

is used in the innermost `for` loop as a test to ensure that the value of `primes[i]` does not exceed the square root of `p`. This test comes directly from the discussions in the last paragraph. (You might want to think about the math a bit.)

We start off by storing 2 and 3 as the first two primes into the array `primes`. This array has been defined to contain 50 elements, even though we obviously won't need that many locations for storing the prime numbers. The variable `prime_index` is initially set to 2, which is the next free slot in the `primes` array. A `for` loop is then set up to run through the odd integers from 5 to 50. After the flag `is_prime` is set to TRUE, another `for` loop is entered. This loop will successively divide the value of `p` by all of the previously generated prime numbers that are stored in the array `primes`. The index variable `i` starts at 1, since it is not necessary to test any values of `p` for divisibilty by `primes[0]` (which is 2). This is true because our program does not even consider even numbers as possible primes. Inside the loop, a test is made to see if the value of `p` is evenly divisible by `primes[i]`, and if it is, then `is_prime` is set FALSE. The `for` loop continues execution so long as the value of `is_prime` is TRUE *and* the value of `primes[i]` does not exceed the square root of `p`.

After exiting the `for` loop, a test of the `is_prime` flag determines whether or not to store the value of `p` as the next prime number inside the `primes` array.

Once all values of `p` have been tried, the program displays each prime number that has been stored inside the `primes` array. The value of the index variable `i` varies from 0 through `prime_index` - 1, since `prime_index` was always set pointing to the *next* free slot in the `primes` array.

Program 7-4

```
/* Modified program to generate prime numbers */

main ()
{
    int  p, is_prime, i, primes[50], prime_index = 2;

    primes[0] = 2;
    primes[1] = 3;

    for ( p = 5;  p <= 50;  p = p + 2 )
    {
        is_prime = 1;

        for ( i = 1;  is_prime &&
                        p / primes[i] >= primes[i]; ++i )
            if ( p % primes[i] == 0 )
                is_prime = 0;

        if ( is_prime )
        {
            primes[prime_index] = p;
            ++prime_index;
        }
    }

    for ( i = 0;  i < prime_index;  ++i )
        printf ("%d  ", primes[i]);

    printf ("\n");
}
```

Program 7-4 Output

```
2  3  5  7  11  13  17  19  23  29  31  37  41  43  47
```

♦ Initializing Array Elements ♦

Just as we can assign initial `values` to variables when they are declared, so can we assign initial values to the elements of an array. This is done by simply listing the initial `values` of the array, starting from the first element. Values in the list are separated by commas and the entire list is enclosed in a pair of braces. Also, in order to assign initial `values` to array elements in this fashion, you must place the word `static` before the declaration.[†] In the next chapter, *static variables* are discussed in detail.

The statement

```
static int   counters[5] = { 0, 0, 0, 0, 0 };
```

will declare an array called `counters` to contain 5 integer values and will initialize each of these elements to zero. In a similar fashion, the statement

```
static int   integers[5] = { 0, 1, 2, 3, 4 };
```

will set the value of `integers[0]` to 0, `integers[1]` to 1, `integers[2]` to 2, and so on.

Arrays of characters are initialized in a similar manner; thus the statement

```
static char   letters[5] = { 'a', 'b', 'c', 'd', 'e' };
```

will define the character array `letters` and will initialize the five elements to the characters `'a'`, `'b'`, `'c'`, `'d'`, and `'e'`, respectively.

It is not necessary to completely initialize an entire array. If less initial values are specified, then only as many elements will be initialized. The remaining values in the array will be set to zero. So the declaration

```
static float   sample_data[500] = { 100.0, 300.0, 500.5 };
```

will initialize the first three values of `sample_data` to 100.0, 300.0, and 500.5 and will set the remaining 497 elements to zero.

Unfortunately, C does not provide any shortcut mechanisms for initializing array elements, such as the type provided in FORTRAN, for example. There is no way to specify a repeat count, so if it were desired to initially set all 500 values of `sample_data` to 1, then all 500 ones would have to be explicitly spelled out. In such a case, it would be better to initialize the array inside the program using an appropriate `for` loop.

Program 7-5 illustrates the two types of array initialization techniques.

---

† This is no longer a requirement. However, most C compilers still require it.

Program 7-5

```
main ()
{
    static int  array_values[10] = { 0, 1, 4, 9, 16 };
    int  i;

    for ( i = 5;  i < 10;  ++i )
       array_values[i] = i * i;

    for ( i = 0;  i < 10;  ++i )
       printf ("array_values[%d] = %d\n", i, array_values[i]);
}
```

Program 7-5 Output

```
array_values[0] = 0
array_values[1] = 1
array_values[2] = 4
array_values[3] = 9
array_values[4] = 16
array_values[5] = 25
array_values[6] = 36
array_values[7] = 49
array_values[8] = 64
array_values[9] = 81
```

In the declaration of the array array_values, the first five elements of the array are initialized to the square of their element number (for example, element number 3 is set equal to 3^2 or 9). The first for loop shows how this same type of initialization can be performed inside a loop. This loop sets each of the elements 5-9 to the square of its element number. The second for loop simply runs through all 10 elements to display their values at the terminal.

♦ Character Arrays ♦

The purpose of Program 7-6 is to simply illustrate how a character array can be used. However, there is one point worthy of discussion. Can you spot it?

Program 7-6

```
main ()
{
    static char  word[] = { 'H', 'e', 'l', 'l', 'o', '!' };
    int    i;

    for ( i = 0;  i < 6;  ++i )
       printf ("%c", word[i]);

    printf ("\n");
}
```

Program 7-6 Output

```
    Hello!
```

The most notable point in the preceding program is the declaration of the character array `word`. There is no mention of the number of elements in the array. The C language allows you to define an array without specifying the number of elements. If this is done, then the size of the array will be determined automatically based on the number of initialization elements. Since in Program 7-6 there are six initial `values` listed for the array `word`, the C language implicitly "dimensions" the array to six elements.

This approach works fine so long as you initialize every element in the array at the point that the array is defined. If this is not to be the case, then you must explicitly dimension the array.

The next program further illustrates the use of integer and character arrays. The task is to develop a program that converts a positive integer from its base 10 representation into its equivalent representation in another base up to base 16. As inputs to the program, we will specifiy the number to be converted and also the base that we would like the number converted to. The program will then convert the keyed-in number to the appropriate base and display the result.

The first step in developing such a program is to devise an algorithm to convert a number from base 10 to another base. An algorithm to generate the digits of the converted number can be informally stated as follows: A digit of the converted number is obtained by taking the modulo of the number by the base. The number is then divided by the base, with any fractional remainder discarded, and the process is repeated until the number reaches 0.

The outlined procedure will generate the digits of the converted number starting from the rightmost digit. Why don't we pick an example and see how it works? Suppose we wanted to convert the number 10 into base 2. The following table shows the steps that would be followed to arrive at the result.

Number	Number modulo 2	Number / 2
10	0	5
5	1	2
2	0	1
1	1	0

The result of converting 10 to base 2 is therefore seen to be 1010, reading the digits of the "number modulo 2" column from the bottom to the top.

In order to write a program that performs the preceding conversion process, we must take a couple of things into account. First of all, the fact that the algorithm generates the digits of the converted number in reverse order is not very nice. We certainly don't expect the user to read the result from right to left, or from the bottom of the page upward. Therefore, we must correct this problem. Rather than simply displaying each digit as it is generated, we can have the program store each digit inside an array. Then, when we have finished converting the number, we can display the contents of the array in the correct order.

The second thing that must be realized is that we specified that the program handle conversion of numbers into bases up to 16. This means that any digits of the converted number that are between 10 and 15 must be displayed using the corresponding letters, A through F. This is where our character array enters the picture.

Examine Program 7-7 to see how these two issues are handled.

The character array base_digits is set up to contain the 16 possible digits that will be displayed for the converted number. The array converted_number is defined to contain a maximum of 64 digits, which will hold the results of converting the largest possible long integer to the smallest possible base (base 2) on just about all machines. We defined the variable number_to_convert to be of type long int so that relatively large numbers can be converted if desired. Finally, the variables base (to contain the desired conversion base) and index (to index into the converted_number array) are both defined to be of type int.

After the user types in the values of the number to be converted and the base—and you will note that the scanf call to read in a long integer value takes the format characters %ld—the program then enters a do loop to perform the conversion. The do was chosen so that at least one digit will appear in the converted_number array even if the user types in the number 0 to be converted.

Inside the loop, the number_to_be_converted modulo the base is computed to determine the next digit. This digit is stored inside the converted_number array, and the index into the array incremented by 1. After dividing the number_to_be_converted by the base, the conditions of the do are checked. If the value of number_to_be_converted is 0, the loop terminates; otherwise the loop is repeated to determine the next digit of the converted number.

Program 7-7

```c
/* Program to convert a positive integer to another base */

main ()
{
    static char  base_digits[16] =
            { '0', '1', '2', '3', '4', '5', '6', '7',
              '8', '9', 'A', 'B', 'C', 'D', 'E', 'F' };
    int          converted_number[64];
    long int  number_to_convert;
    int          next_digit, base, index = 0;

    /* get the number and the base */

    printf ("Number to be converted? ");
    scanf ("%ld", &number_to_convert);
    printf ("Base? ");
    scanf ("%d", &base);

    /* convert to the indicated base */

    do
    {
        converted_number[index] = number_to_convert % base;
        ++index;
        number_to_convert = number_to_convert / base;
    }
    while  ( number_to_convert != 0 );

    /* display the results in reverse order */

    printf ("Converted number = ");

    for ( --index;  index >= 0;  --index )
    {
        next_digit = converted_number[index];
        printf ("%c", base_digits[next_digit]);
    }

    printf ("\n");
}
```

Program 7-7 Output

```
Number to be converted? 10
Base? 2
Converted number = 1010
```

Program 7-7 Output (Re-run)

```
Number to be converted? 128362
Base? 16
Converted number = 1F56A
```

When the do loop is done, the value of the variable index will be the number of digits in the converted number. Since this variable will be incremented one time too many inside the do loop, its value is initially decremented by 1 in the for loop. The purpose of this for loop is to display the converted number at the terminal. The for loop sequences through the converted_number array in *reverse* sequence to display the digits in the correct order.

Each digit from the converted_number array is in turn assigned to the variable next_digit. In order that the numbers 10 through 15 be correctly displayed using the letters A through F, a lookup is then made inside the array base_digits, using the value of next_digit as the index. For the digits 0 through 9, the corresponding location in the array base_digits contains nothing more than the *characters* '0' through '9' (which as you will recall *are* distinct from the integers 0 through 9). Locations 10 through 15 of the array contain the characters 'A' through 'F'. So if the value of next_digit is 10, for example, then the character contained in base_digits[10], or 'A', will be displayed. And if the value of next_digit is 8, then the character '8' as contained in base_digits[8] will be displayed.

When the value of index becomes less than 0, the for loop will be finished. At that point the program will display a newline character and program execution will be terminated.

Incidentally, you might be interested in knowing that we could have easily avoided the intermediate step of assigning the value of converted_number[index] to next_digit by directly specifying this expression as the subscript of the base_digits array in the printf call. In other words, the expression

```
base_digits[ converted_number[index] ]
```

could have been supplied to the printf routine and the same results achieved. Of course, this expression is a bit more cryptic than the two equivalent expressions used by the program.

It should be pointed out that we were a bit sloppy in the preceding program. No check was ever made to ensure that the value of `base` was between 2 and 16. If the user had entered 0 for the value of the base, the division inside the do loop would have been a division by zero. Now we all know that's something we should never let happen. Right? And if the user had keyed in 1 as the value of the base, then the program would go into an infinite loop since the value of `number_to_convert` would never reach zero. If the user entered a base value that was greater than 16, there is a chance that we would have exceeded the bounds of the `base_digits` array later in the program. And we all know that's another "gotcha" that we must be careful of, since the C system does not check this condition for us.

But enough about sloppy programming. In the next chapter, we will rewrite this program and resolve these issues. But now let's take a look at an interesting extension to the notion of an array.

◆ Multidimensional Arrays ◆

The types of arrays that we have been exposed to thus far are all linear arrays—that is, they all dealt with a single dimension. The C language allows arrays of any dimension to be defined. In this section, we will take a look at two-dimensional arrays.

One of the most natural applications for a two-dimensional array arises in the case of a matrix. Consider the 4 x 5 matrix shown next.

$$
\begin{array}{rrrrr}
10 & 5 & -3 & 17 & 82 \\
9 & 0 & 0 & 8 & -7 \\
32 & 20 & 1 & 0 & 14 \\
0 & 0 & 8 & 7 & 6
\end{array}
$$

In mathematics it is quite common to refer to an element of a matrix by use of a double subscript. So if we called the preceding matrix M, then the notation $M_{i,j}$ would refer to the element in the ith row, jth column, where i ranges from 1 through 4, and j ranges from 1 through 5. The notation $M_{3,2}$ would refer to the value 20 which is found in the 3rd row, 2nd column of the matrix. In a similar fashion, $M_{4,5}$ would refer to the element contained in the 4th row, 5th column: the value 6.

In C, there is an analogous notation to be used when referring to elements of a two-dimensional array. However, since C likes to start numbering things at 0, the first row of the matrix is actually row 0, and the first column of the matrix is column 0. The preceding matrix would then have row and column designations as shown in the diagram below.

Row (i)	Column (j)				
	0	1	2	3	4
0	10	5	-3	17	82
1	9	0	0	8	-7
2	32	20	1	0	14
3	0	0	8	7	6

Whereas in mathematics the notation $M_{i,j}$ is used, in C the equivalent notation is

```
M[i][j]
```

Remember, the first index number refers to the row number while the second index number references the column. So the statement

```
sum = M[0][2] + M[2][4];
```

would add the value contained in row 0, column 2—which is -3—to the value contained in row 2, column 4—which is 14—and would assign the result of 11 to the variable sum.

Two-dimensional arrays are declared the same way that one-dimensional arrays are; thus

```
int  M[4][5];
```

declares the array M to be a two-dimensional array consisting of 4 rows and 5 columns, for a total of 20 elements. Each position in the array is defined to contain an integer value.

Two-dimensional arrays may be initialized in a manner analogous to their one-dimensional counterparts. When listing elements for initialization, the values are listed by row. Brace pairs are used to separate the list of initializers for one row from the next. So to define and initialize the array M to the elements listed in the preceding table, a statement such as the following could be used.

```
static int  M[4][5] = {
                 { 10,   5,  -3,  17,  82 },
                 {  9,   0,   0,   8,  -7 },
                 { 32,  20,   1,   0,  14 },
                 {  0,   0,   8,   7,   6 }
             };
```

Pay particular attention to the syntax of the above statement. Note that commas are required after each brace that closes off a row, except in the case of the last row. The use of the inner pairs of braces is actually optional. If not supplied, then initialization proceeds by row. Thus the above statement could also have been written as

```
static int  M[4][5] = { 10, 5, -3, 17, 82, 9, 0, 0,
                         8, -7, 32, 20, 1, 0, 14, 0,
                         0, 8, 7, 6 };
```

As with one-dimensional arrays, it is not required that the entire array be initialized. A statement such as

```
static int  M[4][5] = {
                        { 10,  5, -3 },
                        {  9,  0,  0 },
                        { 32, 20,  1 },
                        {  0,  0,  8 }
                       };
```

would only initialize the first three elements of each row of the matrix to the indicated values. The remaining values will be set to zero. Note that, in this case, the inner pairs of braces *are required* to force the correct initialization. Without them, the first two rows and the first two elements of the third row would have been initialized instead (verify to yourself that this would be the case).

A program example showing the use of multidimensional arrays is deferred to the next chapter, where we will begin our detailed discussion of one of the most important concepts in the C language—the program *function*. Before proceeding to that chapter, however, try to work the exercises that follow.

◆ Exercises ◆

1. If you have access to a computer facility that supports the C programming language, type in and run the seven programs presented in this chapter. Compare the output produced by each program with the output presented after each program.

2. Modify Program 7-1 so that the elements of the array `values` are initially set to zero. Use a `for` loop to perform the initialization.

3. Write a program that calculates the average of an array of 10 floating point `values`.

4. Program 7-2 only permits 20 responses to be entered. Modify that program so that a variable number of responses—up to 1000—may be keyed in. So that the user does not have to count the number of responses in the list, set up the program so that the value 999 can be keyed in by the user to indicate that the last response has been entered.

5. What output would you expect from the following program?

```
main ()
{
    static int   numbers[10] =
                       { 1, 0, 0, 0, 0, 0, 0, 0, 0, 0 };
    int   i, j;

    for ( j = 0;  j < 10;  ++j )
        for ( i = 0;  i < j;  ++i )
            numbers[j]  =  numbers[j] + numbers[i];

    for ( j = 0;  j < 10;  ++j )
        printf ("%d\n", numbers[j]);
}
```

6. Prime numbers may also be generated by an algorithm known as the *Sieve of Erastosthenes*. The algorithm for this procedure is presented below. Write a program that implements this algorithm. Have the program find all prime numbers up to 150. What can you say about this algorithm as compared to the ones used in the text for calculating prime numbers?

Sieve of Erastosthenes Algorithm
To Display All Prime Numbers Between 1 and n

Step 1:   Define an array of integers P. Set all elements P_i to 0, $2 \le i \le n$.

Step 2:   Set i to 2.

Step 3:   If $i > n$, the algorithm terminates.

Step 4:   If P_i is zero, then i is prime.

Step 5:   For all positive integer values of j, such that $i \times j < n$, set $P_{i \times j}$ to 1.

Step 6:   Add 1 to i and go to Step 3.

Functions

Behind all well-written programs in the C programming language lies the same fundamental element—the *function*. We have used functions in every program that we have encountered thus far. The printf and scanf routine are examples of functions. Indeed, each and every program also used a function called main. So you may ask, what is all the fuss about? The truth is that the program function provides the mechanism for producing programs that are easy to write, read, understand, debug, modify, and maintain. Obviously, anything that can accomplish all of these things is worthy of a bit of fanfare.

Let us first understand what a function is, and then proceed to show how it can be most effectively used in the development of programs. If we were to go back to the very first program that we wrote, which displayed the phrase "Programming is fun." at the terminal, and were to change its name from main to print_message, we would end up with the following:

```
print_message ()
{
    printf ("Programming is fun.\n");
}
```

The above statements define a *function* called print_message. In Program 3-1, this function was called main. You will recall in our discussions of that program that we mentioned that main was a specially recognized name in the C system that always indicated where the program was to begin execution. There *always* must be a main routine. So we can add a main routine to the preceding code to end up with a complete program, as shown next.

Program 8-1

```
print_message ()
{
    printf ("Programming is fun.\n");
}

main ()
{
    print_message ();
}
```

Program 8-1 Output

```
Programming is fun.
```

Program 8-1 actually consists of *two* functions: print_message and main. Program execution always begins with the main routine. Inside main, the program statement

```
print_message ();
```

appears. This statement indicates that the function print_message is to be executed. The open and closed parentheses are used to tell the C system that print_message is a function and that no arguments or values are to be passed to this function. When the function call is executed, program execution will be transferred directly to the indicated function. Inside the print_message function, the printf statement will be executed to display the message ''Programming is fun.'' at the terminal. After the message has been displayed, the print_message routine will be finished (as signalled by the closed brace) and the program will *return* to the main routine, where program execution will continue at the point where the function call was executed.

As mentioned above, the idea of calling a function is not new. The printf and scanf routines are both program functions. The main distinction here is that these routines did not have to be written by us since they are a part of the C program library. Whenever we used the printf function to display a message or program results, execution was transferred to the printf function which performed the required tasks and then returned back to the program. In each case, execution was returned to the program statement which immediately followed the call to the function.

Now try to predict the output from the following program.

Program 8-2

```
print_message ()
{
    printf ("Programming is fun.\n");
}

main ()
{
    print_message ();
    print_message ();
}
```

Program 8-2 Output

```
Programming is fun.
Programming is fun.
```

Execution of the preceding program starts at main, which contains two calls to the print_message function. When the first call to the function is executed, control is sent directly to the print_message function which displays the message "Programming is fun." at the terminal and then returns to the main routine. Upon return, another call to the print_message routine is encountered, which results in the execution of the same function a second time. After the return is made from the print_message function, execution is terminated.

As a final example of the print_message function, try to guess the output from the following program.

Program 8-3

```
print_message ()
{
    printf ("Programming is fun.\n");
}

main ()
{
    int  i;

    for ( i = 1;  i <= 5;  ++i )
        print_message ();
}
```

Program 8-3 Output

```
Programming is fun.
Programming is fun.
Programming is fun.
Programming is fun.
Programming is fun.
```

◆ Arguments and Local Variables ◆

When the printf function is called, we always supply one or more values to the function, the first value being the format string and the remaining values the specific program results to be displayed. These values, called *arguments*, greatly increase the usefulness and flexibility of a function. Unlike our print_message routine, which will display the same message each time it is called, the printf function will display whatever you tell it to display.

We can define a function that accepts arguments. In Chapter 5, we developed an assortment of programs for calculating triangular numbers. Here we'll define a function to generate a triangular number. We'll call it, appropriately enough, calculate_triangular_number. As an argument to the function, we will specify which triangular number to calculate. The function will then calculate the desired number and display the results at the terminal. Here then is the function to accomplish the task, and a main routine to "try it out."

Program 8-4

```
/* Function to calculate the nth triangular number */

calculate_triangular_number (n)
int   n;
{
    int   i, triangular_number = 0;

    for ( i = 1;  i <= n;  ++i )
        triangular_number = triangular_number + i;

    printf ("Triangular number %d is %d\n", n,
                            triangular_number);
}

main ()
{
    calculate_triangular_number (10);
    calculate_triangular_number (20);
    calculate_triangular_number (50);
}
```

Program 8-4 Output

```
Triangular number 10 is 55
Triangular number 20 is 210
Triangular number 50 is 1275
```

The function `calculate_triangular_number` requires a bit of explanation. The first line of the function,

```
calculate_triangular_number (n)
```

is called the *function declaration*. It defines the name of the function and also the *number of arguments to the function and their names*. In this case, the function is defined to have one argument called n. The name that is chosen for an argument, called its *formal parameter name*, as well as the name of the function itself, can be any valid name formed by observing the rules outlined in Chapter 4 for forming variable names. For obvious reasons, you should choose meaningful names.

Once the formal parameter name has been defined, it can be used to refer to the argument anywhere inside the body of the function.

As with all variables, formal parameters must also be declared. The line immediately following the function declaration

```
int   n;
```

declares that the formal parameter called n is of type int. Note that the declaration of the formal parameter appears *before* the open brace that defines the body of the function. If this function were to have more than one argument, then each formal parameter would have to be declared after the function declaration and before the open brace.

After the formal parameter n has been named and declared, the body of the function is defined. Since we wish to calculate the nth triangular number, we have to set up a variable to store the value of the triangular number as it is being calculated. We also need a variable to act as our loop index. The variables `triangular_number` and i are defined for these purposes and are declared to be of type int. These variables are defined and intialized in the same manner that we defined and initialized our variables inside the main routine in previous programs. If an initial value is given to a variable, as is done in the case of the variable `triangular_number`, then that initial value will be assigned to the variable *each* time the function is called.

Variables defined inside a function are known as *automatic local* variables, since they are automatically "created" each time the function is called, and since their values are local to the function. This last point means that the value of a local variable can only be accessed by the function in which the variable is defined. Its value cannot be accessed by any other function.

When defining a local variable inside a function, it is more precise in C to use the keyword `auto` before the definition of the variable. An example of this would be the following:

```
auto int  i, triangular_number = 0;
```

Since the C compiler assumes by default that any variable defined inside a function is an automatic local variable, the keyword `auto` is seldom used, and for this reason it will not be used in this book.

Returning to our program example, after the local variables have been defined, the function proceeds to calculate the triangular number and to display the results at the terminal. The closed brace then defines the end of the function.

Inside the `main` routine, the value 10 is passed as the argument in the first call to `calculate_triangular_number`. Execution is then transferred directly to the function where the value 10 *becomes the value of the formal parameter* *n* inside the function. The function then proceeds to calculate the value of the tenth triangular number and display the result.

The next time that `calculate_triangular_number` is called, the argument 20 is passed. In a similar process, as described earlier, this value becomes the value of n inside the function. The function then proceeds to calculate the value of the twentieth triangular number and display the answer at the terminal.

For an example of a function which takes more than one argument, let us rewrite the greatest common divisor program (Program 5-7) in function form. The two arguments to the function will be the two numbers whose greatest common divisor (*gcd*) we wish to calculate.

Program 8-5

```
/* This function finds the Greatest Common Divisor
        of two nonnegative integer values              */

gcd (u, v)
int  u, v;
{
    int  temp;

    printf ("The gcd of %d and %d is ", u, v);

    while ( v != 0 )
    {
        temp = u % v;
        u = v;
        v = temp;
    }

    printf ("%d\n", u);
}
```

```
main ()
{
    gcd (150, 35);
    gcd (1026, 405);
    gcd (83, 240);
}
```

Program 8-5 Output

```
The gcd of 150 and 35 is 5
The gcd of 1026 and 405 is 27
The gcd of 83 and 240 is 1
```

The function gcd is defined to take two arguments as indicated by the formal parameters u and v. These parameters are defined in the very next line to be of type int. After declaring the variable temp to be of type int, the program displays the values of the arguments u and v, together with an appropriate message at the terminal. The function then proceeds to calculate and display the greatest common divisor of the two integers.

You may be wondering why we have two printf statements inside the function gcd. If you reflect a moment on the way that the function operates, the reason will become clear. We must display the values of u and v *before* we enter the while loop, since their values are changed inside the loop. If we waited until after the loop had finished, the values displayed for u and v would not at all resemble the original values that were passed to the routine. Another solution to this problem would have been to assign the values of u and v to two variables before entering the while loop. The values of these two variables could have then been displayed together with the value of u (the greatest common divisor) using a single printf statement after the while loop was completed.

♦ Returning Function Results ♦

The functions in Programs 8-4 and 8-5 performed some straightforward calculations and then displayed the results of the calculations at the terminal. However, we may not always wish to have the results of our calculations displayed. The C language provides us with a convenient mechanism whereby the results of a function may be *returned* back to the calling routine. The syntax of this construct is straightforward enough:

```
return (expression);
```

This statement indicates that the function is to return the value of *expression* back to the calling routine. The parentheses around *expression* are actually optional, but seem to be used by most programmers.

However, an appropriate `return` statement is not enough. When the function declaration is made, we must also declare the *type of value the function returns*. This declaration is placed immediately *before* the function's name. Thus,

```
float   kmh_to_mph (km_speed)
```

would begin the definition of a function `kmh_to_mph`, which takes one argument called `km_speed` and which *returns* a floating point value. Similarly,

```
int   gcd (u, v)
```

defines a function `gcd` with arguments `u` and `v` that returns an integer value. In fact, why don't we modify Program 8-5 so that the greatest common divisor is not displayed by the function `gcd` but is instead returned to the `main` routine.

Program 8-6

```
/* This function finds the Greatest Common Divisor of two
       nonnegative integer values and returns the result    */

int   gcd (u, v)
int   u, v;
{
    int   temp;

    while ( v != 0 )
    {
        temp = u % v;
        u = v;
        v = temp;
    }

    return   (u);
}

main ()
{
    int   result;

    result = gcd (150, 35);
    printf ("The gcd of 150 and 35 is %d\n", result);

    result = gcd (1026, 405);
    printf ("The gcd of 1026 and 405 is %d\n", result);

    printf ("The gcd of 83 and 240 is %d\n", gcd (83, 240));
}
```

Program 8-6 Output

```
The gcd of 150 and 35 is 5
The gcd of 1026 and 405 is 27
The gcd of 83 and 240 is 1
```

The declaration of gcd tells the C system that the function will return an integer value. Once the value of the greatest common divisor has been calculated by the function, the statement

```
return (u);
```

is executed. This has the effect of returning the value of u, which is the value of the greatest common divisor, back to the calling routine.

You might be wondering what we can do with the value that is returned to the calling routine. As you can see from the main routine, in the first two cases, the value that is returned is stored in the variable result. More precisely, the statement

```
result = gcd (150, 35);
```

instructs the C system to execute the function called gcd with the arguments 150 and 35 and to store the value that is returned by this function into the variable result.

The result that is returned by a function call does not have to be assigned to a variable as you will readily observe by the last statement in the main routine. In this case, the result returned by the call

```
gcd (83, 240)
```

is passed directly to the printf function, where its value is displayed.

A C function can only return a single value in the manner that we have just described. Unlike FORTRAN or Pascal, C makes no distinction between subroutines (procedures) and functions. In C, there is only the function, which may or may not return a value.

Default Return Type and the Type void

If the declaration of the type returned by a function is omitted, then the C compiler assumes that the function will return an integer—if it returns a value at all. Many C programmers take advantage of this fact and omit the return type declaration on functions that return integers. This is a bad programming habit that should be avoided. Whenever a program returns a value, make sure that you declare the type of value returned in the function declaration, if only for the sake of improving the program's readability. In this manner, you will always be able to tell from the function declaration not only the function's name and the number and type of its arguments, but also *if* it returns a value and what the type of the returned value is.

A function declaration that is preceded by the keyword void explicitly informs the compiler that the function does not return a value. A subsequent attempt at using the function in an expression, as if a value were returned, will result in a compiler error message. For example, since the calculate_triangular_number function of Program 8-4 did not return a value, the declaration of the function could have been written as

```
void  calculate_triangular_number (n)
   . . .
```

Subsequently attempting to use this function as if it returned a value, as in

```
number = calculate_triangular_number (20);
```

would result in a compiler error.

The void data type is used mainly for the purpose as illustrated above. In a sense, the void data type is actually defining the *absence* of a data type. Therefore, a variable or function declared to be of type void has no value, and cannot be used in an expression as if it does.

In Chapter 6, we wrote a program to calculate and display the absolute value of a number. Let us now write a function which takes the absolute value of its argument and then returns the result. Instead of using integer values as we did in Program 6-1, let us write this function to take a floating value as an argument and to also return the answer as type float.

Program 8-7

```
/* Function to calculate the absolute value */

float   absolute_value (x)
float   x;
{
    if ( x < 0 )
       x = -x;

    return (x);
}

main ()
{
    float   f1 = -15.5, f2 = 20.0, f3 = -5.0;
    int     i1 = -716;
    float   result;
```

```
        result = absolute_value (f1);
        printf ("result = %.2f\n", result);
        printf ("f1 = %.2f\n", f1);

        result = absolute_value (f2) + absolute_value (f3);
        printf ("result = %.2f\n", result);

        result = absolute_value ( (float) i1 );
        printf ("result = %.2f\n", result);

        printf ("%.2f\n", absolute_value (-6.0) / 4 );
    }
```

Program 8-7 Output

```
    result = 15.50
    f1 = -15.50
    result = 25.00
    result = 716.00
    1.50
```

The `absolute_value` function is relatively straightforward. The formal parameter called x is tested against 0. If it is less than 0, the value is negated to take its absolute value. The result is then returned back to the calling routine with an appropriate `return` statement.

There are some interesting points worth mentioning with respect to the `main` routine that tests out the `absolute_value` function. In the first call to the function, the value of the variable `f1`, initially set to -15.5, is passed. Inside the function itself, this value is assigned to the variable x. Since the result of the `if` test will be TRUE, the statement that negates the value of x will be executed, thereby setting the value of x to 15.5. In the next statement, the value of x is returned to the `main` routine where it is assigned to the variable `result` and then displayed.

It should be stressed that when the value of x is changed inside the `absolute_value` function, this in no way affects the value of the variable `f1`. When `f1` was passed to the `absolute_value` function, its *value was automatically copied* into the formal parameter x by the C system. So, any changes made to the value of x inside the function affect only the value of x and not the value of `f1`. This is verified by the second `printf` call, which displays the unchanged value of `f1` at the terminal.

The next two calls to the `absolute_value` function illustrate how the result returned by a function can be used in an arithmetic expression. The absolute value of `f2` is added to the absolute value of `f3` and the sum is assigned to the variable `result`.

The fourth call to the `absolute_value` function introduces the notion that the type of argument that is passed to a function *must agree with the type of the argument as declared inside the function*. Since the function `absolute_value` expects a floating value as its argument, we must first cast our integer variable `i1` to type `float` before the call is made. Failing to do so will result in erroneous results.

The final call to the `absolute_value` function shows that the rules for evaluation of arithmetic expressions also pertain to values returned by functions. Since the value returned by the `absolute_value` function is declared to be of type `float`, the C system treats the division operation as the division of a floating point number by an integer. As you will recall, if one operand of a term is of type `float`, then the operation is performed using floating arithmetic. In accordance with this rule, the division of the absolute value of -6.0 by 4 produces a result of 1.5.

Now that we have defined a function that computes the absolute value of a number, we can use it in any future programs where we might need such a calculation performed. In fact, the next program is just such an example.

♦ Functions Calling Functions Calling ... ♦

With today's pocket calculators as commonplace as wristwatches, it is usually no big deal to find the square root of a particular number should the need arise. But years ago, students were taught manual techniques that could be used to arrive at an approximation of the square root of a number. One such approximation method that lends itself most readily to solution by a computer is known as the *Newton-Raphson Iteration Technique*. In the next program, we'll write a square root function that uses this technique to arrive at an approximation of the square root of a number.

The Newton-Raphson method may be easily described as follows. We begin by selecting a "guess" at the square root of the number. The closer that this guess is to the actual square root, the fewer the number of calculations that will have to be performed to arrive at the square root. For the sake of argument, however, we will assume that we are not very good at guessing and will therefore always make an initial guess of 1.

The number whose square root we wish to obtain is divided by the initial guess and is then added to the value of guess. This intermediate result is then divided by 2. The result of this division become the new guess for another go-around with the formula. That is, the number whose square root we are calculating is divided by this new guess, added into this new guess, and then divided by 2. This result then becomes the new guess and another iteration is performed.

Since we don't wish to continue this iterative process forever, we need some way of knowing when to stop. Since the successive guesses that are derived by repeated evaluation of the formula get closer and closer to the true value of the square root, we can set a limit which we can use for deciding when to terminate the process. The difference between the square of the guess and the number itself can then be compared against this limit—usually called epsilon (ε). If the difference is less than ε, then the desired accuracy for the square root will have been obtained and the iterative process can be terminated.

This procedure can be expressed in terms of an algorithm as shown.

Newton-Raphson Method To Compute the Square Root of x

Step 1:   Set the value of *guess* to 1.

Step 2:   If $|guess^2 - x| < \varepsilon$, proceed to Step 4.

Step 3:   Set the value of *guess* to $(x / guess + guess) / 2$ and return to Step 2.

Step 4:   *guess* is the approximation of the square root.

It is necessary to test the *absolute* difference of $guess^2$ and x against ε in Step 2, since the value of *guess* can approach the square root of x from either side.

Now that we have an algorithm for finding the square root at our disposal, it once again becomes a relatively straightforward task to develop a function to calculate the square root. For the value of ε in the following function, the value .00001 was arbitrarily chosen.

Program 8-8

```
/* Function to calculate the absolute value of a number */

float   absolute_value (x)
float   x;
{
    if ( x < 0 )
        x = -x;

    return (x);
}


/* Function to compute the square root of a number */

float   square_root (x)
float   x;
{
    float   epsilon = .00001;
    float   guess   = 1.0;

    while  ( absolute_value (guess * guess - x) >= epsilon )
        guess = ( x / guess + guess ) / 2.0;

    return (guess);
}
```

```
main ()
{
    printf ("square_root (2.0) = %f\n", square_root (2.0));
    printf ("square_root (144.0) = %f\n", square_root (144.0));
    printf ("square_root (17.5) = %f\n", square_root (17.5));
}
```

Program 8-8 Output

```
    square_root (2.0) = 1.414216
    square_root (144.0) = 12.000000
    square_root (17.5) = 4.183300
```

(The actual values that are displayed by running this program on your computer system may differ slightly in the less-significant digits.)

The above program requires a detailed analysis. The absolute_value function is defined first. This is the same function that was used in Program 8-7.

Next we find the square_root function. This function takes one argument called x and returns a value of type float. Inside the body of the function, two local variables called epsilon and guess are defined. The value of epsilon, which is used to determine when to end the iteration process, is set to .00001. The value of our guess at the square root of the number is initially set to 1.0. These initial values are assigned to these two variables each time that the function is called.

After the local variables have been declared, a while loop is set up to perform the iterative calculations. The statement that immediately follows the while condition will be repetitively executed as long as the absolute difference between guess^2 and x is greater than or equal to epsilon. The expression

```
    guess * guess - x
```

is evaluated and the result of the evaluation is passed to the absolute_value function. The result returned by the absolute_value function is then compared against the value of epsilon. If the value is greater than or equal to epsilon, then the desired accuracy of the square root has not yet been obtained. In that case, another iteration of the loop is performed to calculate the next value of guess.

Eventually the value of guess will be close enough to the true value of the square root and the while loop will terminate. At that point, the value of guess will be returned to the calling program. Inside the main function, this returned value is passed to the printf function where it is displayed.

You may have noticed that *both* the absolute_value function and the square_root function have formal parameters named x. The C compiler doesn't get confused, however, and keeps these two values distinct. In fact, a function always has its own set of formal parameters. So the formal parameter x used inside the `absolute_value` function is distinct from the formal parameter x used inside the `square_root` function.

The same is true for local variables. We can declare local variables with the same name inside as many functions as we desire. The C compiler will not confuse the usage of these variables, since a local variable can only be accessed from within the function where it is defined. Another way of saying this is that the *scope* of a local variable is the function in which it is defined. (As you will see later in the chapter on pointers, C does provide a mechanism for indirectly accessing a local variable from outside of a function.)

Based upon this discussion, you can understand that when the value of $guess^2 - x$ is passed to the `absolute_value` function and assigned to the formal parameter x, this assignment has absolutely *no* effect on the value of x inside the `square_root` function. This is an important concept that you must understand.

Declaring Return Types

We mentioned earlier that the C compiler assumes that a function returns a value of type `int` as the default case. More specifically, whenever a call is made to a function, the compiler will assume that the function returns a value of type `int` unless either of the following has occurred:

1. The function has been defined in the program before the function call is encountered.

2. The value returned by the function has been *declared* before the function call is encountered.

In Program 8-8, the `absolute_value` function is defined before the compiler encounters a call to this function from within the `square_root` function. The compiler will know, therefore, that when this call is encountered, that the `absolute_value` function will return a value of type `float`. Had the `absolute_value` function been defined *after* the `square_root` function, then upon encountering the call to the `absolute_value` function the compiler would have assumed that this function returned an integer value. Many C compilers will catch this error and will generate an appropriate diagnostic message. However, some compilers won't catch this sort of mistake. The net result in that case would be a program that produced incorrect results, because, while the `absolute_value` function would return a value of type `float`, the calling function would be expecting a value of type `int` to be returned. This could be a very subtle bug to uncover (see Appendix F for a discussion of the program `lint`, which can locate these types of problems).

In order to be able to define the `absolute_value` function *after* the `square_root` function (or even in another file—see Chapter 15), we must *declare* the type of the result returned by the `absolute_value` function *before* the function is called. The declaration can be made inside the `square_root` function itself, or outside of any function. In the latter case, the declaration is usually made at the beginning of the program. To declare `absolute_value` as a function that returns a value of type `float`, the following declaration would be used:

```
float   absolute_value ();
```

If a function returns no value, then this fact can also be declared to thwart any attempts at using the function as if it returns a value:

```
void   calculate_triangular_number ();
```

Here are some reminders and suggestions about function types.

1. Remember that, by default, the compiler assumes that a function returns an `int`.

2. When defining a function that returns an `int`, define it as such.

3. When defining a function that doesn't return a value, define it as `void`.

4. Place the definition for a function that doesn't return an `int` before its call, or, safer still, declare *all* functions that don't return `int`s—even if they're previously defined in the file.

Checking Function Arguments

The square root of a negative number takes us away from the realm of real numbers and into the area of imaginary numbers. So what would happen if we were to pass a negative number to our `square_root` function? The fact of the matter is that the Newton-Raphson process would never converge; that is, the value of guess would not get closer to the correct value of the square root with each iteration of the loop. Therefore, the criteria set up for termination of the `while` loop would *never* be satisfied, and the program would go into an infinite loop. Execution of the program would have to be abnormally terminated by typing in some command or hitting a special key at the terminal (such as the *Delete* key under UNIX).

Obviously, modifying the program to correctly account for this situation is what is called for in this case. We could put the burden on the calling routine and mandate that it never pass a negative argument to the `square_root` function. While this approach might seem reasonable, it does have its drawbacks. Eventually, we would develop a program that used the `square_root` function but which forgot to check the argument before calling the function. If a negative number were then passed to the function, the program would go into an infinite loop as described and would have to be aborted. Not very nice!

A much wiser and safer solution to the problem is to place the onus of checking the value of the argument on the square_root function itself. In that way, the function would be "protected" from *any* program that used it. A reasonable approach to take would be to check the value of the argument x inside the function and then (optionally) display a message if the argument were negative. The function could then immediately return without performing its calculations. As an indication to the calling routine that the square_root function did not "work as expected," a value not normally returned by the function could be returned.

The following is a listing of a modified square_root function, which tests the value of its argument.

```
/* Function to compute the square root of a number.
   If a negative argument is passed, then a message
   is displayed and -1.0 is returned.                   */

float   square_root (x)
float   x;
{
    float   epsilon = .00001;
    float   guess   = 1.0;

    if ( x < 0 )
    {
        printf ("Negative argument to square_root.\n");
        return (-1.0);
    }

    while  ( absolute_value (guess * guess - x) >= epsilon )
        guess = ( x / guess + guess ) / 2.0;

    return (guess);
}
```

If a negative argument is passed to the above function, an appropriate message is displayed and the value -1.0 is immediately returned to the calling routine. If the argument is not negative, then calculation of the square root proceeds as previously described.

As you can see from the modified square_root function, we can have more than one return statement in a function. Whenever a return is executed, control is immediately sent back to the calling function; any program statements in the function that appear after the return are not executed. This fact also makes the return statement ideal for use by a function that does not return a value. In such a case, the return statement takes the simpler form

```
    return;
```

since no value is to be returned. Obviously, if the function *is* supposed to return a value, then this form should not be used to return from the function.

◆ Top-Down Programming ◆

The notion of functions that call functions that in turn call functions, and so on, forms the basis for producing good structured programs. In the `main` routine of Program 8-8, the `square_root` function was called several times. All of the details concerned with the actual calculation of the square root are contained within the `square_root` function itself, and not within `main`. Thus, we can write a call to this function before we even write the instructions of the function itself, as `long` as we specify the argument(s) that the function takes and the value that it returns.

Later, when proceeding to write the code for the `square_root` function, this same type of *top-down programming* technique can be applied: we can write a call to the `absolute_value` function without concerning ourselves at that time with the details of operation of that function. All we need to know is that we *can* develop a function to take the absolute value of a number.

The same programming technique which makes programs easier to write also makes them easier to read. Thus the reader of Program 8-8 can easily determine upon examination of the `main` routine that the program is simply calculating and displaying the square root of three numbers. He or she need not sift through all of the details of how the square root is actually calculated in order to glean this information. If the reader wishes to get more involved in details, then the specific code associated with the `square_root` function can be studied. Inside that function, the same discussion applies to the `absolute_value` function: the reader need not know how the absolute value of a number is calculated in order to understand the operation of the `square_root` function. Such details are relegated to the `absolute_value` function itself, which can be studied if a more detailed knowledge of its operation is desired.

◆ Functions and Arrays ◆

As with ordinary variables and values, it is also possible to pass the value of an array element and even an entire array as an argument to a function. To pass a single array element to a function (which is what we were doing in Chapter 7 when we used the `printf` function to display the elements of an array), the array element is specified as an argument to the function in the normal fashion. So, to take the square root of `averages[i]` and assign the result to a variable called `sq_root_result`, a statement such as

```
sq_root_result = square_root (averages[i]);
```

would do the trick. We are, of course, making the assumption here that the argument type expected by the `square_root` function and the type as declared for the array `averages` agree. If not, then the type cast operator could be used to coerce the argument to the proper type. So if the `square_root` function expected a floating argument, and the `averages` array were declared to be of type `int`, then we would need a statement such as

```
sq_root_result = square_root ( (float) averages[i] );
```

to achieve the correct result.

Inside the `square_root` function itself, nothing special has to be done to handle single array elements passed as arguments. So a `square_root` function that defines a formal parameter `x` to be of type `float` would not be affected if an array element of type `float` were passed as an argument to the function. In the same manner as with a simple variable, the value of the array element will be copied into the value of the corresponding formal parameter when the function is called.

Passing an entire array to a function is an entirely new ball game. To pass an array to a function, it is only necessary to list the name of the array, *without any subscripts*, inside the call to the function. As an example, if we assume that `grade_scores` has been declared as an array containing 100 elements, then the expression

```
minimum (grade_scores)
```

will in effect pass the entire 100 elements contained in the array `grade_scores` to the function called `minimum`. Naturally, on the other side of the coin, the `minimum` function must be expecting an entire array to be passed as an argument and must make the appropriate formal parameter declaration. So the `minimum` function might look something like this:

```
int   minimum (values)
int   values[100];
{
      . . .
      return (minimum_value);
}
```

The declaration defines the function `minimum` as returning a value of type `int` and as taking as its argument an array containing 100 integer elements. References made to the formal parameter array `values` will reference the appropriate elements inside the array that was passed to the function. Based upon the function call previously shown and the corresponding function declaration, a reference made to `values[4]`, for example, would actually reference the value of `grade_scores[4]`.

For our first program that illustrates a function that takes an array as an argument, let's write a function `minimum` to find the minimum value in an array of 10 integers. This function, together with a `main` routine to set up the initial values in the array, is shown in Program 8-9.

Program 8-9

```
/* Function to find the minimum in an array */

int   minimum (values)
int   values[10];
{
    int   minimum_value, i;

    minimum_value = values[0];

    for ( i = 1;  i < 10;  ++i )
        if ( values[i] < minimum_value )
            minimum_value = values[i];

    return (minimum_value);
}

main ()
{
    int   scores[10], i, minimum_score;

    printf ("Enter 10 scores\n");

    for ( i = 0;  i < 10;  ++i )
        scanf ("%d", &scores[i]);

    minimum_score = minimum (scores);
    printf ("\nMinimum score is %d\n", minimum_score);
}
```

Program 8-9 Output

```
Enter 10 scores
69
97
65
87
69
86
78
```

```
67
92
90
```

```
Minimum score is 65
```

After the array `scores` is defined, the user is prompted to enter 10 values. The `scanf` call places each number as it is keyed in into `scores[i]`, where `i` ranges from 0 through 9. After all of the values have been entered, the `minimum` function is called with the array `scores` as an argument.

The formal parameter name `values` is used to reference the elements of the array inside the function. It is declared to be an array of 10 integer values. The local variable `minimum_value` is used to store the minimum value in the array and is initially set to `values[0]`, the first value in the array. The `for` loop sequences through the remaining elements of the array, comparing each element in turn against the value of `minimum_value`. If the value of `values[i]` is less than `minimum_value`, then a new minimum in the array has been found. In such a case, the value of `minimum_value` is reassigned to this new minimum value and the scan through the array continues.

When the `for` loop has completed its execution, the value of `minimum_value` is returned to the calling routine where it is assigned to the variable `minimum_score` and is then displayed to the user.

With our general-purpose `minimum` function in hand, we can use it to find the minimum of *any* array containing 10 integers. If we had five different arrays containing 10 integers each, we could simply just call the minimum function five separate times to find the minimum value of each array. And we can just as easily define other functions to perform tasks, such as finding the maximum value, the median value, the mean (average) value, and so on.

By defining small, independent functions that perform well-defined tasks, we can build upon these functions to accomplish more sophisticated tasks, and also make use of them for other related programming applications. For example, we could define a function `statistics`, which takes an array as an argument and perhaps then, in turn calls a `mean` function, a `standard_deviation` function, and so on, to accumulate statistics about an array. This type of program methodology is the very key to the development of programs that are easy to write, understand, modify, and maintain.

Of course, our general-purpose `minimum` function is not so general purpose in the sense that it only works on an array of precisely 10 elements. But this problem is relatively easy to rectify. We can extend the versatility of this function by having it take the number of elements in the array as an argument. In the function declaration, we can then omit the specification of the number of elements contained in the formal parameter array. The C compiler actually ignores this part of the declaration anyway; all the compiler is concerned with is the fact that an array is expected as an argument to the function and not how many elements are in it.

Program 8-10 is a revised version of Program 8-9 in which the `minimum` function finds the minimum value in an integer array of arbitrary length.

Program 8-10

```
/* Function to find the minimum in an array */

int   minimum (values, number_of_elements)
int   values[];
int   number_of_elements;
{
    int   minimum_value, i;

    minimum_value = values[0];

    for ( i = 1;   i < number_of_elements;   ++i )
        if ( values[i] < minimum_value )
            minimum_value = values[i];

    return (minimum_value);
}

main ()
{
    static int   array1[5] = { 157, -28, -37, 26, 10 };
    static int   array2[7] = { 12, 45, 1, 10, 5, 3, 22 };

    printf ("array1 minimum: %d\n", minimum (array1, 5));
    printf ("array2 minimum: %d\n", minimum (array2, 7));
}
```

Program 8-10 Output

```
array1 minimum: -37
array2 minimum: 1
```

This time the function `minimum` is defined to take two arguments: first, the array whose minimum we wish to find, and second, the number of elements in the array. The declaration of the formal parameter array `values` is made with the statement

```
int   values[];
```

The open and closed brackets serve to inform the C compiler that `values` is an array of integers. As was stated, the compiler really doesn't need to know how large it is.

The formal parameter `number_of_elements` replaces the constant 10 as the upper limit inside the `for` statement. So the `for` statement sequences through the array from `values[1]` through `values[number_of_elements - 1]`, which is the last element of the array.

In the `main` routine, two arrays called `array1` and `array2` are defined to contain 5 and 7 elements, respectively. (You will recall that in order to assign initial values to these arrays, your compiler most likely requires that they be declared `static`.)

Inside the first `printf` call, a call is made to the `minimum` function with the arguments `array1` and 5. This second argument specifies the number of elements contained in `array1`. The `minimum` function finds the minimum value in the array and the returned result of -37 is then displayed at the terminal. The second time the minimum function is called, the array `array2` is passed, together with the number of elements in that array. The result of 1 as returned by the function is then passed to the `printf` function to be displayed.

Assignment Operators

Study the following program and try to guess the output *before* looking at the actual program results.

Program 8-11

```
void   multiply_by_two (array, n)
float   array[];
int     n;
{
    int   i;

    for ( i = 0;   i < n;   ++i )
        array[i]  *= 2;
}

main ()
{
    static float   float_values[4] = { 1.2,  -3.7,  6.2,  8.55 };
    int     i;

    multiply_by_two (float_values, 4);

    for ( i = 0;   i < 4;   ++i )
        printf ("%.2f    ", float_values[i]);

    printf ("\n");
}
```

Program 8-11 Output

```
2.40    -7.40    12.40    17.10
```

When you were examining the above program, your attention surely must have been drawn to the statement

```
array[i] *= 2;
```

Hopefully, based upon the name of the function, you were able to determine what this statement is actually doing. This is certainly one of the primary reasons why meaningful function names should always be chosen. The effect of the so-called "times equals" operator *= is to multiply the expression on the left-hand side of the operator by the expression on the right-hand side of the operator and *to store the result back into the variable on the left-hand side of the operator.* So the above expression is equivalent to the statement

```
array[i] = array[i] * 2;
```

The "times equals" operator saves us from having to repeat what appears on the left-hand side of the operator on the right-hand side.

As you might have guessed, there are analagous operators for all binary arithmetic operators in C. These operators are called *assignment operators,* and are formed by listing the normal binary operator immediately followed by the assignment operator =. So the expression

```
counter += 5
```

uses the "plus equals" assignment operator to add 5 to the value of counter, and is equivalent to the expression

```
counter = counter + 5
```

As a slightly more involved expression,

```
a /= b + c
```

divides a by whatever appears to the right of the equals sign—or by the sum of b and c—and stores the result back into a. The reason why the addition is performed first is because the addition operator has higher precedence than the assignment operator. In fact, all operators but the comma operator have higher precedence than the assignment operators (which all have the same precedence). In this case, this expression is identical to

```
a = a / (b + c)
```

The motivations for using assignment operators are threefold. First, the program statement becomes easier to write, since what appears on the left-hand side of the operator does not have to be repeated on the right-hand side. Second, the resulting expression is usually easier to read. Third, the use of these operators can result in programs that execute faster on the computer.

As an example of an expression that is both easier to write and to read, consider the following program statement which subtracts 10 from the value contained in Board[row + col - 5]:

```
Board[row + col - 5]  =  Board[row + col - 5] - 10;
```

With the use of the -= assignment operator, this statement could be written as

```
Board [row + col - 5] -= 10;
```

In the latter case, it is far easier to see that 10 is being subtracted from the indicated element in the Board array, since in the former case, a visual comparison must be made between the element on the left-hand side of the equals side and the element on the right-hand side to determine that the same element of the Board array is being referenced.

Getting back to the main point to be made about the preceding program, you may have realized by now that the function multiply_by_two actually *changes* values inside the float_values array. Isn't this a contradiction to what we have stated before about a function not being able to change the value of its arguments? Not really.

This program example points out one major distinction that must always be kept in mind when dealing with array arguments: *If the function changes the value of an array element, then that change will be made to the original array that was passed to the function.* This change will remain in effect even after the function has completed execution and has returned to the calling routine.

The reason why an array behaves differently from a simple variable or an array element—whose value *cannot* be changed by a function—is worthy of a bit of explanation. We stated that when a function is called, the values that are passed as arguments to the function are copied into the corresponding formal parameters. This statement is still valid. However, when dealing with arrays, the entire contents of the array are *not* copied into the formal parameter array. Instead, the function gets passed information describing *where* in the computer's memory the array is located. Any changes made to the formal parameter array by the function are actually made to the original array passed to the function, and not to a copy of the array. Therefore, when the function returns, these changes still remain in effect.

Remember, the preceding discussion applies only to entire arrays that are passed as arguments, and not to individual elements, whose values are copied into the corresponding formal parameters and therefore cannot be permanently changed by the function. Chapter 11, which deals with *pointers*, discusses these concepts in greater detail.

To further illustrate the idea that a function can change values in an array passed as an argument, we will develop a function to sort (rank) an array of integers. The process of sorting has always received much attention by computer scientists, probably because sorting is an operation that is so commonly performed. Many sophisticated algorithms have been developed in order to sort a set of information in the least amount of time, using as little of the computer's memory as possible. Since the purpose of this book is not to teach such sophisticated algorithms, we will develop a sort function that uses a fairly straightforward algorithm to sort an array into *ascending order*. Sorting an array into ascending order means rearranging the values in the array so that the elements progressively increase in value from the smallest to the largest. By the end of such a sort, the minimum value will be contained in the first location of the array, while the maximum value will be found in the last location of the array, with values that progressively increase in between.

If we wanted to sort an array of *n* elements into ascending order, we could do so by performing a successive comparison of each of the elements of the array. We could begin by comparing the first element in the array against the second. If the first element were greater in value than the second, then we could simply "swap" the two values in the array; that is, exchange the values contained in these two locations.

Next, we could compare the first element in the array (which we now know is less than the second) against the third element in the array. Once again, if the first value were greater than the third, we would exchange these two values. Otherwise, we would leave them alone. Now we would have the smallest of the first three elements contained in the first location of the array.

If we repeated the above process for the remaining elements in the array—comparing the first element against each successive element, and exchanging their values if the former were larger than the latter—then the smallest value of the entire array would be contained in the first location of the array by the end of the process.

If we now did the same thing with the second element of the array, that is, compared it against the third element, then against the fourth, and so on, and if we exchanged any values that were out of order, we would then end up with the next smallest value contained in the second location of the array when the process was completed.

It should now be clear how we can go about sorting the array by performing these successive comparisons and exchanges as needed. The process will stop after we have compared the next-to-last element of the array against the last and have interchanged their values if required. At that point, the entire array will have been sorted into ascending order.

The following algorithm gives a more concise description of the above sorting process. We assume here that we are sorting an array *a* of *n* elements.

Simple Exchange Sort Algorithm

Step 1: Set i to 0.

Step 2: Set j to $i + 1$.

Step 3: If $a[i] > a[j]$, exchange their values.

Step 4: Set j to $j + 1$. If $j < n$, go to Step 3.

Step 5: Set i to $i + 1$. If $i < n - 1$, go to Step 2.

Step 6: a is now sorted in ascending order.

Program 8-12 implements the above algorithm in a function called sort, which takes two arguments: the array to be sorted and the number of elements in the array.

The sort function implements the algorithm as a set of nested for loops. The outermost loop sequences through the array from the first element to the next-to-last element (a[n-2]). For each such element, a second for loop is entered, which starts from the element after the one currently selected by the outer loop, and ranges through the last element of the array.

If the elements are out of order (that is, if a[i] is greater than a[j]) then the elements are switched. The variable temp is used as a temporary storage place while the switch is being made.

When both for loops are finished, the array will have been sorted into ascending order. Execution of the function is then complete.

In the main routine, a static array called array is defined and initialized to 16 integer values. The program then displays the values of the array at the terminal and proceeds to call the sort function, passing as arguments array and 16, the number of elements in array. After the function returns, the program once again displays the values contained in array. As you can see from the output, the function successfully sorted the array into ascending order.

The sort function shown in Program 8-12 is fairly simple. The price that must be paid for such a simplistic approach is one of execution time. If we had to sort an extremely large array of values (arrays containing thousands of elements, perhaps), then the sort routine as we have implemented it here could take a considerable amount of execution time. If this happened, then we would have to resort to one of the more sophisticated algorithms that we alluded to in our discussions. *The Art of Computer Programming, Volume 3, Sorting and Searching* (Donald E. Knuth, Addison-Wesley), is probably the best reference source for such algorithms.

Program 8-12

```c
/* Sort an array of integers into ascending order */

void sort (a, n)
int  a[];
int  n;
{
    int  i, j, temp;

    for ( i = 0;  i < n - 1;  ++i )
        for ( j = i + 1;  j < n;  ++j )
            if ( a[i] > a[j] )
            {
                temp = a[i];
                a[i] = a[j];
                a[j] = temp;
            }
}

main ()
{
    int  i;
    static int  array[16] = { 34, -5, 6, 0, 12, 100, 56, 22,
                             44, -3, -9, 12, 17, 22, 6, 11 };

    printf ("The array before the sort:\n");

    for ( i = 0;  i < 16;  ++i )
        printf ("%d ", array[i]);

    sort (array, 16);

    printf ("\n\nThe array after the sort:\n");

    for ( i = 0;  i < 16;  ++i )
        printf ("%d ", array[i]);

    printf ("\n");
}
```

Program 8-12 Output

```
The array before the sort:
34 -5 6 0 12 100 56 22 44 -3 -9 12 17 22 6 11

The array after the sort:
-9 -5 -3 0 6 6 11 12 12 17 22 22 34 44 56 100
```

Multidimensional Arrays

A multidimensional array element may be passed to a function just as any ordinary variable or single-dimensional array element can. So the statement

```
square_root (matrix[i][j]);
```

will call the `square_root` function, passing the value contained in `matrix[i][j]` as the argument. As with all arguments passed to functions, the type declared for the `matrix` array must correspond to the type expected by the `square_root` function; otherwise, type casting must be used.

An entire multidimensional array can be passed to a function the same way that a single-dimensional array can: you simply list the name of the array. For example, if the matrix `measured_values` is declared to be a two-dimensional array of integers, the C statement

```
scalar_multiply (measured_values, constant);
```

could be used to invoke a function which multiplied each element in the matrix by the value of `constant`. This implies, of course, that the function itself may change the values contained inside the `measured_values` array. The discussion pertaining to this topic for single-dimensional arrays also applies here: an assignment made to any element of the formal parameter array inside the function makes a permanent change to the array that was passed to the function.

When declaring a single-dimensional array as a formal parameter inside a function, it was stated that the actual dimension of the array was not needed. It suffices to simply use a pair of empty brackets to inform the C system that the parameter is in fact an array. This does not totally apply in the case of multidimensional arrays. For a two-dimensional array, the number of rows in the array may be omitted, but the declaration *must* contain the number of columns in the array. So the declarations

```
int   array_values[100][50];
```

and

```
int   array_values[][50];
```

are both valid declarations for a formal parameter array called `array_values` containing 100 rows by 50 columns; but the declarations

```
int   array_values[100][];
```

and

```
int   array_values[][];
```

are not, since the number of columns in the array *must* be specified.

In the next program, we define a function `scalar_multiply`, which multiplies a two-dimensional integer array by a scalar integer value. We will assume for purposes of this example that the array is dimensioned 3 × 5. The `main` routine will call the `scalar_multiply` routine twice. After each call, the array will be passed to the `display_matrix` routine to display the contents of the array. Pay careful attention to the nested `for` loops that are used in both `scalar_mutiply` and `display_matrix` to sequence through each element of the two-dimensional array.

Program 8-13

```
/* Function to multiply a 3 x 5 array by a scalar */

void  scalar_multiply (matrix, scalar)
int   matrix[3][5];
int   scalar;
{
    int  row, column;

    for ( row = 0;  row < 3;  ++row )
        for ( column = 0;  column < 5;  ++column )
            matrix[row][column]  *=  scalar;
}

void  display_matrix (matrix)
int   matrix[3][5];
{
    int  row, column;

    for ( row = 0;  row < 3;  ++row)
    {
        for ( column = 0;  column < 5;  ++column )
            printf ("%5d", matrix[row][column]);

        printf ("\n");
    }
}

main ()
{
    static int  sample_matrix[3][5] =
                {
                    {  7, 16, 55, 13, 12 },
                    { 12, 10, 52,  0,  7 },
                    { -2,  1,  2,  4,  9 }
                };
```

```
    printf ("Original matrix:\n");
    display_matrix (sample_matrix);

    scalar_multiply (sample_matrix, 2);

    printf ("\nMultiplied by 2:\n");
    display_matrix (sample_matrix);

    scalar_multiply (sample_matrix, -1);

    printf ("\nThen multiplied by -1:\n");
    display_matrix (sample_matrix);
}
```

Program 8-13 Output

```
Original matrix:
    7    16    55    13    12
   12    10    52     0     7
   -2     1     2     4     9

Multiplied by 2:
   14    32   110    26    24
   24    20   104     0    14
   -4     2     4     8    18

Then multiplied by -1:
  -14   -32  -110   -26   -24
  -24   -20  -104     0   -14
    4    -2    -4    -8   -18
```

The `main` routine defines the matrix `sample_values` and then proceeds to call the `display_matrix` function to display its initial values at the terminal. Inside the `display_matrix` routine, you will notice the nested `for` statements. The first or outermost `for` statement sequences through each row in the matrix, so the value of the variable `row` varies from 0 through 2. For each value of `row`, the innermost `for` statement is executed. This `for` statement sequences through each column of the particular row, so the value of the variable `column` ranges from 0 through 4.

The `printf` statement displays the value contained in the specified row and column using the format characters `%5d` to ensure that the elements line up in the display. After the innermost `for` loop has finished execution—meaning that an entire row of the matrix has been displayed—a newline character is displayed so that the next row of the matrix is displayed on the next line of the terminal.

The first call to the `scalar_mutiply` function specifies that the `sample_matrix` array is to be multiplied by 2. Inside the function, a simple set of nested `for` loops is set up to sequence through each element in the array. The element contained in `matrix[row][column]` is multiplied by the value of `scalar` in accordance with the use of the assignment operator `*=`. After the function returns to the `main` routine, the `display_matrix` function is once again called to display the contents of the `sample_matrix` array. The program's output verifies that each element in the array has in fact been multiplied by 2.

The `scalar_multiply` function is called a second time to multiply the now-modified elements of the `sample_matrix` array by -1. The modified array is then displayed by a final call to the `display_matrix` function, and program execution is then complete.

◆ Global Variables ◆

We are now ready to tie together many of the principles that we have learned in this chapter, as well as learn some new ones. What we would like to do now is take Program 7-7, which converted a positive integer to another base, and rewrite it in function form. In order to do this, we must conceptually divide the program into logical segments. If you glance back at that program you will see that this is readily accomplished simply by looking at the three comment statements inside `main`. They suggest the three primary functions that the program is performing: getting the number and base from the user, converting the number to the desired base, and then displaying the results.

We can define three functions to perform an analogous task. The first function we will call `get_number_and_base`. This function will prompt the user to enter the number to be converted and the base, and will read these values in from the terminal. Here we will make a slight improvement over what was done in Program 7-7. If the user types in a value of base that is less than 2 or greater than 16, then the program will display an appropriate message at the terminal and set the value of the base to 10. In this manner, the program will end up redisplaying the original number to the user. (Another approach might be to let the user re-enter a new value for the base, but this is left as an exercise.)

The second function we will call `convert_number`. This function will take the value as typed in by the user and convert it to the desired base, storing the digits resulting from the conversion process inside the `converted_number` array.

The third and final function we will call `display_converted_number`. This function will take the digits contained inside the `converted_number` array and will display them to the user in the correct order. For each digit to be displayed, a lookup will be made inside the `base_digits` array so that the correct character is displayed for the corresponding digit.

The three functions that we will define will communicate with each other by means of *global variables*. It has been previously noted that one of the fundamental properties of a local variable is that its value can be accessed only by the function in which the variable is defined. As you might expect, this restriction does not apply to global variables. That is, a global variable's value can be accessed by *any* function in the program.

The distinguishing quality of a global variable declaration versus a local variable declaration is that the former is made *outside* of any function. This indicates its global nature—it does not "belong" to any particular function. *Any* function in the program can then access the value of that variable and can also change its value if desired.

In Program 8-14, four global variables are defined. Each of these variables is used by at least two functions in the program. Since the base_digits array and the variable next_digit are used exclusively by the function display_converted_number, they are *not* defined as global variables. Instead, these two variables are locally defined within the function display_converted_number.

The global variables are defined first in the program. Since they are not defined within any particular function, the C system classifies these variables as global variables, which means, as we have mentioned, that they can now be referenced by any function in the program.

Program 8-14

```
/* Program to convert a positive integer to another base */

int        converted_number[64];
long int   number_to_convert;
int        base;
int        index = 0;

void  get_number_and_base ()
{
    printf ("Number to be converted? ");
    scanf ("%ld", &number_to_convert);

    printf ("Base? ");
    scanf ("%d", &base);

    if  ( base < 2  ||  base > 16 )
    {
        printf ("Bad base - must be between 2 and 16\n");
        base = 10;
    }
}
```

```
void  convert_number ()
{
    do
    {
        converted_number[index] = number_to_convert % base;
        ++index;
        number_to_convert /= base;
    }
    while ( number_to_convert != 0 );
}

void  display_converted_number ()
{
    static char  base_digits[16] =
            { '0', '1', '2', '3', '4', '5', '6', '7',
              '8', '9', 'A', 'B', 'C', 'D', 'E', 'F' };
    int    next_digit;

    printf ("Converted number = ");

    for ( --index;  index >= 0;  --index )
    {
        next_digit = converted_number[index];
        printf ("%c", base_digits[next_digit]);
    }

    printf ("\n");
}

main ()
{
    get_number_and_base ();
    convert_number ();
    display_converted_number ();
}
```

Program 8-14 Output

```
Number to be converted? 100
Base? 8
Converted number = 144
```

Program 8-14 Output (Re-run)

```
Number to be converted? 1983
Base? 0
Bad base - must be between 2 and 16
Converted number = 1983
```

You will notice how the wise choice of function names makes the operation of Program 8-14 clear. Spelled out directly in the `main` routine is the function of the program: to get a number and a base, convert the number, and then display the converted number. The much improved readability of this program over the equivalent program from Chapter 7 is a direct result of the structuring of the program into separate functions that perform small, well-defined tasks. Note that we do not even need comment statements inside the `main` routine to describe what the program is doing—the function names speak for themselves.

The primary use of global variables is in programs in which many functions must access the value of the same variable. Rather than having to pass the value of the variable to each individual function as an argument, the function can explicitly reference the variable instead. Now there is a drawback with this approach. Because the function explicitly references a particular global variable, the generality of the function is somewhat reduced. So, every time that function is to be used, we must make sure that the global variable exists, by its particular name.

For example, the `convert_number` function of Program 8-14 will succeed in converting only a number that is stored in the variable `number_to_convert` to a base as specified by the value of the variable `base`. Furthermore, the variable `index` and the array `converted_number` must be defined. A far more flexible version of this function would allow the arguments to be passed to the function.

The `main` point to be made about global variables is that while their use may reduce the number of arguments that need to be passed to a function, the price that must be paid is reduced function generality and, in some cases, reduced program readability. This latter issue stems from the fact that the variables that are used by a particular function are not all contained within the function itself. Also, a call to a particular function does not indicate to the reader what types of parameters the function needs as inputs or produces as outputs.

Two final things about global variables. First, unlike automatic local variables, they do have default initial values: zero. Second, global arrays can be initialized, and the keyword `static` does not have to precede the declaration. So in the global declaration

```
int data[100] = { 1, 2, 3, 4, 5 };
```

the first five values of `data` are set as shown, with the remaining 95 elements set to zero.

◆ Automatic and Static Variables ◆

When we normally declare a local variable inside a function, as in the declaration of the variables guess and epsilon in our square_root function:

```
float    square_root (x)
float    x;
{
    float    epsilon = .00001;
    float    guess    =  1.0;
        .  .  .
}
```

we are declaring *automatic* local variables. As you will recall, the keyword auto may in fact precede the declaration of such variables, but is optional, since it is the default case. An automatic variable is, in a sense, actually "created" each time the function is called. In the preceding example, the local variables epsilon and guess are "created" whenever the square_root function is called. As soon as the square_root function is finished, these local variables "disappear." This process happens automatically, hence the name automatic variables.

Automatic local variables may be given initial values, as is done with the values of epsilon and guess above. In fact, any valid C expression can be specified as the initial value for a simple automatic variable. The value of the expression will be calculated and assigned to the automatic local variable *each* time that the function is called. And since an automatic variable "disappears" once the function has completed execution, the value of that variable disappears along with it. In other words, the value that an automatic variable has when a function finishes execution is *guaranteed* not to exist the next time the function is called. This is a key concept in the understanding of the operation of automatic variables.

If we stick the word static in front of a variable declaration, then we are in an entirely new ball game. The word static in C refers not to an electric charge but rather to the notion of something that has no movement. This is the key to the concept of a static variable—it does *not* come and go as the function is called and returns. This implies that the value that a static variable has upon leaving a function will be the same value that variable will have the next time that the function is called.

Static variables also differ with respect to their initialization. A static local variable is initialized *once* only at the start of overall program execution and not each time that the function is called. Furthermore, the initial value specified for a static variable *must* be a simple constant or constant expression. Static variables also have default initial values of zero, unlike automatic variables, which have no default initial value.

In the function `auto_static`, which is defined as follows:

```
auto_static ()
{
    static int   static_variable = 0;
                    .
                    .
                    .
}
```

the value of `static_variable` will be initialized to 0 only once when program execution begins. In order to set its value to 0 each time the function is executed, an explicit assignment statement is needed, as in

```
auto_static ()
{
    static int   static_variable;

    static_variable = 0;
                .
                .
                .
}
```

The following program should help make the concepts of automatic and static variables a bit clearer.

Program 8-15

```
/* Illustrate static and automatic variables */

void  auto_static ()
{
    int          auto_variable = 1;
    static int   static_variable = 1;

    printf ("automatic = %d, static = %d\n",
                auto_variable, static_variable);

    ++auto_variable;
    ++static_variable;
}
```

```
main ()
{
    int  i;

    for ( i = 0;  i < 5;  ++i )
        auto_static ();
}
```

Program 8-15 Output

```
automatic = 1, static = 1
automatic = 1, static = 2
automatic = 1, static = 3
automatic = 1, static = 4
automatic = 1, static = 5
```

Inside the auto_static function, two local variables are declared. The first variable, called auto_variable, is an automatic variable of type int with an initial value of 1. The second variable, called static_variable, is a static variable, also of type int and also with an initial value of 1. The function calls the printf routine to display the values of these two variables. After this, the variables are each incremented by 1, and execution of the function is then complete.

The main routine sets up a loop to call the auto_static function 5 times. The output from Program 8-15 points out the difference between the two variable types as per our previous discussions. The value of the automatic variable is listed as 1 for each line of the display. This is because its value is set to 1 each time the function is called. On the other hand, the output shows the value of the static variable steadily increasing from 1 through 5. This is because its value is set equal to 1 only once—when program execution begins—and because its value is retained from one function call to the next.

The choice of whether to use a static variable or automatic variable depends upon the intended use of the variable. If you want the variable to retain its value from one function call to the next (for example, consider a function that counts the number of times that it is called), then use a static variable. Also, if your function uses a variable whose value is set once and then never changes, then you may want to declare the variable static, as it saves the inefficiency of having the variable reinitialized each time that the function is called, and also slightly improves the program's readability.

From the other direction, if the value of a local variable must be initialized at the beginning of each function call, an automatic variable seems the logical choice.

There is another influencing factor over whether to use a static or an automatic variable, and it really has to do with a slight "drawback" with the C language. As we have previously described, most C compilers do not allow for the initialization of automatic arrays. Only static or global arrays may be initialized with a list of values as illustrated in this chapter and in the previous one. Be careful and remember that if a static array is initialized in a function, the initial values will be assigned to the array only once when program execution begins. Any changes made to the array will remain throughout the program's execution.

♦ Recursive Functions ♦

The C language supports a capability known as *recursive* function. Recursive functions can be effectively used to succinctly and efficiently solve problems. They are commonly used in applications in which the solution to a problem can be expressed in terms of successively applying the same solution to subsets of the problem. One example might be in the evaluation of expressions containing nested sets of parenthesized expressions. Other common applications involve the searching and sorting of data structures called *trees* and *lists*.

Recursive functions are most commonly illustrated by an example which calculates the factorial of a number. As you will recall, the factorial of a positive integer n, written $n!$, is simply the product of the successive integers 1 through n. The factorial of 0 is a special case and is defined equal to 1. So 5! is calculated as follows:

$$5! = 5 \times 4 \times 3 \times 2 \times 1$$
$$= 120$$

and

$$6! = 6 \times 5 \times 4 \times 3 \times 2 \times 1$$
$$= 720$$

Comparing the calculation of 6! to the calculation of 5!, you will observe that the former is equal to 6 times the latter; that is, $6! = 6 \times 5!$. In the general case, the factorial of any positive integer n greater than 0 is equal to n multiplied by the factorial of $n - 1$:

$$n! = n \times (n - 1)!$$

The expression of the value of $n!$ in terms of the value of $(n-1)!$ is called a *recursive* definition, since the definition of the value of a factorial is based on the value of another factorial. In fact, we can develop a function which calculates the factorial of an integer n according to this recursive defintion. Such a function is illustrated in the following program.

Program 8-16

```
/* Recursive function to calculate the factorial
            of a positive integer                    */

long int  factorial (n)
int   n;
{
    long int  result;

    if  ( n == 0 )
        result = 1;
    else
        result = n * factorial (n - 1);

    return (result);
}

main ()
{
    int   j;

    for ( j = 0;  j < 11;  ++j )
        printf ("%2d! = %ld\n", j, factorial (j));
}
```

Program 8-16 Output

```
 0! = 1
 1! = 1
 2! = 2
 3! = 6
 4! = 24
 5! = 120
 6! = 720
 7! = 5040
 8! = 40320
 9! = 362880
10! = 3628800
```

The fact that the factorial function includes a call to itself makes this function recursive. Let's see what happens in the case when the function is called to calculate the factorial of 3, for example. When the function is entered, the value of the formal parameter n will be set to 3. Since this value is not zero, the following program statement

```
result = n * factorial (n - 1);
```

will be executed, which, given the value of n, will be evaluated as

```
result = 3 * factorial (2);
```

This expression specifies that the `factorial` function is to be called, this time to calculate the factorial of 2. Therefore, the mutiplication of 3 by this value will be left pending while `factorial (2)` is calculated.

Even though we are again calling the same function, we should conceptualize this as a call to a separate function. Each time that any function is called in C—be it recursive or not—the function gets its own set of local variables and formal parameters to work with. Therefore, the local variable `result` and the formal parameter n that exist when the `factorial` function is called to calculate the factorial of 3 are distinct from the variable `result` and the parameter n when the function is called to calculate the factorial of 2.

With the value of n equal to 2, the `factorial` function will execute the statement

```
result = n * factorial (n - 1);
```

which will be evaluated as

```
result = 2 * factorial (1);
```

Once again, the multiplication of 2 by the factorial of 1 will be left pending while the `factorial` function is called to calculate the factorial of 1.

With the value of n equal to 1, the `factorial` function will once again execute the statement

```
result = n * factorial (n - 1);
```

which will be evaluated as

```
result = 1 * factorial (0);
```

When the `factorial` function is called to calculate the factorial of 0, the function will set the value of `result` to 1 and *return*, thus initiating the evaluation of all of the pending expressions. So the value of `factorial (0)`, or 1, will be returned to the calling function (which happened to be the `factorial` function) which will be multiplied by 1 and assigned to `result`. This value of 1, which represents the value of `factorial (1)`, will then be returned back to the calling function (once again the `factorial` function) where it will be multiplied by 2, stored into `result`, and returned as the value of `factorial (2)`.

Finally, the returned value of 2 will be multiplied by 3, thus completing the pending calculation of factorial (3). The resulting value of 6 will be returned as the final result of the call to the factorial function, to be displayed by the printf function.

In summary, the sequence of operations that is performed in the evaluation of factorial (3) can be conceptualized as follows:

```
factorial (3) = 3 * factorial (2)
              = 3 * 2 * factorial (1)
              = 3 * 2 * 1 * factorial (0)
              = 3 * 2 * 1 * 1
              = 6
```

It might be a good idea for you to trace through the operation of the factorial function with a pencil and paper. Assume that the function is initially called to calculate the factorial of 4. List the values of n and result at each call to the factorial function.

This discussion concludes this chapter on functions and variables. The program function is a powerful tool in the C programming language. Enough cannot be said about the critical importance of structuring a program in terms of small, well-defined functions. Functions will be used heavily throughout the remainder of this book. At this point, you should review any topics that were covered in this chapter that still may seem unclear. Working through the following exercises will also help reinforce the topics that have been discussed.

You should note that ANSI C has a new format for defining and declaring functions. This *prototype* format enables you to specify in the function header not only the type of value returned by the function, but also the number of arguments to the function and their types. With this information, the compiler will then check subsequent calls to the function to ensure that the correct number and type of arguments are being passed. If necessary, it will also convert an argument to match the type expected by the function. Many newer C compilers support this prototyping format, including non-ANSI ones. For more details, consult Appendix B.

◆ Exercises ◆

1. If you have access to a computer facility that supports the C programming language, type in and run the 16 programs presented in this chapter. Compare the output produced by each program with the output presented after each program.

2. Modify Program 8-4 so that the value of triangular_number is returned by the function. Then go back to Program 5-5 and change that program so that it calls the new version of the calculate_triangular_number function.

3. Modify Program 8-8 so that the value of epsilon is passed as an argument to the function. Try experimenting with different values of epsilon to see the effect that it has on the value of the square root.

4. Modify Program 8-8 so that the value of guess is printed each time through the while loop. Notice how quickly the value of guess converges to the square root. What conclusions can you reach about the number of iterations through the loop, the number whose square root is being calculated, and the value of the initial guess?

5. The criteria used for termination of the loop in the square_root function of Program 8-8 is not suitable for use when computing the square root of very large or very small numbers. Rather than comparing the *difference* between the value of x and the value of guess^2, the program should compare the *ratio* of the two values to 1. The closer this ratio gets to 1, the more accurate the approximation of the square root.

   Modify Program 8-8 so that this new termination criteria is used.

6. Modify Program 8-8 so that the square_root function accepts a double precision argument and returns the result as a double precision value. Be sure to change the value of the variable epsilon to reflect the fact that double precision variables are now being used.

7. An equation of the form

   $$ax^2 + bx + c = 0$$

   is known as a *quadratic* equation. The values of a, b, and c in the above example represent constant values. So

   $$4x^2 - 17x - 15 = 0$$

   represents a quadratic equation where a = 4, b = -17, and c = -15. The values of x that satisfy a particular quadratic equation, known as the *roots* of the equation, may be calculated by substituting the values of a, b, and c into the following two formulas:

$$x_1 = \frac{-b + \sqrt{b^2 - 4ac}}{2a}$$

$$x_2 = \frac{-b - \sqrt{b^2 - 4ac}}{2a}$$

If the value of $b^2 - 4ac$, called the *discriminant*, is less than zero, then the roots of the equation, x_1 and x_2, are imaginary numbers.

Write a program to solve a quadratic equation. The program should allow the user to enter the values for a, b, and c. If the discriminant is less than zero, then a message should be displayed that the roots are imaginary; otherwise the program should then proceed to calculate and display the two roots of the equation. (Note: Be sure to make use of the square_root function that we developed in this chapter.)

8. Write a function that raises an integer to a positive integer power. Call the function x_to_the_n taking two integer arguments x and n. Have the function return a long int, which represents the results of calculating x^n.

9. The least common multiple (*lcm*) of two positive integers u and v is the smallest positive integer which is evenly divisible by both u and v. Thus, the *lcm* of 15 and 10, written *lcm* (15, 10) is 30 since 30 is the smallest integer divisible by both 15 and 10. Write a function lcm that takes two integer arguments and returns their *lcm*. The lcm function should calculate the least common multiple by calling the gcd function from Program 8-6 in accordance with the following identity:

$$lcm\ (u, v) = uv \mathbin{/} gcd\ (u, v) \qquad u, v \geq 0$$

10. Write a function prime that returns 1 if its argument is a prime number, and returns 0 otherwise.

11. Write a function called array_sum that takes two arguments: an integer array and the number of elements in the array. Have the function return as its result the sum of the elements in the array.

12. A matrix M with i rows, j columns can be *transposed* into a matrix N having j rows and i columns by simply setting the value of $N_{a,b}$ equal to the value of $M_{b,a}$ for all relevant values of a and b.

Write a function *transpose_matrix* that takes as an argument a 4×5 matrix and a 5×4 matrix. Have the function transpose the 4×5 matrix and store the results into the 5×4 matrix. Also write a main routine to test the function.

13. Rewrite the functions developed in the last four exercises to use global variables instead of arguments. For example, the last exercise should now transpose a globally defined 4×5 matrix, storing the results of the transposition into another globally defined 5×4 matrix.

14. Modify the sort function of Program 8-12 to take a third argument indicating whether the array is to be sorted into ascending or descending order. Then modify the sort algorithm to correctly sort the array into the indicated order.

15. Modify Program 8-14 so that the user is re-asked to type in the value of the base if an invalid base is entered. The modified program should continue to ask for the value of the base until a valid response is given.

16. Modify Program 8-14 so that the user can convert any number of integers. Make provision for the program to terminate when a 0 is typed in as the value of the number to be converted.

♦ ♦ ♦ ♦ ♦ ♦

9

Structures

Chapter 7 introduced the array that permits us to group elements of the same type into a single logical entity. To reference an element in the array, all that was necessary was that the name of the array be given together with the appropriate subscript.

The C language provides another tool for grouping elements together. This falls under the name of *structures* and forms the basis for the discussions in this chapter. As you will see, the structure is a powerful concept that you will use in many C programs that you develop.

Suppose we wished to store today's date—which is 9/18/82—inside a program, perhaps to be used for the heading of some program output, or even for computational purposes. A natural method for storing the date would be to simply assign the month to an integer variable called `month`, the day to an integer variable `day`, and the year to an integer variable `year`. So the statements

```
int  month = 9, day = 18, year = 1982;
```

would work just fine. This is a totally acceptable approach. But what if our program also needed to store the date of purchase of a particular item, for example. We could go about the same procedure of defining three more variables such as `month_of_purchase`, `day_of_purchase`, and `year_of_purchase`. Whenever we needed to use the puchase date, these three variables could then be explicitly accessed.

Using this method, we must keep track of three separate variables for each date that we use in the program—variables that are logically related. It would be much better if we could somehow group these sets of three variables together. This is precisely what the structure in C allows us to do.

We can define a structure called `date` in the C language that consists of three components that represent the month, day, and year. The syntax for such a definition is rather straightforward, as shown by the following:

```
struct   date
{
     int   month;
     int   day;
     int   year;
};
```

The `date` structure just defined contains three integer *members* called `month`, `day`, and `year`. The definition of date in a sense defines a new type in the language in that variables may subsequently be declared to be of type `struct date`, as in the declaration

```
struct date   today;
```

We can also declare a variable `purchase_date` to be of the same type by a separate declaration, such as

```
struct date   purchase_date;
```

or we can simply include the two declarations on the same line, as in

```
struct date   today, purchase_date;
```

Unlike variables of type `int`, `float`, or `char`, a special syntax is needed when dealing with structure variables. A member of a structure is accessed by specifying the variable name, followed by a period, and then the member name. For example, to set the value of the `day` in the variable `today` to 21, you write

```
today.day = 21;
```

Note that there are no spaces permitted between the variable name, the period, and the member name. To set the `year` in `today` to 1989, the expression

```
today.year = 1989;
```

can be used. Finally, to test the value of `month` to see if it is equal to 12, a statement such as

```
if   ( today.month == 12 )
     next_month = 1;
```

will do the trick.

What do you think would be the effect of the following statement?

```
if  ( today.month == 1  &&  today.day == 1 )
    printf ("Happy New Year!!!\n");
```

The following incorporates the preceding discussions into an actual C program.

Program 9-1

```
/* Program to illustrate a structure */

main ()
{
    struct   date
    {
        int   month;
        int   day;
        int   year;
    };

    struct date   today;

    today.month = 9;
    today.day = 25;
    today.year = 1988;

    printf ("Today's date is %d/%d/%d.\n", today.month,
            today.day, today.year % 100);
}
```

Program 9-1 Output

```
Today's date is 9/25/88.
```

The first statement inside main defines the structure called date to consist of three integer members called month, day, and year. In the second statement, the variable today is declared to be of type struct date. Be sure to get these two concepts straight. The first statement simply defines what a date structure looks like to the C compiler, and causes no storage to be reserved inside the computer. The second statement declares a variable to be of type struct date and therefore *does* cause memory to be reserved for storing the three integer values of the variable today.

After today has been declared, the program then proceeds to assign values to each of the three members of today, as depicted in Fig. 9-1.

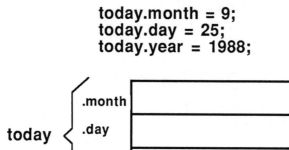

today.month = 9;
today.day = 25;
today.year = 1988;

Fig. 9-1. Assigning values to a structure variable

After the assignments have been made, the values contained inside the structure are displayed by an appropriate `printf` call. The remainder of `today.year` divided by 100 is calculated prior to being passed to the `printf` function so that just 88 is displayed for the year.

When it comes to the evaluation of expressions, `structure` members follow the same rules as do ordinary variables in the C language. So division of an integer `structure` member by another integer would be performed as an integer division, as in

```
century = today.year / 100 + 1;
```

Suppose we wanted to write a simple program that accepted as input today's date and displayed to the user tomorrow's date? Now, at first glance, this seems a perfectly simple task to perform. We can ask the user to enter today's date, and can then proceed to calculate tomorrow's date by a series of statements, such as

```
tomorrow.month = today.month;
tomorrow.day   = today.day + 1;
tomorrow.year  = today.year;
```

Of course, the above statements would work just fine for the majority of dates, but the following two cases would not be properly handled:

1. If today's date fell at the end of a month.

2. If today's date fell at the end of a year (that is, if today's date were December 31).

One way to determine easily if today's date falls at the end of a month is to set up an array of integers that corresponds to the number of days in each month. A lookup inside the array for a particular month will then give the number of days in that month. So the statement

```
static int  days_per_month[12] =
   { 31, 28, 31, 30, 31, 30, 31, 31, 30, 31, 30, 31 };
```

defines an array called `days_per_month` containing 12 integer elements. For each month `i`, the value contained in `days_per_month[i - 1]` corresponds to the number of days in that particular month. Therefore, the number of days in April, which is the fourth month of the year, is given by `days_per_month[3]` which is equal to 30. (We could have defined the array to contain 13 elements, with `days_per_month[i]` corresponding to the number of days in month `i`. Access into the array could then have been made directly based on the month number, rather than on the month number minus 1. The decision of whether to use 12 or 13 elements in this case is strictly a matter of personal preference.)

If it is determined that today's date falls at the end of the month, then we can calculate tomorrow's date by simply adding 1 to the month number, and setting the value of the day equal to 1.

In order to solve the second problem mentioned earlier, we must determine if today's date is at the end of a month and if the month is 12. If this is the case, then tomorrow's day and month must be set equal to 1, and the year appropriately incremented by 1.

Program 9-2 asks the user to enter today's date, calculates tomorrow's date, and displays the results.

If you look at the program's output, you will quickly notice that we seemed to have made a mistake somewhere: the day after February 28, 1988 is listed as March 1, 1988 and *not* as February 29, 1988. I think our program forgot about leap years! But we'll return to this problem shortly. First, let's discuss the program and its logic.

After the `date` structure is defined, two variables of type `struct date`, `today` and `tomorrow`, are declared. The program then proceeds to ask the user to enter today's date. The three integer values that are entered are stored into `today.month`, `today.day`, and `today.year`, respectively.

Program 9-2

```
/* Program to determine tomorrow's date */

main ()
{
    struct  date
    {
        int   month;
        int   day;
        int   year;
    };

    struct date   today, tomorrow;

    static int   days_per_month[12] =
        { 31, 28, 31, 30, 31, 30, 31, 31, 30, 31, 30, 31 };

    printf ("Enter today's date (mm dd yyyy): ");
    scanf ("%d%d%d", &today.month, &today.day, &today.year);

    if  ( today.day != days_per_month[today.month - 1] )
    {
        tomorrow.day = today.day + 1;
        tomorrow.month = today.month;
        tomorrow.year = today.year;
    }
    else if ( today.month == 12 )        /* end of year */
    {
        tomorrow.day = 1;
        tomorrow.month = 1;
        tomorrow.year = today.year + 1;
    }
    else
    {                                    /* end of month */
        tomorrow.day = 1;
        tomorrow.month = today.month + 1;
        tomorrow.year = today.year;
    }

    printf ("Tomorrow's date is %d/%d/%d.\n",tomorrow.month,
            tomorrow.day, tomorrow.year % 100);
}
```

Program 9-2 Output

```
Enter today's date (mm dd yyyy): 7 16 1988
Tomorrow's date is 7/17/88.
```

Program 9-2 Output (Re-run)

```
Enter today's date (mm dd yyyy): 12 31 1989
Tomorrow's date is 1/1/90.
```

Program 9-2 Output (Re-run)

```
Enter today's date (mm dd yyyy): 2 28 1988
Tomorrow's date is 3/1/88.
```

Next, a test is made to determine if the day is at the end of the month, by comparing `today.day` to `days_per_month[today.month - 1]`. If it is not the end of the month, then tomorrow's date is calculated by simply adding one to the day and setting tomorrow's month and year equal to today's month and year.

If today's date does fall at the end of the month, then another test is made to determine if we are at the end of the year. If the month equals 12, meaning that today's date is December 31, then tomorrow's date is set equal to January 1 of the next year. If the month does not equal 12, then tomorrow's date is set to the first day of the following month (of the same year).

After tomorrow's date has been calculated, the values are displayed to the user with an appropriate `printf` statement call, and program execution is complete.

♦ Functions and Structures ♦

Now let's return to the problem that was discovered in the previous program. Our program thinks that February always has 28 days. So, naturally when we ask it for the day after February 28, it will always display March 1 as the answer. What we need to do is to make a special test for the case of a leap year. If the year is a leap year, and the month is February, then the number of days in that month is 29. Otherwise, the normal lookup inside the `days_per_month` array can be made.

A good way to incorporate the required changes into Program 9-2 would be to develop a function called `number_of_days` to determine the number of days in a month. The function would perform the leap year test and the lookup inside the `days_per_month` array as required. Inside the `main` routine all that would have to be changed would be the `if` statement, which compares the value of `today.day` to `days_per_month[today.month - 1]`. Instead, we could now compare the value of `today.day` to the value returned by our number_of_days function.

Study the following program carefully. What is being passed to the number_of_days function as an argument?

Program 9-3

```
/* Program to determine tomorrow's date */

struct   date
{
     int   month;
     int   day;
     int   year;
};

main ()
{
     struct date   today, tomorrow;

     printf ("Enter today's date (mm dd yyyy): ");
     scanf ("%d%d%d", &today.month, &today.day, &today.year);

     if  ( today.day != number_of_days (today) )
     {
         tomorrow.day = today.day + 1;
         tomorrow.month = today.month;
         tomorrow.year = today.year;
     }
     else if ( today.month == 12 )        /* end of year */
     {
         tomorrow.day = 1;
         tomorrow.month = 1;
         tomorrow.year = today.year + 1;
     }
     else                                 /* end of month */
     {
         tomorrow.day = 1;
         tomorrow.month = today.month + 1;
         tomorrow.year = today.year;
     }

     printf ("Tomorrow's date is %d/%d/%d.\n",tomorrow.month,
             tomorrow.day, tomorrow.year % 100);
}
```

```
/* Function to find the number of days in a month */

int   number_of_days   (d)
struct date   d;
{
    int         answer;
    static int  days_per_month[12] =
        { 31, 28, 31, 30, 31, 30, 31, 31, 30, 31, 30, 31 };

    if ( is_leap_year (d)   &&   d.month == 2 )
        answer = 29;
    else
        answer = days_per_month[d.month - 1];

    return (answer);
}

/* Function to determine if it's a leap year */

int   is_leap_year (d)
struct date   d;
{
    int   leap_year_flag;

    if ( (d.year % 4 == 0   &&   d.year % 100 != 0)   ||
                d.year % 400 == 0 )
        leap_year_flag = 1;    /* It's a leap year */
    else
        leap_year_flag = 0;    /* Not a leap year  */

    return (leap_year_flag);
}
```

Program 9-3 Output

```
Enter today's date (mm dd yyyy): 2 28 1988
Tomorrow's date is 2/29/88.
```

Program 9-3 Output (Re-run)

```
Enter today's date (mm dd yyyy): 2 28 1989
Tomorrow's date is 3/1/89.
```

The first thing that will catch your eye in the preceding program is the fact that the definition of the `date` structure appears first and outside of any function. This is because structure definitions behave very much like variables—if a structure is defined within a particular function, then only that function knows of its existence. This is a *local* structure definition. If we define the structure outside of any function, then that definition is *global*. A global structure definition allows any variables that are subsequently defined in the program (either inside or outside of a function) to be declared to be of that structure type.

Inside the `main` routine, which you will notice is listed *first* in this program, the change we discussed earlier was made. That is, instead of comparing the value of `today.day` against `days_per_month[today.month - 1]`, the statement

```
if  ( today.day != number_of_days (today) )
```

was used. As you can see from the function call, we are specifying that the structure `today` is to be passed as an argument. This is perfectly valid in C. Inside the `number_of_days` function, the appropriate declarations must be made to inform the system that a structure is expected as an argument:

```
int  number_of_days  (d)
struct date  d;
```

As with ordinary variables, and unlike arrays, any changes made by the function to the values contained in the structure argument will have no effect on the original structure. They effect only the *copy* of the structure that is created when the function is called.

The `number_of_days` function begins by determining if it is a leap year and if the month is February. The former determination is made by calling another function called `is_leap_year`. We will discuss this function shortly. From reading the `if` statement

```
if ( is_leap_year (d)  &&  d.month == 2 )
```

we can assume that the `is_leap_year` function will return nonzero (TRUE) if it is a leap year, and will return 0 (FALSE) if it is not a leap year. This is directly in line with our discussions of flags back in Chapter 6.

An interesting point to be made about the above `if` statement concerns the choice of the function name `is_leap_year`. This name makes the `if` statement extremely readable, and implies that the function is returning some kind of "yes/no" answer.

Getting back to our program, if the determination is made that we are in February of a leap year, then the value of the variable `answer` is set to 29; otherwise, the value of `answer` is found by indexing the `days_per_month` array with the appropriate month. The value of `answer` is then returned to the `main` routine, where execution is continued as in Program 9-2.

The `is_leap_year` function is straightforward enough—it simply tests the year contained in the `date` structure and returns a 1 if it is a leap year and 0 if it is not.

As an exercise in producing a better structured program, let's take the entire process of determining tomorrow's date and relegate it to a separate function. We can call the new function `date_update` and have it take as its argument today's date. The function will then calculate tomorrow's date and *return* the new date back to us. Can this be done in C? But of course.

Program 9-4

```
/* Program to determine tomorrow's date */

struct   date
{
    int   month;
    int   day;
    int   year;
};

main ()
{
    struct date  date_update ();
    struct date  this_day, next_day;

    printf ("Enter today's date (mm dd yyyy): ");
    scanf ("%d%d%d", &this_day.month, &this_day.day,
            &this_day.year);

    next_day = date_update (this_day);

    printf ("Tomorrow's date is %d/%d/%d.\n",next_day.month,
            next_day.day, next_day.year % 100);
}

/* Function to calculate tomorrow's date */

struct date  date_update (today)
struct date  today;
{
    struct date  tomorrow;

    if ( today.day != number_of_days (today) )
    {
        tomorrow.day = today.day + 1;
        tomorrow.month = today.month;
        tomorrow.year = today.year;
    }
```

```
    else if ( today.month == 12 )        /* end of year */
    {
        tomorrow.day = 1;
        tomorrow.month = 1;
        tomorrow.year = today.year + 1;
    }
    else
    {                                      /* end of month */
        tomorrow.day = 1;
        tomorrow.month = today.month + 1;
        tomorrow.year = today.year;
    }

    return (tomorrow);
}

/* Function to find the number of days in a month */

int  number_of_days  (d)
struct date  d;
{
    int         answer;
    static int  days_per_month[12] =
        { 31, 28, 31, 30, 31, 30, 31, 31, 30, 31, 30, 31 };

    if ( is_leap_year (d)  &&  d.month == 2 )
        answer = 29;
    else
        answer = days_per_month[d.month - 1];

    return (answer);
}

/* Function to determine if it's a leap year */

int  is_leap_year (d)
struct date  d;
{
    int  leap_year_flag;

    if ( (d.year % 4 == 0  &&  d.year % 100 != 0)  ||
                    d.year % 400 == 0 )
        leap_year_flag = 1;    /* It's a leap year */
    else
        leap_year_flag = 0;    /* Not a leap year */

    return (leap_year_flag);
}
```

Program 9-4 Output

```
Enter today's date (mm dd yyyy): 2 28 1988
Tomorrow's date is 2/29/88.
```

Program 9-4 Output (Re-run)

```
Enter today's date (mm dd yyyy): 10 2 1990
Tomorrow's date is 10/3/90.
```

Inside main, the date_update function is declared to return a value of type struct date. This is necessary because the date_update function is defined further on in the program, after it is called, and does not return an int. The statement

```
next_date = date_update (this_day);
```

illustrates the ability to pass a structure to a function and to return one as well. The header of the date_update function has the appropriate declaration to indicate that the function returns a value of type struct date. Inside the function is the same code that was included in the main routine of Program 9-3. The functions number_of_days and is_leap_year remain unchanged from that program.

Make sure that you understand the hierarchy of function calls in the above program: the main function calls date_update, which in turn calls number_of_days, which itself calls the function is_leap_year.

A Structure for Storing the Time

Suppose we had the need to store values inside a program that represented various times expressed as hours, minutes, and seconds. Since we have seen how useful our date structure has been in helping us to logically group the day, month, and year, it seems only natural to use a structure which we could call appropriately enough, time, to group the hours, minutes, and seconds. The structure definition would be straightforward enough, as shown:

```
struct time
{
    int     hour;
    int     minutes;
    int     seconds;
};
```

Most computer installations choose to express the time in terms of a 24-hour clock, known as military time. This representation avoids the "hassle" of having to qualify a time with "AM" or "PM." The hour begins with 0 at 12 midnight and increases by 1 until it reaches 23, which represents 11:00 PM. So, for example, 4:30 means 4:30 AM while 16:30 represents 4:30 PM; and 12:00 represents noon, while 00:01 represents 1 minute after midnight.

Most computer systems have a clock contained within the system that is always running. This clock is used for such diversified purposes as informing the user as to the current time, causing certain events to occur or programs to be executed at specific times, or for recording the time that a particular event occurs. There are one or more computer programs that are usually "associated" with the clock. One of these programs might be executed every second, for example, to update the current time that is stored somewhere in the computer's memory.

Suppose we wished to mimic the function of the program described above—namely develop a program that updates the time by one second. If you think about this for a second (pun intentional), you will realize that this problem is quite analagous to the problem of updating the date by one day.

Just as finding the next day had some special requirements, so does the process of updating the time. In particular, the following special cases must be handled:

1. If the number of seconds reaches 60, the seconds must be reset to 0 and the minutes increased by 1.

2. If the number of minutes reaches 60, the minutes must be reset to 0 and the hour increased by 1.

3. If the number of hours reaches 24, the hours, minutes, and seconds must be reset to 0.

The following program uses a function called time_update, which takes as its argument the current time and returns a time that is one second later.

Program 9-5

```
/* Program to update the time by one second */

struct   time
{
    int   hour;
    int   minutes;
    int   seconds;
};
```

```
main ()
{
    struct  time  time_update ();
    struct  time  current_time, next_time;

    printf ("Enter the time (hh:mm:ss): ");
    scanf ("%d:%d:%d", &current_time.hour,
            &current_time.minutes, &current_time.seconds);

    next_time = time_update (current_time);

    printf ("Updated time is %.2d:%.2d:%.2d\n", next_time.hour,
                next_time.minutes, next_time.seconds );
}


/* Function to update the time by one second */

struct time  time_update(now)
struct time  now;
{
    struct time  new_time;

    new_time = now;
    ++new_time.seconds;

    if ( new_time.seconds == 60 )
    {                                       /* next minute */
        new_time.seconds = 0;
        ++new_time.minutes;

        if ( new_time.minutes == 60 )
        {                                   /* next hour */
            new_time.minutes = 0;
            ++new_time.hour;

            if ( new_time.hour == 24 )
                new_time.hour = 0;    /* midnight */
        }
    }

    return (new_time);
}
```

Program 9-5 Output

```
Enter the time (hh:mm:ss): 12:23:55
Updated time is 12:23:56
```

Program 9-5 Output (Re-run)

```
Enter the time (hh:mm:ss): 16:12:59
Updated time is 16:13:00
```

Program 9-5 Output (Re-run)

```
Enter the time (hh:mm:ss): 23:59:59
Updated time is 00:00:00
```

The `main` routine asks the user to enter in the time. The `scanf` call uses the format string

```
"%d:%d:%d"
```

to read the data. Specifying a non-format character, such as `':'`, in a format string signals to the `scanf` function that the particular character is expected as input. Therefore, the format string listed in Program 9-5 specifies that three integer values are to be input, the first separated from the second by a colon, and the second from the third by a colon. We will see in a later chapter how the `scanf` function returns a value that may be tested to determine if the values were entered in the correct format.

After the time has been entered, the program calls the `time_update` function, passing along the `current_time` as the argument. The result returned by the function is assigned to the `struct time` variable `next_time`, which is then displayed with an appropriate `printf` call. You will recall that the format characters `%.2d` are used to specify that two integer digits are to be displayed with zero fill. This ensures that we get the proper display for times such as `00:00:00`.

The `time_update` function begins execution by copying the values contained in the structure variable `now` to the local structure variable `new_time`. The function then proceeds to "bump" the time in `new_time` by one second. A test is then made to determine if the number of seconds has reached 60. If it has, then the seconds are reset to 0 and the minutes are bumped by 1. Another test is then made to see if the number of minutes has now reached 60, and if it has, the minutes are reset to 0 and the hour is increased by 1. Finally, if the two preceding conditions are satisfied, a test is then made to see if the hour is equal to 24; that is, if it is precisely midnight. If it is, then the hour is reset to 0. The function then returns the value of `new_time`, which contains the updated time, back to the calling routine.

◆ Initializing Structures ◆

Initializing structures is similar to initializing arrays—the elements are simply listed inside a pair of braces, with each element separated by a comma. As with arrays, most C compilers don't permit automatic structure variables to be initialized. However, all compilers will allow you to initialize global and static structure variables. A structure variable is made static simply by placing the keyword static directly before the declaration, as in

```
static struct date  today;
```

To initialize the variable today to July 2, 1988, the statement

```
static struct date  today = { 7, 2, 1988 };
```

can be used. The statement

```
static struct time  this_time = { 3, 29, 55 };
```

defines the struct time variable this_time and sets its value to 3:29:55 AM. As with the initialization of any static variable, a structure can only be initialized with constant values or constant expressions.

As with the initialization of an array, fewer values may be listed than are contained in the structure. So the statement

```
static struct time  time1 = { 12, 10 };
```

sets time1.hour to 12 and time1.minutes to 10, but gives no initial value to time1.seconds. In such a case, its initial value is set to zero by default.

◆ Arrays of Structures ◆

We have seen how useful the structure is in enabling us to logically group related elements together. With the time structure, for instance, it is only necessary to keep track of one variable, instead of three, for each time that it is used by the program. So if we had to handle 10 different times in a program, we would only have to keep track of 10 different variables, instead of 30.

An even better method for handling the 10 different times involves the combination of two powerful features of the C programming language: structures and arrays. C does not limit the programmer to the storing of simple data types inside an array; it is perfectly valid to define an *array of structures*. For example,

```
struct time  experiments[10];
```

defines an array called `experiments`, which consists of 10 elements. Each element inside the array is defined to be of type `struct time`. Similarly, the definition

```
struct date   birthdays[15];
```

defines the array `birthdays` to contain 15 elements of type `struct date`. Referencing a particular structure element inside the array is quite natural. To set the second birthday inside the `birthdays` array to February 4, 1955, the sequence of statements

```
birthdays[1].month = 2;
birthdays[1].day   = 4;
birthdays[1].year  = 1955;
```

will work just fine. To pass the entire `time` structure contained in `experiments[4]` to a function called `check_time`, the array element is specified:

```
check_time (experiments[4]);
```

As is to be expected, the `check_time` function declaration must specify that an argument of type `struct time` is expected:

```
void check_time (t0)
struct time   t0;
{
    .
    .
    .
}
```

Initialization of arrays containing structures is similar to initialization of multidimensional arrays. So the statement

```
static struct time   run_time [5] =
        {  {12, 0, 0},   {12, 30, 0},   {13, 15, 0} };
```

sets the first three times in the array `run_time` to 12:00:00, 12:30:00, and 13:15:00. The inner pairs of braces are optional, meaning that the above statement could be equivalently expressed as

```
static struct time   run_time[5] =
        { 12, 0, 0, 12, 30, 0, 13, 15, 0 };
```

The program that follows sets up an array of time structures called test_times. The program then proceeds to call our time_update function from Program 9-5. The time_update function was not included in the following program listing to conserve space. However, a comment statement was inserted to indicate where in the program the function could be included.

Program 9-6

```
/* Program to illustrate arrays of structures */

struct   time
{
    int   hour;
    int   minutes;
    int   seconds;
};

main ()
{
    struct time  time_update ();
    static struct time  test_times[5] =
        {  { 11, 59, 59 }, { 12, 0, 0 }, { 1, 29, 59 },
           { 23, 59, 59 }, { 19, 12, 27 }};
    int   i;

    for ( i = 0;  i < 5;  ++i )
    {
        printf ("Time is %.2d:%.2d:%.2d", test_times[i].hour,
            test_times[i].minutes, test_times[i].seconds);

        test_times[i] = time_update (test_times[i]);

        printf (" ...one second later it's %.2d:%.2d:%.2d\n",
            test_times[i].hour, test_times[i].minutes,
            test_times[i].seconds);
    }
}

/*** Include the time_update function here ***/
```

Program 9-6 Output

```
Time is 11:59:59 ...one second later it's 12:00:00
Time is 12:00:00 ...one second later it's 12:00:01
Time is 01:29:59 ...one second later it's 01:30:00
Time is 23:59:59 ...one second later it's 00:00:00
Time is 19:12:27 ...one second later it's 19:12:28
```

In the above program, a static array called `test_times` is defined to contain five different times. The elements in this array are assigned initial values that represent the times 11:59:59, 12:00:00, 1:29:59, 23:59:59, and 19:12:27, respectively. Fig. 9-2 can help you to understand what the `test_times` array actually looks like inside the computer's memory. A particular `time` structure stored in the `test_times` array is accessed by using the appropriate index number 0-4. A particular member (`hour`, `minutes`, or `seconds`) is then accessed by appending a period followed by the member name.

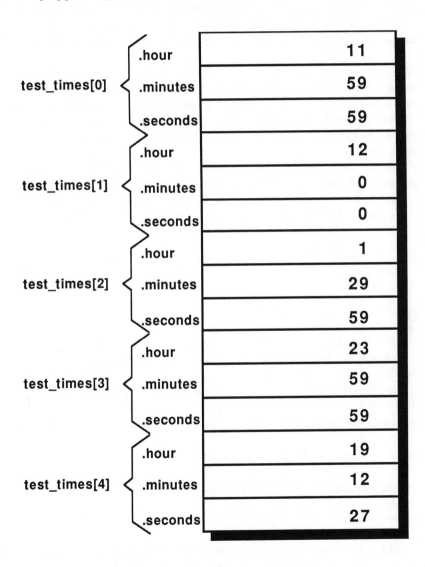

Fig. 9-2. The array `test_times` in memory

For each element in the `test_times` array, Program 9-6 displays the time as represented by that element, calls the `time_update` function, and then displays the updated time.

◆ Structures Within Structures ◆

C provides the user with an enormous amount of flexibility in defining structures. For instance, it is possible to define a structure that itself contains another structure as one or more of its members, as well as define structures that contain arrays.

We have seen how it is possible to logically group the month, day, and year into a structure called `date`, and how to group the hour, minutes, and seconds into a structure called `time`. It is quite possible that in some applications there might arise the need to logically group both a date and a time together. For example, we might need to set up a list of events that are to occur at a particular date and time.

What the above discussion implies is that we would like to have a convenient means for associating *both* the date and the time together. We can do this in C by defining a new structure, called, perhaps, `date_and_time`, which contains as its members two elements: the date and the time.

```
struct date_and_time
{
    struct date    sdate;
    struct time    stime;
};
```

The first member of this structure is of type `struct date` and is called `sdate`. The second member of the `date_and_time` structure is of type `struct time` and is called `stime`. This definition of a `date_and_time` structure requires that a `date` structure and a `time` structure have been previously defined to the compiler.

Variables can now be defined to be of type struct `date_and_time`, as in

```
struct date_and_time  event;
```

To reference the `date` structure of the variable `event`, the syntax is the same:

```
event.sdate
```

So we could call our `date_update` function with this date as the argument and assign the result back to the same place by a statement such as

```
event.sdate = date_update (event.sdate);
```

We can do the same type of thing with the `time` structure contained within our `date_and_time` structure:

```
event.stime = time_update (event.stime);
```

To reference a particular member *inside* one of these structures, a period followed by the member name is tacked onto the end:

```
event.sdate.month = 10;
```

This statement sets the `month` of the `date` structure contained within `event` to October, and the statement

```
++event.stime.seconds;
```

adds one to the `seconds` contained within the `time` structure.

The `event` variable can be initialized in the expected manner:

```
static struct date_and_time  event =
            { { 2, 1, 1988 }, { 3, 30, 0 } };
```

This sets the date in the static variable `event` to February 1, 1988 and sets the time to 3:30:00.

Naturally, it is possible to set up an array of `date_and_time` structures, as is done with the following declaration:

```
struct date_and_time  events[100];
```

The array `events` is declared to contain 100 elements of type `struct date_and_time`. The fourth `date_and_time` contained within the array is referenced in the usual way as `events[3]`, and the twenty-fifth date in the array can be sent to our `date_update` function as follows:

```
events[24].sdate = date_update (events[24].sdate);
```

To set the first time in the array to noon, the series of statements

```
events[0].stime.hour    = 12;
events[0].stime.minutes = 0;
events[0].stime.seconds = 0;
```

can be used.

◆ Structures Containing Arrays ◆

As the heading of this section implies, it is possible to define structures that contain arrays as members. One of the most common applications of this type is in setting up an array of characters inside a structure. For example, suppose we wanted to define a structure called month that contained as its members the number of days in the month as well as a three-character abbreviation for the name of the month. The following definition would do the job:

```
struct  month
{
    int     number_of_days;
    char    name[3];
};
```

This sets up a month structure that contains an integer member called number_of_days and a character member called name. The member name is actually an array of 3 characters. We can now define a variable to be of type struct month in the normal fashion:

```
struct month  a_month;
```

We can set the proper fields inside a_month for January with the following sequence of statements:

```
a_month.number_of_days = 31;
a_month.name[0] = 'J';
a_month.name[1] = 'a';
a_month.name[2] = 'n';
```

Or we can initialize this variable to the same values with the following statement:

```
static struct month  a_month = { 31, { 'J', 'a', 'n' } };
```

And to go one step further, we can set up 12 month structures inside an array to represent each month of the year:

```
struct month  months[12];
```

The following program illustrates the months array defined above. It's purpose is simply to set up the initial values inside the array and then display these values at the terminal.

Program 9-7

```
/* Program to illustrate structures and arrays */

struct   month
{
    int     number_of_days;
    char    name[3];
};

main ()
{
    int  i;

    static struct month  months[12] =
        { { 31, {'J', 'a', 'n'} },   { 28, {'F', 'e', 'b'} },
          { 31, {'M', 'a', 'r'} },   { 30, {'A', 'p', 'r'} },
          { 31, {'M', 'a', 'y'} },   { 30, {'J', 'u', 'n'} },
          { 31, {'J', 'u', 'l'} },   { 31, {'A', 'u', 'g'} },
          { 30, {'S', 'e', 'p'} },   { 31, {'O', 'c', 't'} },
          { 30, {'N', 'o', 'v'} },   { 31, {'D', 'e', 'c'} } };

    printf ("Month     Number of Days\n");
    printf ("-----     --------------\n");

    for ( i = 0;  i < 12;  ++i )
        printf (" %c%c%c              %d\n",
                months[i].name[0], months[i].name[1],
                months[i].name[2], months[i].number_of_days);
}
```

Program 9-7 Output

```
    Month     Number of Days
    -----     --------------
    Jan           31
    Feb           28
    Mar           31
    Apr           30
    May           31
    Jun           30
    Jul           31
    Aug           31
    Sep           30
    Oct           31
    Nov           30
    Dec           31
```

It might be easier for you to conceptualize the notation that is used to reference particular elements of the months array as defined in the program by examining Fig. 9-3.

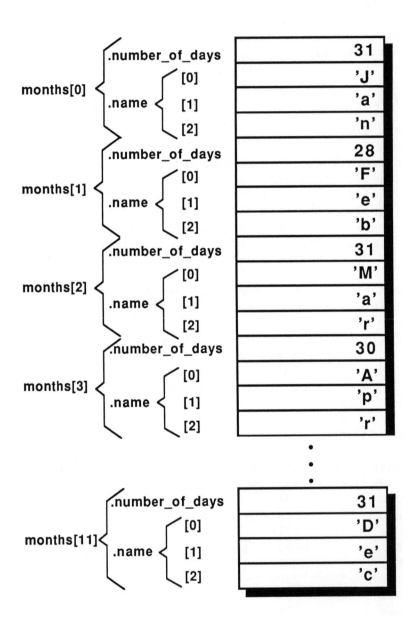

Fig. 9-3. The array months

As you can see from Fig. 9-3, the notation

```
months[0]
```

refers to the *entire* month structure contained in the first location of the months array. The type of this expression is type struct month. Therefore, when passing months[0] to a function as an argument, the corresponding formal parameter inside the function must be declared to be of type struct month.

Going one step further, the expression

```
months[0].number_of_days
```

refers to the number_of_days member of the month structure contained in months[0]. The type of this expression is int. The expression

```
months[0].name
```

references the three-character array called name inside the month structure of months[0]. If passing this expression as an argument to a function, then the corresponding formal parameter would be declared to be an array of type char.

Finally, the expression

```
months[0].name[0]
```

references the first character of the name array contained in months[0] (the character 'J').

◆ Structure Variants ◆

There is some flexibility in defining a structure that we should mention here. First, it is valid to declare a variable to be of a particular structure type at the same time that the structure is defined. This is done simply by including the variable name (or names) before the terminating semicolon of the structure definition. For example, the statement

```
struct   date
{
    int   month;
    int   day;
    int   year;
} todays_date, purchase_date;
```

defines the structure date *and* also declares the variables todays_date and purchase_date to be of this type. We can also assign initial values to the variables in the normal fashion. Thus,

```
static struct   date
{
     int  month;
     int  day;
     int  year;
} todays_date = { 9, 25, 1987 };
```

defines the structure date and the variable todays_date with initial values
as indicated.

If all of the variables of a particular structure type are defined when the
structure is defined, then the structure name can be omitted. So the statement

```
struct
{
     int  month;
     int  day;
     int  year;
}  dates[100];
```

defines an array called dates to consist of 100 elements. Each element is a
structure containing three integer members: month, day, and year. Since we
did not supply a name to the structure, the only way to subsequently declare
variables of the same type would be by explicitly defining the structure again.

♦ Exercises ♦

1. If you have access to a computer facility that supports the C programming language, type in and run the seven programs presented in this chapter. Compare the output produced by each program with the output presented after each program.

2. In certain applications, particularly in the financial area, it is often necessary to calculate the number of elapsed days between two dates. For example, the number of days between July 2, 1983, and July 16, 1983, is obviously 14. But how many days are there between February 3, 1979, and June 21, 1980? This calculation requires a bit more thought.

   Luckily, there is a formula that can be used to calculate the number of days between two dates. This is effected by computing the value of N for each of the two dates and then taking the difference, where N is calculated as follows:

$$N = 1461 \times f(year, month) / 4 + 153 \times g(month) / 5 + day$$

where:

$f(year, month)$	=	$year - 1$	if $month \leq 2$
		$year$	otherwise
$g(month)$	=	$month + 13$	if $month \leq 2$
		$month + 1$	otherwise

As an example of applying the formula, to calculate the number of days between February 3, 1979, and June 21, 1980, we can calculate the values of N_1 and N_2 by substituting the appropriate values into the above formula as shown:

$$
\begin{aligned}
N_1 &= 1461 \times f(1979, 2) / 4 + 153 \times g(2) / 5 + 3 \\
&= (1461 \times 1978) / 4 + (153 \times 15) / 5 + 3 \\
&= 2{,}889{,}858 / 4 + 2295 / 5 + 3 \\
&= 722{,}464 + 459 + 3 \\
&= 722{,}926
\end{aligned}
$$

$$
\begin{aligned}
N_2 &= 1461 \times f(1980, 6) / 4 + 153 \times g(6) / 5 + 21 \\
&= (1461 \times 1980) / 4 + (153 \times 7) / 5 + 21 \\
&= 2{,}892{,}780 / 4 + 1071 / 5 + 21 \\
&= 723{,}195 + 214 + 21 \\
&= 723{,}430
\end{aligned}
$$

$$
\begin{aligned}
\textit{Number of elapsed days} &= N_2 - N_1 \\
&= 723{,}430 - 722{,}926 \\
&= 504
\end{aligned}
$$

So the number of days between the two dates is shown to be 504. The above formula is applicable for any dates after March 1, 1900 (1 must be added to N for dates from March 1, 1800, to February 28, 1900, and 2 must be added for dates between March 1, 1700, and February 28, 1800).

Write a program that permits the user to type in two dates and then calculates the number of elapsed days between the two dates. Try to structure the program logically into separate functions. For example, you should have a function that accepts as an argument a date structure and returns the value of N computed as above. This function can then be called twice, once for each date, and the difference taken to determine the number of elapsed days. One word of advice: be careful about the calculation of N as you will be dealing with very large numbers. Use long int variables and make sure that the necessary calculations are performed with long integer arithmetic.

3. If we take the value of N as computed above, subtract 621,049 from it, and then take that result modulo 7, we get a number from 0 to 6 that represents the day of the week (Sunday through Saturday, respectively) that the particular day falls on. For example, the value of N computed for February 3, 1979, is 722,926 as derived above. 722,926 - 621,049 gives 101,877, and 101,877 % 7 gives 6, indicating that this date fell on a Saturday.

Use the functions developed in the previous exercise to develop a program that displays the day of the week that a particular date falls on. Make sure that the program displays the day of the week in English (such as "Monday").

4. Write a function elapsed_time that takes as its arguments two time structures and returns a time structure that represents the elapsed time (in hours, minutes, and seconds) between the two times. So the call

```
elapsed_time (time1, time2)
```

where time1 represents 3:45:15 and time2 represents 9:44:03, should return a time structure that represents 5 hours, 58 minutes, and 48 seconds. Be careful with times that cross midnight.

5. Write a function called clock_keeper that takes as its argument a date_and_time structure as defined in this chapter. The function should call the time_update function and, if the time reaches midnight, the function should call the date_update function to switch over to the next day. Have the function return the updated date_and_time structure.

10

Character Strings

Now we are ready to take a look at character strings in more detail. You were first introduced to character strings back in Chapter 3 when we wrote our first C program. In the statement

```
printf ("Programming in C is fun.\n");
```

the argument that is passed to the `printf` function is the character string

```
"Programming in C is fun.\n"
```

The double quote signs are used to delimit the character string, which can contain any combinations of letters, numbers, or special characters, other than a double quote sign. But as we shall see shortly, it is even possible to include a double quote sign inside a character string.

When we introduced the data type `char`, we mentioned that a variable that was declared to be of this type could contain only a *single* character. To assign a single character to such a variable, the character was enclosed within a pair of single quote marks. Thus the assignment

```
plus_sign = '+';
```

would have the effect of assigning the character `'+'` to the variable `plus_sign`, which we assume has been appropriately declared. We also pointed out that there *is* a distinction made between the single quote and double quote marks, and that if `plus_sign` were declared to be of type `char`, then the statement

```
plus_sign = "+";
```

would be incorrect.

But we would like to be able to deal with variables that can hold more than a single character, and this is precisely where the array of characters comes into play.

In Program 7-6, we defined an array of characters called word as follows

```
static char  word [] = { 'H', 'e', 'l', 'l', 'o', '!' };
```

Remembering that in the absence of a particular array size, the C system automatically computes the number of elements in the array based upon the number of initializers, this statement would reserve space in memory for exactly six characters as shown in Fig. 10-1.

word[0]	'H'
word[1]	'e'
word[2]	'l'
word[3]	'l'
word[4]	'o'
word[5]	'!'

Fig. 10-1. The array word in memory

In order to print out the contents of the array word, we ran through each element in the array and displayed it using the %c format characters.

With this technique, we can begin to build an assortment of useful functions for dealing with character strings. Some of the more commonly performed operations on character strings include combining two character strings together, (concatenation), copying one character string to another, extracting a portion of a character string (substring), and determining if two character strings are equal (i.e., contain the same characters). Why don't we take the first mentioned operation, concatenation, and develop a function to perform this task. We can define a call to our concatenate function as follows:

```
concatenate (string1, n1, string2, n2, result);
```

where string1 and string2 represent the two character arrays that are to be

concatenated and n1 and n2 represent the number of characters in the respec-
tive arrays. This makes the function flexible enough so that we can concatenate
two character arrays of arbitrary length. The argument result represents the
character array that is to be the destination of the concatenated character arrays
string1 followed by string2.

Program 10-1

```
/* Function to concatenate two character arrays */

void concatenate (string1, n1, string2, n2, result)
char   string1[], string2[], result[];
int    n1, n2;
{
    int  i, j;

    /* copy string1 to result */

    for ( i = 0;  i < n1;  ++i )
        result[i] = string1[i];

    /* copy string2 to result */

    for ( j = 0;  j < n2;  ++j )
        result[n1 + j] = string2[j];
}

main ()
{
    static char   s1[5] = { 'T', 'e', 's', 't', ' ' };
    static char   s2[6] = { 'w', 'o', 'r', 'k', 's', '.' };
    char          s3[11];
    int           i;

    concatenate (s1, 5, s2, 6, s3);

    for ( i = 0;  i < 11;  ++i )
        printf ("%c", s3[i]);

    printf ("\n");
}
```

Program 10-1 Output

```
Test works.
```

The function `concatenate` is defined as discussed above. You will notice that in declaring the formal parameters it is not necessary that they be defined in the precise order that they appear in the function header. All that matters is that they *are* defined before the open brace that introduces the body of the function.

The first `for` loop inside the `concatenate` function copies the characters from the `string1` array into the `result` array. This loop is executed `n1` times, which is the number of characters contained inside the `string1` array.

The second `for` loop copies `string2` into the `result` array. Since `string1` was `n1` characters long, copying into `result` begins at `result[n1]`—the position immediately following the one occupied by the last character of `string1`. After this `for` loop is done, the `result` array will contain the n1+n2 characters of `string2` concatenated to the end of `string1`.

Inside the `main` routine, two static character arrays, `s1` and `s2`, are defined. The first array is initialized to the characters `'T'`, `'e'`, `'s'`, `'t'`, and `' '`. This last character represents a blank space and is a perfectly valid character constant. The second array is initially set to the characters `'w'`, `'o'`, `'r'`, `'k'`, `'s'`, and `'.'`. A third character array, `s3`, is defined with enough space to hold `s1` concatenated to `s2`—11 characters. It is not declared to be static because there are no initial values assigned to it. Of course, it would have made no difference if it had been declared `static`.

The function call

```
concatenate (s1, 5, s2, 6, s3);
```

calls the `concatenate` function to concatenate the character arrays `s1` and `s2`, with the destination array `s3`. The arguments 5 and 6 are passed to the function to indicate the number of characters in `s1` and `s2`, respectively.

After the `concatenate` function has completed execution and returns to the main routine, a `for` loop is set up to display the results of the function call. The 11 elements of `s3` are displayed at the terminal, and as can be seen from the program's output, the `concatenate` function seems to be working properly.

It should be pointed out that in the preceding program example that it is the user's responsibility to ensure that the last argument to the `concatenate` function—the result array—contains enough space to hold the resulting concatenated character arrays. Failure to do so can produce unpredictable results when the program is run.

◆ Variable Length Character Strings ◆

We can adopt a similar approach to that used by the `concatenate` function for defining other functions to deal with character arrays. That is, we can develop a set of routines, each of which has as its arguments one or more character arrays plus the number of characters contained in each such array. Unfortunately, after working with these functions for a while, you will find that it gets a bit tedious trying to keep track of the number of characters contained in each character array that you are using in the program—especially if you are using your arrays to store characters strings of varying sizes. What we need is a method for dealing with character arrays without having to worry about precisely how many characters we have stored in them.

There is such a method, and it is based upon the idea of placing a special character at the end of every character string. In this manner, the function can then determine for itself when it has reached the end of a character string once it encounters this special character. By developing all of our functions to deal with character strings in this fashion, we can thus eliminate the need to specify the number of characters that are contained inside a character string.

In the C language, the special character that is used to signal the end of a string is known as the *null* character, and is written as '\0'. So the statement

```
static char  word [] = { 'H', 'e', 'l', 'l', 'o', '!', '\0' };
```

defines a character array called word that contains *seven* characters, the last of which is the null character (you will recall that the backslash character (\) is a special character in the C language and does not count as a separate character; therefore, '\0' represents a single character in C). The array word is depicted in Fig. 10-2.

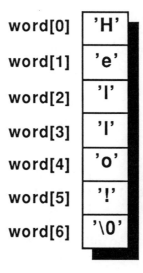

Fig. 10-2. The array word with terminating null character

To begin with an illustration of how these *variable length* character strings are used, let us write a function that counts the number of characters in a character string. We will call our function `string_length` and have it take as its argument a character array that is terminated by the null character. The function will determine the number of characters in the array and will return this value back to the calling routine. We will define the number of characters in the array as the number of characters up to, but not including, the terminating null character. So the function call

```
string_length (character_string)
```

should return the value 3 if `character_string` were defined as follows:

```
static  char  character_string[] = { 'c', 'a', 't', '\0' };
```

Program 10-2

```
/* Function to count the number of characters in a string */

int  string_length (string)
char  string[];
{
    int  count = 0;

    while ( string[count] != '\0' )
        ++count;

    return (count);
}

main ()
{
    static char  word1[] = { 'a', 's', 't', 'e', 'r', '\0' };
    static char  word2[] = { 'a', 't', '\0' };
    static char  word3[] = { 'a', 'w', 'e', '\0' };

    printf ("%d   %d   %d\n", string_length (word1),
            string_length (word2), string_length (word3));
}
```

Program 10-2 Output

```
5   2   3
```

Inside the `string_length` function, the variable count is defined and its value set to 0. The program then enters a `while` loop to sequence through the `string` array until the null character is reached. When the function finally hits upon this character, signaling the end of the character string, the `while` loop is exited and the value of count returned. This value represents the number of characters in the string, excluding the null character. You might want to trace through the operation of this loop on a small character array to verify that the value of count when the loop is exited is in fact equal to the number of characters in the array, excluding the null character.

In the `main` routine, three character arrays, word1, word2, and word3, are defined. The `printf` function call displays the results of calling the `string_length` function for each of these three character arrays.

Initializing and Displaying Character Strings

Now it is time to go back to the `concatenate` function developed in Program 10-1 and rewrite it to work with variable-length character strings. Obviously, the function must be changed somewhat since we no longer wish to pass as arguments the number of characters in the two arrays. The function will now take only three arguments: the two character arrays to be concatenated and the character array to place the result into.

Before presenting this program, now would be a good time to discuss two of the nice features that C provides for dealing with character strings.

The first feature involves the initialization of character arrays. C permits a character array to be initialized by simply specifying a constant character string rather than a list of individual characters. So, for example, the statement

```
static char  word[] = { "Hello!" };
```

can be used to set up an array of characters called word with the initial characters 'H', 'e', 'l', 'l', 'o', and '\0', respectively. This statement is equivalent to the statement

```
static char  word[] = { 'H', 'e', 'l', 'l', 'o', '!', '\0' };
```

Obviously, the first form is easier to type and to read.

The preceding discussion implies that character-string constants in the C language are automatically terminated by the null character. This is precisely the case. This fact helps functions such as `printf` determine when the end of a character string has been reached. So in the call

```
printf ("Programming in C is fun.\n");
```

the null character is automatically placed after the newline character in the character string, thereby enabling the `printf` function to determine when it has reached the end of the format string.

The other feature to be mentioned here involves the display of character strings. The special format characters %s inside a printf format string can be used to display an array of characters that is terminated by the the null character. So with the definition of word given earlier, the printf call

```
printf ("%s\n", word);
```

can be used to display the entire contents of the word array at the terminal. The printf function assumes when it encounters the %s format characters that the corresponding argument is a character string that is terminated by a null character.

The two features just described were incorporated into the main routine of the following program, which illustrates our revised concatenate function. Since we are no longer passing the number of characters in each string as arguments to the function, the function must determine when the end of each string is reached by testing for the null character. Also, when string1 is copied into the result array, we want to be sure *not* to also copy the null character, since this would end the string in the result array right there. We do need, however, to place a null character into the result array *after* string2 has been copied so as to signal the end of the newly created string.

Program 10-3

```
/* Function to concatenate two character strings */

void concatenate (string1, string2, result)
char   string1[], string2[], result[];
{
    int   i, j;

    /* copy string1 to result */

    for ( i = 0;  string1[i] != '\0';  ++i )
        result[i] = string1[i];

    /* copy string2 to result */

    for ( j = 0;  string2[j] != '\0';  ++j )
        result[i + j] = string2[j];

    /* Terminate the concatenated string with a null */

    result [i + j] = '\0';
}
```

```
main ()
{
    static char    s1[] = { "Test " };
    static char    s2[] = { "works." };
    char           s3[20];

    concatenate (s1, s2, s3);

    printf ("%s\n", s3);
}
```

Program 10-3 Output

```
Test works.
```

In the first for loop of the concatenate function, the characters contained inside string1 are copied into the result array until the null character is reached. Since the for loop will terminate as soon as the null character is matched, it will not get copied into the result array.

In the second loop, the characters from string2 are copied into the result array directly after the last character from string1. This loop makes use of the fact that when the previous for loop finished execution, the value of i was equal to the number of characters in string1, excluding the null character. Therefore, the assignment statement

```
result[i + j] = string2[j];
```

is used to copy the characters from string2 into the proper locations of result.

After the second loop is completed, the concatenate function puts a null character at the end of the string. Study the function to make sure that you understand the use of i and j. Many program errors when dealing with character strings involve the use of an index number that is off by 1 in either direction. Remember, to reference the first character of the array, an index number of 0 is used. And if the character string contains n characters, excluding the null byte, then string[n - 1] references the last (non-null) character in the string while string[n] references the null. Furthermore, string must be defined to contain at least n + 1 characters, bearing in mind that the null character occupies a location in the array.

Returning to our program, the main routine defines two char arrays, s1 and s2, and sets their values using the new initialization technique previously described. The array s3 is defined to contain 20 characters, thus ensuring that sufficient space is reserved for the concatenated character string and also saving us from the trouble of having to precisely calculate its size.

The `concatenate` function is then called with the three strings `s1`, `s2`, and `s3` passed as arguments. The final result, as contained in `s3` after the concatenate function returns, is displayed using the `%s` format characters. Although `s3` is defined to contain 20 characters, the `printf` function only displays characters from the array up to the null character.

Testing Two Character Strings for Equality

We cannot directly test two strings to see if they are equal with a statement in C such as

```
if ( string1 == string2 )
    . . .
```

since the equality operator can only be applied to simple variable types such as `floats`, `ints` or `chars` and not to more sophisticated types such as structures or arrays.

In order to determine if two strings are equal, we therefore must explicitly compare the two character strings character by character. If we reach the end of both character strings at the same time, and if all of the characters up to that point are identical, then the two strings are equal; otherwise they are not.

It might be a good idea to develop a function which could be used to compare two character strings for us. We can call the function `equal_strings` and have it take as arguments the two character strings to be compared. Since we are only interested in determining if the two character strings are equal or not, we can have the function return 1 (TRUE) if in fact the two strings are identical and 0 (FALSE) if they are not. In this way, the function can be used directly inside test statements, such as in

```
if  ( equal_strings (string1, string2) )
    . . .
```

Program 10-4

```
/* Function to determine if two strings are equal */

int   equal_strings (s1, s2)
char   s1[], s2[];
{
     int  i = 0, answer;

     while ( s1[i] == s2 [i]  &&
               s1[i] != '\0' &&   s2[i] != '\0' )
          ++i;
```

```
        if ( s1[i] == '\0'  &&  s2[i] == '\0' )
            answer = 1;        /* strings equal */
        else
            answer = 0;        /* not equal     */

        return (answer);
    }

main ()
{
        static  char  stra[] = "string compare test";
        static  char  strb[] = "string";

        printf ("%d\n", equal_strings (stra, strb));
        printf ("%d\n", equal_strings (stra, stra));
        printf ("%d\n", equal_strings (strb, "string"));
}
```

Program 10-4 Output

```
    0
    1
    1
```

The equal_strings function uses a while loop to sequence through the character strings s1 and s2. The loop will be executed so long as the two character strings are equal (s1[i] == s2[i]) and so long as the end of either string is not reached (s1[i] != '\0' && s2[i] != '\0'). The variable i, which is used as the index number for both arrays, is incremented each time through the while loop.

The if statement that is executed after the while loop has terminated determines if we have simultaneously reached the end of both strings s1 and s2. (Why could we have used the statement

```
    if ( s1[i] == s2[i] )
        . . .
```

instead to achieve the same results?) If we *are* at the end of both strings, then the strings must be identical, in which case answer is set to 1 and returned to the calling routine. Otherwise, the strings are not identical and answer is set to 0 and returned.

In main, two character arrays stra and strb are set up and assigned the indicated initial values. The first call to the equal_strings function passes these two character arrays as arguments. Since these two strings are not equal, the function correctly returns the value 0.

The second call to the equal_strings function passes the string stra twice. The function correctly returns the value 1 to indicate that the two strings are equal, as verified by the program's output.

The third call to the equal_strings function is a bit more interesting. As you can see from this example, we can pass a constant character string to a function that is expecting an array of characters as an argument. In the next chapter, which deals with pointers, you will see how this works. The equal_strings function compares the character string contained in strb to the character string "string" and returns 1 to indicate that the two strings are equal.

Inputting Character Strings

By now you are used to the idea of displaying a character string using the %s format characters. But what about reading in a character string from the terminal? Well, on your particular system, there are probably several library functions that you can use to input character strings. The scanf function can be used with the %s format characters to read in a string of characters up to a blank space, tab character, or the end of line, whichever occurs first. So the statements

```
char    string[81];

scanf ("%s", string);
```

will have the effect of reading in a character string from the terminal and storing it inside the character array string. Note that unlike previous scanf calls, in the case of reading strings, the & is *not* placed before the array name (the reason for this will also be explained in the next chapter).

If the preceding scanf call were executed, and the following characters typed in at the terminal:

```
Shawshank
```

then the string "Shawshank" would be read in by the scanf function and stored inside the string array. If the following line of text were typed instead:

```
scanf test
```

then just the string "scanf" would be stored inside the string array, since the blank space after the word scanf would terminate the string. If the scanf call were executed again, this time the string "test" would be stored inside the string array, as the scanf function always continues scanning from the last character that was read in.

The scanf function automatically terminates the string that is read in with a null character. So execution of the preceding scanf call with the line of text

```
abcdefghijklmnopqrstuvwxyz
```

would result in the entire lowercase alphabet being stored in the first 26 locations of the string array, with string[26] being automatically set to the null character.

If s1, s2, and s3 were defined to be character arrays of appropriate sizes, the execution of the statement

```
scanf ("%s%s%s", s1, s2, s3);
```

with the line of text

```
micro computer system
```

would result in the assignment of the string "micro" to s1, "computer" to s2, and "system" to s3. If the following line of text were typed instead

```
system expansion
```

it would result in the assignment of the string "system" to s1, and "expansion" to s2. Since no further characters appear on the line, the scanf function would then wait for more input to be entered from the terminal.

Program 10-5

```
/* Program to illustrate the %s scanf format characters */

main ()
{
    char  s1[81], s2[81], s3[81];

    printf ("Enter text:\n");
    scanf ("%s%s%s", s1, s2, s3);
    printf ("\ns1 = %s\ns2 = %s\ns3 = %s\n", s1, s2, s3);
}
```

Program 10-5 Output

```
Enter text:
system expansion
bus

s1 = system
s2 = expansion
s3 = bus
```

The `scanf` function was called to read in three character strings: `s1`, `s2`, and `s3`. Since the first line of text contained only two character strings—where the definition of a character string to `scanf` is a sequence of characters up to a space, tab, or the end of the line—the program waited for more text to be entered. After this was done, the `printf` call was used to verify that the strings `"system"`, `"expansion"`, and `"bus"` were correctly stored inside the string arrays `s1`, `s2`, and `s3`, respectively.

Single-Character Input

Most computer installations that support the C language provide functions for the express purposes of reading and writing single characters and entire character strings. On such systems, a function called `getchar` can be used to read in a single character from the terminal. Repeated calls to the `getchar` function will return successive single characters from the input. When the end of the line has been reached, the function will return the newline character `'\n'`. So if the characters "abc" are typed at the terminal, followed immediately by the "Return" key, then the first call to the `getchar` function will return the character `'a'`, the second call the character `'b'`, the third call `'c'`, and the fourth call the newline character `'\n'`. A fifth call to this function will cause the program to wait for more input to be entered from the terminal.

You may be wondering why we need the `getchar` function when we already know how to read in a single character with the `%c` format characters of the `scanf` function. The fact of the matter is that using the `scanf` function for this purpose is a perfectly valid approach. However, the `getchar` function is a more direct approach, as its sole purpose is for reading in single characters and therefore does not require any arguments. The function returns a single character that may be assigned to a variable or used as desired by the program.

In many text-processing applications, we need to read in an entire line of text from the terminal. This line of text is frequently stored in a single place—generally called a "buffer"—where it will be processed further. Using the `scanf` call with the `%s` format characters will not work in this case since the string is terminated as soon as a space is encountered in the input.

Available from the function library on most systems that support C is a function called `gets`. The sole purpose of this function—you guessed it—is to read in a single line of text from the terminal. As an interesting program exercise, we will show how a function similar to the `gets` function—we will call it `read_line` here—can be developed using the `getchar` function. The function will take a single argument: a character array where the line of text is to be stored. Characters read from the terminal up to, but not including, the newline character will be stored into this array by the function.

Before proceeding with this program, it is necessary to point out that on most systems, a special program statement must be inserted at the beginning of the program in order to use the `getchar` function. On most systems, this statement takes the following form:

```
#include <stdio.h>
```

The #include statement will be described in detail in Chapter 13. For now, just remember to insert it at the beginning of any program which uses the getchar function.

Program 10-6

```
#include <stdio.h>

/* Function to read a line of text from the terminal */

void read_line (buffer)
char  buffer[];
{
    char   character;
    int    i = 0;

    do
    {
        character = getchar ();
        buffer[i] = character;
        ++i;
    }
    while ( character != '\n' );

    buffer[i - 1] = '\0';
}

main ()
{
    int    i;
    char   line[81];

    for ( i = 0; i < 3; ++i )
    {
        read_line (line);
        printf ("%s\n\n", line);
    }
}
```

Program 10-6 Output

```
This is a sample line of text.
This is a sample line of text.

abcdefghijklmnopqrstuvwxyz
abcdefghijklmnopqrstuvwxyz

runtime library routines
runtime library routines
```

The do loop in the read_line function is used to build up the input line inside the character array buffer. Each character that is returned by the getchar function is stored into the next location of the array. When the newline character is reached—signaling the end of the line—the loop is exited. The null character is then stored inside the array to terminate the character string, replacing the newline character that was stored there the last time that the loop was executed. The index number i – 1 indexes the correct position in the array, since the index number was incremented one extra time inside the loop the last time it was executed.

The main routine defines a character array called line with enough space reserved to hold 81 characters. This will ensure that an entire line from most terminals (80 characters + the null character) can be stored inside the array. (However, even on terminals that have 80 characters per line, we are still in danger of overflowing the array if we were to continue typing past the end of the line without pressing the "Return" key on the keyboard. It would be a good idea to extend the read_line function to accept as a second argument the size of the buffer. In this way, the function can ensure that the capacity of the buffer is not exceeded.)

The program then enters a for loop, which simply calls the read_line function three times. Each time that this function is called, a new line of text is read from the terminal. This line is simply echoed back at the terminal in order to verify proper operation of the function. After the third line of text has been displayed, execution of Program 10-6 is then complete.

For our next program example, let us consider a practical text-processing application: counting the number of words in a portion of text. We will develop a function called count_words, which will take as its argument a character string and which will return the number of words contained in that string. For the sake of simplicity, we will assume here that a "word" will be defined as a sequence of one or more alphabetic characters. The function can scan the character string for the occurrence of the first alphabetic character, and will consider all subsequent characters up to the first nonalphabetic character as part of the same word. Then the function can continue scanning the string for the next alphabetic character, which identifies the start of a new word.

Program 10-7

```
/* Function to determine if a character is alphabetic */

int  alphabetic (c)
char   c;
{
    if  ( (c >= 'a'  &&  c <= 'z') || (c >= 'A'  &&  c <= 'Z') )
        return (1);
    else
        return (0);
}

/* Function to count the number of words in a string */

int  count_words (string)
char  string[];
{
    int  i, looking_for_word = 1, word_count = 0;

    for ( i = 0;  string[i] != '\0';  ++i )
        if ( alphabetic (string[i]) )
        {
            if ( looking_for_word )
            {
                ++word_count;
                looking_for_word = 0;
            }
        }
        else
            looking_for_word = 1;

    return (word_count);
}

main ()
{
    static char  text1[] = "Well, here goes.";
    static char  text2[] = "And here we go...again.";

    printf ("%s -- words = %d\n", text1, count_words (text1));
    printf ("%s -- words = %d\n", text2, count_words (text2));
}
```

Program 10-7 Output

```
Well, here goes. -- words = 3
And here we go...again. -- words = 5
```

The `alphabetic` function is straightforward enough—it simply tests the value of the character passed to it to determine if it is either a lowercase or uppercase letter. If it is either, the function returns 1, indicating that the character is alphabetic; otherwise, the function returns 0.

The `count_words` function is not as straightforward. The integer variable `i` is used as an index number to sequence through each character in the string. The integer variable `looking_for_word` is used as a flag to indicate whether we are currently in the process of looking for the start of a new word. At the beginning of the execution of the function, we obviously *are* looking for the start of a new word, so this flag is set to 1. The local variable `word_count` is used for the obvious purpose of counting the number of words in the character string.

For each character inside the character string, a call to the `alphabetic` function is made to determine if the character is alphabetic or not. If the character is alphabetic, then the `looking_for_word` flag is tested to determine if we are in the process of looking for a new word. If we are, then the value of `word_count` is incremented by 1, and the `looking_for_word` flag is set FALSE, indicating that we are no longer looking for the start of a new word.

If the character is alphabetic and the `looking_for_word` flag is FALSE, this means that we are currently scanning *inside* a word. In such a case, the `for` loop is continued with the next character in the string.

If the character is not alphabetic—meaning that either we have reached the end of a word or that we have still not found the beginning of the next word— then the flag `looking_for_word` is set TRUE (even though it may already be TRUE).

When all of the characters inside the character string have been examined, the function returns the value of `word_count` to indicate the number of words that were found in the character string.

It would be helpful to present a table of the values of the various variables in the `count_words` function to see how the algorithm works. Table 10-1 shows such a table, with the first call to the `count_words` function from the above program as an example. The first line of Table 10-1 shows the initial value of the variables `word_count` and `looking_for_word` before the `for` loop is entered. Subsequent lines depict the values of the indicated variables each time through the `for` loop. So the second line of the table shows that the value of `word_count` has been set to 1 and the `looking_for_word` flag set FALSE (0) after the first time through the loop (after the `'W'` has been processed). The last line of the table shows the final values of the variables when the end of the string is reached. You should spend some time studying this table, verifying the values of the indicated variables against the logic of the `count_words` function. Once this has been accomplished, you should then feel comfortable with the algorithm that is used by the function to count the number of words in a string.

TABLE 10-1. Execution of the `count_words` function

i	string[i]	word_count	looking_for_word
		0	1
0	'W'	1	0
1	'e'	1	0
2	'l'	1	0
3	'l'	1	0
4	','	1	1
5	' '	1	1
6	'h'	2	0
7	'e'	2	0
8	'r'	2	0
9	'e'	2	0
10	' '	2	1
11	'g'	3	0
12	'o'	3	0
13	'e'	3	0
14	's'	3	0
15	'.'	3	1
16	'\0'	3	1

The Null String

Now let us see a slightly more practical example of the use of the `count_words` function. This time we will make use of our `read_line` function to allow the user to type in multiple lines of text at the terminal. The program will then count the total number of words in the text and will then display the result.

In order to make the program more flexible, we would rather not have to limit or specify the number of lines of text that are entered. Therefore, we must have a way for the user to "tell" the program when he or she is done entering text. One way to do this is to have the user simply press the "Return" key an extra time after the last line of text has been entered. When the `read_line` function is called to read in such a line, the function will immediately encounter the newline character, and as a result will store the null character as the first (and only) character in the buffer. Our program can check for this special case and can know that the last line of text has been entered once a line containing no characters has been read.

A character string which contains no characters other than the null character has a special name in the C language; it is called the *null string*. When you think about it, the use of the null string is still perfectly consistent with all of the functions that we have defined so far in this chapter. The string_length function will correctly return 0 as the size of the null string; our concatenate function will also properly concatenate "nothing" onto the end of another string; even our equal_strings function will work correctly if either string is null or if both strings are null (and in the latter case, the function will correctly call these strings equal).

Sometimes it becomes desirable to set the value of a character string to the null string. In C, the null string is denoted by an adjacent pair of double quotes. So the statement

```
static char  buffer[100] = "";
```

defines a character array called buffer and sets its value to the null string. Note the fact that the character string "" is *not* the same as the character string " ", since the second string contains a single blank character. (If you are doubtful, send both strings to the equal_strings function and see what result comes back.)

The following program uses the read_line, alphabetic, and count_words functions from previous programs. They have not been shown in the program listing to conserve space.

Program 10-8

```
#include <stdio.h>

/*****  Insert alphabetic function here    *****/

/*****  Insert read_line function here     *****/

/*****  Insert count_words function here   *****/

main ()
{
    char   text[81];
    int    end_of_text = 0, total_words = 0;

    printf ("Type in your text.\n");
    printf ("When you are done, press 'RETURN'.\n\n");
```

```
        while ( ! end_of_text )
        {
            read_line (text);

            if ( text[0] == '\0' )
                end_of_text = 1;
            else
                total_words += count_words (text);
        }

        printf ("\nThere are %d words in the above text.\n",
                    total_words);
    }
```

Program 10-8 Output

```
    Type in your text.
    When you are done, press 'RETURN'.
```

**Wendy glanced up at the ceiling where the mound of
lasagna loomed like a mottled mountain range. Within
seconds, she was crowned with ricotta ringlets and a
tomato sauce tiara. Bits of beef formed meaty moles
on her forehead. After the second thud, her culinary
coronation was complete.**
RETURN

```
    There are 48 words in the above text.
```

(The line labeled *RETURN* indicates the pressing of the "Return" key at the terminal.)

The `end_of_text` variable is used as a flag to indicate when the end of the input text has been reached. The `while` loop will be executed as long as this flag is FALSE. Inside this loop, the program calls the `read_line` function to read a line of text from the terminal. The `if` statement then tests the input line that is stored inside the `text` array to see if just the "Return" key were pressed. If so, then the buffer will contain the null string, in which case the `end_of_text` flag will be set TRUE to signal that all of the text has been entered.

If the buffer does contain some text, then the `count_words` function is called to count the number of words in the `text` array. The value that is returned by this function is added into the value of `total_words`, which contains the cumulative number of words from all lines of text entered thus far.

After the `while` loop is exited, the program displays the value of `total_words`, along with some informative text, at the terminal.

It might seem that the preceding program does not help to reduce our work efforts much because we still have to manually enter in all of the text at the terminal. But as we will see in a later chapter, this same program can also be used to count the number of words contained in a file stored on a disk, for example. So an author using a computer system for the preparation of a manuscript might find this program extremely valuable as it could be used to quickly determine the number of words contained in the manuscript.

♦ Escape Characters ♦

We have alluded to the fact that the backslash character has a special significance that extends beyond its use in forming the newline and null characters. Just as the backslash and the letter n, when used in combination, cause subsequent printing to begin on a new line, so can other characters be combined with the backslash character to perform "special" functions. These various "backslash characters," often referred to as *escape characters*, are summarized in the following table.

TABLE 10-2. Escape Characters

Escape Character	Name
\b	backspace
\f	form feed
\n	newline
\r	carriage return
\t	horizontal tab
\v	vertical tab
\\	backslash
\"	double quote
\'	single quote
\ (*carriage return*)	line continuation
nnn	character value *nnn*

The first six characters listed in Table 10-2 will perform the indicated function on most video terminals when they are displayed. For example, including the backspace character ' \b' inside a character string will cause the terminal to backspace one character at the point where the character appears in the string, provided that the terminal has the appropriate capabilities for performing this function. Similarly, the function call

```
printf ("%d\t%d\t%d\n", a, b, c);
```

will display the value of a, space over to the next tab setting, display the value of b, space over to the next tab setting, and then display the value of c. The horizontal tab character is particularly useful for lining up data in columns.

In order to include the backslash character itself inside a character string, two backslash characters are necessary, so the printf call

```
printf ("\\t is the horizontal tab character.\n");
```

will display the following at the terminal:

```
\t is the horizontal tab character.
```

(Note that since the \\ is encountered first in the string, a tab is not displayed in this case.)

In order to include a double quote character inside a character string, it must be preceded by a backslash. So the printf call

```
printf ("\"Hello\", he said.\n");
```

will result in the display of the message

```
"Hello", he said.
```

To assign a single quote character to a character variable, the backslash character must be placed before the quote. If c were declared to be a variable of type char, then the statement

```
c = '\'';
```

would assign a single quote character to c.

The backslash character, followed immediately by a carriage return, is used to tell the C compiler to ignore the end of the line. It is used primarily for continuing long character strings onto the next line and, as we will see in Chapter 13, for continuing a *macro* definition onto the next line.

Without the line continuation character, most C compilers will generate an error message if an attempt is made to initialize a character string across multiple lines; for example, as in

```
        static char  letters[] =
               { "abcdefghijklmnopqrstuvwxyz
ABCDEFGHIJKLMNOPQRSTUVWXYZ" };
```

By placing a backslash character at the end of each line to be continued, a character string constant can be written over mutiple lines:

```
      static char   letters[] =
            { "abcdefghijklmnopqrstuvwxyz\
ABCDEFGHIJKLMNOPQRSTUVWXYZ" };
```

It is necessary to begin the continuation of the character string constant at the *beginning* of the next line because, otherwise, the leading blank spaces on the line would get stored into the character string. The preceding statement would therefore have the net result of defining the character array letters and of initializing its elements to the character string

```
"abcdefghijklmnopqrstuvwxyzABCDEFGHIJKLMNOPQRSTUVWXYZ"
```

The last entry in the table of escape characters (Table 10-2) enables *any* character to be included in a character string. In the escape character `'\nnn'`, *nnn* is a one- to three-digit *octal* number that represents the *value* of the character. This enables characters which may not be directly available from the keyboard to be coded into a character string. For example, in the ASCII character representation, the "bell" character has the value 7. On most terminals, displaying this character will cause a bell or short beep to sound at the terminal. In order to include a bell character in a string, the escape character `'\7'` (or `'\07'`, or `'\007'`) can be coded directly into the string. So the printf call

```
      printf ("\7\7\7SYSTEM SHUT DOWN IN 5 MINUTES!!\n");
```

will sound three bells at the terminal and display the indicated message.

The null character `'\0'` is a special case of the above. It represents the character that has a value of 0. In fact, since the value of the null character *is* 0, this knowledge is frequently used by programmers in tests and loops dealing with variable-length character strings. For example, the loop to count the length of a character string in the function string_length from Program 10-2 can also be equivalently coded as follows:

```
      while  ( string[count] )
          ++count;
```

The value of string[count] will be nonzero until the null character is reached, at which point the while loop will be exited.

Before leaving this discussion of escape characters, it should once again be pointed out that these characters are only considered a single character inside a string. So the character string `"\007\"Hello\"\n"` actually consists of nine characters: the bell character `'\007'`, the double quote character `'\"'`, the five characters in the word Hello, the double quote character once again, and the newline character. Try passing the preceding character string to the string_length function to verify that nine is indeed the number of characters in the string.

♦ Character Strings, Structures, and Arrays ♦

There are many ways to combine the basic elements of the C programming language to form very powerful programming constructs. In the previous chapter, for example, we saw how we could easily define an array of structures. The next program example further illustrates the notion of arrays of structures, combined with the variable length character string.

Suppose we wanted to write a computer program that acted as a dictionary. If we had such a program, we could then use it whenever we came across a word whose meaning was not clear. We could type the word into the program, and the program could then automatically "look up" the word inside the dictionary and tell us the definition of the word.

If we were to contemplate developing such a program, one of the first thoughts that would come to mind would be the representation of the word and its definition inside the computer. Obviously, since the word and its definition are logically related, the notion of a structure comes immediately to mind. We can define a structure called entry, for example, to hold the word and its defintion:

```
struct   entry
{
    char   word[10];
    char   definition[50];
};
```

In the above structure definition, we have defined enough space for a 9-letter word (remember, we are dealing with variable length character strings, so we need to leave room for the null character) plus a 49-character definition. The following would be an example of a variable defined to be of type struct entry that is initialized to contain the word "blob" and its definition.

```
static struct entry   word1 =
                { "blob", "an amorphous mass" };
```

Since we would like to provide for many words inside our dictionary, it seems logical to define an array of entry structures, such as in

```
struct entry   dictionary[100];
```

which would allow for a dictionary of 100 words. Obviously, this is far from sufficient if we are interested in setting up an English language dictionary, which would require at least 50,000 entries to make a decent dictionary. If such were the case, then it would not be very practical to define such a dictionary with a statement such as

```
struct entry English_dictionary[50000];
```

as this would impose severe storage requirements on the computer. (Each character occupies one storage unit known as a *byte* inside most computer systems; 50,000 multiplied by 60 bytes—10 for the word plus 50 for the definition—equals 3,000,000 bytes, a very large amount of storage.) So the above approach would really not work if we were interested in such a large dictionary. We would need to adopt a more sophisticated approach, one that would involve storing the dictionary on the computer's disk, as opposed to storing it in memory.

Despite the preceding objections, we will proceed with this example, since it is quite illustrative and can still be used for smaller-sized dictionaries, perhaps for a specialized technical dictionary, for example.

Having defined the structure of our dictionary, we should now think a bit about its organization. Most dictionaries are organized alphabetically. Does it make much sense to organize ours the same way? The answer to this question is "yes." For now, let us assume that the reason for this is because it makes the dictionary easier to read. Later we will see the real motivation for such an organization.

Now it is time to think about the development of the program. It would be convenient to define a function to look up a word inside the dictionary. If the word were found, then the function could return the entry number of the word inside the dictionary; otherwise the function could return -1 to indicate that the word was not found in the dictionary. So a typical call to this function, which we can call `lookup`, might appear as follows:

```
entry_number = lookup (dictionary, word, entries);
```

In this case, the `lookup` function would search `dictionary` for the word as contained in the character string `word`. The function would search the dictionary for the specified word and would return the entry number in the dictionary if the word were found, or -1 if the word were not found. The last argument to `lookup`, `entries`, specifies the number of entries contained in the dictionary.

In the program that follows, the `lookup` function will use the `equal_strings` function defined in Program 10-4 to determine when the specified word matches an entry in the dictionary.

Program 10-9

```
/* Dictionary lookup program */

struct   entry
{
    char   word[10];
    char   definition[50];
};

/***** Insert equal_strings function here *****/
```

```
/* function to lookup a word inside a dictionary */

int   lookup (dictionary, search, number_of_entries)
struct entry  dictionary[];
char          search[];
int           number_of_entries;
{
    int  i;

    for ( i = 0;  i < number_of_entries;  ++i )
        if ( equal_strings (search, dictionary[i].word) )
            return (i);

    return (-1);
}

main ()
{
    static struct entry  dictionary[100] =
        { { "aardvark",  "a burrowing African mammal"         },
          { "abyss",     "a bottomless pit"                    },
          { "acumen",    "mentally sharp; keen"                },
          { "addle",     "to become confused"                 },
          { "aerie",     "a high nest"                        },
          { "affix",     "to append; attach"                   },
          { "agar",      "a jelly made from seaweed"          },
          { "ahoy",      "a nautical call of greeting"         },
          { "aigrette",  "an ornamental cluster of feathers" },
          { "ajar",      "partially opened"                   } };

    int    entries = 10;
    char   word[10];
    int    entry_number;

    printf ("Enter word: ");
    scanf ("%s", word);
    entry_number = lookup (dictionary, word, entries);

    if ( entry_number != -1 )
        printf ("%s\n", dictionary[entry_number].definition);
    else
        printf ("Sorry, that word is not in my dictionary.\n");
}
```

Program 10-9 Output

```
Enter word: agar
a jelly made from seaweed
```

Program 10-9 Output (Re-run)

```
Enter word: accede
Sorry, that word is not in my dictionary.
```

The `lookup` function sequences through each entry in the dictionary. For each such entry, the function calls the `equal_strings` function to determine if the character string `search` matches the `word` member of the particular dictionary entry. If it does match, then the function returns the value of the variable `i`, which is the entry number of the word that was found in the dictionary. The function is exited immediately upon execution of the `return` statement, despite the fact that the function is in the middle of executing a `for` loop.

If the `lookup` function exhausts all of the entries in the dictionary without finding a match, then the `return` statement after the `for` loop will be executed to return the "not found" indication (-1) back to the caller.

A Better Search Method

The method used by the `lookup` function to search for a particular word in the dictionary was straightforward enough; the function simply performed a sequential search through all of the entries in the dictionary until either a match was made or the end of the dictionary was reached. For a small-sized dictionary like the one in our program, this approach is perfectly fine. However, if we start dealing with large dictionaries containing hundreds or perhaps even thousands of entries, this approach is no longer so fine. The reason for this is because of the time it takes to sequentially search through all of the entries, which can be considerable—where considerable in this case could mean several seconds. One of the prime considerations that must be given to any sort of "information retrieval" program is that of speed. And since the searching process is one that is so frequently used in computer applications, much attention has been given by computer scientists to developing efficient algorithms for searching (almost as much attention as has been given to the process of sorting).

We can make use of the fact that our dictionary is in alphabetical order to develop a more efficient `lookup` function. The first obvious optimization that comes to mind is in the case where the word that we are looking for does not exist in the dictionary. We can make our `lookup` function "intelligent" enough to recognize when it has gone "too far" in its search. For example, if we were looking up the word "active" in the dictionary defined in Program 10-9, then as soon as we reached the word "acumen" in the dictionary, we could conclude that "active" is not there because, if it were, it would have appeared in the dictionary *before* the word "acumen."

As was mentioned, the above optimization strategy does help to reduce our search time somewhat, but only in the case where a particular word is *not* present in the dictionary. What we are really looking for is an algorithm that reduces the search time in most cases, not just in one particluar case. Such an algorithm exists under the name of the *binary search*.

The strategy behind the binary search is relatively simple to understand. To illustrate how this algorithm works, let's take an analogous situation of a simple guessing game. Suppose I pick a number from 1 to 99 and then tell you to try to guess the number in the fewest number of guesses. For each guess that you make, I can tell you if you are too low, too high, or if your guess is correct. After a few tries at the game, you will probably realize that a good way to narrow in on the answer is by using a halving process. For example, if you take 50 as your first guess, then an answer of either "too high" or "too low" will narrow the possibilities down from 100 to 49. So if the answer was "too high," then the number must be from 1 to 49, inclusive. And if the answer were "too low," then the number must be from 51 to 99, inclusive.

We can now repeat the halving process with the remaining 49 numbers. So if the first answer were "too low," then the next guess should be halfway between 51 and 99, which is 75. This process can be continued until we finally narrow in on the answer. On the average, this procedure will take far less time to arrive at the answer than any other search method.

The preceding discussion describes precisely how the binary search algorithm works. The following provides a formal description of the algorithm. In this algorithm, we are looking for an element x inside an array M which contains n elements. The algorithm assumes that the array M is sorted in ascending order.

Binary Search Algorithm

Step 1: Set *low* to 0, *high* to $n - 1$.

Step 2: If *low* > *high*, then x does not exist in M and the algorithm terminates.

Step 3: Set *mid* to (*low* + *high*) / 2.

Step 4: If M[*mid*] < x, then set *low* to *mid* + 1 and go to Step 2.

Step 5: If M[*mid*] > x, then set *high* to *mid* - 1 and go to Step 2.

Step 6: M[*mid*] equals x and the algorithm terminates.

The division performed in Step 3 is an integer division, so if *low* were 0 and *high* were 49, the value of *mid* would be 24.

Now that we have the algorithm for performing a binary search, we can rewrite our `lookup` function to use this new search strategy. Since the binary search must be able to determine if one value is less than, greater than, or equal to another value, we might want to replace our `equal_strings` function with another function which makes this type of determination for two character strings. We'll call the function `compare_strings` and have it return the value -1 if the first string is lexicographically less than the second string, 0 if the two strings are equal, and 1 if the first string is lexicographically greater than the second string. So the function call

```
compare_strings ("alpha", "altered")
```

would return the value -1 since the first string is lexicographically less than the second string (think of this to mean that the first string would occur *before* the second string in a dictionary). And the function call

```
compare_strings ("zioty", "yucca");
```

would return the value 1 since "zioty" is lexicographically greater than "yucca."

In Program 10-10 that follows, the new `compare_strings` function is presented. The `lookup` function now uses the binary search method to scan through the dictionary. The main routine remains unchanged from the previous program.

The `compare_strings` function is identical to the `equal_strings` function up through the end of the `while` loop. When the `while` loop is exited, the function analyzes the two characters that resulted in the termination of the `while` loop. If `s1[i]` is less than `s2[i]`, then `s1` must be lexicographically less than `s2`. In such a case, -1 is returned. If `s1[i]` is equal to `s2[i]`, the two strings are equal and 0 is returned. If neither is true, then s1 must be lexicographically greater than s2, in which case the value 1 is returned.

Program 10-10

```
/* Dictionary lookup program */

struct   entry
{
    char   word[10];
    char   definition[50];
};
```

```
/* Function to compare two character strings */

int   compare_strings (s1, s2)
char   s1[], s2[];
{
    int   i = 0, answer;

    while ( s1[i] == s2[i] && s1[i] != '\0'&& s2[i] != '\0' )
        ++i;

    if ( s1[i] < s2[i] )
        answer = -1;                     /* s1 < s2  */
    else if ( s1[i] == s2[i] )
        answer = 0;                      /* s1 == s2 */
    else
        answer = 1;                      /* s1 > s2  */

    return (answer);
}

/* Function to look up a word inside a dictionary */

int   lookup (dictionary, search, number_of_entries)
struct entry  dictionary[];
char          search[];
int           number_of_entries;
{
    int   low = 0;
    int   high = number_of_entries - 1;
    int   mid, result;

    while  ( low <= high )
    {
        mid = (low + high) / 2;
        result = compare_strings (dictionary[mid].word, search);

        if ( result == -1 )
            low = mid + 1;
        else if ( result == 1 )
            high = mid - 1;
        else
            return (mid);     /* found it */
    }

    return (-1);              /* not found */
}
```

```
main ()
{
    static struct entry  dictionary[100] =
        { { "aardvark", "a burrowing African mammal"        },
          { "abyss",    "a bottomless pit"                   },
          { "acumen",   "mentally sharp; keen"               },
          { "addle",    "to become confused"                 },
          { "aerie",    "a high nest"                        },
          { "affix",    "to append; attach"                  },
          { "agar",     "a jelly made from seaweed"          },
          { "ahoy",     "a nautical call of greeting"        },
          { "aigrette", "an ornamental cluster of feathers" },
          { "ajar",     "partially opened"                   } };

    int    entries = 10;
    char   word[10];
    int    entry_number;

    printf ("Enter word: ");
    scanf ("%s", word);

    entry_number = lookup (dictionary, word, entries);

    if ( entry_number != -1 )
        printf ("%s\n", dictionary[entry_number].definition);
    else
        printf ("Sorry, that word is not in my dictionary.\n");
}
```

Program 10-10 Output

```
Enter word: aigrette
an ornamental cluster of feathers
```

Program 10-10 Output (Re-run)

```
Enter word: acerb
Sorry, that word is not in my dictionary.
```

The lookup function defines the int variables low and high, and assigns them initial values as per the binary search algorithm. The while loop executes as long as the value of low does not exceed the value of high. Inside the loop, the value of mid is calculated by adding low and high and dividing the result by 2. The compare_strings function is then called with the word contained in dictionary[mid] and the word we are searching for as arguments. The returned value is assigned to the variable result.

If `compare_strings` returns a value of -1—indicating that `dictionary[mid].word` is less than `search`—then `lookup` sets the value of `low` equal to `mid + 1`. If `compare_strings` returns a 1—indicating that `dictionary[mid].search` is greater than `search`—then `lookup` sets the value of `high` equal to `mid - 1`. If neither -1 nor 1 is returned, the two strings must be equal, and, in that case, `lookup` returns the value of `mid`, which is the entry number of the word in the dictionary.

If the value of `low` eventually exceeds the value of `high`, then the word is not present in the dictionary. In that case, `lookup` returns -1 to indicate this "not found" condition.

◆ Character Operations ◆

Character variables and constants are frequently used in relational and arithmetic expressions. In order to properly use characters in such situations, it is necessary for you to understand how they are handled by the C compiler.

Whenever a character constant or variable is used in an expression in C, it is automatically converted to, and subsequently treated as, an integer value. This applies when characters are passed as arguments to functions as well: *they are automatically converted to integers by the system.*

In Chapter 6, we saw how the expression

```
c >= 'a'   &&   c <= 'z'
```

could be used to determine if the character variable `c` contained a lowercase letter. We mentioned there that such an expression could be used on systems that used an ASCII character representation since the lowercase letters are represented sequentially in ASCII, with no other characters in between. The first part of the preceding expression, which compares the value of `c` against the value of the character constant `'a'`, is actually comparing the value of `c` against the internal representation of the character `'a'`. In ASCII, the character `'a'` has the value 97, the character `'b'` the value 98, and so on. Therefore, the expression `c >= 'a'` will be TRUE (nonzero) for any lowercase character contained in `c`, since it will have a value that is greater than or equal to 97. However, since there are characters other than the lowercase letters whose ASCII values are greater than 97 (such as the open and closed braces), the test must be bounded on the other end to ensure that the result of the expression is TRUE for lowercase characters only. For this reason, `c` is compared against the character `'z'`, which, in ASCII, has the value 122.

Since comparing the value of `c` against the characters `'a'` and `'z'` in the preceding expression actually compares `c` to the numerical representations of `'a'` and `'z'`, the expression

```
c >= 97   &&   c <= 122
```

could be equivalently used to determine if c were a lowercase letter. The first expression is to be preferred, however, because it does not require the knowledge of the specific numerical values of the characters ′a′ and ′z′, and because its intentions are less obscure.

Because the C compiler automatically converts all characters that are used in expressions or passed as function arguments into integers, the printf call

```
printf ("%d\n", c);
```

can be used to print out the value that is used to internally represent the character stored inside c on your machine. If your machine uses ASCII, then the statement

```
printf ("%d\n", 'a');
```

will result in the display of 97 at the terminal, for example.

What do you think the following two statements would produce?

```
c = 'a' + 1;
printf ("%c\n", c);
```

Since the value of ′a′ is 97 in ASCII, the effect of the first statement would be to assign the value 98 to the character variable c. Since this value represents the character ′b′ in ASCII, this is the character that would be displayed by the printf call.

While adding one to a character constant hardly seems practical, the preceding example gives way to an important technique that is used to convert the characters ′0′ through ′9′ into their corresponding numerical values 0 through 9. You will recall that we stressed the fact that the character ′0′ is not the same as the integer 0, the character ′1′ is not the same as the integer 1, and so on. In fact, the character ′0′ has the numerical value 48 in ASCII, which is what would be displayed by the following printf call:

```
printf ("%d\n", '0');
```

Suppose the character variable c contained one of the characters ′0′ through ′9′ and that we wished to convert this value into the corresponding integer 0 through 9. Since the digits of virtually all character sets are represented by sequential integer values, we can easily convert c into its integer equivalent by subtracting the character constant ′0′ from it. Therefore, if i is defined as an integer variable, the statement

```
i = c - '0';
```

will have the effect of converting the character digit contained in c into its equivalent integer value. Suppose c contained the character '5', which, in ASCII, is the number 53. The ASCII value of '0' is 48, so execution of the above statement would result in the integer subtraction of 48 from 53, which would result in the integer value 5 being assigned to i. On a machine that used a character set other then ASCII, the same result would most likely be obtained, even though the internal representations of '5' and '0' might differ.

The above technique can be extended to convert a character string consisting of digits into its equivalent numerical representation. This has been done in the following program in which a function called string_to_integer is presented to convert the character string passed as its argument into an integer value. The function ends its scan of the character string once a nondigit character is encountered, and returns the result back to the calling routine. It is assumed that an int variable is large enough to hold the value of the converted number.

Program 10-11

```
/* Function to convert a string to an integer */

int   string_to_integer (string)
char   string[];
{
    int   i, integer_value, result = 0;

    for  ( i = 0; string[i] >= '0' && string[i] <= '9'; ++i )
    {
        integer_value = string[i] - '0';
        result = result * 10 + integer_value;
    }

    return (result);
}

main ()
{
    printf ("%d\n", string_to_integer("245"));
    printf ("%d\n", string_to_integer("100") + 25);
    printf ("%d\n", string_to_integer("13x5"));
}
```

Program 10-11 Output

```
245
125
13
```

The `for` loop is executed as long as the character contained in `string[i]` is a digit character. Each time through the loop, the character contained in `string[i]` is converted into its equivalent integer value and is then added into the value of `result` multiplied by 10. To see how this technique works, consider execution of this loop when the function is called with the character string `"245"` as an argument: The first time through the loop, `integer_value` will be assigned the value of `string[0]` - `'0'`. Since `string[0]` will contain the character `'2'`, this will result in the value 2 being assigned to `integer_value`. Since the value of `result` is 0 the first time through the loop, multiplying it by 10 will produce 0, which will be added to `integer_value` and stored back into `result`. So by the end of the first pass through the loop, `result` will contain the value 2.

The second time through the loop, `integer_value` will be set equal to 4, as calculated by subtracting `'0'` from `'4'`. Multiplying `result` by 10 will produce 20, which will be added to the value of `integer_value`, producing 24 as the value stored into `result`.

The third time through the loop, `integer_value` will be equal to `'5'` - `'0'`, or 5, which will be added into the value of `result` mutiplied by 10 (240). Thus, the value 245 will be the value of `result` after the loop has been executed for the third time.

Upon encountering the terminating null character, the `for` loop will be exited and the value of `result`, 245, will be returned to the calling routine.

The `string_to_integer` function could be improved in two ways. First, it doesn't handle negative numbers. Second, it doesn't let you know whether or not the string contained *any* valid digit characters at all (for example, `string_to_integer ("xxx")` returns 0). These improvements are left as an exercise.

This discussion concludes this chapter on character strings. As you can see, C provides capabilities that enable character strings to be efficiently and easily manipulated. Chances are that your system offers a wide variety of library functions for performing operations on strings. For example, most systems offer the functions `strlen`, to calculate the length of a character string; `strcmp`, to compare two strings; `strcat`, to concatenate two strings; and `strcpy`, to copy one string to another. Check your system documentation, or consult Appendix C which lists a number of the functions available under most systems.

◆ Exercises ◆

1. If you have access to a computer facility that supports the C programming language, type in and run the 11 programs presented in this chapter. Compare the output produced by each program with the output presented after each program.

2. Why could we have replaced the `while` statement of the `equal_strings` function of Program 10-4 with the statement

   ```
   while ( s1[i] == s2[i]  &&  s1[i] != '\0' )
   ```

   to achieve the same results?

3. The `count_words` function from Programs 10-7 and 10-8 will incorrectly count a word that contains an apostrophe as two separate words. Modify this function to correctly handle this situation. Also extend the function to count a sequence of numbers, including any embedded commas and periods, as a single word. Finally, have the function handle the special case where a word is hyphenated across two lines and make sure that the sequence of letters at the beginning of the next line is not counted as a new word.

4. Write a function called `substring` to extract a portion of a character string. The function should be called as follows:

   ```
   substring (source, start, count, result);
   ```

   where `source` is the character string from which we are extracting the substring, `start` is an index number into `source` indicating the first character of the `substring`, `count` is the number of characters to be extracted from the `source` string, and `result` is an array of characters that is to contain the extracted substring. For example, the call

   ```
   substring ("character", 4, 3, result_array);
   ```

   will extract the substring `"act"` (3 characters starting with character number 4) from the string `"character"` and will place the result in `result_array`.

   Make sure the function inserts a null character at the end of the substring in the `result` array. Also, have the function check that the requested number of characters does in fact exist in the string, and if this is not the case then have the function end the substring when it reaches the end of the `source` string. (So, for example, a call such as

   ```
   substring ("two words", 4, 20, result);
   ```

should just place the string `"words"` inside the `result` array, even though 20 characters were requested by the call.)

5. Write a function called `find_string` to determine if one character string exists inside another string. The first argument to the function should be the character string that is to be searched and the second argument is the string we are interested in finding. If the function finds the specified string, then have it return the location in the source string where the string was found. If the function does not find the string, then have it return -1. So, for example, the call

```
index = find_string ("a chatterbox", "hat");
```

will search the string `"a chatterbox"` for the string `"hat"`. Since `"hat"` does exist inside the source string, the function will return 3 to indicate the starting position inside the source string where `"hat"` was found.

6. Write a function called `remove_string` to remove a specified number of characters from a character string. The function should take three arguments: the source string, the starting index number in the source string, and the number of characters to remove. So if the character array `text` contained the string `"the wrong son"` then the call

```
remove_string (text, 4, 6);
```

would have the effect of removing the characters "wrong " (the word "wrong" plus the space that follows) from the array `text`. The resulting string inside `text` would then be `"the son"`.

7. Write a function called `insert_string` to insert one character string into another string. The arguments to the function should consist of the source string, the string to be inserted, and the position in the source string where the string is to be inserted. So the call

```
insert_string (text, "per", 10);
```

with `text` as originally defined in the previous exercise, would result in the character string `"per"` being inserted inside `text`, beginning at `text[10]`. Therefore, the character string `"the wrong person"` would be stored inside the `text` array after the function returned.

8. Using the `find_string`, `remove_string`, and `insert_string` functions from preceding exercises, write a function called `replace_string` that takes three character string arguments as follows

```
replace_string (source, s1, s2);
```

and which will replace s1 inside source with the character string s2. The function should call the find_string function to locate s1 inside source, then call the remove_string function to remove s1 from source, and finally call the insert_string function to insert s2 into source at the proper location.

So the function call

```
replace_string (text, "1", "one");
```

will replace the first occurrence of the character string "1" inside the character string text, if it exists, with the string "one". Similarly, the function call

```
replace_string (text, "*", "");
```

will have the effect of removing the first asterisk inside the text array, since the replacement string is the null string.

9. We can extend even further the usefulness of the replace_string function from the preceding exercise if we have it return a value that indicates if the replacement succeeded, where succeeded means that the string to be replaced was found inside the source string. So if the function returns 1 if the replacement succeeds and 0 if it does not, then the loop

```
do
      still_found = replace_string (text, " ", "");
while ( still_found );
```

could be used to remove *all* blank spaces from text, for example.

Incorporate this change into the replace_strings function and try it with various character strings to make sure that it works properly.

10. Write a function called dictionary_sort that sorts a dictionary, as defined in Programs 10-9 and 10-10, into alphabetical order.

11. Extend the string_to_integer function from Program 10-11 so that if the first character of the string is a minus sign, then the value that follows is taken as a negative number.

12. Write a function called string_to_float that will convert a character string into a floating point value. Have the function accept an optional leading minus sign. So the call

```
string_to_float ("-867.6921");
```

should return the value -867.6921.

13. Write a function called `integer_to_string` that will convert an integer value into a character string. Make sure the function handles negative integers properly.

14. If c is a lowercase character, then the expression

```
c - 'a' + 'A'
```

will produce the uppercase equivalent of c, assuming an ASCII character set. Write a function called uppercase that converts all lowercase characters in a string into their uppercase equivalents.

11

Pointers

In this chapter, we will examine one of the most sophisticated features of the C programming language: *pointers*. In fact, the power and flexibility that C provides in dealing with pointers serve to set it apart from other programming languages such as Pascal. Pointers enable you to effectively represent complex data structures, to change values passed as arguments to functions, to work with memory that has been allocated "dynamically" (see Chapter 17), and to more concisely and efficiently deal with arrays.

To understand the way in which pointers operate, it is first necessary to understand the concept of *indirection*. We are used to this concept in our everyday life. For example, suppose that I needed to buy a new ribbon for my printer. In the company that I work for, all purchases are handled by the purchasing department. So I would call Jim in purchasing and ask him to order the new ribbon for me. Jim, in turn, would call the local supply store to order the ribbon. The approach that I would take in obtaining my new ribbon would actually be an indirect one, since I would not be ordering the ribbon directly from the supply store myself.

This same notion of indirection applies to the way pointers work in C. A pointer provides an indirect means of accessing the value of a particular data item. And just as there are reasons why it makes sense to go through the purchasing department to order new ribbons (I don't have to know which particular store the ribbons are being ordered from, for example), so are there good reasons why, at times, it makes sense to use pointers in C.

But enough talk—it's time to see how pointers actually work. Suppose we define a variable called count as follows:

```
int   count = 10;
```

We can define another variable, called int_pointer, that will enable us to indirectly access the value of count by the declaration

```
int   *int_pointer;
```

The asterisk defines to the C system that the variable int_pointer is of type *pointer to int*. This means that int_pointer will be used in the program to indirectly access the value of one or more integer variables.

We have seen how the & operator was used in the scanf calls of previous programs. This unary operator, known as the *address* operator, is used to make a pointer to an object in C. So if x is a variable of a particular type, then the expression &x is a pointer to that variable. The expression &x can be assigned to any pointer variable, if desired, that has been declared to be a pointer to the same type as x.

Therefore, with the definitions of count and int_pointer as given, we can write a statement such as

```
int_pointer = &count;
```

to set up the indirect reference between int_pointer and count. The address operator has the effect of assigning to the variable int_pointer, not the value of count, but a *pointer* to the variable count. The link that has been made between int_pointer and count is conceptualized in Fig. 11-1. The directed line illustrates the idea that int_pointer does not directly contain the value of count, but a pointer to the variable count.

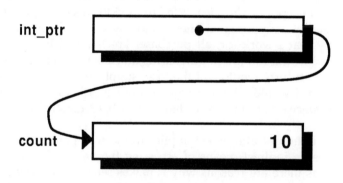

Fig. 11-1. Pointer to an integer

In order to reference the contents of count through the pointer variable int_pointer, we use the *indirection* operator, which is the asterisk *. So if x were defined to be of type int, then the statement

```
x = *int_pointer;
```

would assign the value that is indirectly referenced through int_pointer to the variable x. Since int_pointer was previously set pointing to count, this statement would have the effect of assigning the value contained in the variable count—which is 10—to the variable x.

The previous statements have been incorporated into the following program, which illustrates the two fundamental pointer operators: the address operator, &, and the indirection operator, *.

Program 11-1

```
/* Program to illustrate pointers */

main ()
{
    int    count = 10, x;
    int    *int_pointer;

    int_pointer = &count;
    x = *int_pointer;

    printf ("count = %d, x = %d\n", count, x);
}
```

Program 11-1 Output

```
count = 10, x = 10
```

The variables count and x are declared to be integer variables in the normal fashion. On the next line, the variable int_pointer is declared to be of type "pointer to int." Note that the two lines of declarations could have been combined into the single line

```
int    count = 10, x, *int_pointer;
```

Next, the address operator is applied to the variable count. This has the effect of creating a pointer to this variable, which is then assigned by the program to the variable int_pointer.

Execution of the next statement in the program,

```
x = *int_pointer;
```

proceeds as follows: the indirection operator tells the C system to treat the variable int_pointer as containing a pointer to another data item. This pointer is then used to access the desired data item, whose type is specified by the declaration of the pointer variable. Since we told the compiler that int_pointer points to integers when we declared the varible, the compiler knows that the value referenced by the expression *int_pointer is an integer. And since we set int_pointer to point to the integer variable count in the previous program statement, it is the value of count that is indirectly accessed by this expression.

It should be realized that the program we have just presented is a manufactured example of the use of pointers and does not show a practical use for them in a program. Such motivation will be presented shortly, after you have become familiar with the basic ways in which pointers may be defined and manipulated in a program.

Program 11-2 illustrates some interesting properties of pointer variables. Here a pointer to a character is used.

Program 11-2

```
/* Further examples of pointers */

main ()
{
    char   c = 'Q';
    char   *char_pointer = &c;

    printf ("%c %c\n", c, *char_pointer);

    c = '/';
    printf ("%c %c\n", c, *char_pointer);

    *char_pointer = '(';
    printf ("%c %c\n", c, *char_pointer);
}
```

Program 11-2 Output

```
Q Q
/ /
( (
```

The character variable c is defined and initialized to the character 'Q'. In the next line of the program, the variable char_pointer is defined to be of type "pointer to char", meaning that whatever value is stored inside this variable should be treated as an indirect reference (pointer) to a character. You will notice that we can assign an initial value to this variable in the normal fashion. The value that we assign to char_pointer in the program is a pointer to the variable c, which is obtained by applying the address operator to the variable c. (Note that this initialization would have generated a compiler error had c been defined *after* this statement, since a variable must always be declared *before* its value may be referenced in an expression.)

The declaration of the variable `char_pointer` and the assigment of its initial value could have been equivalently expressed in two separate statements as

```
char   *char_pointer;
char_pointer = &c;
```

(and *not* by the statements

```
char   *char_pointer;
*char_pointer = &c;
```

as may be implied from the single line declaration).

The first `printf` call simply displays the contents of the variable `c` and the contents of the variable that is referenced by `char_pointer`. Since we set `char_pointer` to point to the variable `c`, the value that is displayed is the contents of `c`, as verified by the first line of the program's output.

In the next line of the program, the character `'/'` is assigned to the character variable `c`. Since `char_pointer` still points to the variable `c`, displaying the value of `*char_pointer` in the subsequent `printf` call correctly displays this new value of `c` at the terminal. This is an important concept. Unless the value of `char_pointer` is changed, the expression `*char_pointer` will *always* access the value of `c`. So as the value of `c` changes, so does the value of `*char_pointer`.

The previous discussion can help you to understand how the program statement that appears next in the program works. We mentioned that unless `char_pointer` were changed, the expression `*char_pointer` would always reference the value of `c`. Therefore, in the expression

```
*char_pointer = '(';
```

we are assigning the left parenthesis character to `c`. More formally, the character `'('` is assigned to the variable that is pointed to by `char_pointer`. We know that this variable is `c`, since we placed a pointer to `c` in `char_pointer` at the beginning of the program.

The above concepts are the key to your understanding of the operation of pointers. Please review them at this point if they still seem a bit unclear.

In the next program, two integer pointers, `p1` and `p2`, are defined. Notice how the value referenced by a pointer can be used in an arithmetic expression. If `p1` is defined to be of type "pointer to integer", what conclusion do you think can be made about the use of `*p1` in an expression?

Program 11-3

```
/* More on pointers */

main ()
{
    int   i1, i2;
    int   *p1, *p2;

    i1 = 5;
    p1 = &i1;
    i2 = *p1 / 2 + 10;
    p2 = p1;

    printf ("i1 = %d, i2 = %d, *p1 = %d, *p2 = %d\n",
              i1, i2, *p1, *p2);
}
```

Program 11-3 Output

```
i1 = 5, i2 = 12, *p1 = 5, *p2 = 5
```

After defining the integer variables i1 and i2 and the integer pointer variables p1 and p2, the program then proceeds to assign the value 5 to i1 and to store a pointer to i1 inside p1. Next, the value of i2 is calculated with the following expression:

```
i2 = *p1 / 2 + 10;
```

We implied from our discussions of Program 11-2 that if a pointer px points to a variable x, and px has been defined to be a pointer to the same data type as is x, then use of *px in an expression is in all respects identical to the use of x in the same expression.

Since in Program 11-3 the variable p1 is defined to be an integer pointer, the preceding expression is evaluated using the rules of integer arithmetic. And since the value of *p1 is 5 (p1 points to i1), the final result of the evaluation of the preceding expression is 12, which is the value that is assigned to i2. (As you would expect, the pointer reference operator * has higher precedence than the arithmetic operation of division. In fact, this operator, as well as the address operator &, have higher precedence than *all* binary operators in C.)

In the next statement, the value of the pointer p1 is assigned to p2. This assignment is perfectly valid, and has the effect of setting p2 to point to the same data item that p1 points to. Since p1 points to i1, after the assignment statement has been executed, p2 will *also* point to i1 (and we can have as many pointers to the same item as we desire in C).

The `printf` call verifies that the values of `i1`, `*p1`, and `*p2` are all the same (5) and that the value of `i2` was set to 12 by the program.

♦ Pointers and Structures ♦

We have seen how a pointer can be defined to point to a basic data type such as an `int` or a `char`. But pointers can also be defined to point to structures as well. In Chapter 9, we defined our `date` structure as follows:

```
struct date
{
    int   month;
    int   day;
    int   year;
};
```

Just as we defined variables to be of type `struct date`, as in

```
struct date    todays_date;
```

so can we define a variable to be a pointer to a `struct date` variable:

```
struct date    *date_pointer;
```

The variable `date_pointer`, as just defined, can then be used in the expected fashion. For example, we can set it to point to `todays_date` with the assignment statement

```
date_pointer = &todays_date;
```

Once such an assignment has been made, we can then indirectly access any of the members of the `date` structure pointed to by `date_pointer` in the following way:

```
(*date_pointer).day = 21;
```

This statement will have the effect of setting the day of the `date` structure pointed to by `date_pointer` to 21. The parentheses are required since the structure member operator `.` has higher precedence than the indirection operator `*`.

To test the value of `month` stored in the `date` structure pointed to by `date_pointer`, a statement such as

```
if   ( (*date_pointer).month == 12   )
      . . .
```

can be used.

Pointers to structures are so often used in C that a special operator exists in the language. The structure pointer operator ->, which is the dash followed by the greater than sign, permits expressions that would otherwise be written as

```
(*x).y
```

to be more clearly expressed as

```
x->y
```

So the if statement from above can be conveniently written as

```
if   ( date_pointer->month == 12 )
      . . .
```

Program 9-1, which was the first program that illustrated structures, was rewritten using the concept of structure pointers. This program is presented below.

Program 11-4

```
/* Program to illustrate structure pointers */

main ()
{
    struct date
    {
        int   month;
        int   day;
        int   year;
    };

    struct date   today, *date_pointer;

    date_pointer = &today;
    date_pointer->month = 9;
    date_pointer->day = 25;
    date_pointer->year = 1988;

    printf ("Today's date is %d/%d/%d.\n",
            date_pointer->month, date_pointer->day,
            date_pointer->year % 100);
}
```

Program 11-4 Output

```
Today's date is 9/25/88.
```

Figure 11-2 depicts how the variables today and date_pointer would look after all of the assignment statements from the preceding program have been executed.

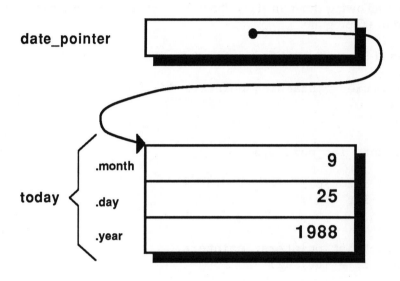

Fig. 11-2. Pointer to a structure

Once again, it should be pointed out that there is no real motivation shown here as to why we should even bother using a structure pointer when it seems as though we can get along just fine without it (as we did in Program 9-1). We will get to the motivation shortly.

Structures Containing Pointers

Naturally, a pointer can also be a member of a structure. In the structure definition

```
struct   int_pointers
{
    int   *p1;
    int   *p2;
};
```

a structure called int_pointers is defined to contain two integer pointers, the first one called p1 and the second one p2. We can define a variable of type struct int_pointers in the usual way:

```
struct int_pointers  pointers;
```

The variable pointers can now be used in the normal fashion, remembering that pointers itself is *not* a pointer, but a structure variable that has two pointers as its members.

The following program shows how the int_pointers structure can be handled in a C program.

Program 11-5

```
/* Structures containing pointers */

main ()
{
    struct   int_pointers
    {
        int   *p1;
        int   *p2;
    };

    struct int_pointers  pointers;
    int   i1 = 100, i2;

    pointers.p1 = &i1;
    pointers.p2 = &i2;
    *pointers.p2 = -97;

    printf ("i1 = %d, *pointers.p1 = %d\n", i1, *pointers.p1);
    printf ("i2 = %d, *pointers.p2 = %d\n", i2, *pointers.p2);
}
```

Program 11-5 Output

```
i1 = 100, *pointers.p1 = 100
i2 = -97, *pointers.p2 = -97
```

After the variables have been defined, the assignment statement

```
pointers.p1 = &i1;
```

sets the p1 member of pointers pointing to the integer variable i1, while the next statement

```
pointers.p2 = &i2;
```

sets the p2 member pointing to i2. Next, -97 is assigned to the variable that is pointed to by pointers.p2. Since we just set this to point to i2, -97 is stored in i2. No parentheses are needed in this assignment statement, since as we mentioned previously, the structure member operator . has higher precedence than the indirection operator. Therefore, the pointer is correctly referenced from the structure *before* the indirection operator is applied. Of course, parentheses could have been used just to play it safe, as at times it can be difficult to try to remember which of two operators has higher precedence.

The two printf calls that follow in the preceding program verify that the correct assignments were made.

Fig. 11-3 has been provided to help you understand the relationship between the variables i1, i2, and pointers after the assignment statements from the Program 11-5 have been executed. As you can see in Fig. 11-3, the p1 member points to the variable i1, which contains the value 100, while the p2 member points to the variable i2, which contains the value -97.

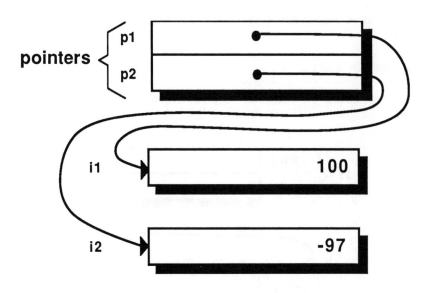

Fig. 11-3. Structure containing pointers

Linked Lists

The concepts of pointers to structures and structures containing pointers are very powerful ones in C, for they enable us to create sophisticated data structures, such as *linked lists, doubly linked lists,* and *trees.*

Suppose we define a structure as follows:

```
struct entry
{
    int         value;
    struct entry  *next;
};
```

This defines a structure called entry, which contains two members. The first member of the structure is a simple integer called value. The second member of the structure is a member called next, which is a *pointer to an entry structure*. Think about this for a moment. Contained inside an entry structure is a pointer to another entry structure. This is a perfectly valid concept in the C language. Now suppose we define two variables to be of type struct entry as follows:

```
struct entry  n1, n2;
```

We set the next pointer of structure n1 to point to structure n2 by executing the statement

```
n1.next = &n2;
```

This statement effectively makes a "link" between n1 and n2, as depicted in Fig. 11-4.

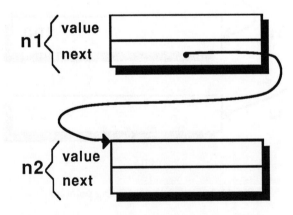

Fig. 11-4. Linked structures

Assuming a variable n3 were also defined to be of type struct entry, then we could add another "link" with the statement

```
n2.next = &n3;
```

This resulting chain of linked entries, known more formally as a *linked list,* is illustrated in Fig. 11-5. Program 11-6 illustrates this linked list.

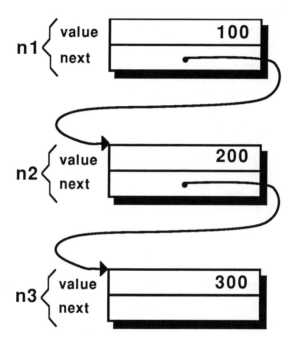

Fig. 11-5. A linked list

The structures n1, n2, and n3 are defined to be of type struct entry, which consists of an integer member called value and a pointer to an entry structure called next. The program then assigns the values 100, 200, and 300 to the value members of n1, n2, and n3, respectively.

The next two statements in the program:

```
n1.next = &n2;
n2.next = &n3;
```

set up the linked list, with the next member of n1 pointing to n2 and the next member of n2 pointing to n3.

Program 11-6

```
/* Linked Lists */

main ()
{
    struct   entry
    {
        int             value;
        struct entry  *next;
    };

    struct entry n1, n2, n3;
    int             i;

    n1.value = 100;
    n2.value = 200;
    n3.value = 300;

    n1.next = &n2;
    n2.next = &n3;

    i = n1.next->value;
    printf ("%d  ", i);

    printf ("%d\n", n2.next->value);
}
```

Program 11-6 Output

```
200   300
```

Execution of the statement

```
i = n1.next->value;
```

proceeds as follows: the value member of the entry structure pointed to by n1.next is accessed and assigned to the integer variable i. Since we set n1.next to point to n2, the value member of n2 is accessed by this state-

ment. Therefore, this statement has the net result of assigning 200 to `i`, as verified by the `printf` call that follows in the program. You may want to verify
that the expression `n1.next->value` is the correct one to use and not
`n1.next.value`, since the `n1.next` field contains a pointer to a structure, and
not the structure itself. This distinction is important and can quickly lead to programming errors if it is not fully understood.

The structure member operator `.` and the structure pointer operator `->`
have the same precedence in the C language. In expressions such as the preceding one, where both operators are used, the operators are evaluated from left to
right. Therefore, the expression is evaluated as

```
i = (n1.next)->value;
```

which is what was intended.

The second `printf` call in Program 11-6 displays the `value` member that
is pointed to by `n2.next`. Since we set `n2.next` to point to `n3`, the contents
of `n3.value` are displayed by the program.

As mentioned, the concept of a linked list is a very powerful one in programming. Linked lists greatly simplify operations such as the insertion and
removal of elements from large lists of sorted items. For example, if `n1`, `n2`,
and `n3` are as defined above, then we can easily remove `n2` from the list simply
by setting the `next` field of `n1` to point to whatever `n2` is pointing to:

```
n1.next = n2.next;
```

This statement has the effect of copying the pointer contained in `n2.next` into
`n1.next`, and, since `n2.next` was set to point to `n3`, `n1.next` will now be
pointing to `n3`. Furthermore, since `n1` no longer points to `n2`, we have effectively removed it from our list. Fig. 11-6 depicts this situation after the above
statement is executed. Of course, we could have set `n1` pointing to `n3` directly
with the statement

```
n1.next = &n3;
```

but this latter statement is not as general, since we must know in advance that
`n2` was pointing to `n3`.

Inserting an element into a list is just as straightforward. If we wanted to
insert a `struct entry` called `n2_3` after `n2` in the list, we could simply set
`n2_3.next` to point to whatever `n2.next` was pointing to, and then set
`n2.next` to point to `n2_3`. So the sequence of statements

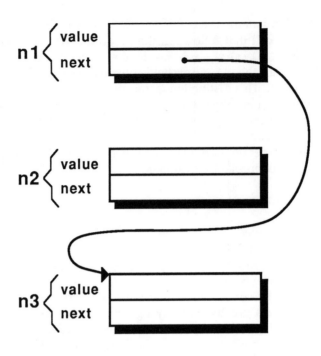

Fig. 11-6. Removing an entry from a linked list

```
n2_3.next = n2.next;
n2.next = &n2_3;
```

would insert n2_3 into the list, immediately after entry n2. Note that the sequence of the above statements is important, since executing the second statement first would overwrite the pointer stored in n2.next before it had a chance to be assigned to n2_3.next. The inserted element n2_3 is depicted in Fig. 11-7. You will notice that we did not show n2_3 between n1 and n3. This is to emphasize the fact that n2_3 can be anywhere in the computer's memory, and does not have to physically occur after n1 and before n3. This is one of the main motivations for the use of a linked list approach for storing information: entries of the list do not have to be stored sequentially in memory, as *is* the case with elements contained in an array.

Before we start developing some functions to work with linked lists, two more issues must be discussed. Usually associated with a linked list is at least one pointer to the list. Often, a pointer to the start of the list is kept. So, for our

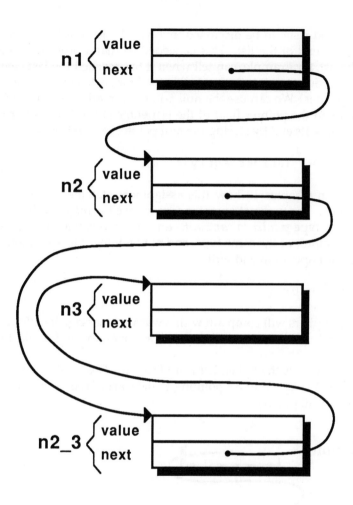

Fig. 11-7. Inserting an element into a linked list

original three-element list, which consisted of n1, n2, and n3, we can define a variable called `list_pointer` and set it to point to the beginning of the list with the statement

```
struct entry   *list_pointer = &n1;
```

(assuming here that n1 has been previously defined). A pointer to a list is useful for sequencing through the entries in the list, as we shall see shortly.

The second issue to be discussed involves the idea of having some way of identifying the end of the list. This is needed so that a procedure that searches through the list, for example, can tell when it has reached the last element in the list. By convention, a pointer value of 0 is used for such a purpose, and is known as the *null* pointer. We can use the null pointer to mark the end of a list by storing this value in the pointer field of the last entry of the list. In our three-entry list, we can mark its end by storing the null pointer into n3.next:

```
n3.next =  (struct entry *) 0;
```

(We will see in Chapter 13 how this assignment statement can be made a bit more readable.) The typecast operator says to take the *integer* value 0 and to convert it to be of type *pointer to struct entry*. In this way, we are assigning a pointer to a pointer of the same type, and not an integer to a pointer. If you forget the typecast operation and write

```
n3.next = 0;
```

then some compilers will complain with a warning message like "different levels of indirection." It's better to use the typecast operator and avoid the warning message.

Fig. 11-8 depicts the linked list from Program 11-6, with a struct entry pointer called list_pointer pointing to the start of the list and the n3.next field set to the null pointer.

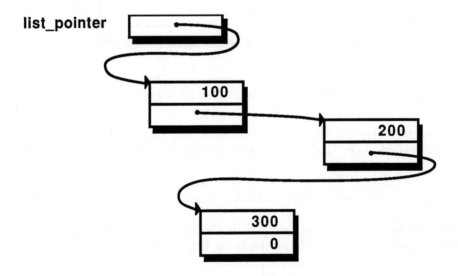

Fig. 11-8. Linked list showing list pointer and terminating null

Program 11-7 incorporates the concepts we have just described. The program uses a for loop to sequence through the list and display the value member of each entry in the list.

Program 11-7

```
/* List traversal */

main ()
{
    struct entry
    {
        int             value;
        struct entry    *next;
    };

    struct entry    n1, n2, n3;
    struct entry    *list_pointer = &n1;

    n1.value = 100;
    n1.next  = &n2;

    n2.value = 200;
    n2.next  = &n3;

    n3.value = 300;
    n3.next  = (struct entry *) 0;

    while ( list_pointer != (struct entry *) 0 )
    {
        printf ("%d\n", list_pointer->value);
        list_pointer = list_pointer->next;
    }
}
```

Program 11-7 Output

```
100
200
300
```

The program defines the variables n1, n2, and n3 and the pointer variable list_pointer, which is initially set to point to n1, the first entry in the list. The next program statements link together the three elements of the list, with the next member of n3 set to the null pointer to mark the end of the list.

A while loop is then set up to sequence through each element of the list. This loop will be executed as long as the value of list_pointer is not equal to the null pointer (once again, the typecast operator is used to ensure that we're comparing two pointers, and not a pointer and an integer). The printf call inside the while loop displays the value member of the entry currently pointed to by list_pointer.

The statement that follows the printf call,

```
list_pointer = list_pointer->next;
```

has the effect of taking the pointer from the next member of the structure pointed to by list_pointer and assigning it to list_pointer. So the first time through the loop, this statement takes the pointer contained in n1.next (remember, list_pointer was initially set pointing to n1) and assigns it to list_pointer. Since this value is not null—it's a pointer to the entry structure n2—the while loop is repeated.

The second time through the while loop results in the display of n2.value, which is 200. The next member of n2 is then copied into list_pointer, and since we set this value to point to n3, list_pointer will point to n3 by the end of the second pass through the loop.

When the while loop is executed for the third time, the printf call displays the value of 300 as contained in n3.value. At that point, list_pointer->next (which is actually n3.next) is copied into list_pointer, and, since we set this member to the null pointer, the while loop will terminate after it has been executed three times.

Trace through the operation of the while loop just discussed, using a pencil and paper, if necessary, to keep track of the values of the various variables. Understanding of the operation of this loop is the key to your understanding of the operation of pointers in C. Incidentally, it should be noted that this same while loop can be used to sequence through the elements of a list of any size, provided the end of the list is marked by the null pointer.

◆ Pointers and Functions ◆

Pointers and functions get along quite well together. That is, we can pass a pointer as an argument to a function in the normal fashion, and we can also have a function return a pointer as its result.

The first case cited above, passing pointer arguments, is straightforward enough: the pointer is simply included in the list of arguments to the function in the normal fashion. So to pass the pointer list_pointer from the previous program to a function called print_list, you can write

```
print_list (list_pointer);
```

Inside the `print_list` routine, the formal parameter must be declared to be a pointer to the appropriate type:

```
print_list   (pointer)
struct entry   *pointer;
{
     ...
}
```

The formal parameter `pointer` can then be used in the same way as a normal pointer variable. One thing worth remembering when dealing with pointers that are sent to functions as arguments: the value of the pointer is copied into the formal parameter when the function is called. Therefore, any change made to the formal parameter by the function will *not* effect the pointer that was passed to the function. But here's the catch: while the pointer cannot be changed by the function, the data elements that the pointer references *can* be changed! The next program example will help clarify this point.

Program 11-8

```
/* pointers and functions */

void test (int_pointer)
int   *int_pointer;
{
    *int_pointer = 100;
}

main ()
{
    int   i = 50, *p = &i;

    printf ("i before the call to test = %d\n", i);

    test (p);
    printf ("i after the call to test = %d\n", i);
}
```

Program 11-8 Output

```
i before the call to test = 50
i after the call to test = 100
```

The function test is defined to take as its argument a pointer to an integer. Inside the function, a single statement is executed to set the integer pointed to by int_pointer to the value 100.

The main routine defines an integer variable i with an initial value of 50 and a pointer to an integer called p that is set to point to i. The program then displays the value of i and calls the test function, passing the pointer p as the argument. As you can see from the second line of the program's output, the test function did in fact change the value of i to 100.

Now consider the following program.

Program 11-9

```
/* More on pointers and functions */

void exchange (pint1, pint2)
int *pint1, *pint2;
{
    int   temp;

    temp = *pint1;
    *pint1 = *pint2;
    *pint2 = temp;
}

main ()
{
    int i1 = -5, i2 = 66, *p1 = &i1, *p2 = &i2;

    printf ("i1 = %d, i2 = %d\n", i1, i2);

    exchange (p1, p2);
    printf ("i1 = %d, i2 = %d\n", i1, i2);

    exchange (&i1, &i2);
    printf ("i1 = %d, i2 = %d\n", i1, i2);
}
```

Program 11-9 Output

```
i1 = -5, i2 = 66
i1 = 66, i2 = -5
i1 = -5, i2 = 66
```

The purpose of the exchange function is to interchange the two integer values pointed to by its two arguments. The local integer variable temp is used to hold one of the integer values while the exchange is made. Its value is set equal to the integer that is pointed to by pint1. The integer pointed to by pint2 is then copied into the integer pointed to by pint1, and the value of temp is then stored into the integer pointed to by pint2, thus making the exchange complete.

The main routine defines integers i1 and i2 with values of -5 and 66, respectively. Two integer pointers, p1 and p2, are then defined and are set to point to i1 and i2, respectively. The program then displays the values of i1 and i2 and calls the exchange function, passing the two pointers, p1 and p2, as arguments. The exchange function exchanges the value contained in the integer pointed to by p1 with the value contained in the integer pointed to by p2. Since p1 points to i1, and p2 to i2, the values of i1 and i2 end up getting exchanged by the function. The output from the second printf call verifies that the exchange worked properly.

The second call to exchange is a bit more interesting. This time, the arguments that are passed to the function are pointers to i1 and i2 that are "manufactured right on the spot" by applying the address operator to these two variables. Since the expression &i1 produces a pointer to the integer variable i1, this is right in line with the type of argument that our function expects for the first argument (a pointer to an integer). The same applies for the second argument as well. And as can be seen from the program's output, the exchange function did its job and switched the values of i1 and i2 back to their original values.

You should realize that without the use of pointers we could not have written our exchange function to exchange the value of two integers, since we are limited to returning only a single value from a function, and since a function cannot permanently change the value of its arguments.

The next program example shows how a function can return a pointer. The program defines a function called find_entry whose purpose is to search through a linked list to find a specified value. When the specified value has been found, the program returns a pointer to the entry in the list. If the desired value is not found, then the program returns the null pointer.

Program 11-10

```
struct entry
{
    int            value;
    struct entry   *next;
};

struct entry  *find_entry (lpointer, match_value)
struct entry  *lpointer;
int            match_value;
{
    while  ( lpointer != (struct entry *) 0 )
        if ( lpointer->value == match_value )
            return (lpointer);
        else
            lpointer = lpointer->next;

    return ( (struct entry *) 0 );
}

main ()
{
    struct entry  n1, n2, n3;
    struct entry  *lptr, *list_start = &n1;
    int           i, search;

    n1.value = 100;
    n1.next =   &n2;

    n2.value = 200;
    n2.next =   &n3;

    n3.value = 300;
    n3.next =   (struct entry *) 0;

    printf ("Enter value to locate: ");
    scanf ("%d", &search);

    lptr = find_entry (list_start, search);

    if ( lptr != (struct entry *) 0 )
        printf ("Found %d\n.", lptr->value);
    else
        printf ("Not found.\n");
}
```

Program 11-10 Output

```
Enter value: 200
Found 200.
```

Program 11-10 Output (Re-run)

```
Enter value to locate: 400
Not found.
```

Program 11-10 Output (Re-run)

```
Enter value to locate: 300
Found 300.
```

The function header

```
struct entry  *find_entry (lpointer, match_value)
```

specifies that the function find_entry will return a pointer to an entry structure. After the formal parameters lpointer and match_value have been declared, the function enters a while loop to sequence through the elements of the list. This loop is executed until either match_value is found equal to one of the value entries in the list (in which case the value of lpointer is immediately returned), or until the null pointer is reached (in which case the while loop will be exited and a null pointer will be returned).

After setting up the list as in previous programs, the main routine asks the user for a value to locate in the list and then proceeds to call the find_entry function with a pointer to the start of the list (list_start) and the value entered by the user (search) as arguments. The pointer that is returned by find_entry is assigned to the struct entry pointer variable lptr. If lptr is not null, then the value member pointed to by lptr is displayed. This should be the same as the value entered by the user. If lptr is null, then a "Not found." message is displayed.

The program's output verifies that the values 200 and 300 were correctly located in the list, and the value 400 was properly not found.

The pointer that is returned by the find_entry function in the program does not seem to serve any useful purpose. However, in more practical situations, this pointer might be used to access other elements contained in the particular entry of the list. For example, we could have a linked list of our dictionary entries from the previous chapter. Then, we could call the find_entry function (or rename it lookup as it was called in that chapter) to search the linked list of dictionary entries for the given word. The pointer returned by the lookup function could then be used to access the definition member of the entry.

Organizing the dictionary as a linked list has several advantages. Inserting a new word into the dictionary is easy: once it has been determined where in the list the new entry is to be inserted, it can be done so by simply adjusting some pointers, as illustrated earlier in this chapter. Removing an entry from the dictionary is also simple. Finally, as you will learn in Chapter 17, this approach also provides the framework that enables us to "dynamically" expand the size of the dictionary.

However, the linked list approach for the organization of the dictionary does suffer from one major drawback: we can not apply our fast binary search algorithm to such a list. This algorithm only works with an array of elements that can be directly indexed. Unfortunately, there is no faster way to search our linked list other than by a straight sequential search, since each entry in the list can only be accessed from the previous one.

One way to glean the benefits of easy insertion and removal of elements, as well as fast search time, is by using a different type of data structure known as a *tree*. The reader is respectfully referred elsewhere—such as to *The Art of Computer Programming, Volume 1, Fundamental Algorithms* (Donald E. Knuth, Addison-Wesley)—for a discussion of this type of data structure, which can be easily implemented in C with the techniques we have already described.

♦ Pointers and Arrays ♦

One of the most common uses of pointers in C is as pointers to arrays. The main reasons for using pointers to arrays are ones of notational convenience and of program efficiency. Pointers to arrays generally result in code that uses less memory space and executes faster. The reason why this is so will become apparent through our discussions in this section.

If we have an array of 100 integers called `values`, then we can define a pointer called `values_pointer`, which can be used to access the integers contained in this array with the statement

```
int   *values_pointer;
```

When we define a pointer that will be used to point to the elements of an array, we don't designate the pointer as type "pointer to array"; rather we designate the pointer as pointing to the type of element that is contained in the array.

If we had an array of characters called `text`, then we could similarly define a pointer to be used to point to elements in `text` with the statement

```
char *text_pointer;
```

In order to set `values_pointer` to point to the first element in the `values` array, we simply write

```
values_pointer = values;
```

The address operator is not used in this case since the C compiler treats the occurrence of an array name without a subscript as a pointer to the array. Therefore, simply specifying `values` without a subscript has the effect of producing a pointer to the first element of values (see Fig. 11-9).

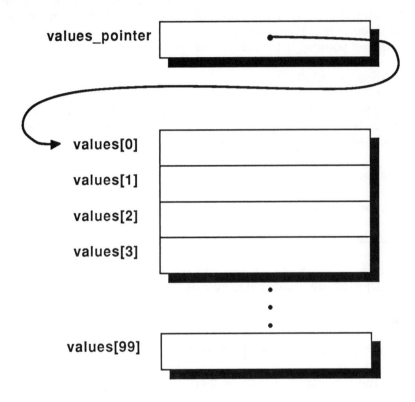

Fig. 11-9. Pointer to an array element

An equivalent way of producing a pointer to the start of `values` is to apply the address operator to the first element of the array. Thus the statement

```
values_pointer = &values[0];
```

can be used to serve the same purpose of placing a pointer to the first element of `values` in the pointer variable `values_pointer`.

To set `text_pointer` to point to the first character inside the `text` array, either the statement

```
text_pointer = text;
```

or

```
text_pointer = &text[0];
```

can be used. Whichever statement you choose to use is strictly a matter of taste.

The real power of using pointers to arrays comes into play when we wish to sequence through the elements of an array. If `values_pointer` is defined as above and is set pointing to the first element of `values`, then the expression

```
*values_pointer
```

can be used to access the first integer of the `values` array, i.e., `values[0]`. To reference `values[3]` through the `values_pointer` variable, we can add 3 to `values_pointer` and then apply the indirection operator:

```
*(values_pointer + 3)
```

In general, the expression

```
*(values_pointer + i)
```

can be used to access the value contained in `values[i]`. So, to set `values[10]` to 27, we could obviously write the expression

```
values[10] = 27;
```

or, using `values_pointer`, we could write

```
*(values_pointer + 10) = 27;
```

To set `values_pointer` to point to the second element of the `values` array, we can apply the address operator to `values[1]` and assign the result to `values_pointer`:

```
values_pointer = &values[1];
```

If `values_pointer` points to `values[0]`, then we can set it to point to `values[1]` by simply adding 1 to the value of `values_pointer`:

```
values_pointer += 1;
```

This is a perfectly valid expression in C and can be used for pointers to *any* data type.

So, in general, if a is an array of elements of type x, px is of type "pointer to x," and i and n are integer constants of variables, then the statement

```
px = a;
```

will set px to point to the first element of a, and the expression

```
*(px + i)
```

will subsequently reference the value contained in a[i]. Furthermore, the statement

```
px += n;
```

will set px to point n elements further in the array, *no matter what type of element is contained in the array.*

The increment and decrement operators ++ and -- are particularly handy when dealing with pointers. Applying the increment operator to a pointer has the same effect as adding one to the pointer, while applying the decrement operator has the same effect as subtracting one from the pointer. So if text_pointer were defined as a char pointer, and were set pointing to the beginning of an array of chars called text, then the statement

```
++text_pointer;
```

would set text_pointer pointing to the next character in text, which is text[1]. In a similar fashion, the statement

```
--text_pointer;
```

would set text_pointer pointing to the previous character in text, assuming of course that text_pointer was not pointing to the beginning of text prior to the execution of this statement.

It is perfectly valid to compare two pointer variables in C. This is particularly useful when comparing two pointers into the same array. For example, we could test the pointer values_pointer to see if it points past the end of an array containing 100 elements by comparing it to a pointer to the last element in the array. So the expression

```
values_pointer > &values[99]
```

would be TRUE (nonzero) if values_pointer was pointing past the last element in the values array, and would be FALSE (zero) otherwise. From our previous discussions, we can replace the above expression with its equivalent

```
values_pointer > values + 99
```

since `values` used without a subscript is a pointer to the beginnning of the `values` array.

We can apply the same technique to determine if a pointer has gone too far in the other direction (that is, before the begining of an array) with an expression such as

```
values_pointer < &values[0]
```

or, equivalently,

```
values_pointer < values
```

The next program illustrates pointers to arrays. The `array_sum` function calculates the sum of the elements contained in an array of integers.

Program 11-11

```
/* Function to sum the elements of an integer array */

int   array_sum (array, n)
int   array[];
int   n;
{
    int   sum = 0, *ptr;
    int   *array_end = array + n;

    for (  ptr = array;  ptr < array_end;  ++ptr )
        sum += *ptr;

    return (sum);
}

main ()
{
    static int   values[10] = { 3, 7, -9, 3, 6, -1,
                                7, 9, 1, -5 };

    printf ("The sum is %d\n", array_sum (values, 10));
}
```

Program 11-11 Output

```
The sum is 21
```

Inside the `array_sum` function, the integer pointer `array_end` is defined and set pointing immediately after the last element of `array`. A `for` loop is then set up to sequence through the elements of `array`. The value of `ptr` is set to point to the beginning of `array` when the loop is entered. Each time through the loop, the element of `array` pointed to by `ptr` is added into `sum`. The value of `ptr` is then incremented by the `for` loop to set it pointing to the next element in `array`. When `ptr` points past the end of `array`, the `for` loop is exited, and the value of `sum` is returned to the callng routine.

A Slight Digression about Program Optimization

It is pointed out that the local variable `array_end` was not actually needed by the function, as we could have explicitly compared the value of `ptr` to the end of the array inside the `for` loop:

```
for ( ...; pointer <= array + n; ... )
```

The sole motivation for using `array_end` was one of optimization. Each time through the `for` loop, the looping conditions are evaluated. Since the expression `array + n` is never changed from within the loop, its value is constant throughout the execution of the `for` loop. By evaluating it once *before* the loop is entered, we therefore save the time that would otherwise be spent reevaluating this expression each time through the loop. While there is virtually no savings in time for a 10-element array, especially if the `array_sum` function is called only once by the program, there could be a more substantial savings of time if this function were heavily used by a program for summing large-sized arrays, for example.

The other issue to be discussd about program optimizaton concerns the very use of pointers themselves in a program. In the `array_sum` function discussed earlier, the expression `*ptr` is used inside the `for` loop to access the elements in the array. Conventionally, we would have written our `array_sum` function with a `for` loop that used an index variable, such as `i`, and then would have added the value of `array[i]` into `sum` inside the loop. In general, the process of indexing an array takes more time to execute than does the process of accessing the contents of a pointer. In fact, this is one of the main reasons why pointers are used to access the elements of an array—the code that is generated is generally more efficient. Of course, if access to the array is not generally sequential, then pointers accomplish nothing, as far as this issue is concerned, since the expression `*(pointer + j)` will take just as long to execute as will the expression `array[j]`.

Is It an Array or Is It a Pointer?

You will recall that in order to pass an array to a function, we simply specify the name of the array, as we did previously with the call to the array_sum function. But we also mentioned in this section that in order to produce a pointer to an array that we need only specify the name of the array. This implies that in the call to the array_sum function, what was passed to the function was actually a *pointer* to the array values. This is precisely the case, and explains why we are able to change the elements of an array from within a function.

But if it is indeed the case that a pointer to the array is passed to the function, then why isn't the formal parameter inside the function declared to be a pointer? In other words, in the declaration of array in the array_sum function, why isn't the declaration

```
int   *array;
```

used? Shouldn't all references to an array from within a function be made using pointer variables?

To answer these questions, we must first reiterate what we have said before about pointers and arrays. We mentioned that if values_pointer points to the same type of element as contained in an array called values, then the expression *(values_pointer + i) is in all ways equivalent to the expression values[i], assuming that values_pointer has been set to point to the beginning of values. What follows from this is that we can also use the expression *(values + i) to reference the ith element of the array values, and, in general, if x is an array of any type, then the expression x[i] can always be equivalently expressed in C as *(x + i).

As you can see, pointers and arrays are intimately related in C, and this is why we can declare array to be of type "array of ints" inside the array_sum function *or* to be of type "pointer to int." Either declaration works just fine in the preceding program—try it and see.

If you are going to be using index numbers to reference the elements of an array that is passed to a function, then declare the corresponding formal parameter to be an array. This will more correctly reflect the usage of the array by the function. Similarly, if you will be using the argument as a pointer to the array, then declare it to be of type pointer.

Realizing now that we could have declared array to be an int pointer in the last program example, and then could have subsequently used it as such, we can eliminate the variable ptr from the function and use array instead. We have done just this in the program that follows.

Program 11-12

```
/* Function to sum the elements of an integer array
             Version 2                                  */

int   array_sum (array, n)
int   *array;
int   n;
{
     int   sum = 0;
     int   *array_end = array + n;

     for (  ; array < array_end;  ++array )
       sum += *array;

     return (sum);
}

main ()
{
     static int   values[10] = { 3, 7, -9, 3, 6, -1,
                                 7, 9, 1, -5 };

     printf ("The sum is %d\n", array_sum (values, 10));
}
```

Program 11-12 Output

```
The sum is 21
```

The program is fairly self-explanatory. The first expression inside the for loop was omitted because no value had to be initialized before the loop was started. One point worth repeating is that when the array_sum function is called, a pointer to the values array is passed, where it is called array inside the function. Changes to the value of array (as opposed to the values referenced by array) do not in any way effect the contents of the values array. So the increment operator that is applied to array is just incrementing a pointer to the array values, and not affecting its contents. (Of course, we know that we *can* change values in the array if we want to, simply by assigning values to the element referenced by the pointer.)

Pointers to Character Strings

One of the most common applications of using a pointer to an array is as a pointer to a character string. The reasons are ones of notational convenience and efficiency. To show how easily pointers to character strings can be used, let's write a function called `copy_string` to copy one string into another. If we were writing this function using our normal array indexing methods, then the function might be coded as follows:

```
void copy_string (from, to)
char from[], to[];
{
    int  i;

    for ( i = 0;  from[i] != '\0';  ++i )
        to[i] = from[i];

    to[i] = '\0';
}
```

The `for` loop is exited before the null character is copied into the `to` array, thus explaining the need for the last statement in the function.

If we write `copy_string` using pointers, then we no longer need the index variable `i`. A pointer version is shown in the following program.

Program 11-13

```
void copy_string (from, to)
char *from, *to;
{
    for ( ;  *from != '\0';  ++from, ++to )
        *to = *from;

    *to = '\0';
}

main ()
{
    static char string1[] = "A string to be copied.";
    static char string2[50];

    copy_string (string1, string2);
    printf ("%s\n", string2);

    copy_string ("So is this.", string2);
    printf ("%s\n", string2);
}
```

Program 11-13 Output

```
A string to be copied.
So is this.
```

The `copy_string` function defines the two formal parameters `from` and `to` as character pointers and not as character arrays as was done in the previous version of `copy_string`. This reflects how these two variables will be used by the function.

A `for` loop is then entered (with no initial conditions) to copy the string pointed to by `from` into the string pointed to by `to`. Each time through the loop, the `from` and `to` pointers are each incremented by one. This sets the `from` pointer pointing to the next character that is to be copied from the source string, and sets the `to` pointer pointing to the location in the destination string where the next character is to be stored.

When the `from` pointer points to the null character, the `for` loop is exited. The function then places the null character at the end of the destination string.

In the `main` routine, the `copy_string` function is called twice, the first time to copy the contents of `string1` into `string2`, and the second time to copy the contents of the constant character string `"So is this."` into `string2`.

Constant Character Strings and Pointers

The fact that the call

```
copy_string ("So is this.", string2);
```

works in the previous program implies that when a constant character string is passed as an argument to a function, what is actually passed is a pointer to that character string. Not only is this true in this case, but it can also be generalized by saying that *whenever* a constant character string is used in C, it is a pointer to that character string that is produced. So if `text_pointer` is declared to be a character pointer, as in

```
char   *text_pointer;
```

then the statement

```
text_pointer = "A character string.";
```

will assign to `text_pointer` a *pointer* to the constant character string `"A character string."` Be careful to make the distinction here between character pointers and character arrays, as the type of assignment shown above does *not* apply to character arrays. So, for example, if `text` were defined to be an array of `chars`, with a statement such as

```
char   text[80];
```

then we *could not* write a statement such as

```
text = "This is not valid.";
```

The *only* time that C lets you get away with performing this type of assignment is when defining and initializing a character array, as in

```
static char   text[80] = { "This is okay." };
```

Initializing the text array in this manner does not have the effect of storing a pointer to the character string "This is okay." inside text, but rather the actual characters themselves. This is actually a slight anomaly with the language.

If text were instead defined to be a character pointer, then initializing text with the statement

```
char *text =   "This is okay.";
```

would assign to text a pointer to the character string "This is okay." Note that, in this case, it is not necessary to declare text as a static variable, since we are initializing a pointer and not an array in this case.

As another example of the distinction between character strings and character string pointers, the following sets up an array called days which contains *pointers* to the names of the days of the week.

```
static char *days[] =
    { "Sunday", "Monday", "Tuesday", "Wednesday",
      "Thursday", "Friday", "Saturday" };
```

The array days is defined to contain seven entries, each a pointer to a character string. So days[0] contains a pointer to the character string "Sunday", days[1] a pointer to the string "Monday", and so on (see Fig. 11-10). We could display the name of the third weekday, for example, with the following statement:

```
printf ("%s\n", days[3]);
```

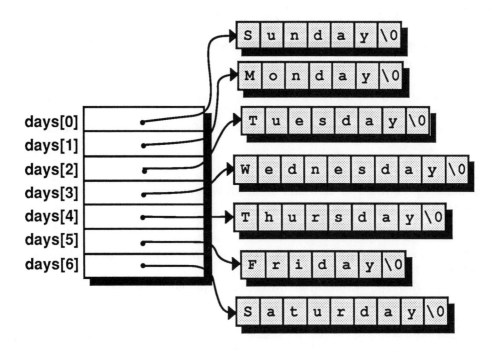

Fig. 11-10. Array of pointers

The Increment and Decrement Operators Revisited

Up to this point, whenever we used the increment or decrement operator it was the only operator that appeared in the expression. When we write the expression ++x, we know that this has the effect of adding 1 to the value of the variable x. And as we have just seen, if x is a pointer to an array, then this has the effect of setting x to point to the next element of the array.

The increment and decrement operators can be used in expressions in which other operators also appear. In such cases, it becomes important to know more precisely how these operators work.

Whenever we used the increment and decrement operators, we always placed them *before* the variables that were being incremented or decremented. So, to increment a variable i, we simply wrote

```
++i;
```

Actually, it is also perfectly valid to place the increment operator *after* the variable, as in

```
i++;
```

Both expressions are perfectly valid and both achieve the same result—namely, of incrementing the value of `i`. In the first case, where the `++` is placed before its operand, the increment operation is more precisely identified as a *pre-increment*. In the second case, where the `++` is placed after its operand, the operation is identified as a *post-increment*.

The same discussion applies to the decrement operator. So the statement

```
--i;
```

technically performs a *pre-decrement* of `i`, whereas the statement

```
i--;
```

performs a *post-decrement* of `i`. Both have the same net result of subtracting 1 from the value of `i`.

It is when the increment and decrement operators are used in more complex expressions that the distinction between the *pre-* and *post-* nature of these operators is realized.

Suppose we have two integers called `i` and `j`. If we set the value of `i` to 0 and then write the statement

```
j = ++i;
```

the value that gets assigned to `j` is 1, and not 0 as you might expect. In the case of the pre-increment operator, the variable is incremented *before* its value is used in an expression. So in the above expression, the value of `i` is first incremented from 0 to 1 and then its value is assigned to `j`, as if the following two statements had been written instead:

```
++i;
j = i;
```

If we use the post-increment operator in the statement

```
j = i++;
```

then `i` will be incremented *after* its value has been assigned to `j`. So if `i` were 0 before the above statement were executed, 0 would be assigned to `j` and *then* `i` would be incremented by 1, as if the statements

```
j = i;
++i;
```

were used instead.

As another example, if `i` is equal to 1, then the statement

```
x = a[--i];
```

has the effect of assigning the value of `a[0]` to `x`, since the variable `i` will be decremented before its value is used to index into `a`. The statement

```
x = a[i--];
```

used instead would have the effect of assigning the value of `a[1]` to `x`, since `i` would be decremented after its value had been used to index into `a`.

As a third example of the distinction between the pre- and post- operators, the function call

```
printf ("%d\n", ++i);
```

will increment `i` and then send its value to the `printf` function, while the call

```
printf ("%d\n", i++);
```

will increment `i` after its value has been sent to the function. So if `i` were equal to 100, then the first `printf` call would display 101 at the terminal, whereas the second `printf` call would display 100. In either case, the value of `i` would be equal to 101 after the statement had been executed.

As a final example on this topic before we present a program, if `text_pointer` is a character pointer, then the expression

```
*(++text_pointer)
```

first increments `text_pointer` and then fetches the character it points to, whereas the expression

```
*(text_pointer++)
```

fetches the character pointed to by `text_pointer` before its value is incremented. In either case, the parentheses are not required, since the `*` and `++` operators have equal precedence but associate from right to left.

Now let's go back to the `copy_string` function from Program 11-13 and rewrite it to incorporate the increment operations directly into the assignment statement.

Since the `to` and `from` pointers are incremented each time after the assignment statement inside the `for` loop is executed, they should be incorporated into the assignment statement as post-increment operations. The revised `for` loop of Program 11-13 then becomes

```
for (  ;   *from != '\0';   )
    *to++ = *from++;
```

Execution of the assignment statement inside the loop would proceed as follows. The character pointed to by from would be retrieved and then from would be incremented to point to the next character in the source string. The referenced character would then be stored inside the location pointed to by to, and then to would be incremented to point to the next location in the destination string.

Study the preceding assignment statement until you fully understand its operation. Statements of this type are so commonly used in C programs, that it's important that you understand the principles involved here.

The for statement above hardly seems worthwhile, since it has no initial expression and no looping expression. In fact, the logic would be better served when expressed in the form of a while loop. This has been done in Program 11-14. This program presents our new version of the copy_string function. The while loop uses the fact that the null character is equal to the value zero, as is commonly done by experienced C programmers.

Program 11-14

```
/* Function to copy one string to another
        pointer version 2                    */

void copy_string (from, to)
char *from, *to;
{
    while ( *from )
        *to++ = *from++;

    *to = '\0';
}

main ()
{
    static char string1[] = "A string to be copied.";
    static char string2[50];

    copy_string (string1, string2);
    printf ("%s\n", string2);

    copy_string ("So is this.", string2);
    printf ("%s\n", string2);
}
```

Program 11-14 Output

```
A string to be copied.
So is this.
```

♦ Operations on Pointers ♦

As we have seen in this chapter, we can add or subtract integer values from pointers. Furthermore, we can compare two pointers to see if they are equal or not, or if one pointer is less than or greater than another pointer. The only other operation that is permitted on pointers is the subtraction of two pointers. The result of subtracting two pointers in C is the number of elements contained between the two pointers. So if a points to an array of elements of any type, and b points to another element somewhere further along in the same array, then the expression b - a represents the number of elements between these two pointers. For example, if p points to some element in an array x, then the statement

```
n = p - x;
```

will have the effect of assigning to the variable n (assumed here to be an integer variable) the index number of the element inside x that p points to. Therefore, if p had been set pointing to the hundredth element in x by a statement such as

```
p = &x[99];
```

then the value of n after the above subtraction were performed would be 99.

As a practical application of this newly learned fact about pointer subtraction, let us present a new version of the string_length function from Chapter 10.

In Program 11-15, the character pointer cptr is used to sequence through the characters pointed to by string until the null character is reached. At that point, string is subtracted from cptr to obtain the number of elements (characters) contained in the string. The program's output verifies that the function is working correctly.

Program 11-15

```
/* Function to count the characters in a string
            pointer version                        */

int   string_length (string)
char   *string;
{
    char   *cptr = string;

    while ( *cptr )
        ++cptr;

    return ( cptr - string );
}

main ()
{
    printf ("%d  ", string_length ("string_length test"));
    printf ("%d  ", string_length (""));
    printf ("%d\n", string_length ("complete"));
}
```

Program 11-15 Output

```
    18   0   8
```

◆ Pointers to Functions ◆

Of a slightly more advanced nature, but presented here for the sake of completeness, is the notion of a pointer to a function. When working with pointers to functions, the C compiler needs to know not only that the pointer variable points to a function, but also what type of value is returned by that function. To declare a variable `fn_pointer` to be of type "pointer to a function that returns an int," the declaration

```
    int   (*fn_pointer) ();
```

can be written. The parentheses around `*fn_pointer` are required, as otherwise the C compiler would treat the preceding statement as the declaration of a function called `fn_pointer` that returns a pointer to an `int` (because the functional call operator `()` has higher precedence that the pointer indirection operator `*`).

In order to set our function pointer pointing to a specific function, we simply assign the name of the function to it. So if `lookup` is a function that returns an `int`, then the statement

```
fn_pointer = lookup;
```

stores a pointer to this function inside the function pointer variable `fn_pointer`. Writing a function name without a subsequent set of parentheses is treated in an analogous way as writing an array name without a subscript. The C compiler automatically produces a pointer to the specified function.

If the `lookup` function has not been previously defined in the program, it will be necessary to declare the function before the above assignment can be made, *even if the function returns an integer.* So a statement such as

```
int  lookup ();
```

would be needed before a pointer to this function could be assigned to the variable `fn_pointer`.

We can call the function that is indirectly referenced through a pointer variable by applying the indirection operator to the variable and by including a set of parentheses after the variable, optionally containing a list of arguments to be passed to the function. For example,

```
entry = (*fn_pointer) (dictionary, word, entries);
```

would call the function pointed to by `fn_pointer`, passing `dictionary`, `word`, and `entries` as arguments to the function. The value returned by the function would be stored inside the variable `entry`. In a similar fashion,

```
(*fn_pointer) ();
```

would simply call the function with no arguments. Once again, the parentheses are needed around `*fn_pointer` to force the indirection operator to be applied before the function call operator.

One common application for pointers to functions is in passing them as arguments to other functions. The UNIX operating system uses this, for example, in the function `qsort`, which performs a "quicksort" on an array of data elements. This function takes as one of its arguments a pointer to a function that is called whenever `qsort` needs to compare two elements in the array being sorted. In this manner, `qsort` can be used to sort arrays of any type, as the actual comparison of any two elements in the array is made by a user-supplied function, and not by the `qsort` function itself.

As you can see from this brief discussion of pointers to functions, the pointer is a very powerful construct in C. The flexibility in defining pointer variables extends beyond those illustrated in this chapter. For example, we can define a pointer to a pointer, and even a pointer to a pointer to a pointer. But these types of constructs are beyond the scope of this book.

♦ Pointers and Memory Addresses ♦

Before we end this discussion of pointers in C, we should point out the details of how they are actually implemented. A computer's memory can be conceptualized as a sequential collection of storage "cells." Each cell of the computer's memory has a number, called an *address,* associated with it. Typically, the first address of a computer's memory is numbered 0. On most computer systems, a "cell" is called a *byte.*

The computer uses memory for storing the instructions of your computer program, and also for storing the values of the variables that are associated with a program. So, if we declare a variable called count to be of type int, then the system would assign location(s) in memory to hold the value of count while the program is executing. This location might be at address 500, for example, inside the computer's memory.

Luckily, one of the advantages of higher-level programming languages such as C is that we don't need to concern ourselves with the particular memory addresses that are assigned to variables—they are automatically handled by the system. However, the knowledge that associated with each variable is a unique memory address will help you to understand the way pointers operate.

Whenever we apply the address operator to a variable in C, the value that is generated is the actual address of that variable inside the computer's memory. (Obviously, this is where the address operator gets its name.) So the statement

```
int_pointer = &count;
```

will assign to int_pointer the address in the computer's memory that has been assigned to the variable count. So if count were located at address 500, then this statement would assign the value 500 to int_pointer.

Applying the indirection operator to a pointer variable, as in the expression

```
*int_pointer
```

has the effect of treating the value contained in the pointer variable as a memory address. The value stored at that memory address is then fetched and interpreted in accordance with the type declared for the pointer variable. So if int_pointer were of type pointer to int, then the value stored in the memory address given by *int_pointer would be interpreted as an integer by the system.

At times, systems programmers must access particular locations inside the computer's memory. In such cases, this knowledge of the way that pointer variables operate will prove helpful.

This concludes the discussion on pointers in C. This topic is probably the hardest for novices to grasp. You should reread any sections of this chapter that still seem unclear before proceeding. Solving the exercises that follow will also help you to understand the material. Finally, for a more thorough (and advanced) treatment of pointers, consult *Topics in C Programming*, Kochan & Wood, Hayden Books, 1987.

◆ Exercises ◆

1. If you have access to a computer facility that supports the C programming language, type in and run the 15 programs presented in this chapter. Compare the output produced by each program with the output presented after each program.

2. Write a function called `insert_entry` to insert a new entry into a linked list. Have the procedure take as arguments a pointer to the list entry to be inserted (of type `struct entry` as defined in this chapter), and a pointer to an element in the list *after* which the new `entry` is to be inserted.

3. The function developed in the previous exercise only inserts an element after an existing element in the list, thereby preventing us from inserting a new entry at the front of the list. How can we use this same function and yet overcome this problem? (Hint: think about setting up a special structure to point to the beginning of the list.)

4. Write a function called `remove_entry` to remove an `entry` from a linked list. The sole argument to the procedure should be a pointer into the list. Have the function remove the entry *after* the one pointed to by the argument. (Why can't we remove the entry pointed to by the argument?) You will need to use the special structure you set up in the previous exercise to handle the special case of removing the first element from the list.

5. A *doubly linked list* is a list in which each entry contains a pointer to the preceding entry in the list as well as a pointer to the next entry in the list. Define the appropriate structure definition for a doubly linked list entry and then write a small program that implements a small doubly linked list and prints out the elements of the list.

6. Develop `insert_entry` and `remove_entry` functions for a doubly linked list that are similar in function to those developed in previous exercises for a singly linked list. Why can our `remove_entry` function now take as its argument a direct pointer to the entry to be removed from the list?

7. Write a pointer version of the `sort` function from Chapter 8. Make sure that pointers are exclusively used by the function, including as index variables in the loops.

8. Write a function called `sort3` to sort three integers into ascending order. (This function is not to be implemented with arrays.)

9. Rewrite the `read_line` function from Chapter 10 so that it uses a character pointer rather than an array.

10. Rewrite the `compare_strings` function from Chapter 10 to use character pointers instead of arrays.

11. Given the definition of a `date` structure as defined in this chapter, write a function called `date_update` that takes a pointer to a `date` structure as its argument and which updates the structure to the following day (see Program 9-4).

♦ ♦ ♦ **12** ♦ ♦ ♦

Operations on Bits

On several occasions, we have remarked that the C language was developed with systems programming applications in mind. Pointers are the perfect case in point, since they give the programmer an enormous amount of control over and access into the computer's memory. Along these same lines, systems programmers frequently must get in and "twiddle with the bits" of particular computer words. In this area, C once again shines above other programming languages, such as Pascal, because it provides a host of operators specifically designed for performing operations on individual bits.

In our discussions of the previous chapter, we talked about the concept of a *byte*. On most computer systems, a byte consists of 8 smaller units called *bits*. A bit can assume either of two values: 1 or 0. So a byte stored at address 1000 in a computer's memory, for example, might be conceptualized as a string of 8 binary digits as shown:

```
01100100
```

The rightmost bit of a byte is known as the *least significant* or *low-order* bit, while the leftmost bit is known as the *most significant* or *high-order* bit. If we treat the string of bits as an integer, then the rightmost bit of the above byte represents 2^0 or 1, the bit immediately to its left represents 2^1 or 2, the next bit 2^2 or 4, and so on. Therefore, the preceding binary number represents the value $2^2 + 2^5 + 2^6 = 4 + 32 + 64 = 100$ decimal.

The representation of negative numbers is handled slightly differently. Most computers choose to represent such numbers using a so-called "twos complement" notation. Using this notation, the leftmost bit represents the *sign* bit. If this bit is 1, the number is negative; otherwise, the bit is zero and the number is positive. The remaining bits represent the value of the number. In twos complement notation, the value -1 is represented by all bits being equal to 1:

```
11111111
```

A convenient way to convert a negative number from decimal to binary is to first add 1 to the value, express the absolute value of the result in binary, and then "complement" all the bits—i.e., change all 1s to 0s and 0s to 1s. So, for example, to convert -5 to binary, 1 is added which gives -4; 4 expressed in binary is 00000100, and complementing the bits produces 11111011.

To convert a negative number from binary back to decimal, first complement all of the bits, convert the result to decimal, change the sign of the result and then subtract 1.

Given the above discussion about twos complement representation, the largest positive number that can be stored into n bits is $2^{n-1}-1$. So in 8 bits, we can store a value up to $2^7 - 1$, or 127. Similarly, the smallest negative number that can be stored into n bits is -2^{n-1}, which in an 8-bit byte comes to -128. (Can you figure out why the largest positive and smallest negative values are not of the same magnitude?)

On many minicomputers, integers occupy two contiguous bytes, or 16 bits, in the computer's memory. The largest positive value that can therefore be stored into such an integer is $2^{15}-1$ or 32,767, while the smallest negative number that can be stored is -32,768.

In Chapter 4, we introduced the `unsigned` modifier and mentioned that it could be used to effectively increase the accuracy of a variable. This is because the leftmost bit is no longer needed to store the sign of the number, since we are only dealing with positive integers. This "extra" bit is used to increase the magnitude of the value stored in that variable by a factor of 2. More precisely, n bits can now be used to store values up to 2^n-1. On a machine that stores integers in 16 bits, this means that unsigned integers can range in value from 0 through 65,535.

♦ Bit Operators ♦

Now that we have completed some preliminaries, it is time to discuss the various bit operators that are available. The operators that C provides for manipulating bits are presented in Table 12-1.

TABLE 12-1. Bit Operators

Symbol	Operation
&	Bitwise AND
|	Bitwise Inclusive-OR
^	Bitwise Exclusive-OR
~	Ones Complement
<<	Left Shift
>>	Right Shift

All of the operators listed in Table 12-1, with the exception of the ones complement operator ~, are binary operators and as such take two operands. Bit operations can be performed on any type of integer value in C—be it short, long or unsigned—and on characters, but cannot be performed on floating point values.

The Bitwise AND Operator

When two values are ANDed in C, the binary representations of the values are "compared" bit by bit. Each corresponding bit that is a 1 in the first value *and* a 1 in the second value produces a 1 in the corresponding bit position of the result; anything else produces a 0. If $b1$ and $b2$ represent corresponding bits of the two operands, then the following table, called a *truth table*, shows the result of $b1$ ANDed with $b2$ for all possible values of $b1$ and $b2$.

$b1$	$b2$	$b1$ & $b2$
0	0	0
0	1	0
1	0	0
1	1	1

So, for example, if w1 and w2 are defined as ints, and w1 is set equal to 25 and w2 is set equal to 77, then the C statement

```
w3 = w1 & w2;
```

will assign the value 9 to w3. This can be more easily seen by treating the values of w1, w2, and w3 as binary numbers. Here we will assume that we are dealing with an int size of 16 bits.

w1	0000000000011001	25
w2	0000000001001101	& 77
w3	0000000000001001	9

If you think about the way the logical AND operator && works (TRUE only if both operands are TRUE), you will be able to more easily remember the way the bitwise AND operator works. Incidentally, make sure that you don't get these two operators confused! The logical AND operator && is used in logical expressions for producing a TRUE/FALSE result; it does not perform a bitwise AND.

Bitwise ANDing is frequently used for "masking" operations. That is, this operator can be used to easily set specific bits of a data item to 0. For example, the statement

```
w3 = w1 & 3;
```

will assign to w3 the value of w1 bitwise ANDed with the constant 3. This has the effect of setting all of the bits in w3, other than the rightmost two bits, to 0, and of "preserving" the rightmost two bits from w1.

As with all binary arithmetic operators in C, the binary bit operators can also be used as assignment operators by "tacking" on an equal sign. So the statement

```
word &= 15;
```

will perform the same function as

```
word = word & 15;
```

and will have the effect of setting all but the rightmost four bits of word to 0.

When using constants in performing bitwise operations, it is usually more convenient to express the constants in either octal or hexadecimal notation. The choice as to which to use is usually influenced by the size of the data that you are dealing with. For example, when dealing with 16-bit computers, hexadecimal notation is often used, since 16 is an even multiple of 4 (the number of bits in a hexadecimal digit).

The following program is presented to illustrate the bitwise AND operator. Since we are dealing with only positive values in this program, we have declared all integers as unsigned int variables.

Program 12-1

```
/* Demonstration of the bitwise AND operator */

main ()
{
    unsigned int   word1 = 077, word2 = 0150,
                   word3 = 0210;

    printf ("%o  ", word1 & word2);
    printf ("%o  ", word1 & word1);
    printf ("%o  ", word1 & word2 & word3);
    printf ("%o\n", word1 & 1);
}
```

Program 12-1 Output

```
50  77  10  1
```

You will recall that if an integer constant has a leading 0 it represents an octal (base 8) constant in C. Therefore, the three unsigned ints, word1, word2, and word3, are given initial *octal* values of 077, 0150, and 0210, respectively.

The first printf call displays octal 50 as the result of bitwise ANDing word1 with word2. The following depicts how this value was calculated:

```
word1    ... 000 111 111      077
word2    ... 001 101 000    & 0150
         ... 000 101 000      050
```

We have shown only the rightmost nine bits of the above values, since all bits to the left are 0. The binary numbers have been arranged in groups of three bits to make it easier to translate back and forth between binary and octal.

The second printf call results in the display of octal 77, which is the result of ANDing word1 with itself. By definition, any quantity *x*, when ANDed with itself, will produce *x*.

The third printf call displays the result of ANDing word1, word2, and word3 together. The operation of bitwise ANDing is such that it makes no difference whether an expression such as a & b & c is evaluated as (a & b) & c or as a & (b & c), but for the record, evaluation proceeds from left to right. It is left as an exercise to you to verify that the displayed result of octal 10 is the correct result of ANDing word1 with word2 with word3.

The final printf call has the effect of extracting the rightmost bit of word1. This is actually another way of testing if an integer is even or odd, since that rightmost bit of any odd integer is 1 and of any even integer is 0. Therefore when the if statement

```
if ( word1 & 1 )
   ...
```

gets executed, the expression will be TRUE if word1 is odd (since the result of the AND operation will be 1) and FALSE if it is even (since the result of the AND operation will be 0). (Note: On machines which use a ones complement representation for negative numbers, this will not work for negative integers.)

The Bitwise Inclusive-OR Operator

When two values are bitwise Inclusive-ORed in C, the binary representation of the two values are once again "compared" bit by bit. This time, each bit that is a 1 in the first value *or* a 1 in the second value will produce a 1 in the corresponding bit of the result. The truth table for the Inclusive-OR operator is shown next.

b1	b2	b1 | b2
0	0	0
0	1	1
1	0	1
1	1	1

So if `w1` is an unsigned int equal to octal 0431 and `w2` is an unsigned int equal to octal 0152, then a bitwise Inclusive-OR of `w1` and `w2` will produce a result of octal 0573 as shown:

```
w1    ... 100 011 001      0431
w2    ... 001 101 010   |  0152
      ... 101 111 011      0573
```

As was pointed out with the bitwise AND operator, be sure not to confuse the operation of bitwise ORing (|) with that of logical ORing (||), the latter operation being used to determine if either of two logical values is TRUE.

Bitwise Inclusive-ORing, frequently called just bitwise ORing, is used when it is desired to set some specified bits of a word to 1. For example, the statement

```
w1 = w1 | 07;
```

will set the three rightmost bits of `w1` to 1, regardless of the state of these bits before the operation was performed. Of course, we could have used a special assignment operator in the statement, as in

```
w1 |= 07;
```

We will defer presentation of a program example illustrating the use of the Inclusive-OR operator until later.

The Bitwise Exclusive-OR Operator

The bitwise Exclusive-OR operator, which is often called the XOR operator, works as follows: for corresponding bits of the two operands, if either bit is a 1—but not both—the corresponding bit of the result is a 1; otherwise it is a 0. The truth table for this operator is as shown.

b1	b2	b1 ^ b2
0	0	0
0	1	1
1	0	1
1	1	0

If `w1` and `w2`, were set equal to octal 0536 and octal 0266, respectively, then the result of `w1` Exclusive-ORed with `w2` would be octal 0750, as illustrated:

```
w1   ... 101 011 110      0536
w2   ... 010 110 110    ^ 0266
     ... 111 101 000      0750
```

One interesting property of the Exclusive-OR operator is that any value Exclusive-ORed with itself produces 0. This trick is frequently used by assembly language programmers as a fast way to set a value to 0, or to compare two values to see if they are equal. This method is not recommended for use in C programs, however, as it won't save any time and will most likely make the program more obscure.

Another interesting application of the Exclusive-OR operator is that it can be used to effectively exchange two values without the need for an extra memory location. We all know that normally we would interchange two integers called `i1` and `i2` with a sequence of statements such as

```
temp = i1;
i1 = i2;
i2 = temp;
```

(We assume in the above sequence of statements that `temp` has been appropriately declared.) Using the Exclusive-OR operator, we can exchange values without the need of the temporary storage location:

```
i1 ^= i2;
i2 ^= i1;
i1 ^= i2;
```

It is left as an exercise to you to verify that the above statements do in fact succeed in interchanging the values of `i1` and `i2`.

The Ones Complement Operator

The ones complement operator is a unary operator, and its effect is to simply "flip" the bits of its operand. So each bit of the operand that is a 1 is changed to a 0, and each bit that is a 0 is changed to a 1. The truth table is provided below simply for the sake of completeness.

b1	~b1
0	1
1	0

If w1 is an int 16 bits long, and is set equal to octal 0122457, then taking the ones complement of this value will produce a result of octal 0055320

```
w1    1 010 010 100 101 111        0122457
~w1   0 101 101 011 010 000        0055320
```

The ones complement operator (~) should not be confused with the arithmetic minus operator (-) or with the logical negation operator (!). So if w1 is defined as an int, and set equal to 0, then -w1 still results in 0. If we apply the ones complement operator to w1, we end up with w1 being set to all ones, which is -1 when treated as a signed value. Finally, applying the logical negation operator to w1 produces the result TRUE (1), since w1 is FALSE (0).

The ones complement operator is useful in operations where we don't know the precise bit size of the quantity that we are dealing with. Its use can help make a program more "portable"—i.e., less dependent on the particular computer that the program is running on, and therefore easier to get running on a different machine. For example, in order to set the low-order bit of an int called w1 to 0, we can AND w1 with an int consisting of all 1s except for a single 0 in the rightmost bit. So a statement in C such as

```
w1 &= 0177776;
```

will work fine on machines in which an integer is represented by 16 bits. However, on machines that represent integers using more than 16 bits, this statement will not produce the desired results.

If we replace the preceding statement with

```
w1 &= ~1;
```

then w1 will get ANDed with the correct value on any machine, since the ones complement of 1 will be calculated and will consist of as many leftmost one bits as are necessary to fill the size of an int (15 leftmost bits on a 16-bit integer machine, and 31 leftmost bits on a 32-bit integer machine).

Now it's time to present a program that summarizes the various bitwise operators presented thus far. Before proceeding, however, we should mention the precedences of the various operators. The AND, OR, and Exclusive-OR operators each have lower precedence than any of the arithmetic or relational operators, but higher precedence than the logical AND and logical OR operators. The bitwise AND is higher in precedence than the bitwise Exclusive-OR, which in turn is higher in precedence than the bitwise OR. The unary ones complement operator has higher precedence than *any* binary operator. For a summary of these operator precedences, the reader is once again respectfully referred to Appendix A.

Program 12-2

```
/* Bitwise operators illustrated */

main ()
{
    unsigned int  w1 = 0525, w2 = 0707, w3 = 0122;

    printf ("%o\t%o\t%o\n", w1 & w2, w1 | w2, w1 ^ w2);
    printf ("%o\t%o\t%o\n", ~w1, ~w2, ~w3);
    printf ("%o\t%o\t%o\n", w1 ^ w1, w1 & ~w2, w1 | w2 | w3);
    printf ("%o\t%o\n", w1 | w2 & w3, w1 | w2 & ~w3);
    printf ("%o\t%o\n", ~(~w1 & ~w2), ~(~w1 | ~w2));

    w1 ^= w2;
    w2 ^= w1;
    w1 ^= w2;
    printf ("w1 = %o, w2 = %o\n", w1, w2);
}
```

Program 12-2 Output

```
505      727      222
177252 177070   177655
0        20       727
527      725
727      505
w1 = 707, w2 = 525
```

(We used the tab character '\t' in the display of the program's result to help make the output more readable.)

You should work out each of the operations from Program 12-2 with a paper and pencil to verify that you understand how the results were obtained. The program was run on a computer that uses 16 bits to represent an int.

In the fourth printf call, it is important to remember that the bitwise AND operator has higher precendence than the bitwise OR, because this fact influences the resulting value of the expression.

The fifth printf call illustrates DeMorgan's rule, namely that ~(~a & ~b) is equal to a | b, and that ~(~a | ~b) is equal to a & b. The sequence of statements that follow next in the program verifies that the exchange operation works as discussed in the section on the Exclusive-OR operator.

Bitwise Operations on Different Sized Data Items

When a bitwise operation is performed between two values that are of different sizes (such as between a long int and a short int), the system aligns the operands on the right. If the shorter of the two items is a signed quantity, and the value is negative, then the sign is *extended* to the left to match the number of bits contained in the larger-sized value. So if the shorter value is negative, 1s are filled in on the left, and if the value is positive, then 0s are filled in. For example, if s were defined to be of type `short int` and occupied 16 bits on our particular computer and i were defined to be of type `int` and occupied 32 bits, then s would effectively be extended 16 bits to the left when a bitwise operation was performed between s and i. If s were negative, then these leftmost 16 bits would all be set to 1, otherwise they would all be set to 0.

If the smaller-sized data item is unsigned, it is always filled from the left with 0s when performing bitwise operations with larger-sized data items.

The Left Shift Operator

When a left shift operation is performed on a value, the bits contained in the value are literally shifted to the left. Associated with this operation is the number of places (bits) that the value is to be shifted. Bits that are shifted out through the high-order bit of the data item are lost, and 0s are always shifted in through the low-order bit of the value. So if w1 is equal to 3, then the expression

```
w1 = w1 << 1;
```

which can also be expressed as

```
w1 <<= 1;
```

will result in 3 being shifted 1 place to the left, which will result in 6 being assigned to w1:

```
w1          ... 000 011    03
w1 << 1  ... 000 110    06
```

The operand on the left of the << operator is the value to be shifted, while the operand on the right is the number of bit positions the value is to be shifted by. If we were to shift w1 one more place to the left, we would end up with octal 014 as the value of w1:

```
w1          ... 000 110     06
w1 << 1  ... 001 100     014
```

Left shifting actually has the effect of multiplying the value that is shifted by two. In fact, some C compilers will automatically perform multiplication by a power of two by left shifting the value the appropriate number of places, since shifting is a much faster operation than multiplication on most computers.

A program example illustrating the left shift operator will be presented after the right shift operator has been described.

The Right Shift Operator

As implied from its name, the right shift operator >> shifts the bits of a value to the right. Bits shifted out of the low-order bit of the value are lost. Right shifting an unsigned value will always result in 0s being shifted in on the left, i.e., through the high-order bits. What is shifted in on the left for signed values depends on the sign of the value that is being shifted and also on how this operation is implemented on your particular computer system. If the sign bit is 0 (meaning the value is positive), then 0s will be shifted in no matter what machine we are talking about. However if the sign bit is 1, then on some machines 1s will be shifted in, and on others 0s will be shifted in. This former type of operation is known as an *arithmetic* right shift, while the latter is known as a *logical* right shift.

So, for example, if w1 is an unsigned int, which is represented in 16 bits, and w1 is set equal to octal 0155667, then shifting w1 one place to the right with the statement

```
w1 >>= 1;
```

will set w1 equal to octal 0066733:

```
w1            1  101 101 110 110 111     0155667
w1 >> 1       0  110 110 111 011 011     0066733
```

If w1 were declared to be a (signed) int, then the same result would be produced on some computers, while, on others, the result would be 0166733 if the operation were performed as an arithmetic right shift.

It should be noted that the C language does not produce a defined result if an attempt is made to shift a value to the left or right by an amount that is greater than or equal to the number of bits in the size of the data item. So on a machine that represents integers in 32 bits, for example, shifting an integer to the left or right by 32 or more bits is not guaranteed to produce a defined result in your program.

Now it is time to put the left and right shift operators to work in an actual program example. Some computers have a single machine instruction to shift a value to the left if the shift count is positive and to the right if the shift count is negative. Let us now write a function in C to mimic this type of operation. We can have the function take two arguments: the value to be shifted and the shift count. If the shift count is positive, the value will be shifted left the designated number of places; otherwise, the value will be shifted right the number of places as specified by the absolute value of the shift count.

Program 12-3

```
/* Function to shift an unsigned int left if
   the count is positive, and right if negative */

unsigned int  shift (value, n)
unsigned int  value;
int           n;
{
    unsigned int  result;

    if ( n > 0 )      /* left shift */
        result = value << n;
    else              /* right shift */
        result = value >> -n;

    return (result);
}

main ()
{
    unsigned int  w1 = 0177777, w2 = 0444;

    printf ("%o\t%o\n", shift (w1, 5), w1 << 5);
    printf ("%o\t%o\n", shift (w1, -6), w1 >> 6);
    printf ("%o\t%o\n", shift (w2, 0), w2 >> 0);
    printf ("%o\n", shift (shift (w1, -3), 3));
}
```

Program 12-3 Output

```
177740 177740
1777    1777
444     444
177770
```

The shift function declares the type of the argument value to be unsigned int, thus ensuring that a right shift of value will be zero filled (i.e., performed as a logical right shift).

If the value of n, which is the shift count, is greater than zero, the function shifts value left n bits. If n is negative (or zero), the function performs a right shift, where the number of places that the value is shifted is obtained by negating the value of n. In either case, the result of the shift is assigned to the variable result, whose value is then returned by the function.

The first call to the shift function from the main routine specifies that the value of w1 is to be left shifted five bits. The printf call that displays the result of the call to the shift function also displays the result of directly shifting w1 left five places so that these values can be compared.

The second call to the shift function has the effect of shifting w1 six places to the right. The result returned by the function is identical to the result obtained by directly shifting w1 to the right six places, as verified by the program's output.

In the third call to shift, a shift count of 0 is specified. In this case, the shift function will perform a right shift of value by 0 bits, which, as you can see from the program's output, has no effect on the value.

The last printf call illustrates nested function calls to the shift function. The innermost call to shift is executed first. This call specifies that w1 is to be shifted right three places. The result of this function call, which is 0017777, is then passed to the shift function to be shifted to the left three places. As you can see from the program's output, this has the net effect of setting the low-order three bits of w1 to zero. (Of course, we know by now that this could also have been done by simply ANDing w1 with ~7.)

For the next program example, which ties together some of the bit operations we have presented in this chapter, we will develop a function to rotate a value to the left or right. The process of rotation is similar to shifting, except that when a value is rotated to the left, the bits that are shifted out of the high-order bits are shifted back into the low-order bits. When a value is rotated to the right, the bits that are shifted out of the low-order bits of the value are shifted back into the high-order bits. So, if we are dealing with 16-bit unsigned integers, the value octal 0100000 rotated to the left by one bit would produce octal 0000001, since the 1 from the sign bit that would normally be lost by a left shift of one bit would be brought around and shifted back into the low-order bit.

We will have our function take two arguments, the first, the value to be rotated, and the second, the number of bits the object is to be rotated by. If this second argument is positive, then we will rotate the value to the left; otherwise we will rotate the value to the right.

We can adopt a fairly straightforward approach to implementing our rotate function. For example, in order to compute the result of rotating x to the left by n bits, where x is of type int and n ranges from 0 to the number of bits in an int minus 1, we can extract the leftmost n bits of x, shift x to the left by n bits, and then put the extracted bits back into x at the right. A similar algorithm can be also used to implement the right rotate function.

The program that follows implements the rotate function using the algorithm described above. This function makes the assumption that an int uses 16 bits on the computer. In an exercise at the end of this chapter, we will discuss a way to modify the function so that this assumption does not have to be made.

The function handles the special cases where the rotate count is specified as 0, -16, or 16. In either of these three cases, the function returns the original value (which happens to be the correct answer) as the function result.

Program 12-4

```
/* Function to rotate an unsigned int left or right */

unsigned int  rotate (value, n)
unsigned int  value;
int           n;
{
    unsigned int  result, bits;

    if  ( n == 0  ||  n == -16  ||  n == 16 )
        return (value);
    else if ( n > 0 )      /* left rotate */
    {
        bits = value >> (16 - n);
        result = value << n  |  bits;
    }
    else                   /* right rotate */
    {
        n = -n;
        bits = value << (16 - n);
        result = value >> n  |  bits;
    }

    return (result);
}

main ()
{
    unsigned int  w1 = 0xa1b5, w2 = 0xff22;

    printf ("%x\n", rotate (w1, 4));
    printf ("%x\n", rotate (w1, -4));
    printf ("%x\n", rotate (w2, 8));
    printf ("%x\n", rotate (w2, -2));
    printf ("%x\n", rotate (w1, 0));
}
```

Program 12-4 Output

```
1b5a
5a1b
22ff
bfc8
a1b5
```

An n-bit rotation to the left is divided into three steps by the function. First, the n leftmost bits of value are extracted and shifted to the right. This is done by shifting value to the right by the size of an int (in our case, 16) minus n. Next, value is shifted n bits to the left, and finally, the extracted bits are ORed back in. A similar procedure is followed to rotate value to the right.

In the main routine, we resorted to the use of hexadecimal notation for a change. The first call to the rotate function specifies that the value of w1 is to be rotated four bits to the left. As can be seen from the program's output, the hexadecimal value 1b5a is returned by the rotate function, which is in fact a1b5 rotated to the left four bits (which conveniently happens to be the number of bits in a hexadecimal digit).

The second call to the rotate function has the effect of rotating the value of w1 four bits to the right; and as you can see from the program's output, the 5 that was in the low-order four bits of w1 was correctly rotated around into the high-order four bits.

The next two calls to the rotate function do similar things with the value of w2, and are fairly self-explanatory. The last call to rotate specifies a rotate count of 0. The program's output verifies that in such a case the function simply returns the value unchanged.

• Bit Fields •

With the bit operators discussed above, we can proceed to perform all sorts of sophisticated operations on bits. Bit operations are frequently performed on data items that contain "packed" information. Just as a short int can be used to conserve memory space on many computers, so can we pack information into the bits of a byte or word if we do not need to use the entire byte or word to represent the data. For example, flags that are used for a boolean TRUE or FALSE condition can be represented in a single bit on a computer. Declaring a variable that will be used as a flag will use at least 8 bits (one byte), and most likely at least 16 bits on most computer systems. And if we needed to store many flags inside a large table, then the amount of memory that would be "wasted" could become significant.

There are two methods in C that can be used to pack information together to make better use of memory. One way is to simply represent the data inside a normal int, for example, and then access the desired bits of the int using the bit operators we have just described. Another way is to define a structure of packed information using a C construct known as a *bit field*.

To illustrate how the first method can be used, suppose we needed to pack five data values into a single word because we had to maintain a very large table of these values in memory. Assume that three of these data values are flags, which we will call *f1*, *f2*, and *f3*; the fourth value is an integer called *type* which ranges from 1 through 12; and the final value an integer called *index*, which ranges from 0 to 500.

In order to store the values of the flags *f1*, *f2*, and *f3*, we would only require three bits of storage, one bit for the TRUE/FALSE value of each flag. To store the value of the integer *type*, which ranges from 1 to 12, would require four bits of storage. Finally, to store the value of the integer *index*, which can assume a value from 0 to 500, we would need nine bits. Therefore, the total amount of storage needed to store the five data values *f1*, *f2*, *f3*, *type*, and *index*, would (conveniently) be 16 bits. We could define an integer variable that could be used to contain all five of these values, as in

```
unsigned int   packed_data;
```

and could then arbitrarily assign specific bits or *fields* inside `packed_data` to be used to store the five data values. One such assignment is depicted in Fig. 12-1, which assumes that the size of `packed_data` is 16 bits. If it were larger than 16 bits, then we could still conceptualize these field assignments as occupying the 16 rightmost bits of the integer.

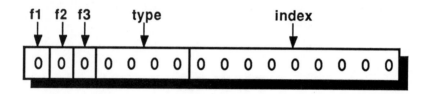

Fig. 12-1. Bit field assignments in `packed_data`

We can now apply the correct sequence of bit operations to `packed_data` to set and retrieve values to and from the various fields of the integer. For example, we can set the *type* field of `packed_data` to 7 by shifting the value 7 the appropriate number of places to the left and then ORing it into `packed_data`:

```
packed_data |= 7 << 9;
```

Or we can set the *type* field to the value n, where n is between 0 and 15, by the statement

```
packed_data |= n << 9;
```

(To ensure that n is between 0 and 15, we can AND it with 0xf before it is shifted.) Of course, the preceding statements will work only if we know that the *type* field is zero, otherwise we must zero it first by ANDing it with a value (frequently called a mask) that consists of 0s in the four bit locations of the *type* field and 1s everywhere else:

```
packed_data &= 0xe1ff;
```

To save us the bother of having to explicitly calculate the preceding mask, and also to make the operation independent of the size of an integer, the following statement could be used instead to set the type field to zero:

```
packed_data &= ~(0xf << 9);
```

Combining the statements described above, we can set the *type* field of packed_data to the value contained in the four low-order bits of n, irrespective of any value previously stored in this field, with the statement

```
packed_data = (packed_data & ~(0xf << 9)) | ((n & 0xf) << 9);
```

(Some of the parentheses are superfluous but were added to aid readability.)

You can see how complex the above expression is for accomplishing the relatively simple task of setting the bits in the *type* field to a specified value. Extracting a value from one of these fields is not as bad: the field can be shifted into the low-order bits of the word and then ANDed with a mask of the appropriate bit length. So, to extract the *type* field of packed_data and assign it to n, the statement

```
n = (packed_data >> 9) & 0xf;
```

will do the trick.

The C language does provide a more convenient way of dealing with bit fields. This method employs the use of a special syntax in the structure definition that allows you to define a field of bits and assign a name to that field. Whenever the term "bit fields" is applied to C, it is this approach that is referenced.

In order to define the bit field assignments previously mentioned, we can define a structure called packed_struct, for example, as follows:

```
struct   packed_struct
{
    unsigned int   f1:1;
    unsigned int   f2:1;
    unsigned int   f3:1;
    unsigned int   type:4;
    unsigned int   index:9;
};
```

The structure packed_struct is defined to contain five members. The first member, called f1, is an unsigned int. The :1 that immediately follows the member name specifies that this member is to be stored in one bit. The flags f2 and f3 are similarly defined as being a single bit in length. The member type is defined to occupy four bits, while the member index is defined as being nine bits long.

The C compiler automatically packs the preceding bit field definitions together. The nice thing about this approach is that the fields of a variable defined to be of type `packed_struct` can now be referenced in the same convenient way normal structure members are referenced. So, if we were to declare a variable called `packed_data` as follows:

```
struct packed_struct   packed_data;
```

then we could easily set the `type` field of `packed_data` to 7 with the simple statement

```
packed_data.type = 7;
```

or we could set this field to the value of `n` with the similar statement

```
packed_data.type = n;
```

In this last case, we needn't worry about whether the value of `n` is too large to fit into the `type` field; only the low-order four bits of `n` will be assigned to `packed_data.type`.

Extraction of the value from a bit field is also automatically handled, so the statement

```
n = packed_data.type;
```

will extract the `type` field from `packed_data` (automatically shifting it into the low-order bits as required) and assign it to `n`.

Bit fields can be used in normal expressions, and are automatically converted to integers. So the statement

```
i = packed_data.index / 5 + 1;
```

is perfectly valid, as is

```
if   ( packed_data.f2 )
   ...
```

which tests if flag `f2` is TRUE or FALSE. One thing worth noting about bit fields is that there is no guarantee as to whether the fields are assigned inside the word from left to right or from right to left. On the PDP-11, bit fields are assigned from right to left, which means that `f1` would be in the low-order bit position, `f2` in the bit position immediately to the left of `f1`, and so on. This should not present a problem unless you are dealing with data that was created by a different program or by a different machine. In such cases, you must know how the bit fields are assigned and make the declarations appropriately. (We could have defined the structure `packed_struct` as

```
struct   packed_struct
{
     unsigned int   index:9;
     unsigned int   type:4;
     unsigned int   f3:1;
     unsigned int   f2:1;
     unsigned int   f1:1;
};
```

to achieve the same representation on the PDP-11 as depicted in Fig. 12-1.)

We can also include "normal" data types within a structure that contains bit fields. So if we wanted to define a structure that contained an int, a char, and two one-bit flags, the following definition would be valid:

```
struct   table_entry
{
     int               count;
     char              c;
     unsigned int   f1:1;
     unsigned int   f2:1;
};
```

Certain points are worth mentioning with respect to bit fields. Bit fields may always be treated as unsigned on some machines, whether or not they are declared as such. Furthermore, some C compilers do not support bit fields that are larger than the size of a word. A bit field cannot be dimensioned; that is, we cannot have an array of fields, such as flag:1[5]. Finally, we cannot take the address of a bit field, and since this is the case, there is obviously no such thing as a variable of type "pointer to bit field."

Bit fields are packed into words as they appear in the structure definition. If a particular field does not fit into a word, then the remainder of the word is skipped and the field is placed into the next word. If the following structure definition were used

```
struct   bits
{
     unsigned int   f1:1;
     int               word;
     unsigned int   f3:1;
};
```

then f1 and f2 would not get packed into the same word since the definition of word comes between them. The C compiler will *not* rearrange the bit field definitions to try to optimize storage space.

A bit field that has no name can be specified to cause bits inside a word to be "skipped." So the definition

```
struct   x_entry
{
    unsigned int   type:4;
    unsigned int   :3;
    unsigned int   count:9;
};
```

would define a structure x_entry that contained a four-bit field called type and a nine-bit field called count. The unnamed field specifies that three bits separate the type from the count field.

A final point concerning the specification of fields concerns the special case of an unnamed field of length 0. This may be used to force alignment of the next field in the structure at the start of a word boundary.

This concludes our discussion of bit operations in C. You can see how much power and flexibility the C language provides for the efficient manipulation of bits. In the next chapter, we will see how another powerful feature known as the *preprocessor* can be used to effectively customize the C language to one's particular tastes and to enable programs to be developed that are easier to write and to read.

♦ Exercises ♦

1. If you have access to a computer facility that supports the C programming language, type in and run the four programs presented in this chapter. Compare the output produced by each program with the output presented after each program.

2. Write a program that determines whether your particular computer performs an arithmetic or a logical right shift.

3. Modify the `rotate` function so that rotate counts greater than 16 (or less than -16) produce the correct results.

4. Given that the expression `~0` produces an integer that contains all 1s, write a function called `int_size` that returns the number of bits contained in an `int` on your particular machine.

5. Using the result obtained in the exercise above, modify the `rotate` function from Program 12-4 so that it no longer makes any assumptions about the size of an `int`.

6. Write a function that implements the `rotate` function without making an assumption about the size of an `int` or how right shifts are performed (that is, arithmetic or logical).

7. Write a program that determines whether bit fields are packed left to right or right to left on your machine.

8. Write a function called `bit_search` that looks for the occurrence of a specified pattern of bits inside an `int`. The function should take three arguments and should be called as shown:

   ```
   bit_search (source, pattern, n)
   ```

   The function will search the integer `source`, starting at the leftmost bit, to see if the rightmost n bits of `pattern` occur in `source`. If the pattern is found, then have the function return the number of the bit that the pattern begins at, where the leftmost bit is bit number 0. If the pattern is not found, then have the function return -1. So, for example, the call

   ```
   index = bit_search (0xe1f4, 0x5, 3);
   ```

   will cause the `bit_search` function to search the number 0xe1f4 (= 1110 0001 1111 0100 binary) for the occurrence of the three-bit pattern 0x5 (= 101 binary). The function would return 11 to indicate that the pattern was found in the source beginning with bit number 11.

Make sure that the function makes no assumptions about the size of an int (see Exercise 4, this chapter).

9. Write a function called `bit_set` to set a specified set of bits to a particular value. The function should take four arguments: a pointer to an int in which the specified bits are to be set; another int containing the value that the specified bits are to be set to, right adjusted in the int; a third int that specifies the starting bit number (with the leftmost bit numbered 0); and a fourth int specifying the size of the field. So the call

```
bit_set (&x, 0, 2, 5);
```

would have the effect of setting the five bits contained in x, beginning with the third bit from the left (bit number 2), to zero. Similarly, the call

```
bit_set (&x, 0x55, 0, 8);
```

would set the eight leftmost bits of x to hexadecimal 55.

Make no assumptions about the particular size of an int (refer to Exercise 4, this chapter).

C H A P T E R

•   •   •   **13**   •   •   •

The Preprocessor

This chapter describes yet another unique feature of the C language that is not found in most other higher-level programming languages. The C preprocessor provides the tools that enable the programmer to develop programs that are easier to develop, easier to read, easier to modify, and easier to transport to a different computer system. The programmer can also use the preprocessor to literally customize the C language to suit a particular programming application or to satisfy one's own programming style. If you have ever had any dealings with a macro processor, you will be one step ahead in our discussions of the C preprocessor.

The preprocessor is a part of the C compilation process that recognizes special statements that may be interspersed throughout a C program. As its name implies, the preprocessor actually analyzes these statements *before* analysis of the C program itself takes place. Preprocessor statements are identified by the presence of a pound sign, #, which must be the *first* character on the line. As you will see, preprocessor statements have a syntax that is slightly different from that of normal C statements. We will begin by examining the the #define statement.

• The **#define** Statement •

One of the primary uses of the #define statement is for assigning symbolic names to program constants. The preprocessor statement

```
#define    TRUE    1
```

defines the name TRUE and makes it equivalent to the value 1. The name TRUE can subsequently be used anywhere in the program where the constant 1 could be used. Whenever this name appears, its defined value of 1 will be automatically substituted into the program by the preprocessor. For example, we might have the following C statement that uses the defined name TRUE:

```
game_over = TRUE;
```

This statement would assign the value of TRUE to game_over. We don't need to concern ourselves with the actual value that we defined for TRUE, but since we do know that we defined it to be 1, the preceding statement would have the effect of assigning 1 to game_over. The preprocessor statement

```
#define    FALSE    0
```

would define the name FALSE and would make its subsequent use in the program equivalent to specifying the value 0. Therefore, the statement

```
game_over = FALSE;
```

would assign the value of FALSE to game_over, and the statement

```
if ( game_over == FALSE )
   . . .
```

would compare the value of game_over against the defined value of FALSE. Just about the only place that we *cannot* used a defined name is inside a character string; so the statement

```
char   *char_pointer = "TRUE";
```

sets char_pointer pointing to the string "TRUE" and not to the string "1".

A defined name is *not* a variable. Therefore, we cannot assign a value to it. Whenever a defined name is used in a program, whatever appears to the right of the defined name in the #define statement gets automatically substituted into the program by the preprocessor.

You will notice that the #define statement has a special syntax: there is no equal sign used to assign the value 1 to TRUE. Furthermore, a semicolon does *not* appear at the end of the statement. Soon you will understand why this special syntax exists. But first, let's take a look at a small program that uses the TRUE and FALSE defines as illustrated above. The function is_even in the following program simply returns TRUE if its argument is even and FALSE if its argument is odd.

Program 13-1

```
#define    TRUE     1
#define    FALSE    0
```

```
/* Function to determine if an integer is even */

int   is_even (number)
int   number;
{
    int   answer;

    if ( number % 2 == 0 )
        answer = TRUE;
    else
        answer = FALSE;

    return (answer);
}

main ()
{
    if ( is_even (17) == TRUE )
        printf ("yes ");
    else
        printf ("no ");

    if ( is_even (20) == TRUE )
        printf ("yes\n");
    else
        printf ("no\n");
}
```

Program 13-1 Output

```
no yes
```

The #define statements appear first in the program. This is not required; they can appear *anywhere* in the program. All that is required is that a name be defined before it is referenced by the program. Defined names do not behave the same way that variables do: There is no such thing as a "local" define. Once a name has been defined in a program, either inside a function or outside a function, it can subsequently be used anywhere in the program. Most programmers tend to group their defines at the beginning of the program (or inside an *include* file[†] where they may be quickly referenced.

---

† Read on to learn how defines can be set up inside special files that you can "include" in your program.

The defined name NULL is frequently used by programmers to represent the null pointer.[†] By including a definition such as

```
#define   NULL   0
```

in a program, we can then write more readable statements, such as

```
while ( list_pointer != (struct entry *) NULL )
      . . .
```

to set up a while loop that will execute as long as the value of list_pointer is not equal to the null pointer.

As another example of the use of a defined name, suppose we wanted to write three functions to find the area of a circle, the circumference of a circle, and the volume of a sphere of a given radius. Since all of these functions need to use the constant π, which is not a particularly easy constant to remember, it would make sense to define the value of this constant once at the start of the program and then use this value where needed in each function.

Program 13-2

```
/* Function to calculate the area and circumference of a
   circle, and the volume of a sphere of a given radius   */

#define   PI        3.141592654

double   area (r)
double   r;
{
    return ( PI * r * r );
}

double   circumference (r)
double   r;
{
    return ( 2.0 * PI * r );
}

double   volume (r)
double r;
{
    return ( 4.0 / 3.0   *   PI * r * r * r );
}
```

---

† NULL is probably already defined on your system inside a file named stdio.h. We talked briefly about this file in Chapter 10.

```
main ()
{
    printf ("radius = 1: %.4f    %.4f    %.4f\n",
            area(1.0), circumference(1.0), volume(1.0));

    printf ("radius = 4.98: %.4f    %.4f    %.4f\n",
            area(4.98), circumference(4.98), volume(4.98));
}
```

Program 13-2 Output

```
radius = 1: 3.1416    6.2832    4.1888
radius = 4.98: 77.9128    31.2903    517.3403
```

The symbolic name PI is defined as the value 3.141592654 at the beginning of the program. Subsequent use of the name PI inside the area, circumference, and volume functions has the effect of causing its defined value to be automatically substituted at the appropriate point.

Assignment of a constant to a symbolic name frees us from having to remember the particular constant value every time we wish to use it in a program. Furthermore, if we ever needed to change the value of the constant (if perhaps we found out that we were using the wrong value, for example), then we would only have to change the value in one place in the program: in the #define statement. Without this approach, we would have to otherwise search throughout the program and explicitly change the value of the constant whenever it was used.

You may have realized that all of the defines that we have shown so far (TRUE, FALSE, and PI) have been written in capital letters. This is not required, but has more or less become a convention among C programmers. The reason this is done is to visually distinguish a defined value from a variable. By adopting the convention that all defined names be capitalized, it then becomes easy to determine when a name represents a variable and when it represents a defined name.

Program Extendability

Using a defined name for a constant value helps to make programs more readily extendable. For example, we know that when we define an array, we must specify the number of elements in the array—either explicitly or implicitly (by specifying a list of initializers). Subsequent program statements will likely use the knowledge of the number of elements contained inside the array. For example, if the array data_values were defined in a program as follows:

```
float   data_values[1000];
```

then there is a good chance that we would see statements in the program that used the fact that `data_values` contains 1000 elements. For instance, in a `for` loop

```
for ( i = 0;  i < 1000;  ++i )
    . . .
```

we would use the value 1000 as an upper bound for sequencing through the elements of the array. A statement such as

```
if ( index  > 999 )
    . . .
```

might also be used in the program to test if an index value exceeded the maximum size of the array.

Now suppose that we had to increase the size of the `data_values` array from 1000 to 2000 elements. This would necessitate changing all statements which used the fact that `data_values` contained 1000 elements.

A better way of dealing with array bounds, which makes programs easier to extend, is to define a name for the upper array bound. So, if we define a name such as `MAXIMUM_DATA_VALUES` with an appropriate `#define` statement:

```
#define   MAXIMUM_DATA_VALUES     1000
```

then we can subsequently define the `data_values` array to contain `MAXIMUM_DATA_VALUES` elements with the following program line:

```
float  data_values[MAXIMUM_DATA_VALUES];
```

Statements that use the upper array bound can also make use of this defined name. To sequence through the elements in `data_values`, for example, the `for` statement

```
for ( i = 0;  i < MAXIMUM_DATA_VALUES;  ++i )
    . . .
```

could be used. To test if an index value were greater than the upper bound of the array, we could write

```
if  ( index > MAXIMUM_DATA_VALUES - 1 )
    . . .
```

and so on. The nicest thing about the preceding approach is that we can now easily change the size of the `data_values` array to 2000 elements by simply changing the definition:

```
#define  MAXIMUM_DATA_VALUES   2000
```

And if the program was written to use MAXIMUM_DATA_VALUES in all cases where the size of the array was used, the preceding definition would probably be *the only statement in the program that would have to be changed.*

Program Portability

Another nice use of the define is that it helps to make programs more portable from one computer system to another. At times, it may be necessary to use constant values that are related to the particular computer that the program is running on. This might have to do with the use of a particular computer memory address, or the number of bits contained in a computer word, for example. You will recall that our rotate function from Program 12-4 used the knowledge that an int contained 16 bits on the machine that the program was executed on. If we wanted to execute this program on a different machine, such as on the VAX-11, where an int contains 32 bits, then the rotate function would not work correctly. Study the following code.

```
#define  INT_SIZE  16   /*** machine dependent !!! ***/

/* Function to rotate an unsigned int left or right */

unsigned int  rotate (value, n)
unsigned int  value;
int           n;
{
    unsigned int  result, bits;

    if ( n == 0  ||  n == INT_SIZE  ||  n == -INT_SIZE )
        return (value);
    else if ( n > 0 )      /* left rotate */
    {
        bits = value >> (INT_SIZE - n);
        result = value << n  |  bits;
    }
    else                        /* right rotate */
    {
        n = -n;
        bits = value << (INT_SIZE - n);
        result = value >> n  |  bits;
    }

    return (result);
}
```

In cases where the program *must* be written to make use of machine dependent values (and we know that we could have developed our `rotate` function so that it did not have to rely on a constant value for the number of bits contained in an `int`), it makes sense to isolate such dependencies from the program as much as possible. The `#define` statement can help significantly in this respect. For example, the version of the `rotate` function shown previously would be easier to port to another machine, even though it is a rather simple case in point.

More Advanced Types of Definitions

A definition for a name can include more than a simple constant value. It can include an expression, and, as we will see shortly, just about anything else!

If you're working with linked lists, and each element of the list is of type `struct entry`, then the following define may be convenient:

```
#define  NULLPTR   (struct entry *) 0
```

Here `NULLPTR` is defined to be a null `entry` structure pointer. Now you can write an `if` statement to see if `list_pointer` is null, like this:

```
if ( list_pointer == NULLPTR )
    printf ("Entry not found in list\n");
```

The following defines the name `TWO_PI` as the product of 2.0 and 3.141592654:

```
#define  TWO_PI   2.0 * 3.141592654
```

We can subsequently use this defined name anywhere in a program where the expression "2.0 * 3.141592654" would be valid. So we could have replaced the `return` statement of the `circumference` function from the previous program with the following statement, for example:

```
return ( TWO_PI * r );
```

Whenever a defined name is encountered in a C program, *everything* that appears to the right of the defined name in the #define statement is literally substituted for the name at that point in the program. So, when the C preprocessor encounters the name `TWO_PI` in the above `return` statement, it substitutes for this name whatever appeared in the `#define` statement for this name. Therefore, `2.0 * 3.141592654` is literally substituted by the preprocessor whenever the defined name `TWO_PI` occurs in the program.

The fact that the preprocessor performs a literal text substitution whenever the defined name occurs explains why you don't usually want to end your `#define` statement with a semicolon. If you did, then the semicolon would also

be substituted into the program wherever the defined name appeared. So if we
had defined PI as

```
#define   PI            3.141592654;
```

and then wrote

```
return ( 2.0 * PI * r );
```

the preprocessor would replace the occurrence of the defined name PI by
3.141592654;. The compiler would therefore see this statement as

```
return ( 2.0 * 3.141592654; * r );
```

after the preprocessor had made its substitution, which would result in a syntax
error.

A preprocessor definition does not have to be a valid C expression in its
own right—just so long as wherever it is used the resulting expression is valid.
For instance, the definition

```
#define   LEFT_SHIFT_8     << 8
```

is legitimate, even though what appears after LEFT_SHIFT_8 is not a syntacti-
cally valid expression. We can use our definition of LEFT_SHIFT_8 in a statement such as

```
x = y   LEFT_SHIFT_8;
```

to shift the contents of y to the left eight bits and assign the result to x. Of a
much more practical nature, we can set up the definitions

```
#define   AND          &&
#define   OR           ||
```

and then write expressions such as

```
if ( x > 0   AND   x < 10 )
    . . .
```

and

```
if ( y == 0   OR   y == value )
    . . .
```

We can even include a define for the equality test:

```
#define  EQUALS     ==
```

and then write the statement

```
if  ( y  EQUALS 0  OR  y EQUALS value )
    . . .
```

thus removing the very real possibility of mistakenly using a single equals sign for the equality test, as well as improving the statement's readability.

To make things even more interesting, a defined value can itself reference another defined value. So the two defines

```
#define  PI        3.141592654
#define  TWO_PI     2.0 * PI
```

are perfectly valid. The name TWO_PI is defined in terms of the previously defined name PI, thus obviating the need to spell out the value 3.141592654 again.

Good use of defines will oftentimes reduce the need for comments within the program. Consider the following statement:

```
if ( year % 4 == 0  &&  year % 100 != 0  ||  year % 400 == 0 )
    . . .
```

We know from previous programs in this book that the above expression tests if the variable year is a leap year or not. Now consider the following define and the subsequent if statement:

```
#define  IS_LEAP_YEAR    year % 4 == 0  &&  year % 100 != 0 \
                    || year % 400 == 0

    . . .
if  ( IS_LEAP_YEAR )
    . . .
```

Normally, the preprocessor assumes that a definition is contained on a single line of the program. If a second line is needed, then the last character on the line must be a backslash character. This character signals a continuation to the preprocessor, and is otherwise ignored. The same holds true for more than one continuation line; each line to be continued must be ended with a backslash character.

The preceding if statement is far easier to understand than the one shown directly before it. There is no need for a comment as the statement is self-explanatory. The purpose that the define IS_LEAP_YEAR serves is analogous to that served by a function. We could have used a call to a function called is_leap_year to achieve the same degree of readability. The choice of which to use in this case is completely subjective. Of course, the is_leap_year function could be made more general than the above define, since it could be written to take an argument. This would enable us to test if the value of any variable were a leap year and not just the variable `year` as the `IS_LEAP_YEAR` define restricts us to. Actually, we *can* write a definition to take one or more arguments, which leads us to our next point of discussion.

`IS_LEAP_YEAR` can be defined to take an argument called `y` as follows:

```
#define  IS_LEAP_YEAR(y)    y % 4 == 0  &&  y % 100 != 0  \
                         || y % 400 == 0
```

Unlike a function, we do not define the type of the argument `y` here, since we are merely performing a literal text substitution and not invoking a function. Pay careful attention to note that no spaces are permitted between the defined name and the left parenthesis of the argument list.

With the above definition, we can write a statement such as

```
if ( IS_LEAP_YEAR (year) )
    . . .
```

to test if the value of `year` were a leap year or not, or

```
if ( IS_LEAP_YEAR (next_year) )
    . . .
```

to test if the value of `next_year` were a leap year or not. In the preceding statement, the definition for `IS_LEAP_YEAR` would be directly substituted inside the `if` statement, with the argument `next_year` replacing `y` wherever it appeared in the definition. So the `if` statement would actually be seen by the compiler as

```
if ( next_year % 4 == 0  &&  next_year % 100 != 0
        || next_year % 400 == 0 )
    . . .
```

In C, definitions are frequently called *macros*. This terminology is more often applied to definitions which take one or more arguments. An advantage of implementing something in C as a macro, as opposed to as a function, is that in the former case the type of the argument is not important. For example, consider a macro called `SQUARE` that simply squares its argument. The definition

```
#define  SQUARE(x)   x * x
```

enables us to subsequently write statements, such as

```
y = SQUARE (v);
```

to assign the value of v^2 to y. The point to be made here is that v can be of type int, or of type long, or of type float, for example, and the *same* macro can be used. If SQUARE were implemented as a function, we would need a different function for each argument type. One thing to bear in mind about macro definitions: since they are directly substituted into the program by the preprocessor, they will inevitably use more memory space than an equivalently defined function. On the other hand, since a function takes time to call and to return, this "overhead" is avoided when a macro definition is used instead.

While the macro definition for SQUARE is straightforward, there is an interesting pitfall that you must be careful to avoid when defining macros. As we have described, the statement

```
y = SQUARE (v);
```

will assign the value of v^2 to y. What do you think would happen in the case of the statement

```
y = SQUARE (v + 1);                    ?
```

This statement will *not* assign the value of $(v + 1)^2$ to y as you would expect. Since the preprocessor performs a literal text substitution of the argument into the macro definition, the preceding expression would actually be evaluated as

```
y = v + 1 * v + 1;
```

which would obviously not produce the expected results. In order to handle this situation properly, parentheses are needed in the definition of the SQUARE macro:

```
#define  SQUARE(x)    (x) * (x)
```

While the above definition might look strange, remember that it is the entire expression as given to the SQUARE macro that will be literally substituted wherever x appears in the definition. With our new macro definition for SQUARE, the statement

```
y = SQUARE (v + 1);
```

will then be correctly evaluated as

```
y = (v + 1) * (v + 1);
```

The conditional expression operator can be particularly handy when defining macros. The following defines a macro called MAX that gives the maximum of two values:

```
#define  MAX(a,b)    ( ((a) > (b)) ? (a) : (b) )
```

This macro enables us to subsequently write statements such as

```
limit = MAX (x + y, min_value);
```

which would assign to `limit` the maximum of `x + y` and `min_value`. Parentheses were placed around the entire `MAX` definition to ensure that an expression such as

```
MAX (x, y) * 100
```

gets evaluated properly; and parentheses were individually placed around each argument to ensure that expressions such as

```
MAX (x & y, z)
```

get correctly evaluated.

The following macro can be used to test if a character is a lowercase character:

```
#define  IS_LOWER_CASE(x)   ( ((x) >= 'a') && ((x) <= 'z') )
```

and thereby permits expressions such as

```
if ( IS_LOWER_CASE (c) )
       . . .
```

to be written. We can even use this macro in a subsequent macro definition to convert a character from lowercase to uppercase, leaving any non-lowercase character unchanged:

```
#define  TO_UPPER(x) ( IS_LOWER_CASE (x) ? (x) - 'a' + 'A' : (x) )
```

The program loop

```
while ( *string != '\0' )
{
     *string = TO_UPPER (*string);
     ++string;
}
```

would sequence through the characters pointed to by `string`, converting any lowercase characters in the string to uppercase.

After you have programmed in C for a while, you will find yourself developing your own set of macros that you will want to use in each of your programs. On most systems, there are many predefined macros that are available to the programmer. Many of these macros are written with lowercase letters, thereby making them indistinguishable from function calls to the user. For example, the getchar "function" that we used in Chapter 10 to read a single character from the terminal is actually implemented under UNIX as a macro.

♦ The #include Statement ♦

As we mentioned in the preceding paragraph, after you have developed several programs in C, you will probably begin to collect a set of macros that you will want to use in each of your programs. But instead of having to type these macros into each new program that you write, the preprocessor enables you to collect all of your definitions into a separate file and then *include* them in your program, using the #include statement.

Suppose we were writing a series of programs for performing various metric conversions. We might want to set up some defines for all of the various constants that we would need for performing our conversions:

```
#define   INCHES_PER_CENTIMETER   0.394
#define   CENTIMETERS_PER_INCH    1 / INCHES_PER_CENTIMETER

#define   QUARTS_PER_LITER        1.057
#define   LITERS_PER_QUART        1 / QUARTS_PER_LITER

#define   OUNCES_PER_GRAM         0.035
#define   GRAMS_PER_OUNCE         1 / OUNCES_PER_GRAM
   ...
```

Suppose we entered the above definitions into a separate file on the system called metric.h. (Under many systems, the appendage .h is commonly used for files such as these, called *header* files.) Any program that subsequently needed to use any of the definitions contained in the metric.h file could then do so by simply issuing the preprocessor directive

```
#include "metric.h"
```

This statement must appear before any of the defines contained in metric.h are referenced and is typically placed at the beginning of the source file. The preprocessor will look for the specified file on the system and will effectively copy the contents of the file into the program at the precise point that the #include statement appears. So any statements inside the file will be treated just as if they had been directly typed into the program at that point.

The double quote signs around the include file name instruct the preprocessor to look for the specified file in the same *file directory* that contains the source file. If the file is not found there, then the preprocessor will automatically search other directories, as may have been set up by the system manager. (On the UNIX system, one other directory, /usr/include, will be searched.) Enclosing the file name within the characters < and > instead, as in

```
#include <stdio.h>
```

has the same effect as above, except that the file directory that contains the source file is *not* searched.

To see how include files are used in an actual program example, type the six defines given above into a file called metric.h. Then type in and run the following program in the normal manner.

Program 13-3

```
/* Illustrate the use of the #include statement
   Note: This program assumes that definitions are
   set up in a file called metric.h              */

#include "metric.h"

main ()
{
    float   liters, gallons;

    printf ("*** Liters to Gallons ***\n\n");
    printf ("Enter the number of liters: ");
    scanf ("%f", &liters);

    gallons = liters * QUARTS_PER_LITER / 4.0;
    printf ("%.2f liters = %.2f gallons\n",
                    liters, gallons);
}
```

Program 13-3 Output

```
*** Liters to Gallons ***

Enter the number of liters: 55.75
55.75 liters = 14.73 gallons.
```

The preceding example is a rather simple one as it only shows a single defined value (QUARTS_PER_LITER) being referenced from the included file metric.h. Nevertheless, the point is well made: once the definitions have been entered into metric.h, they can be used in any program that uses an appropriate #include statement.

One of the nicest things about the include file capability is that it enables us to centralize our definitions, thus assuring that all programs reference the same value. Furthermore, errors discovered in one of the values contained in the include file need only be corrected in that one spot, thus eliminating the need to correct each and every program that uses the value. Any program that referenced the incorrect value would simply have to be recompiled and would not have to be modified.

We can actually put anything we want in an include file, and not just #define statements as may have been implied. In fact, include files are frequently used to contain structure definitions, variable declarations, and function return type declarations, as we will describe in Chapter 15.

It is permitted to have more than one file included in a program. In such a case, separate #include statements must be used. Be careful though, because if a statement contained in one include file references a value defined in another include file, then the latter file must be included in the program first.

One last point to be made about include files in this chapter: include files may be nested. That is, an include file can itself include another file, and so on.

♦ Conditional Compilation ♦

The C preprocessor offers a feature known as *conditional compilation*. If you have some experience with assembly language programming, then this concept may not be new to you. Conditional compilation is often used to have one program that can run on different computer systems. It is also often used to "switch" on or off various statements in the program, such as debugging statements that print out the values of various variables or trace the flow of program execution.

The #ifdef, #endif, #else, and #ifndef Statements

In our discussions of the C preprocessor, we described how we could make the rotate function from Chapter 12 more portable. We showed how the use of a define would help in this regard. So the definition

```
#define   INT_SIZE   16
```

was used to isolate the dependency on the specific number of bits contained in an int. We mentioned that this definition would be used for running the program on a IBM-PC, for example, but that if we wanted the rotate function to run on a VAX-11/780, we would need to change this define to 32:

```
#define  INT_SIZE  32
```

If we had a large program that had many such dependencies on the particular hardware of the computer system (and this should be minimized as much as possible), then we might end up with many defines whose values would have to be changed when the program was moved to another computer system.

We can help reduce the problem of having to change these defines when the program is moved, and can incorporate into the program the values of these defines for each different machine by using the conditional compilation capabilities of the preprocessor. As a simple example, the statements

```
#ifdef  IBMPC
#    define  INT_SIZE   16
#else
#    define  INT_SIZE   32
#endif
```

will have the effect of defining INT_SIZE to 16 if the symbol IBMPC has been previously defined and to 32 otherwise. The #ifdef, #else, and #endif statements behave as you would expect. If the symbol specified on the #ifdef line has been already defined—through a #define statement or through the command line when the program is compiled—then lines that follow up to a #else, #elif, or #endif are processed by the compiler; otherwise, they are ignored.

In order to define the symbol IBMPC to the preprocessor, the statement

```
#define  IBMPC    1
```

or even just

```
#define  IBMPC
```

will suffice. Under UNIX, the name IBMPC can also be defined when the program is compiled by using a special option to the cc command. The command line

```
cc -D IBMPC program.c
```

will define the name IBMPC to the preprocessor, causing all #ifdef IBMPC statements inside program.c to evaluate as TRUE (note that the -D IBMPC must be type *before* the program name on the command line). This technique enables names to be defined *without* having to edit the source program.

Along the same lines as the #ifdef statement, there exists the preprocessor statement #ifndef. This statement is used the same way the #ifdef statement is used, except that it causes the subsequent lines to be processed if the indicated symbol is *not* defined.

As already mentioned, conditional compilation is useful when debugging programs. We may have many `printf` calls embedded in our program that are used to display intermediate results and trace the flow of execution. These statements can be "turned on" by conditionally compiling them into the program if a particular name, say DEBUG, is defined. For example, suppose we had some program that set up some data into an array called `data`. We might want to display the values contained inside this array at the terminal as a way of verifying the proper operation of the program. A sequence of statements such as the following could be used to display the elements of `data` only if the program had been compiled with the name DEBUG defined.

```
#ifdef DEBUG
    printf ("data elements:\n");

    for ( i = 0; i < MAX_DATA_VALUES; ++i )
        printf ("%d  %f\n", i, data[i]);
#endif
```

We might have many such debugging statements throughout the program. Whenever the program is being debugged, it can be compiled under UNIX with the -D DEBUG command-line option to have all of the debugging statements compiled. When the program is working correctly, it can be recompiled without the -D option. This will also have the added benefit of reducing the size of the program, since the debugging statements will not be compiled in.

The #if and #elif Preprocessor Statements

The #if preprocessor statement offers a more general way of controlling conditional compilation. The #if statement can be used to test whether a constant expression evaluates to nonzero or not. If the result of the expression is nonzero, then subsequent lines up to a #else, #elif, or #endif are processed; otherwise, they are skipped. As an example of how this may be used, assume we define the name MACHINE, which is set to 1 if the machine is a DEC PDP-11, to 2 if the machine is a DEC VAX-11, to 3 if the machine is an IBM PC, and so on. We could write a sequence of statements to conditionally compile statements based upon the value of MACHINE as follows:

```
#if  MACHINE == 1      /* PDP-11 */
  ...
#elif  MACHINE == 2  /* VAX-11 */
  ...
#elif  MACHINE == 3  /* IBM PC */
  ...
#else
  ...
#endif
```

Under UNIX, we can assign a value to the name MACHINE on the command line using the -D option discussed earlier. The command

```
cc -D MACHINE=2 program.c
```

will compile program.c with the name MACHINE defined as 2. This will cause the program to be compiled to run on a VAX-11.

The special "operator"

```
defined (name)
```

can also be used in #if statements. The sets of preprocessor statements

```
#if  defined (DEBUG)
    ...
#endif
```

and

```
#ifdef DEBUG
    ...
#endif
```

do the same thing. The statements

```
#if defined (PDP11) || defined (IBMPC)
#   define INT_SIZE   16
#else
#   define INT_SIZE   32
#endif
```

say to define INT_SIZE to 16 if either PDP11 or IBMPC is defined and to 32 otherwise.

The #undef Statement

On some occasions, it may be desirable to cause a defined name to become "undefined." This can be accomplished by means of the #undef preprocessor statement. In order to remove the definition of a particular name, the statement

```
#undef  name
```

can be used. So the statement

```
#undef  PDP11
```

would cause the definition of `PDP11` to be removed from the system. All subsequent `#ifdef PDP11` or `#if defined (PDP11)` statements would evaluate FALSE.

◆ Exercises ◆

1. If you have access to a computer facility that supports the C programming language, type in and run the three programs presented in this chapter, remembering to type in the include file associated with Program 13-3. Compare the output produced by each program with the output presented.

2. Locate the header file `stdio.h` on your system (on UNIX systems, look inside the `/usr/include` directory). Examine the file to see what's in it.

3. Define a macro `MIN` that gives the minimum of two values. Then write a program to test the macro definition.

4. Define a macro `MAX3` that gives the maximum of three values. Write a program to test the definition.

5. Write a macro `SHIFT` to perform the identical purpose as the `shift` function of Program 12-3.

6. Write a macro `IS_UPPER_CASE` that gives a nonzero value if a character is an uppercase letter.

7. Write a macro `IS_ALPHABETIC` that gives a nonzero value if a character is an alphabetic character. Have the macro use the `IS_LOWER_CASE` macro defined in the chapter text and the `IS_UPPER_CASE` macro defined in the previous exercise.

8. Write a macro `IS_DIGIT` that gives a nonzero value if a character is a digit `'0'` through `'9'`. Use this macro in the definition of another macro `IS_SPECIAL`, which gives a nonzero result if a character is a special character; that is, not alphabetic and not a digit. Be sure to use the `IS_ALPHABETIC` macro developed in the preceding exercise.

9. Write a macro `ABSOLUTE_VALUE` that computes the absolute value of its argument. Make sure that an expression such as `ABSOLUTE_VALUE (x + delta)` is properly evaluated by the macro.

C H A P T E R

♦   ♦   ♦   ♦   ♦
14

More on Data Types

T his chapter discusses a data type which we have not yet described: the *enumerated* data type. Also described in this chapter is the `typedef` statement, which enables us to assign our own names to basic data types or to derived data types. Finally, this chapter discusses the precise rules that are used by the compiler in the conversion of data types in an expression.

♦ Enumerated Data Types ♦

One of the qualities of a variable that is used as a flag in a C program is that it will usually be assigned one of two values: either TRUE or FALSE. In the preceding chapter, we saw how we could define the names TRUE or FALSE to the preprocessor and then subsequently use these names when dealing with flags. This approach is a valid one; however, it does not prevent us from inadvertently assigning a value other than TRUE or FALSE to a variable that is used as a flag in a program. Furthermore, such variables are usually declared to be of type `int`, or of type `short int`, thus somewhat obscuring their usage in the program. Wouldn't it be nice if we could define a variable to be of type `flag`, and then somehow specify that variables declared to be of this type could only be assigned the values `true` and `false` and nothing else? This is precisely the type of capability that is provided by the enumerated data type.

An enumerated data type definition is initiated by the keyword `enum`. Immediately following this keyword is the name of the enumerated data type, followed by a list of the permissible values that can be assigned to the type. For example, the statement

```
enum flag  { true, false };
```

defines a data type `flag`. This data type can be assigned the values `true` and `false` inside the program, *and no other values*. An attempt at assigning any other value to such a variable will cause a compiler error message to be issued on many machines.

To declare a variable to be of type `enum flag`, we again use the keyword enum, followed by the enumerated type name, followed by the variable list. So the statement

```
enum flag  end_of_data, match_found;
```

defines the two variables `end_of_data` and `match_found` to be of type `flag`. The only permissible values that can be assigned to these variables are the names `true` and `false`. So statements such as

```
end_of_data = true;
```

and

```
if ( match_found == false )
    . . .
```

are valid. As another example of an enumerated data type definition, the following defines the type `enum month`, with permissible values that can be assigned to a variable of this type being the months of the year:

```
enum   month   { january, february, march, april, may,
                 june, july, august, september, october,
                 november, december };
```

Enumerated values are actually treated as constants by the C compiler. Beginning with the first name in the list, the compiler assigns sequential integers values to these names, starting with 0. If we executed a statement, such as the following:

```
this_month = february;
```

where `this_month` had been appropriately declared to be of type `enum month`, then the value 1 would be assigned to `this_month` (and not the name `february`).

If it is desired to have a specific integer value associated with an enumerated value, then the integer can be assigned to the value when the data type is defined. Enumerated values that subsequently appear in the list will be assigned sequential values beginning with the specified integer value plus one. For example, in the definition

```
enum   direction   { up, down, left = 10, right };
```

an enumerated data type `direction` is defined with the values `up`, `down`, `left,` and `right.` The compiler assigns the value 0 to `up,` since it appears first in the list; 1 to `down` since it appears next; 10 to `left` since it is explicitly assigned this value; and 11 to `right` since it appears immediately after `left` in the list.

If we need to explicitly assign an integer value to an enumerated data type variable, this can be done with the type cast operator. So if `month_value` were an integer variable that had the value 6, for example, then the expression

```
this_month = (enum month) (month_value - 1);
```

would be permissible and would have the effect of assigning the sixth enumerated data value, or `june,` to the variable `this_month.`

When writing programs with enumerated data type variables, you should try not to rely on the fact that the enumerated values are treated as integer constants. Instead, these variables should be treated as distinct variable types.

The variations permitted when defining an enumerated data type are similar to those permitted with structure definitions: the name of the data type can be omitted, and variables can be declared to be of the particular enumerated data type when the type is defined. As an example showing both of these options, the statement

```
enum{ east, west, south, north } location;
```

defines an (unnamed) enumerated data type with values `east, west, south,` or `north,` and declares a variable `location` to be of that type.

Enumerated type definitions behave like structure and variable definitions as far as their scope is concerned: defining an enumerated data type within a function restricts usage of that definition to variables defined within the function. On the other hand, defining an enumerated data type at the beginning of the program, outside of any function, makes the type definition global to the file.

By the way, when defining an enumerated data type, you must make certain that the enumerated value names are unique with respect to other variable names and enumerated value names defined within the same scope as the enumerated type.

♦ The `typedef` Statement ♦

C provides a capability that enables the programmer to assign an alternate name to a data type. This is done with a statement known as `typedef.` The statement

```
typedef  int  COUNTER;
```

defines the name COUNTER to be equivalent to the C data type `int.` Variables can subsequently be declared to be of type COUNTER, as in the statement

```
COUNTER   j, n;
```

The C compiler actually treats the declaration of the variables j and n, shown above, as normal integer variables. The main advantage of the use of the typedef in this case is in the added readability that it lends to the definition of the variables. It is clear from the definition of j and n what the intended purpose of these variables is in the program. Declaring them to be of type int in the traditional fashion would not have made the intended use of these variables at all clear.

In many instances, a typedef statement can be equivalently substituted by the appropriate #define statement. For example, we could have used the statement

```
#define   COUNTER   int
```

instead to achieve the same results as above. However, because the typedef is handled by the C compiler proper, and not by the preprocessor, the typedef statement provides more flexibility than does the #define when it comes to assigning names to "derived" data types. For example, the following typedef statement,

```
typedef   char   STRING[81];
```

defines a type called STRING, which is an array of 81 characters. Subsequently declaring variables to be of type STRING, as in

```
STRING   text, input_line;
```

has the effect of defining the variables text and input_line to be character arrays containing 81 characters. This is equivalent to the following declaration:

```
char   text[81], input_line[81];
```

You will note that, in this case, STRING could *not* have been equivalently defined with a #define preprocessor statement.

The following typedef defines a type name STRING_POINTER to be a char pointer:

```
typedef   char *STRING_POINTER;
```

Variables subsequently declared to be of type STRING_POINTER, as in

```
STRING_POINTER   buffer;
```

will be treated as character pointers by the C compiler.

In order to define a new type name, you should follow this procedure:

1. Write the statement as if a variable of the desired type were being declared.

2. Where the name of the declared variable would normally appear, substitute the new type name.

3. In front of everything, place the keyword `typedef`.

As an example of the preceding procedure, to define a type called DATE to be a structure containing three integer members called `month`, `day`, and `year`, we write out the structure definition, substituting the name DATE where the variable name would normally appear (before the last semicolon). Before everything, we place the keyword `typedef`:

```
typedef   struct
          {
                int    month;
                int    day;
                int    year;
          } DATE;
```

With this `typedef` in place, we could subsequently declare variables to be of type DATE, as in

```
DATE   birthdays[100];
```

This defines `birthdays` as an array containing 100 DATE elements.

By convention, `typedef` names are usually written in uppercase letters to alert the reader of the program that they are user-defined type names. When working on programs in which the source code is contained in more than one file (as described in the next chapter), it's a good idea to place the common `typedefs` into a separate file that can be included into each source file with a `#include` statement.

Remember, use of the `typedef` statement does not actually define a new type—only a new type *name*. Variables defined to be of the new type name are not treated any differently by the C compiler. So the variables `j` and `n`, as defined in the beginning of this section, would in all respects be treated as normal `int` variables by the C compiler.

◆ Data Type Conversions ◆

In Chapter 4, we briefly addressed the fact that sometimes conversions are implicitly made by the system when expressions are evaluated. The case that we examined was with the data types `float` and `int`. We saw how an operation which involved a `float` and an `int` was carried out as a floating point operation, the integer data item being automatically converted to floating point.

We have also seen how the type cast operator can be used to explicitly dictate a conversion. So in the statement

```
average = (float) total / n;
```

the value of the variable `total` is converted to type `float` before the operation is performed, thereby guaranteeing that the division will be carried out as a floating point operation.

The C compiler adheres to very strict rules when it comes to evaluating expressions that consist of different data types. The compiler also has two rules that it uses for converting arguments that are passed to functions: (1) any argument of type `float` is automatically converted to type `double`; and (2) any argument of type `char` or `short int` is automatically converted to type `int`. As is pointed out in Chapter 16, this interesting little fact explains why either the value of a `float` *or* a `double` can be displayed using the format characters `%f` or `%e`; the `printf` function always sees the argument as type `double`, regardless of whether a `float` or a `double` is passed. This might seem to imply that we shouldn't declare a formal parameter to be of type `float`, `char`, or `short`. We can still go ahead and make these declarations, since the compiler handles the situation properly. In other words, if you declare a formal parameter to be of type `float`, the compiler knows that what actually will be passed to the function is an argument of type `double`, and handles the situation properly.

Getting back to the rules that are used for expression evaluation, the following summarizes the order in which conversions take place in the evaluation of two operands in an expression.

Conversion of Operands in An Expression

Step 1: If either operand is of type `float`, it is converted to type `double`. If either operand is of type `char` or of type `short int` (signed or unsigned), it is converted to type `int` (signed or unsigned).

Step 2: If either operand is of type `double`, the other operand is converted to type `double`, and that is the type of the result.

Step 3: If either operand is of type `long int`, the other operand is converted to type `long`, and that is the type of the result.

Step 4: If either operand is of type `unsigned`, the other operand is converted to type `unsigned`, and that is the type of the result.

Step 5: If this step is reached, then both operands must be of type `int`, and that is the type of the result.

As an example of how to follow these steps, let us see how the following expression would be evaluated, where f is defined to be a float, i an int, l a long int, and s a short int variable:

```
f * i + l / s
```

Consider first the multiplication of f by i, which is the multiplication of a float by an int. From Step 1, we find that since f is of type float it will be converted to type double. Since one of the operands is of type double, the other will also be converted to type double, as indicated by Step 2. This step also specifies that the result of the mutiplication of f by i will be of type double.

Next we proceed to the division of l by s, which is the division of a long int by a short int. We find from Step 3 that since one of the operands (l) is long, the other operand (s) will be converted to type long, which will also be the type of the result. This division will therefore be performed as a long int division, with any fractional part resulting from the division truncated.

Finally, Step 2 indicates that if one of the operands in an expression is of type double (as is the result of multiplying f * i), then the other operand will be converted to type double, which will be the type of the result. Therefore, *after* the division of l by s has been performed, the result of the operation will be converted to type double and then added into the product of f and i. The final result of the preceding expression will therefore be a value of type double.

The type cast operator can always be used to explicitly force conversions and thereby control the way that a particular expression is evaluated. For example, if we didn't want the result of dividing l by s to be truncated in the preceding expression evaluation, we could have type cast one of the operands to type double, thereby forcing the evaluation to be performed as a double floating point division:

```
f * i + (double) l / s
```

In this expression, l would be converted to double before the division operation was performed, since the type cast operator has higher precedence than the division operator. Since one of the operands of the division would then be of type double, the other (s) would be automatically converted to type double, and that would be the type of the result.

You should note that the conversion of all floats to doubles is not required but is implemented by most existing C compilers. So there is a chance that your C compiler may perform single-precision floating point arithmetic. Check at your installation to find out. Realize that even if your system doesn't convert floats to doubles when evaluating expressions, it still will convert them when passing them as arguments to functions.

Whenever a signed `int` or signed `short int` is converted into an integer of a larger size, the sign is extended to the `left` when the conversion is performed. This ensures that a `short int` having a value of -5, for example, will also have the value -5 when it is converted into a `long int`. Whenever an `unsigned` integer is converted into an integer of a larger size, as you would expect, no sign extension occurs.

On some systems (such as on the PDP-11 and the VAX-11), characters are treated as signed quantities. This means that if a character is converted to an integer, then sign extension will occur. As long as characters are used from the standard character set, this fact will never pose a problem. However, if a character value is used that is not part of the standard character set, then its sign may be extended when used in an expression or when passed as an argument to a function. For example, on some machines, the character constant '\377' will be converted into the value -1 because its value is negative when treated as a signed 8-bit quantity.

The C language permits character variables to be declared `unsigned`, thus avoiding this potential problem.

♦ Exercises ♦

1. Write a function called month_name that takes as its argument a value of type enum month (as defined in this chapter) and returns a pointer to a character string containing the name of the month. In this way, we can display the value of an enum month variable with a statement such as:

   ```
   printf ("%s\n", month_name (this_month));
   ```

2. Define a type FUNCTION_POINTER (using typedef) that represents a pointer to a function that returns an int. Refer to Chapter 11 for the details on how to declare a variable of this type.

3. Given the following variable declarations:

   ```
   short int   s = 10;
   int         i = 25;
   long int    l = 50L;
   float       f = 0.5;
   double      d = 1.5;
   ```

   what would be the value and the type of the following expressions?

   ```
   f + s * i - l
   i / f + s * d
   i / s * f
   (double) i / s * f
   l / i + (int) d / f
   ```

```
C   H   A   P   T   E   R
◆   ◆   ◆   15   ◆   ◆   ◆
```

Working with Larger Programs

The programs that we have illustrated throughout this book have all been
very small and relatively simple. Unfortunately, the programs that you
will have to develop to solve your particular problems will probably be neither
as small nor as simple. Learning the proper techniques for dealing with such
programs is the topic of this chapter. As you will see, C provides all of the
features necessary for the efficient development of large programs.

◆ Separate Compilations ◆

In every program that we have shown, we always assumed that the entire program was entered into a single file on the system—presumably via a text editor such as vi under UNIX—and then compiled and executed. In this single file
was included all of the functions that the program used, except of couse for the
"system" functions, such as printf and scanf.

This approach works fine when dealing with small programs; that is, programs that contain up to 100 statements or so. However, when you start dealing
with larger programs, this approach no longer suffices. As the number of statements in the program increase, so does the time it takes to edit the program and
to subsequently recompile it. Not only that, large programming applications frequently require the efforts of more than one programmer. Having everyone
work on the same source file, or even on their own copy of the same source file,
would be unmanageable.

C very much supports the notion of modular programming in that it does
not require that all of the statements for a particular program be contained in a
single file. This means that you can enter your code for a particular module into
one file, for another module into a different file, and so on. Here, when we use
the term "module," we are referring either to a single function or to a number of
related functions which we choose to group logically.

For example, suppose we have conceptually divided our program into two modules and have entered the statements for the first module into a file called mod1.c and the statements for the second module into a file called mod2.c. In order to tell the system that these two modules actually belong to the same program, we simply include the names of both files when we enter the command to compile. For example, under UNIX, the command

```
cc mod1.c mod2.c
```

would have the effect of compiling the code contained in mod1.c and the code contained in mod2.c. Errors discovered in either mod1.c or mod2.c would be separately identified by the compiler. Obviously, if there were errors discovered in both modules, then we would have to edit both modules to correct the mistakes. But if an error were discovered only in mod1.c, for example, then we would only have to edit this file to fix the mistake. And, since we have not made any changes to mod2.c since the last time it was compiled, we can tell the C system to recompile only mod1.c and *not* mod2.c. Under UNIX, this would be done as follows:

```
cc mod1.c mod2.o
```

Replacing the c from the file name mod2.c with an o instructs the C compiler to use the object file that was produced the last time mod2.c was compiled.[†] So, not only do we not have to reedit mod2.c if no errors are discovered by the compiler, but we don't have to recompile it either.

If no errors are discovered in compiling mod1.c, the UNIX C compiler will place the final executable object into the file a.out, which can then be executed by simply typing the command

```
a.out
```

at the terminal. (Appendix E shows how you can specify a different name for the executable object.) We should reiterate something we have mentioned on several occasions in this book: in either of the two files mod1.c or mod2.c (but not in both), there *must* exist a function called main to indicate to the system where program execution is to begin.

If we extend the preceding example to programs that consist of more than two modules, then you can see how this mechanism of separate compilations can enable us to develop large programs more efficiently. For example, the UNIX command

---

† The UNIX C compiler places the resulting object code from compiling mod.c into the file mod.o by default. When a program consisting of only one module is compiled and linked—such as would be the case with all of the program examples in this book—this object file is automatically deleted by the system. However, when the program is divided into multiple modules, these separate .o files are retained.

```
cc legal.c makemove.o exec.o enumerator.o evaluator.o
```

could be used to compile a program consisting of five modules, in which only the module `legal.c` is to be recompiled.

◆ Communication Between Modules ◆

There are several methods that can be used so that the modules contained in separate files can effectively communicate. If a function from one file needs to call a function contained inside another file, then the function call can be made in the normal fashion and arguments can be passed and returned in the usual way. Of course, if the function from the other file does not return a value of type `int`, then its return type *must* be declared in the program that calls the function.

It's important to remember that even though two or more modules may be specified to the compiler at the same time on the command line, the *compiler compiles each module independently*. That means, for example, that no knowledge about structure definitions or function return types is shared across module compilations by the compiler. It's totally up to you to ensure that each module that needs to use a particular structure defines it. And each module that calls a function that does not return an `int` must declare that fact (unless, of course, the function is defined earlier inside the same module that the call appears in).

External Variables

Functions contained in separate files can also communicate through so-called *external variables*, which are effectively an extension to the concept of the global variable that we discussed in Chapter 8.

An external variable is one whose value can be accessed and changed by another module. Inside the module that wishes to access the external variable, the variable is declared in the normal fashion and the keyword `extern` is placed before the declaration. This signals to the system that a globally defined variable from another file is to be accessed.

Suppose we wished to define an `int` variable called `move_number` whose value we wished to access and possibly modify from within a function contained in another file. In Chapter 8, we noted that if we wrote the statement

```
int  move_number = 0;
```

at the beginning of our program, outside of any function, then its value could be referenced by any function within that program. In such a case, we said that `move_number` was defined as a global variable.

Actually, this very same definition of the variable `move_number` also makes its value accessible by functions contained in other files. Specifically, the preceding statement defines the variable move_number not just as a global variable, but in fact as an *external global* variable. In order to reference the value of an external global from another module, we must declare the type of the variable to be accessed, preceding the declaration with the keyword extern:

```
extern int  move_number;
```

The value of move_number can now be accessed and modified by the module in which the preceding declaration appeared. Other modules can also access the value of move_number by using a similar extern declaration in the file.

Here is one important concept that you must keep straight when working with external variables: the external variable can be assigned an initial value in one place and one place only—at the place where it is defined. Due to various peculiarities, and also due to the fact that the keyword extern is optional on some systems, some systems *require* that an external variable be assigned an initial value when it is defined (but still, only in one place).

Let's take a look at a small program example to illustrate the use of external variables. Suppose we type the following code into a file called main.c:

```
int  i = 5;

main ()
{
    printf ("%d  ", i);

    foo ();

    printf ("%d\n", i);
}
```

The definition of the global variable i in the above program makes its value accessible by any module that uses an appropriate extern declaration. Suppose we now type the following statements into a file called foo.c:

```
extern int i;

foo ()
{
    i = 100;
}
```

Compiling the two modules main.c and foo.c together under UNIX with the command

```
cc main.c foo.c
```

and subsequently executing the program with the command

```
a.out
```

would produce the following output at the terminal:

```
5   100
```

which would verify that the function `foo` was able to access and change the value of the external variable `i`.

Since the value of the external variable `i` is referenced *inside* the function `foo`, we could have placed the `extern` declaration of `i` inside the function itself, as in:

```
foo ()
{
    extern int  i;

    i = 100;
}
```

If there were many functions in the file `foo.c` that needed to access the value of `i`, then it would be easier to make the `extern` declaration just once at the front of the file. However, if only one function or a small number of functions needed to access this value, then there would be something to be said for making separate `extern` declarations in each such function; it would make the program more organized and would isolate the use of the particular variable to those functions that actually used it.

When declaring an external array, it is not necessary to give its size. Thus the declaration

```
extern char  text[];
```

would enable us to reference a character array `text` that is defined elsewhere. As with formal parameter arrays, if the external array is multidimensional, then all but the first dimension must be specified. Thus the declaration

```
extern int  matrix[][50];
```

would suffice to declare a two-dimensional external array `matrix` that contained 50 columns.

Some things are worth noting with respect to external variable names. On some systems, the number of characters that are significant for an external variable name may not be the same as the number that is significant for non-external variable names. For example, on the PDP-11, only the first seven characters of an external variable name are significant. External variables, which have the same first seven characters (as in `pointera` and `pointerb`), will therefore not be distinguishable and will lead to an error on this machine.

A second point worth noting is that on some systems, lowercase and upper-case letters are indistinguishable in external variable names. On such systems, external variables called `stack` and `Stack`, for example, would be treated as the same variable. Check your system documentation to find out any limitations that may exist with respect to external variable names.

Static vs. Extern Variables and Functions

We now know that any variable defined outside of a function is not only a global variable, but is an external variable as well. There are many situations that arise in which we would like to define a variable to be global but *not* external. In other words, we would like to define a global variable to be local to a particular module (file). It would make sense to want to define a variable this way if no functions other than those contained inside a particular file needed access to the particular variable. This can be accomplished in C by defining the variable to be `static`.

The statement

```
static int   move_number = 0;
```

if made outside of any function, makes the value of `move_number` accessible from any subsequent point in the file in which the definition appears, *but not from functions contained in other files*.

If you need to define a global variable whose value does not have to be accessed from another file, then declare the variable to be `static`. This is a cleaner approach to programming: the `static` declaration more accurately reflects the variable's usage, there can be no "conflicts" created by two modules that unknowingly both use different external global variables of the same name, and the process of "linking" the program together will actually be more efficient.

We mentioned earlier in this chapter that we can directly call a function from another file. Unlike variables, no special mechanisms are required; that is, to call a function contained in another file, we don't need an `extern` declaration for that function.

When a function is *defined*, it can be declared to be either `extern` or `static`, the former case being the default. A statically defined function can only be called from within the same file as the function appears. So if we had a func-tion called `square_root`, placing the keyword `static` before the function header declaration for this function would make it callable only from within the file in which it is defined:

```
static double  square_root (x)
double x;
{
    ...
}
```

The definition of the `square_root` function effectively becomes local to the file in which it is defined. It cannot be called from outside this file, and any attempts at doing so would cause an error.

The same motivations previously cited for using static variables also apply in the case of static functions.

Fig. 15-1 summarizes communication between different modules. Here we depict two modules, `mod1.c` and `mod2.c`.

```
double  x;
static  double  result;


static  void  dosquare  ()
{
   double square  ();

   x = 2.0;
   result  =  square  ();
}

main  ()
{
   dosquare  ();
   printf  ("%f\n",  result);
}
```

```
extern double  x;


double  square  ()
{
    return  (x * x);
}
```

mod1.c   **mod2.c**

Fig. 15-1. Communication between modules

In `mod1.c`, we define two functions: `dosquare` and `main`. The way things are set up here, `main` calls `dosquare`, which in turn calls `square`. This last function is defined in the module `mod2.c`.

Because `dosquare` is declared `static`, it can only be called from within `mod1.c`, and by no other module.

mod1.c defines two global variables: x and result, both of type double. x can be accessed by any module that is linked together with mod1.c. On the other hand, the keyword static in front of the definition of result means that it can only be accessed by functions defined inside mod1.c (namely main and dosquare).

When execution begins, the main routine calls dosquare. dosquare assigns the value 2.0 to the global variable x and then calls the function square. Since square is defined in another source file (inside mod2.c), and since it doesn't return an int, dosquare properly includes an appropriate declaration at the start of the function.

The square function returns as its value the square of the value of the global variable x. Since square wishes to access the value of this variable, which is defined in another source file (in mod1.c), an appropriate extern declaration appears in mod2.c (and, in this case, it makes no difference whether the declaration occurs inside or outside the square function).

The value that is returned by square is assigned to the global variable result inside dosquare, which then returns back to main. Inside main, the value of the global variable result is displayed. This example, when run, will produce a result of 4.0 at the terminal (since that's obviously the square of 2.0).

Study this example until you feel comfortable with it. This small—albeit impractical—example illustrates very important concepts about communicating between modules and it's necessary that you understand these concepts to work effectively with larger programs.

Include Files

In Chapter 13, we introduced the concept of the include file. We stated there that we could group all of our commonly used definitions inside such a file and then simply include the file in any program that needed to use those definitions. Nowhere is the usefulness of the #include facility greater than in developing programs that have been divided into separate program modules.

If more than one programmer is working on developing a particular program, then include files provide a means of standardization: each programmer will be using the same definitions which have the same values. Furthermore, each programmer is thus spared the time-consuming and error-prone task of typing these definitions into each file that must use them. These last two points are made even stronger when we start placing common structure definitions, external variable declarations, typedef definitions, and function return type declarations into include files. Various modules of a large programming system will invariably deal with common data structures. By centralizing the definition of these data structures into one or more include files, we eliminate the error that would be caused by two modules that used different definitions for the same data structure. Furthermore, if a change had to be made to the definition of a particular data structure, it could be done so in one place only—inside the include file.

16

Input and Output

All of the reading and writing of data up to this point has been done through the terminal. When we wished to input some information, we either used the `scanf` or `getchar` functions. All program results were displayed at the terminal with a call to the `printf` function.

The C language itself does not have any special statements for performing Input/Output (I/O) operations. Unlike FORTRAN, for example, which has the `READ` and `WRITE` statements defined as part of the language, all I/O operations in C must be carried out through function calls. Since these functions are not a part of the language itself, they may differ slightly from one machine to the next. However, several functions, such as `printf` and `scanf`, have more or less become standardized in the C language and will most likely exist and work the same from one machine to the next. These functions form part of what has become known as the *Standard I/O Library*. If you confine all of your I/O operations to use of functions from this Library, then your program stands a good chance of running on any machine that supports the C language, with little or no changes—as far as I/O operations are concerned.

You will recall the use of the include statement

```
#include <stdio.h>
```

from previous programs that used the `getchar` function. This include file contains declarations and macro definitions associated with the Standard I/O Library. Therefore, whenever using a function from this Library, you should include this file at the front of your program. When using `printf` and `scanf`, this header file is normally not required.

In this chapter, we will describe many of the functions that are provided in the Standard I/O Library. Unfortunately, space does not permit us to go into much detail about these functions or discuss each function that is offered. Refer to Appendix D for a list of many of the functions in the Standard I/O Library, and consult *Topics in C Programming* (Kochan & Wood, Hayden Books, 1987) for an in-depth treatment of the Standard I/O Library.

♦ Character I/O: `getchar` and `putchar` ♦

The `getchar` function proved convenient when we wished to read data from the terminal a single character at a time. We saw how we could develop a function called `read_line` to read in an entire line of text from the terminal. This function repeatedly called the `getchar` function until the newline character was read.

There is an analagous function for writing data to the terminal a single character at a time. The name of this function is `putchar`.[†]

A call to the `putchar` function is quite simple: the only argument it takes is the character to be displayed. So the call

```
putchar (c);
```

where `c` is defined of type `char`, would have the effect of displaying the character contained in `c` at the terminal. The call

```
putchar ('\n');
```

would have the effect of displaying the newline character at the terminal which, as we know, would cause the cursor to move to the beginning of the next line.

♦ Formatted I/O: `printf` and `scanf` ♦

We have been using the `printf` and `scanf` functions throughout this book. In this section, we will summarize all of the options that are available for formatting data with these functions.

The first argument to both `printf` and `scanf` is the format string. This string specifies how the remaining arguments to the function are to be displayed in the case of `printf`, and how the data that is read is to be interpreted in the case of `scanf`.

The `printf` Function

We have seen in various program examples how we could place certain characters between the `%` character and the specific so-called conversion character to more precisely control the formatting of the output. For example, we saw in Program 5-3A how an integer value before the conversion character could be used to specify a *field width*. The format characters `%2d` specified the display of an integer value right-justified in a field width of 2 columns. We also saw in Exercise 6 in Chapter 5 how a minus sign could be used to left-justify a value in a field.

[†] Even though `putchar` is actually defined as a macro under UNIX inside `stdio.h` (as is `getchar`), we will still refer to it as a function here.

The general format of a printf conversion specification is

%[*flags*][*width*][.*prec*][l]*type*

Optional fields are enclosed in brackets, and must appear in the order shown. Table 16-1 summarizes all possible characters and values that can be placed directly after the % sign and before the *type* specification inside a format string.

TABLE 16-1. printf conversion modifiers

Modifier		Meaning
flags	– + (*space*) #	Left justify value Precede value with + or – Precede positive value with space character Precede octal value with 0, hexadecimal value with 0x (or 0X); display decimal point for floats; leave trailing zeroes for g or G format
width		Minimum size of field; * means take next argument as field width
prec		Minimum number of digits to display for integers; number of decimal places for e or f formats; maximum number of significant digits to display for g; maximum number of characters for s format; * means take next argument as size
l		Display long integer
type		Type conversion character

Table 16-2 lists all of the conversion characters that may be specified in the format string.

Table 16-1 and 16-2 may appear a bit overwhelming. As you can see, there are many different combinations that can be used to precisely control the format of your output. The best way to become familiar with the various possibilities is through experimentation. Just make sure that the number of arguments you give to the printf function matches the number of % signs in the format string (with %% the exception of course). And, in the case of using an * in place of an integer for the field width or precision modifiers, remember that printf will be expecting an argument for each asterisk as well.

TABLE 16-2. printf conversion characters

Char	Use for printing
d	Integers
u	Unsigned integers
o	Octal integers
x	Hexadecimal integers, using a-f
X	Hexadecimal integers, using A-F
f	Floating point numbers
e	Floating point numbers in exponential format, using e before exponent
E	Floating point numbers in exponential format, using E before exponent
g	Floating point numbers in f or e format
G	Floating point numbers in f or E format
c	Single characters
s	Null-terminated character strings
%	Percent signs

Program 16-1 shows some of the formatting possibilities using printf.

Program 16-1

```
/* Program to illustrate various printf formats */

main ()
{
    char            c = 'X';
    static char     s[] = "abcdefghijklmnopqrstuvwxyz";
    int             i = 425;
    short int       j = 17;
    unsigned int    u = 0xf179;
    long int        l = 75000L;
    float           f = 12.978;
    double          d = -97.4583;

    printf ("Integers:\n");
    printf ("%d  %o  %x  %u\n", i, i, i, i);
    printf ("%x  %X  %#x %#X\n", i, i, i, i);
    printf ("%d  %o  %x  %u\n", j, j, j, j);
    printf ("%d  %o  %x  %u\n", u, u, u, u);
    printf ("%ld  %lo  %lx  %lu\n", l, l, l, l);

    printf ("\nFloats and Doubles:\n");
    printf ("%f  %e  %g\n", f, f, f);
    printf ("%.2f  %.2e\n", f, f);
```

```
        printf ("%.0f   %.0e\n", f, f);
        printf ("%7.2f   %7.2e\n", f, f);
        printf ("%f   %e   %g\n", d, d, d);
        printf ("%.*f\n", 3, d);
        printf ("%*.*f\n", 8, 2, d);

        printf ("\nCharacters:\n");
        printf ("%c\n", c);
        printf ("%3c%3c\n", c, c);
        printf ("%x\n", c);

        printf ("\nStrings:\n");
        printf ("%s\n", s);
        printf ("%.5s\n", s);
        printf ("%30s\n", s);
        printf ("%20.5s\n", s);
        printf ("%-20.5s|\n", s);
}
```

Program 16-1 Output

```
Integers:
425   651   1a9   425
1a9   1A9   0x1a9  0X1A9
17   21   11   17
-3719   170571   f179   61817
75000   222370   124f8   75000

Floats and Doubles:
12.978000   1.297800e+01   12.978
12.98   1.30e+01
13   1e+01
   12.98   1.30e+01
-97.458300   -9.745830e+01   -97.4583
-97.458
   -97.46

Characters:
X
  X  X
58

Strings:
abcdefghijklmnopqrstuvwxyz
abcde
     abcdefghijklmnopqrstuvwxyz
                abcde
abcde                   |
```

It's worthwhile to take some time to explain the output in detail. The first 'set" of output deals with the display of integers: short, long, unsigned, and "normal" ints. The first line displays i in decimal (%d), octal (%o), hexadecimal (%x), and unsigned (%u) formats. You will notice that octal numbers are not preceded by a leading 0 when they are displayed.

The next line of output displays the value of i again. First, i is displayed in hexadecimal notation using %x. The use of a capital X (%#X) causes printf to use uppercase letters A-F instead of lowercase letters when displaying numbers in hexadecimal. The # modifier (%#x) causes a leading 0x to appear before the number, and causes a leading 0X to appear when the capital X is used as the conversion character (%#X).

The fourth printf call displays the value of the short int variable j in various formats. Any integer format can be specified, since, as you'll recall, short ints automatically get converted to ints when passed as arguments to functions.

The next printf call shows what happens when %d is used to display the value of an unsigned int. Since the value assigned to u was larger than the maximum positive value that could be stored in a signed int on the machine that this program was run on, it is displayed as a negative number when the %d format characters are used.

The sixth printf call shows how the l modifier is used to display long integers.

The second set of output illustrates various formatting possibilities for displaying floats and doubles. The first output line of this set shows the result of displaying a float value using %f, %e, and %g formats. As we mentioned, unless specified otherwise, the %f and %e formats default to six decimal places. With the %g format, printf decides whether to display the value in either %e or %f format, depending upon the magnitude of the value and on the specified precision. With this format, trailing zeroes are also automatically removed, and a decimal point is displayed only if nonzero digits follow it. In general, %g is the best format to use for displaying floating point numbers.

In the next line of output, the precision modifier .2 was specified to limit the display of f to two decimal places. As you can see, printf was nice enough to automatically round the value of f for us. The line that immediately follows shows the use of the .0 precision modifier to suppress the display of any decimal places, including the decimal point in the %f format. Once again, the value of f was automatically rounded for us.

The modifiers 7.2, as used for generating the next line of output, specify that the value is to be displayed in a minimum of seven columns, to two decimal places of accuracy. Since both values need fewer than seven columns to be displayed, printf right-justifies the value (adding spaces on the left) within the specified field width.

In the next three lines of output, the value of the double variable d is displayed with various formats. The same format characters are used for the display of floats and double values, since, as you'll once again recall, floats are automatically converted to doubles when passed as arguments to functions. The `printf` call

```
printf ("%.*f\n", 3, d);
```

specifies that the value of d is to be displayed to three decimal places. The asterisk after the period in the format specification instructs `printf` to take the next argument to the function as the value of the precision. In this case, the next argument is 3. This value could have also been specified by a variable, as in

```
printf ("%.*f\n", accuracy, d);
```

which makes this feature useful for dynamically changing the format of a display.

The final line of the "Floats and Doubles" set shows the result of using the format characters `%*.*f` for displaying the value of d. In this case, both the field width and the precision are given as arguments to the function, as indicated by the two asterisks in the format string. Since the first argument after the format string is 8, this is taken as the field width. The next argument, 2, is taken as the precision. The value of d is therefore displayed to two decimal places in a field size of eight characters. You will notice that the minus sign as well as the decimal point are included in the field-width count. This is true for any field specifier.

In the next set of program output, the character c, which was initially set to the character X, is displayed in various formats. The first time it is displayed using the familiar `%c` format characters. On the next line, it is displayed twice with a field width specification of 3. This results in the display of the character with two leading spaces.

A character can be displayed using any integer format specification. In the next line of output, the value of c is displayed in hexadecimal. The output indicates that on this machine the character X is internally represented by the number hexadecimal 58.

In the final set of program output, the character string s is displayed. The first time it's displayed with the normal `%s` format characters. Then, a precision specification of 5 is used to display just the first five characters from the string. This results in the display of the first five letters of the alphabet.

In the third output line from this set, the entire character string is once again displayed, this time using a field width specification of 30. As you can see, the string is displayed right-justified in the field.

The final two lines of the program's output show five characters from the string s being displayed in a field-width size of 20. The first time, these five characters are displayed right-adjusted in the field. The second time, the minus sign results in the display of the first five letters left-adjusted in the field. The vertical bar character was printed to verify that the format characters `%-20.5s` actually result in the display of 20 characters at the terminal (five letters followed by 15 spaces).

The scanf Function

Like the printf function, there are many more formatting options that can be specified inside the format string of a scanf call than have been illustrated up to this point. As with printf, scanf takes optional modifiers between the % and the conversion character. These optional modifiers are summarized in Table 16-3. The possible conversion characters that may be specified are summarized in Table 16-4.

When the scanf function searches the input stream for a value to be read, it will always bypass any leading so-called *white space* characters, where *white space* refers to either a blank space, tab ('\t'), newline ('\n'), or form-feed character ('\f'). The exceptions are in the case of the %c format characters—in which case, the next character from the input, no matter what it is, is read—and in the case of the bracketed character string read—in which case, the characters contained in the brackets (or *not* contained in the brackets) specify the permissible characters of the string.

When scanf reads in a particular value, reading of the value will terminate as soon as the number of characters specified by the field width is reached (if supplied), or until a character that is not valid for the value being read is encountered. In the case of integers, valid characters are an optionally signed sequence of digits that are valid for the base of the integer that is being read (decimal: 0-9, octal: 0-7, hexadecimal: 0-9, a-f, or A-F). For floats, permissible characters are an optionally signed sequence of decimal digits, followed by an optional decimal point and another sequence of decimal digits, all of which may be followed by the letter e (or E) and an optionally signed exponent. For character strings read in with the %s format, any nonwhite space character is valid. In the case of %c format, all characters are valid. Finally, in the case of the bracketed string read, valid characters are only those enclosed within the brackets (or not enclosd within the brackets if the ^ character is used after the open bracket).

TABLE 16-3. scanf conversion modifiers

Modifier	Meaning
*	Field is to be skipped and not assigned
size	Maximum size of the input field
l	Value is to be stored in long int or double
h	Value to be read is to be stored in a short int
type	Conversion character

TABLE 16-4. scanf conversion characters

Character	Action
d	The value to be read is expressed in decimal notation; the corresponding argument is a pointer to an `int` unless the `l` or `h` modifier is used, in which case the argument is a pointer to a `long` or `short int`, respectively.
u	The value to be read is an integer and the corresponding argument is a pointer to an `unsigned int`.
o	The value to be read is expressed in octal notation; the corresponding argument is a pointer to an `int`, unless an `l` or an `h` precedes the `x`, in which case the argument is a pointer to a `long` or a `short`, respectively.
x	The value to be read is expressed in hexadecimal notation; the corresponding argument is a pointer to an `int`, unless an `l` or an `h` modifies the `x`.
e, f, or g	The value to be read is expressed in floating point notation; the value may be optionally preceded by a sign and may optionally be expressed in exponential notation (as in `3.45e3`); the corresponding argument is a pointer to a float, unless an `l` modifier is used, in which case it is a pointer to a `double`.
c	The value to be read is a single character; the next character that appears on the input is read, even if it a space, tab, newline, or form-feed character; the corresponding argument is a pointer to a character; an optional count before the `c` specifies the number of characters to read; in such a case, the corresponding argument is a pointer to a character array.
s	The value to be read is a sequence of characters; the sequence begins with the first nonwhite space character and is terminated by the first white space character; the corresponding argument is a pointer to a character array, which must contain enough characters to contain the characters that are read plus the null character that is automatically added to the end of the string; if a number precedes the `s`, then the specified number of characters is read, unless a white space character is encountered first.
[. . .]	Characters enclosed within brackets indicate that a character string is to be read, as in `%s`; the characters within the brackets indicate the permissible characters in in the string; if any character other than that specified in the brackets is encountered, then the string will be terminated; the sense of how these characters are treated may be "inverted" by placing a `^` as the first character inside the brackets; in such a case, the subsequent characters are taken to be the ones that will terminate the string; that is, if any of the subsequent characters is found on the input, then the string will be terminated.

When we wrote the programs in Chapter 9 that prompted us to enter the time from the terminal, we mentioned there that any nonformat characters that were specified in the format string of the `scanf` call would be expected on the input. So, for example, the `scanf` call

```
scanf ("%d:%d:%d", &hour, &minutes, &seconds);
```

meant that three integers values were to be read in and stored into the variables `hour`, `minutes`, and `seconds`, respectively. Inside the format string, the `:` characters specified that colons were expected as separators between the three integer values. In order to specify that a percent sign is expected as input, double percent signs are included in the format string, as in

```
scanf ("%d%%", &percentage);
```

White space characters inside a format string match an arbitrary number of white space characters on the input. So the call

```
scanf ("%d%c", &i, &c);
```

with the line of text

```
            29      w
```

would assign the value 29 to `i` and a blank space character to `c`, since this is the character that appears immediately after the characters `29` on the input. If the following `scanf` call were made instead:

```
scanf ("%d %c", &i, &c);
```

and the same line of text entered, then the value 29 would be assigned to `i` and the character `'w'` to `c` since the blank space in the format string would cause the `scanf` function to ignore any leading white space characters after the characters `29` had been read.

In Table 16-3, it was indicated that an asterisk may be used to skip fields. If the `scanf` call

```
scanf ("%d %5c %*f %s", &i1, text, string);
```

were executed and the following line of text were typed in at the terminal:

```
    144abcde     736.55        (wine and cheese)
```

then the value 144 would get stored into `i1`; the 5 characters `abcde` into the character array `text`; the floating value 736.55 would be skipped; and the character string `"(wine"` would be stored into `string`, terminated by a null. The next call to `scanf` would *pick up where the last one left off.* So a subsequent call such as

```
scanf ("%s %s %d", string2, string3, &i2);
```

would have the effect of storing the character string `"and"` into `string2`, the string `"cheese)"` into `string3` and would cause the function to wait for an integer value to be typed.

It must be remembered that the `scanf` call must take pointers to the variables where the values that are read in are to be stored. We know from the chapter on pointers why this is necessary (so that `scanf` can make changes to the variables; that is, store the values that it read into them). You will also remember that to specify a pointer to an array, that only the name of the array need be specified. So if `text` is defined as an appropriately sized array of characters, then the `scanf` call

```
scanf ("%80c", text);
```

would read the next 80 characters from the input and store it into `text`.

The `scanf` call

```
scanf ("%[^/]", text);
```

indicates that the string to be read in can consist of any character except for a slash. Using the above call on the line of text

```
(wine and cheese)/
```

would have the effect of storing the string `"(wine and cheese)"` into `text`, since the string would not be terminated until the `/` was matched (which would also be the next character read by `scanf` on the next call).

To read an entire line from the terminal into the character array `buf`, you can specify that the newline character at the end of the line is your string terminator:

```
scanf ("%[^\n]\n", buf)
```

The newline character is repeated outside the brackets so that `scanf` will match it and not read it the next time it's called (remember, `scanf` always continues reading from the character that terminated its last call).

When a value is read that does not match a value expected by `scanf` (for example, typing in the character `x` when an integer is expected), `scanf` does not read any further items from the input and immediately returns. Since the function returns the number of items that were succesfully read, this value can be tested to determine if any errors occurred on the input. For example, the call

```
if ( scanf ("%d %f %d", &i, &f, &l) != 3 )
    printf ("Error on input\n");
```

will test to make sure that scanf succesfully read and assigned three values. If not, an appropriate message is displayed.

Remember, the return value from scanf indicates the number of values read *and assigned*, so the call

```
scanf ("%d %*d %d", &i1, &i3)
```

returns 2 when successful and not 3, since we are reading and assigning *two* integers (skipping one in between).

It is left as an exercise to experiment with the various formatting options provided by the scanf function. As with the printf function, a good under-standing of these various formats will be obtained only through trying them in actual program examples. Consult *Topics in C Programming* (mentioned at the start of this chapter) for a more detailed discussion of scanf and its various peculiarities.

◆ File I/O ◆

Redirection of I/O to a File

Whenever a call was made to the scanf function by one of the programs in this book, the data that was requested by the call was always read in from the termi-nal. Similarly, all calls to the printf function resulted in the display of the desired information at the terminal.

The need frequently arises to either read in information from a file that is stored on the system, or to write data out to a file on the system. Both of these operations can be easily performed under many operating systems like UNIX and MS-DOS without anything special being done at all to the program. If we wished to write all of our program results into a file called data, for example, then all that we would have to do under UNIX (or MS-DOS) would be to redirect the output from the program into the file data by executing the program with the following command:

```
a.out > data
```

This command instructs the system to execute the program a.out but to take all of the output that is normally written to the terminal by the program and redirect it into a file called data instead. So any values displayed by printf would not be appear at the terminal but instead would be written into the file called data.

To see how this works, type in the very first program we wrote, Program 3-1, and compile the program in the usual way. Now execute the program as you normally would by typing in the command

```
a.out
```

at the terminal. If all goes well, you should get the output

```
Programming is fun.
```

at the terminal. Now issue the following command at the terminal:

```
a.out > data
```

This time you will notice that you did not get any output at the terminal. This is because the output was redirected into the file called data. We can examine the contents of the file data under UNIX by issuing the command

```
cat data
```

which will result in the display of the following at the terminal:

```
Programming is fun.
```

This verifies that the output from the program went into the file data as we described. You might want to try the preceding sequence of commands with a program that produces more lines of output to verify that the preceding process works properly in such cases.

We can do a similar type of redirection for the input to our program. Any call to a function that normally reads data from the terminal, such as scanf and getchar, can be easily made to read its information from a file. Program 5-8 was designed to reverse the digits of a number. The program uses scanf to read in the value of the number to be reversed from the terminal. We can have the program get its input from a file called number, for example, by redirecting the input to the program when the program is executed:

```
a.out < number
```

If we typed the number 2001 into a file called number before issuing the above command, then the following output would appear at the terminal after this command was entered:

```
Enter your number.
1002
```

You will notice that the program requested that a number be entered but did not wait for you to type in a number. This is because the input to the program—but not its output—was redirected to the file called `number`. Therefore, the `scanf` call from the program had the effect of reading the value from the file `number` and not from the terminal. The information must be entered in the file the same way that it would be typed in from the terminal. The `scanf` function itself does not actually know (or care) whether its input is coming from the terminal or a file; all that it cares about is that it is properly formatted.

Naturally, we can redirect the input and the output to a program at the same time. The command

```
a.out < number > data
```

causes execution of the program contained in `a.out` to read all program input from the file `number`, and to write all program results into the file `data`. So if we executed the above command for Program 5-8, the input would once again be taken from the file `number`, and the output would be written into the file `data`.

There are many cases where the method of redirecting the program's input and/or its output will be practical. For example, suppose we were writing an article for a magazine and had typed the text into a file called `article`. Program 10-8 counted the number of words that appeared in lines of text entered at the terminal. We could use this very same program to count the number of words in our article simply by typing in the command

```
a.out < article
```

Of course, we would have to remember to include an extra carriage return at the end of the `article` file, since our program was designed to recognize an "end of data" condition by the presence of a single newline character on a line.

End of File

The preceding point brings up an interesting topic of discussion: end of data. When dealing with files, this condition is called "end of file." An end of file condition exists when the last piece of data has been read from a file. Attempting to read past the end of the file may cause the program to terminate with an error, or else it may cause the program to go into an infinite loop if this condition is not checked by the program (the latter being the case for the UNIX system). Luckily, most of the functions from the Standard I/O Library return a special flag to indicate when a program has reached the end of a file. The value of this flag is equal to a special name called `EOF`, which is defined in the Standard I/O Library include file.

As an example of the use of the `EOF` test in combination with the `getchar` function, the following program will read in characters and echo them back at the terminal until an end of file is reached. Notice the expression contained inside the `while` loop. As you can see, an assignment does not have to be made in a separate statement.

Program 16-2

```
/* Program to echo characters until an end of file */

#include <stdio.h>

main ()
{
    int   c;

    while ( (c = getchar ()) != EOF )
        putchar (c);
}
```

If we were to compile and execute the preceding program, redirecting the input to a file with a command such as

```
a.out < infile
```

then the effect of the program would be to display the contents of the file infile at the terminal. Try it and see! Actually, the program serves the same basic function as the cat command under UNIX, and we could use it to display the contents of any text file we chose.

In the while loop of Program 16-2, the character that is returned by the getchar function is assigned to the variable c and is then compared against the defined value of EOF. If the values are equal, then this means that we have read the last character from the file. One important point must be mentioned with respect to the EOF value that is returned by the getchar function: The function actually returns an int and not a char. This is because the EOF value must be unique; that is, it cannot be equal to the value of any character that would normally be returned by getchar. Therefore, the value returned by getchar is assigned to an int and not a char variable in the preceding program. This works out okay, because the C language allows us to store characters inside ints, even though, in general, it may not be the best of programming practices.

The fact that we can make an assignment inside the conditional expression of the while loop illustrates the flexibility that C provides in the formation of expressions. The parentheses are required around the assignment because the assignment operator has lower precedence than the not equals operator.

Even though we stated earlier that the putchar function takes a character as its argument, we can get away with passing it an integer because of the way arguments are passed in C. Since a character is automatically converted to an integer when it is passed as an argument to a function, there is no harm in directly passing an integer value to the putchar function instead of a character. This discussion does not imply that you can or should use ints interchangeably with chars. Character arrays must be defined to contain chars and not ints if they are to work with any of the library functions, such as `printf` or `scanf`. Furthermore, `char`s will most likely take up less memory space on the machine than will `int`s.

♦ Special Functions for Handling Files ♦

It is very likely that many of the programs that you will develop will be able to perform all of their I/O operations using just the `getchar`, `putchar`, `scanf`, and `printf` functions and the notion of I/O redirection. However, situations do arise where you will need more flexibility to work with files. For example, you may need to read data from two or more different files, or to write output results into several different files. To handle these situations, special functions have been designed expressly for the purpose of working with files. Several of these functions will now be described.

The `fopen` Function

Before you can begin to do any I/O operations on a file, the file must first be *opened*. In order to open a file, we must specify to the system the name of the file. The system will then check to make sure that this file actually exists and, in certain instances, will create the file for you if it does not. When a file is opened, we must also specify to the system the type of I/O operations that we intend to perform with the file. If the file is to be used to read in data, then we would normally specify that the file be opened in *read mode*. If we wish to write data into the file, then the file must be opened in *write mode*. Finally, if we wish to append information to the end of a file that already contains some data, then the file must be opened in *append mode*. In the last two cases, write and append mode, if the specified file does not exist on the system, then the system will create the file for you. In the case of read mode, if the file does not exist, then the system will report an error.

Since a program can have many different files open at the same time, we need a way of identifying a particular file in the program whenever we wish to perform some I/O operation on the file. This is done by means of a *file pointer*.

The function called `fopen` in the Standard I/O Library serves the function of opening a file on the system and of returning a unique file pointer with which to subsequently identify the file. The function takes two arguments: the first is a character string specifying the name of the file to be opened; the second is also a character string that indicates the mode in which the file is to be opened. The function returns a file pointer that is used by other Standard I/O Library functions to identify a particular file.

If the file cannot be opened for some reason, then the function returns the value `NULL`, which is defined in the Standard I/O include file. Also defined in this file is the definition of a type called `FILE`. In order to store the result returned by the `fopen` function in our program, we must define a variable of type "pointer to `FILE`."

Taking the preceding comments into account, the statements

```
#include <stdio.h>

FILE   *input_file;

input_file = fopen ("data", "r");
```

will have the effect of opening a file called data in read mode. (Write mode is specified by the string "w" and append mode is specified by the string "a".) The fopen call will return an identifier for the opened file that will be assigned to the FILE pointer variable input_file. Subsequent testing of this variable against the defined value NULL (which happens to simply be defined as 0 inside stdio.h), as in

```
if ( input_file == (FILE *) NULL )
     printf ("*** data could not be opened.\n");
```

will tell us if the open were successful or not (recall the use of the type cast operator to ensure that we are comparing two FILE pointers and not a FILE pointer and an integer).

Frequently, the fopen call, the assignment of the returned FILE pointer variable, and the test against the NULL pointer are combined into a single statement, as in

```
if ( (input_file = fopen ("data", "r")) == (FILE *) NULL )
     printf ("*** data could not be opened.\n");
```

The fopen function also supports three other types of modes, called *update* modes ("r+", "w+", and "a+"). These modes will not be described here.

The getc and putc Functions

The function getc enables you to read in a single character from a file. This function behaves identically to the getchar function that we have encountered. The only difference is that the getc function takes an argument: a FILE pointer that identifies the file from which the character is to be read. So if fopen were called as shown above, then subsequent execution of the statement

```
c = getc (input_file);
```

would have the effect of reading a single character from the file data. Subsequent characters could be read from the file simply by making additional calls to the getc function.

The getc function returns the value EOF when the end of file is reached, and as with the getchar function, the value returned by getc should be stored in a variable of type int.

As you might have guessed, the putc function is equivalent to the putchar function, only it takes two arguments instead of one. The first argument to putc is the character that is to be written into the file. The second argument is the FILE pointer. So the call

```
putc ('\n', output_file);
```

would write a newline character into the file identified by the FILE pointer output_file. Of course, the identified file must have been previously opened in either write or append mode in order for this call to succeed.

With the functions putc and getc, we can now proceed to write a program which will copy one file to another. The program will prompt the user for the name of the file to be copied and the name of the resultant copied file. This program is based upon Program 16-2 that was presented earlier. You may want to refer to that program for comparison purposes.

Program 16-3

```
/* Program to copy one file to another */

#include <stdio.h>

main ()
{
    char  in_name[25], out_name[25];
    FILE  *in, *out;
    int   c;

    printf ("Enter name of file to be copied: ");
    scanf ("%24s", in_name);
    printf ("Enter name of output file: ");
    scanf ("%24s", out_name);

    if ( (in = fopen (in_name, "r"))  ==  (FILE *) NULL )
        printf ("Couldn't open %s for reading.\n", in_name);
    else if  ( (out = fopen (out_name, "w")) == (FILE *) NULL )
        printf ("Couldn't open %s for writing.\n", out_name);
    else
    {
        while ( (c = getc (in)) != EOF )
            putc (c, out);

        printf ("File has been copied.\n");
    }
}
```

Type the following three lines of text into the file `copyme`:

```
This is a test of the file copy program
that we have just developed using the
fopen, getc and putc functions.
```

and then execute the above program.

Program 16-3 Output

```
Enter name of file to be copied: copyme
Enter name of output file: here
File has been copied.
```

Now examine the contents of the file `here` (under UNIX use the `cat` command). The file should contain the same three lines of text as contained in the `copyme` file.

The `scanf` function call in the beginning of the program was given a field-width count of 24 just to ensure that we didn't overflow our `in_name` or `out_name` character arrays. The program then proceeds to open the specified input file for reading, and the specified output file for writing. If the output file already exists and is opened in write mode, then its previous contents will be destroyed under most systems.

If either of the two `fopen` calls is unsuccessful, then the program displays an appropriate message at the terminal and proceeds no further. Otherwise, the file is copied one character at a time, by means of successive `getc` and `putc` calls, until the end of the file is encountered.

The `fclose` Function

One operation that we can perform on a file, which must be mentioned, is that of closing the file. The `fclose` function in a sense does the opposite of what the `fopen` does: it tells the system that we no longer need to access the file. Whenever a file is closed, the system performs some necessary housekeeping chores (such as write all of the data that it may be keeping in a buffer in memory to the file), and then dissociates the particular file identifier from the file. Once a file has been closed, it can no longer be read from or written to unless it is reopened.

Whenever you have completed your operations on a file, it is a good habit to close the file. We did not do so in the preceding program because of the fact that when a program terminates normally, the system automatically closes any open files for us. It is generally better programming practice to close a file as soon as you are done with it. This can be beneficial if your program has to deal with a large number of files, as there are practical limits on the number of files that can be simultaneously open by a program at any given point in time (20 files can be simultaneously open under UNIX).

By the way, the argument to the fclose function is the FILE pointer of the file to be closed. So the call

```
fclose (input);
```

would close the file associated with the FILE pointer input.

The feof Function

In order to test for an end of file condition on a file, the function feof is provided. The single argument to the function is a FILE pointer. The function returns an integer value that is nonzero if an attempt has been made to read past the end of a file, and is zero otherwise. So, the statements

```
if ( feof (in_file) )
      printf ("Ran out of data.\n");
```

will have the effect of displaying the message "Ran out of data." at the terminal if an end of file condition exists on the file identified by in_file.

Remember, feof tells you that an attempt has been made to read past the end of the file, which is not the same as telling you that you just read the last data item from a file. You have to read "one past" the last data item for feof to return nonzero.

The fprintf and fscanf Functions

The functions fprintf and fscanf are provided to perform the analagous operations of the printf and scanf functions on a file. These functions take an additional argument, which is the FILE pointer that identifies the file to which the data is to be written or from which the data is to be read. So to write the character string "Programming in C is fun.\n" into the file identified by out_file, we can write the statement

```
fprintf (out_file, "Programming in C is fun.\n");
```

Similarly, to read in the next floating point value from the file identified by in_file into the variable fv, the statement

```
fscanf (in_file, "%f", &fv);
```

could be used. As with scanf, fscanf returns the number of arguments that are successfully read and assigned, or the value EOF if the end of the file is reached before any data items have been read.

The `fgets` and `fputs` Functions

For reading and writing entire lines of data from and to a file, the `fputs` and `fgets` functions can be used. The `fgets` function is called as follows:

>   fgets   (*buffer, n, file_pointer*) ;

buffer is a pointer to a character array where the line that is read in will be stored; *n* is an integer value that represents the maximum number of characters that are to be stored into *buffer*; and *file_pointer* identifies the file from which the line is to be read.

The `fgets` function reads characters from the specified file until a newline character has been read (which *will* get stored into the buffer) or until *n-1* characters have been read, whichever occurs first. The function automatically places a null character after the last character in *buffer*. It returns the value of *buffer* (the first argument) if the read is successful and the value `NULL` if an error occurs on the read or if an attempt is made to read past the end of the file.

The `fputs` function writes a line of characters to a specified file. The function is called as shown

>   fputs   (*buffer, file_pointer*) ;

Characters stored in the array pointed to by *buffer* are written to the file identified by *file_pointer* until the null character is reached. The terminating null character is *not* written to the file.

There are also analgous functions called `gets` and `puts` that can be used to read a line from the terminal and write a line to the terminal, respectively. These functions are described in Appendix C.

`stdin`, `stdout`, and `stderr`

Whenever a C program is executed, three "files" are automatically opened by the system for use by the program. These files are identified by the *constant* `FILE` pointers `stdin`, `stdout`, and `stderr`, which are defined in the Standard I/O include file. The `FILE` pointer `stdin` identifies the standard input of the program, and is normally associated with your terminal. All Standard I/O functions that perform input and do not take a `FILE` pointer as an argument get their input from `stdin`. For example, the `scanf` function reads its input from `stdin`, and a call to this function is equivalent to a call to the `fscanf` function with `stdin` as the first argument. So the call

```
fscanf (stdin, "%d", &i);
```

will read in the next integer value from the standard input, which will normally be your terminal. If the input to your program has been redirected to a file, then this call will read the next integer value from the file that the standard input has been redirected to.

As you might have guessed, stdout refers to the standard output, which is normally also associated with your terminal. So a call such as

```
printf ("hello there.\n");
```

can be replaced by an equivalent call to the fprintf function with stdout as the first argument:

```
fprintf (stdout, "hello there.\n");
```

The putchar function on your system is most likely actually implemented as a macro definition that simply calls the putc function with stdout as the argument for the FILE pointer:

```
#define   putchar(c)      putc (c, stdout)
```

The same is most likely true for the getchar "function" with respect to the function getc:

```
#define   getchar()       getc (stdin)
```

(On your system, putc and getc themselves may be implemented as macro definitions as well.)

The FILE pointer stderr identifies the standard error file. This is where most of the error messages produced by the system are written, and is also normally associated with your terminal. The reason why stderr exists is so that error messages can be logged to a device or file other than that where the normal output is written. This is particularly desirable whenever the program's output is redirected to a file. In such a case, the normal output will be written into the file but any system error messages will still appear at the terminal. You might want to write your own error messages to stderr for this same reason. As an example, the fprintf call in the following statement

```
if ( (in_file = fopen (."data", "r")) == (FILE *) NULL )
{
      fprintf (stderr, "Can't open data for reading.\n");
      ...
}
```

will write the indicated error message to stderr if the file data cannot be opened for reading. And if the the standard output had been redirected to a file, then this message would still appear at the terminal.

The exit Function

At times, it may be desirable to force the termination of a program, such as when an error condition is detected by a program. We know that program execution is automatically terminated whenever the last statement in main is executed. But in order to explicitly terminate a function, the exit function can be called. The function call

```
exit (n);
```

has the effect of terminating (exiting from) the current program. Any open files will be automatically closed by the system. The integer value *n* is called the *exit status*. Under UNIX, this value is 0 by convention for a program that terminates normally, and nonzero for a program that terminates due to some detected error condition. This condition code may be tested by other processes to determine whether the program successfully completed execution or not.

As an example of the use of the exit function, the following sequence of statements will cause the program to terminate with a condition code value of 1 if the file data cannot be opened for reading.

```
if ( (in_file = fopen ("data", "r")) == (FILE *) NULL )
{
    fprintf (stderr, "Can't open data for reading.\n");
    exit (1);
}
```

This concludes our discussion of I/O operations under C. As mentioned, we have not covered all of the library functions here for reasons of space. You should check the system documentation at your computer installation to find out about other functions that are available—not just in the Standard I/O Library, but in other function libraries as well. Also consult the book noted at the start of this chapter. Most likely, your installation offers a wide selection of functions for performing operations with character strings, for *random* I/O, and for dynamic memory management. Most systems also provide a wide selection of mathematical functions. Appendix C lists many of the functions supplied by most operating systems.

◆ Exercises ◆

1. If you have access to a computer facility that supports the C programming language, type in and run the three programs presented in this chapter. Compare the output produced by each program with the output presented.

2. Go back to programs developed earlier in this book and experiment with redirecting their input and output to files.

3. Write a program to copy one file to another, replacing all lowercase characters with their uppercase equivalents.

4. Write a program that merges lines alternately from two files and writes the results to stdout. If one file has less lines than the other, the remaining lines from the larger file should be simply copied to stdout.

5. Write a program that writes columns m through n of each line of a file to stdout. Have the program accept the values of m and n from the terminal.

6. Write a program that displays the contents of a file at the terminal 20 lines at a time. At the end of each 20 lines, have the program wait for a character to be entered from the terminal. If the character is the letter q, then the program should stop the display of the file; any other character should cause the next 20 lines from the file to be displayed.

Miscellaneous and Advanced Features

This chapter discusses some miscellaneous features of the C language that we have not yet covered and also provides a discussion of some more advanced topics, such as command line arguments and dynamic memory allocation.

The goto Statement

Anyone who has learned about structured programming knows of the reputation afforded to the goto statement. Virtually every computer language has such a statement.

Execution of a goto statement causes a direct branch to be made to a specified point in the program. This branch is made immediately and unconditionally upon execution of the goto. In order to identify where in the program the branch is to be made, a *label* is needed. A label is a name that is formed with the same rules as variable names, and must be immediately followed by a colon. The label is placed directly before the statement to which the branch is to be made, and must appear in the same function as the goto.

So, for example, the statement

```
goto out_of_data;
```

will cause the program to branch immediately to the statement that is preceded by the label out_of_data:. This label can be located anywhere in the function, before or after the goto, and might be used as shown:

```
out_of_data:  printf ("Ran out of data.\n");
    ...
```

Programmers who are lazy will frequently use a goto statement to exit from a deeply nested loop. The way to "gracefully" exit such a loop is by using a flag and testing the value of the flag at each point in the loop. For example, suppose the preceding goto statement were used to exit from inside a loop nested three levels deep when an end of file occurred on the input:

```
while ( a < b )
    for ( i = 0;  i < n;  ++i )
        for ( j = 0;  j < m;  ++j )
        {
            . . .
            if ( eof_flag == EOF )
                goto end_of_data;
            . . .
        }
return;

end_of_data:
        printf ("Ran out of data\n");
        . . .
```

We could rewrite the above sequence of statements without the use of the goto as follows:

```
int  eof_flag = 0;

while ( a < b  &&  eof_flag != EOF )
    for ( i = 0;  i < n  &&  eof_flag != EOF;  ++i )
        for ( j = 0;  j < m  &&  eof_flag != EOF;  ++j )
        {
            . . .
            if ( eof_flag != EOF )
                . . .
        }

if ( eof_flag != EOF )
    return;

printf ("Ran out of data.\n");
    . . .
```

In this example, when the value of eof_flag becomes equal to EOF, the program will "back out" of each loop because the looping condition will no longer be satisfied. This sort of technique can always be used to avoid the use of a goto statement.

The `goto` statement interrupts the normal sequential flow of a program. As a result, programs are harder to follow. Using many `goto`s in a program can make it impossible to decipher. For this reason, `goto` statements are not considered part of a good programming style.

The Null Statement

C permits a solitary semicolon to be placed wherever a normal program statement can appear. The effect of such a statement, known as the *null* statement, is that nothing is done. While this may seem quite useless, it is very often used by C programmers in `while`, `for`, and `do` statements. For example, the purpose of the following statement is to store all of the characters read in from the standard input into the character array pointed to by `text` until a newline character is encountered.

```
while ( (*text++ = getchar ()) != '\n' )
    ;
```

All of the operations are performed inside the looping-conditions part of the `while` statement. The null statement is needed because the compiler takes the statement that follows the looping expression as the body of the loop. Without the null statement, whatever statement that follows in the program would be treated as the body of the program loop by the compiler.

The following `for` statement copies characters from the standard input to the standard output until the end of file is encountered:

```
for (  ; (c = getchar ()) != EOF;  putchar (c) )
    ;
```

The next `for` statement counts the number of characters that appear in the standard input:

```
for ( count = 0;  getchar () != EOF;  ++count )
    ;
```

As a final example illustrating the null statement, the following loop sums the integers in an array named a, which contains n elements:

```
for ( sum = 0, i = 0;  i < n;  sum += a[i++] )
    ;
```

The reader is advised that there is a tendency among certain programmers to try to "squeeze" as much as possible into the condition part of the `while`, or into the condition or looping part of the `for`. Try not to become one of those programmers. In general, only those expressions involved with testing the condition of a loop should be included inside the condition part. Everything else should form the body of the loop. The only case to be made for forming such complex expressions might be one of execution efficiency. Unless execution speed is that critical, you should avoid using these types of expressions.

So the preceding `for` statement is clearer when written like this:

```
for ( sum = 0, i = 0;  i < n;   ++i )
    sum += a[i];
```

Unions

One of the more unusual constructs in the C programming language is the *union*. This construct is used mainly in more advanced programming applications where it is necessary to store different types of data into the same storage area. For example, if we wanted to define a single variable called x, which could be used to store a single character, a floating point number, or an integer, we would first define a union, called, perhaps, `mixed`, as follows:

```
union   mixed
{
      char    c;
      float   f;
      int     i;
};
```

The declaration for a union is identical to that of a structure, except the keyword `union` is used where the keyword `struct` is otherwise specified. The real difference between structures and unions has to do with the way memory is allocated. Declaring a variable to be of type `union mixed`, as in

```
union mixed  x;
```

does *not* define x to contain three distinct members called c, f, and i, but rather defines x to contain a *single* member that is called *either* c, f, or i. In this way, the variable x can be used to store either a `char` or a `float` or an `int`, but not all three (or not even two of the three). We can store a character into the variable x with the following statement:

```
x.c = 'K';
```

The character stored in x can subsequently be retrieved in the same manner. So to display its value at the terminal, for example, the following could be used:

```
printf ("Character = %c\n", x.c);
```

To store a floating point value into x, the notation x.f is used:

```
x.f = 786.3869;
```

Finally, to store the result of dividing an integer `count` by 2 into `x`, the statement

```
x.i = count / 2;
```

could be used.

Since the `float`, `char`, and `int` members of `x` all co-exist in the same place in memory, only one value can be stored into `x` at a time. Furthermore, it is your responsibility to ensure that the value retrieved from a union is consistent with the way it was last stored in the union.

A union member follows the same rules of arithmetic as the type of the member that is used in the expression. So in

```
x.i / 2
```

the expression is evaluated according to the rules of integer arithmetic, since `x.i` and 2 are both integers.

A union can be defined to contain as many members as desired. The C compiler ensures that enough storage is allocated to accommodate the largest member of the union. Structures can be defined that contain unions, as can arrays. When defining a union, the name of the union is not required, and variables can be declared at the same time that the union is defined. Pointers to unions can also be declared, and their syntax and rules for performing operations are the same as for structures.

The use of a union enables you to define arrays that can be used to store elements of different data types. For example, the statement

```
struct
{
    char    *name;
    int     type;
    union
    {
        int     i;
        float   f;
        char    c;
    } data;
}   table [TABLE_ENTRIES];
```

sets up an array called `table`, consisting of `TABLE_ENTRIES` elements. Each element of the array contains a structure consisting of a character pointer called name, an integer member called `type`, and a union member called `data`. Each data member of the array can contain either an `int`, a `float`, or a `char`. The integer member `type` might be used to keep track of the type of value stored in the member `data`. For example, we could assign it the value `INTEGER` (defined appropriately, we assume) if it contained an `int`, `FLOATING` if it contained a `float`, and `CHARACTER` if it contained a `char`. This information would enable us to know how to reference the particular `data` member of a particular array element.

To store the character `'#'` into `table[5]`, and subsequently set the `type` field to indicate that a character is stored in that location, the following two statements could be used:

```
table[5].data.c = '#';
table[5].type = CHARACTER;
```

When sequencing through the elements of `table`, we could determine the type of data value stored in each element by setting up an appropriate series of test statements. For example, the following loop would display each name and its associated value from `table` at the terminal.

```
#define     INTEGER    0
#define     FLOATING   1
#define     CHARACTER  2
     . . .

for ( j = 0;  j < TABLE_ENTRIES;  ++j )
{
    printf ("%s   ", table[j].name);

    switch ( table[j].type )
    {
        case INTEGER:
            printf ("%d\n", table[j].data.i);
            break;
        case FLOATING:
            printf ("%f\n", table[j].data.f);
            break;
        case CHARACTER:
            printf ("%c\n", table[j].data.c);
            break;
        default:
            printf ("Unknown type (%d), element %d\n",
                    table[j].type, j );
            break;
    }
}
```

The type of application illustrated above might be very practical for storage of a symbol table, for example, which might contain the name of each symbol, its type, and its value (and perhaps other information about the symbol as well).

The Comma Operator

At the bottom of the precedence totem pole, so to speak, is the comma operator. In Chapter 5, we pointed out that inside a `for` statement we could include more than one expression in any of the fields by separating each expression with a comma. For example, the `for` statement that begins

```
for ( i = 0, j = 100;  i != 10;  ++i, j -= 10 )
    ...
```

initializes the value of `i` to 0 *and* `j` to 100 before the loop begins, and increments the value of `i` *and* subtracts 10 from the value of `j` each time after the body of the loop is executed.

The comma operator can be used to separate multiple expressions anywhere that a valid C expression can be used. However, this operator is primarily used in `for` statements. Since all operators in C produce a value, the value of the comma operator is that of the rightmost expression.

Note that a comma used to separate arguments in a function call, or variable names in a list of declarations, for example, is a separate syntactic entity and is *not* an example of the use of the comma operator.

Register Variables

The C compiler provides a mechanism that enables the programmer to have some influence over the efficiency of the code that is generated by the compiler. If a function uses a particular variable heavily, then you can request that the value of that variable be stored in one of the machine's registers whenever the function is executed. This is done by prefixing the declaration of the variable by the keyword `register`, as in

```
register int    index;
register char   *text_pointer;
```

Both local variables and formal parameters can be declared as `register` variables. The types of variables that can be assigned to registers vary among machines. The basic data types can usually be assigned to registers, as well as pointers to any data type. As you would expect, arrays and structures cannot be declared as register variables.

Even if your compiler lets you declare a variable as a register variable, it is still not guaranteed that it will in fact be assigned to a register. Each machine has different limitations on the number of register variables that are permitted. In any case, variables that cannot be assigned to a register will not cause an error—the declaration will simply be ignored by the compiler.

It is worth noting that you cannot apply the address operator to a register variable. Otherwise, register variables behave just as ordinary variables.

◆ Command Line Arguments ◆

Many times a program will be developed that requires the user to enter a small amount of information at the terminal. Based upon programs presented in this book, this information might consist of a number indicating the triangular number that we would like to have calculated, or a word which we would like to have looked up inside a dictionary.

Rather than having the program request this type of information from the user we can supply the information to the program *at the time that the program is executed*. This capability is provided by what is known as *command line arguments*.

We have pointed out that the only distinguishing quality of the function main is that its name is special; it specifies where program execution is to begin. In fact, the function main is actually *called* upon the start of program execution by the C system (known more formally as the *runtime* system), just as you would call a function from within your own C program. When main completes execution, control is returned to the runtime system, which then knows that your program has completed execution.

When main is called by the runtime system, two arguments are actually passed to the function. The first argument, which is called argc by convention (for *arg*ument *c*ount), is an integer value that specifies the number of arguments typed on the command line. The second argument to main is an array of character pointers, which is called argv by convention (for *arg*ument *v*ector). There will be argc character pointers contained in this array, where argc always has a minimum value of 1. The first entry in this array is always a pointer to the name of the program that is executing. Subsequent entries in the array point to the values that were specified on the same line as the command which initiated execution of the program.

In order to access the command line arguments, the main function must be appropriately declared as taking two arguments. The conventional declaration that is used appears as follows:

```
main (argc, argv)
int    argc;
char   *argv[];
{
    ...
}
```

Remember, the declaration of argv defines an array that contains elements of type "pointer to char." As a practical use of command line arguments, recall Program 10-10, which looked up a word inside a dictionary and printed its meaning. We can make use of command line arguments so that the word whose meaning we wish to find can be specified at the same time that the program is executed, as in the UNIX command

```
a.out  aerie
```

This eliminates the need for the program to prompt the user to enter a word and also reduces the number of steps required on the part of the user to have a word looked up inside the dictionary.

If the command shown above were executed, then the system would automatically pass to the main function a pointer to the character string "aerie" in argv[1]. As you will recall, argv[0] would contain a pointer to the name of the program, which in this case would be "a.out".

The main routine might appear as shown:

```
main (argc, argv)
int    argc;
char   *argv[];
{
    static struct entry  dictionary[100] =
       { { "aardvark",  "a burrowing African mammal"        },
         { "abyss",     "a bottomless pit"                  },
         { "acumen",    "mentally sharp; keen"              },
         { "addle",     "to become confused"                },
         { "aerie",     "a high nest"                       },
         { "affix",     "to append; attach"                 },
         { "agar",      "a jelly made from seaweed"         },
         { "ahoy",      "a nautical call of greeting"       },
         { "aigrette",  "an ornamental cluster of feathers" },
         { "ajar",      "partially opened"                  } };

    int    entries = 10;
    int    entry_number;

    if ( argc != 2 )
    {
        fprintf (stderr, "No word typed on the command line.\n");
        exit (1);
    }

    entry_number = lookup (dictionary, argv[1], entries);

    if ( entry_number != -1 )
        printf ("%s\n", dictionary[entry_number].definition);
    else
        printf ("Sorry, %s is not in my dictionary.\n", argv[1]);
}
```

The main routine tests to make sure that a word was typed after the program name when the program was executed. If it wasn't, or if more than one word was typed, then the value of argc will not be equal to 2. In that case, the program will write an error message to standard error and would then terminate.

If argc is equal to 2, then the lookup function will be called to find the word pointed to by argv[1] in the dictionary. If the word is found, then its definition will be displayed.

By changing the name of the executable object to something more meaningful, such as lookup, the command to execute the program to find the word "addle" in the dictionary would be

```
lookup addle
```

(The name of the executable file can be specified to be lookup when the program is compiled, or the executable file can easily be renamed with a simple command after the program has been compiled.)

As another example of command line arguments, Program 16-3 was a file copying program. Program 17-1, which follows, takes the two file names from the command line, rather than prompting the user to type them in.

Program 17-1

```
/* Program to copy one file to another -- version 2 */

#include <stdio.h>

main (argc, argv)
int     argc;
char    *argv[];
{
    FILE    *in, *out;
    int     c;

    if ( argc != 3 )
    {
        fprintf (stderr, "Specify two files on command line\n");
        exit (1);
    }

    if ( (in = fopen (argv[1], "r"))   ==   (FILE *) NULL )
    {
        fprintf (stderr, "Can't read %s.\n", argv[1]);
        exit (2);
    }

    if ( (out = fopen (argv[2], "w"))  ==  (FILE *) NULL )
    {
        fprintf (stderr, "Can't write %s.\n", argv[2]);
        exit (3);
    }
```

```
while ( (c = getc (in)) != EOF )
    putc (c, out);

printf ("File has been copied.\n");

exit (0);
}
```

The program first checks to make sure that two arguments were typed after the program name. If so, then the name of the input file will be pointed to by argv[1], and the name of the output file by argv[2]. After opening the first file for reading and the second file for writing, and checking the results of both opens to make sure they succeeded, the program copies the file character by character as before.

Note the use of the exit status in this program example. There are four different ways for the program to terminate: incorrect number of command line arguments, can't open the file to be copied for reading, can't open the file to place the copy into for writing, and successful termination. In order to be able to detect which way this program terminates (and the way to do that under the UNIX system is beyond the scope of this text), the program exits with a different exit status in each case. Note that if you're going to be using this exit status, you should *always* terminate the program with a call to exit. If your program terminates simply by returning from main, it will return a *random* exit status.

If Program 16-3 were called copyf, and the program was executed with the following command line:

```
copyf foo fool
```

then the argv array would look like Fig. 17-1 when main gets entered.

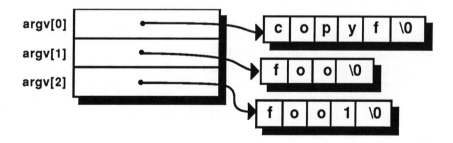

Fig. 17-1. argv array on startup of copyf

It should be remembered that command line arguments are *always* stored as character strings. So execution of the program power with the command line arguments 2 and 16, as in

```
power 2 16
```

will store a pointer to the character string `"2"` inside `argv[1]`, and a pointer to the string `"16"` inside `argv[2]`. If the arguments are to be interpreted as numbers by the program (as we suspect is the case in the `power` program), then they must be converted by the program itself. There are probably several routines in your program library for doing such conversions, such as `sscanf`, `atof`, and `atoi`.

◆ Dynamic Memory Allocation ◆

Whenever we define a variable in C—whether it is a simple data type, an array, or a structure—we are effectively reserving one or more locations in the computer's memory to contain the values that will be stored in that variable. The C compiler automatically allocates the correct amount of storage for us.

It is frequently desirable, if not necessary, to be able to *dynamically* allocate storage while a program is running. Suppose we had a program that was designed to read in a set of data from a file into an array in memory. If we were unsure precisely how many data elements were contained in the file, or if the amount could vary from one run of the program to the next, then we would have to define our array to contain the maximum number of elements that would be read into the array, as in the following:

```
#define  MAX_ELEMENTS    1000

struct data_entry  data_array [MAX_ELEMENTS];
```

Now as long as the data file contains 1000 elements or less, we're in business. But what happens when the number of elements exceeds this amount? In that case, we must go back to the program, change the value of MAX_ELEMENTS, and recompile it. Of course, no matter what value we select, we always have the chance of running into the same problem again in the future.

The preceding problem becomes much worse if we are dealing with many different arrays in our program, each of which can contain a variable number of elements. In order to handle the situation properly, we must reserve the maximum number of elements in each array. In many cases, this approach may be infeasible. We might know, for example, that the *total* number of elements that would be stored into three different arrays would be a maximum of 10,000, but that each individual array might contain up to 8,000 elements. Reserving 8,000 elements for each array might exceed the memory capacity of the computer system, whereas we know that 10,000 total elements could be easily handled. What could we do?

Dynamic memory allocation enables us to get storage as we need it. That is, this approach enables us to allocate memory as the program is executing, and thereby eliminates the need to completely define our storage requirements when the program is compiled. In order to use dynamic memory allocation, we must first learn about three functions and one new operator.

The `calloc` and `malloc` Functions

In order to allocate storage while a program is executing, a call must be made to a special function. On most systems, two functions, called `calloc` and `malloc`, can be used. The `calloc` function takes two arguments that specify the number of elements to be reserved, and the size of each element in *bytes*. The function returns a pointer to the beginning of the allocated storage area in memory. The storage area is also automatically set to zero.

The pointer that is returned by `calloc` can be assigned to a pointer variable of the appropriate type, and should first be type cast into the same data type as the variable to ensure that everything is *aligned* properly. (A detail that you need not concern yourself with as long as you remember the type casting.) The pointer variable can subsequently be used as a normal pointer variable in C.

The `malloc` function works similarly, except that it only takes a single argument—the total number of bytes of storage to allocate—and also doesn't automatically set the storage area to zero.

The `sizeof` Operator

In order to determine the size of data elements to be reserved by `calloc` or `malloc`, the C `sizeof` operator should be used. The `sizeof` operator returns the size of the specified item in bytes. The argument to the `sizeof` operator can be a variable, an array name, the name of a basic data type, the name of a derived data type, or an expression. For example, writing

```
sizeof (int)
```

gives the number of bytes needed to store an integer. On the PDP-11, this will have the value 2, since an integer occupies that many bytes on the machine. If `x` were defined to be an array of 100 integers, then the expression

```
sizeof (x)
```

would give the amount of storage required for the 100 integers of `x`. The expression

```
sizeof (struct data_entry)
```

will have as its value the amount of storage required to contain one `data_entry` structure. Finally, if `data` is defined as an array of `struct` data_entry elements, then the expression

```
sizeof (data) / sizeof (struct data_entry)
```

will have as its value the number of elements contained in data (data must be a previously defined array, and not a formal parameter or externally referenced array).

You should remember that sizeof is actually an operator, and not a function, even though it looks like one. Also, this operator is evaluated at compile time and not at run time. This means that the compiler automatically calculates the value of the sizeof expression and replaces it with the result of the calculation; also, the value of this operator is considered a constant.

So if you wanted to allocate enough storage in your program to store 1000 integers, you can call calloc as shown:

```
intptr = (int *) calloc (sizeof (int), 1000);
```

Using malloc, you would write instead

```
intptr = (int *) malloc (1000 * sizeof (int));
```

Both malloc and calloc are defined to return a pointer to a char and must be declared as such. The pointer that is returned should be type cast to the appropriate pointer type. In the preceding example, the pointer is type cast to an integer pointer and then assigned to int_pointer.

Whether you use calloc or malloc, be sure to test the pointer that is returned to ensure that the allocation succeeded. For example, if you ask for more memory then the system has available, calloc (or malloc) will return a null (i.e., zero) pointer. The following code segment allocates space for 1000 integer pointers and tests the pointer that is returned. If the allocation fails, the program writes an error message to standard error and then exits.

```
int   *intptr;
char *calloc ();
    ...
intptr = (int *) calloc (sizeof (int), 1000);

if ( intptr == (int *) 0 )
{
    fprintf (stderr, "calloc failed\n");
    exit (1);
}
```

If the allocation succeeds, then the integer pointer variable intptr can be used as if it were pointing to an array of 1000 integers. So, to set all 1000 elements to -1, you could write

```
for ( p = intptr; p < intptr + 1000; ++p )
    *p = -1;
```

assuming p is declared to be an integer pointer.

To reserve storage for *n* elements of type struct data_entry, we would first need to define a pointer of the appropriate type:

```
struct data_entry  *data_pointer;
```

and could then proceed to call the calloc function to reserve the appropriate number of elements:

```
data_pointer = (struct data_entry *)
                   calloc (n, sizeof (struct data_entry));
```

Execution of the above statement proceeds as follows: (1) the calloc function is called with two arguments, the first specifying that storage for n elements is to be dynamically allocated, and the second specifying the size of each element. (2) The calloc function returns a pointer in memory to the allocated storage area. If the storage cannot be allocated then the null pointer will be returned. (3) The pointer is type cast into a pointer of type "pointer to struct data_entry" and is then assigned to the pointer variable data_pointer.

Once again, the value of data_pointer should be subsequently tested to ensure that the allocation succeeded. If it did, then its value will be nonnull. This pointer could then be used in the normal fashion, as if it were pointing to an array of n data_entry elements. For example, if data_entry contained an integer member called index, we could assign 100 to this member as pointed to by data_pointer with the statement

```
data_pointer->index = 100;
```

The free Function

When you have finished working with the memory that has been dynamically allocated by calloc or malloc, you can "give it back" to the system by calling the free function. The single argument to the function is a pointer to the beginning of the allocated memory, as returned by a calloc or malloc call. So the call

```
free (data_pointer);
```

will return the memory allocated by the calloc call shown above, provided that the value of data_pointer still points to the *beginning* of the allocated memory.

The free function does not return a value.

The memory that is freed by free can be reused by a later call to calloc or malloc. For programs that need to allocate more storage space than would otherwise be available if it were all allocated at once, this is worth remembering.

Dynamic memory allocation proves very useful when dealing with linked structures, such as linked lists. Whenever we wish to add a new entry to the list, we can dynamically allocate storage for one entry in the list and link it into the list with the pointer returned by calloc or malloc. For example, assume that list_end points to the end of a singly linked list of type struct entry, defined as follows:

```
struct entry
{
    int          value;
    struct entry *next;
};
```

Here is a function called add_entry that takes as its argument a pointer to the start of the linked list and that adds a new entry to the end of the list.

```
#define NULL    0

/* add new entry to end of list */

struct entry *add_entry (list_ptr)
struct entry *list_ptr;
{
    /* find the end of the list */

    while ( list_ptr->next != (struct entry *) NULL )
        list_ptr = list_ptr->next;

    /* get storage for new entry */

    list_ptr->next = (struct entry *)
                        malloc (sizeof (struct entry));

    if ( list_ptr->next != (struct entry *) NULL )
        /* add null to the new end of the list */
        (list_ptr->next)->next = (struct entry *) NULL;

    return (list_ptr->next);
}
```

If the allocation succeeds, a null pointer is placed in the `next` member of the newly allocated linked list entry (pointed to by `list_ptr->next`).

The function returns a pointer to the new list entry, or the null pointer if the allocation fails (verify that this is in fact what happens). If you draw a picture of a linked list and trace through the execution of `add_entry`, it will help you to understand how the function works.

A

Language Summary

This section summarizes the C language in a format suitable for quick reference. It is not intended that this section be a complete definition of the language, but rather a concise summary of all of its features. You should thoroughly read the material in this section after you have completed the text. Doing so will not only reinforce the material you have learned, but will also provide you with a better global understanding of C.

◆ 1.0 Identifiers ◆

An *identifier* in C consists of a sequence of letters (upper- or lowercase), digits, or underscore characters. The first character of an identifier must be a letter or an underscore character. Only the first eight characters of an identifier are guaranteed to be significant, even though more characters may be used. On some systems, external names may be significant to less than eight characters. Furthermore, on some systems upper- and lowercase letters may not be distinguishable in an external name.

Table A-1 lists the identifiers that are reserved by the C compiler and cannot be otherwise used in a program.

◆ 2.0 Comments ◆

A comment begins with the two characters /* and ends as soon as the characters */ are encountered. Any characters may be included inside the comment, which can extend over multiple lines of the program. A comment can be used anywhere in the program where a blank space is allowed. Comments cannot be nested.

TABLE A-1. Reserved identifiers

asm	double	if	struct
auto	else	int	switch
break	enum	long	typedef
case	extern	register	union
char	float	return	unsigned
continue	for	short	void
default	fortran	sizeof	while
do	goto	static	

♦ 3.0 Constants ♦

3.1 Integer Constants

An integer constant is a sequence of digits, optionally preceded by a minus sign (an optional plus sign is *not* acceptable because there is no unary plus operator in C). If the first digit is 0, then the integer is taken as an octal constant, in which case all digits that follow must be from 0 through 7. If the first digit is 0 and is immediately followed by the letter x (or X), then the integer is taken as a hexadecimal constant, and the digits that follow may be in the range of 0-9 or a-f (or A-F).

An integer constant is taken as a long integer constant if (1) it is a decimal integer constant and is greater in value than the largest value that can be stored in a signed integer; (2) it is an octal or hexadecimal constant and is greater in value than the largest value that can be stored in an unsigned integer; or (3) the letter l (or L) immediately follows the integer constant.

3.2 Floating Point Constants

A floating point constant consists of a sequence of decimal digits, a decimal point, and another sequence of decimal digits. A minus sign may precede the value to denote a negative value. Either the sequence of digits before the decimal point or after the decimal point may be omitted, but not both.

If the floating point constant is immediately followed by the letter e (or E) and an optionally signed integer, then the constant is expressed in scientific notation. This integer (the *exponent*) represents the power of 10 that the value preceding the letter e (the *mantissa*) is multiplied by (e.g., 1.5e-2 represents 1.5×10^{-2} or .015).

Floating point constants are treated as double precision values by most compilers, although this is no longer a requirement.

3.3 Character Constants

A character that is enclosed within single quotes is a character constant. Special escape characters are recognized and are introduced by the backslash character. These escape characters are listed below.

Character	Meaning
\b	backspace
\f	form feed
\n	newline
\r	carriage return
\t	horizontal tab
\v	vertical tab
\\	backslash
\"	double quote
\'	single quote
\(*carriage return*)	line continuation
nnn	octal character value

In the last case, from one to three octal digits can be specified.

3.4 Character String Constants

A sequence of zero or more characters enclosed within double quotes represents a character string constant. Any valid character can be included in the string, including any of the escape characters listed above. The compiler automatically inserts a null character (' \0 ') at the end of the string, and produces a pointer to the first character in the string.

3.5 Enumeration Constants

An identifier that has been declared as a value for an enumerated type is taken as a constant of that particular type, and is otherwise treated as an integer by the compiler.

♦ 4.0 Data Types and Declarations ♦

This section summarizes the basic data types, derived data types, enumerated data types, and typedef. Also summarized in this section is the format for declaring variables.

4.1 Definitions vs. Declarations

The *definition* of a particular structure, union, enumerated data type, or typedef does not cause any storage to be reserved by the compiler; it merely sets up the definition for the particular data type and (optionally) associates a name with it. A definition can be made either inside or outside a function. In the former case, only the function knows of its existence; in the latter case, the definition is known throughout the remainder of the file.

Once the definition has been made, variables can subsequently be *declared* to be of that particular data type. A variable that is declared to be of *any* data type *will* have storage reserved for it (the exception is the extern storage class—see section 6.0). The language also allows variables to be declared at the same time that a particular structure, union, or enumerated data type is defined. This is done by simply listing the variables before the terminating semicolon of the definition.

4.2 Basic Data Types

The basic C data types are summarized in Table A-2. A variable can be declared to be of a particular basic data type using the format

> *type name = initial_value;*

The assignment of an initial value to the variable is optional, and is subject to the rules summarized in Section 6.2. More than one variable can be declared at once using the general format

> *type name = initial_value, name = initial_value, ... ;*

Before the type declaration, an optional storage class may also be specified, as summarized in Section 6.2. If a storage class is specified, and the type of the variable is int, then int can be omitted. For example,

```
static   counter;
```

declares counter to be a static int variable.

4.3 Derived Data Types

A derived data type is one that is built up from one or more of the basic data types. Derived data types are arrays, structures, unions, and pointers. A function that returns a value of a specified type is also considered a derived data type. Each of these, with the exception of functions, is summarized below. Functions are separately covered in section 7.0.

TABLE A-2. Summary of basic data types

Type	Meaning
int	Integer value; i.e., value that contains no decimal point
short int	Integer value of reduced accuracy; takes half as much memory as an int on some machines
long int	Integer value of extended accuracy; takes twice as much memory as an int on some machines
unsigned int	Positive integer value; variables declared of this type can store positive values up to twice as large as an int
float	Floating point value; that is, a value that may contain decimal places
double	Extended accuracy floating point value (roughly twice the accuracy of a float)
char	Single character value; on some systems, sign extension may occur when used in an expression
unsigned char	Same as char, except ensures that sign extension will not occur
void	No type; used to ensure that a function that does not return a value is not used as if it does

4.3.1 Arrays

Single-Dimensional Arrays

Arrays can be defined to contain any basic data type or any derived data type. Arrays of functions are not permitted (although arrays of function pointers are).

The declaration of an array has the following basic format:

type name[*n*]   = { *initial_value, initial_value, ...* } ;

The constant expression *n* determines the number of elements in the array *name*, and may be omitted provided a list of initial values is specified. In such a case, the size of the array will be determined based on the number of initial values listed. Each initial value must be a constant expression, and most compilers only allow static or extern arrays to be initialized. There can be less values in the initialization list than there are elements in the array, but there cannot be more. If less values are specified, then only that many elements of the array will be initialized, beginning with the first element. The remaining elements will be set to zero.

A special case of array initialization occurs in the case of character arrays, which may be initialized by a constant character string. For example,

```
char today[] = "Monday";
```

declares `today` as an array of characters. This array will be initialized to the characters `'M'`, `'o'`, `'n'`, `'d'`, `'a'`, `'y'`, and `'\0'`, respectively.

Multidimensional Arrays

The general format for declaring a multidimensional array is as follows:

type name [*d1*] [*d2*]...[*dn*] = *initialization_list;*

The array *name* is defined to contain *d1 x d2 x ... x dn* elements of the specified type, where *d1, d2, ..., dn* are constant expressions. For example,

```
int  three_d [5][2][20];
```

defines a three-dimensional array, `three_d`, containing 200 integers.

A particular element is referenced from a multidimensional array by enclosing the desired subscript for each dimension in its own set of brackets. For example, the statement

```
three_d [4][0][15] = 100;
```

stores 100 into the indicated element of the array `three_d`.

Multidimensional arrays can be initialized in the same manner as one-dimensional arrays. Nested pairs of braces can be used to control the assignment of values to the elements in the array.

The following declares `matrix` to be a two-dimensional array containing four rows and three columns:

```
static int matrix[4][3] =
             {  { 1, 2, 3 },
                { 4, 5, 6 },
                { 7, 8, 9 } };
```

Elements in the first row of `matrix` are set to the values 1, 2, and 3, respectively;

in the second row to 4, 5, and 6, respectively; and in the third row to 7, 8, and 9, respectively. The elements in the fourth row are set to 0, since no values are specified for that row. The declaration

```
static int matrix[4][3] =
            { 1, 2, 3, 4, 5, 6, 7, 8, 9 };
```

initializes `matrix` to the same values, since the elements of a multidimensional array are initialized in "dimension-order" (i.e., from leftmost to rightmost dimension).

Finally, the declaration

```
static int matrix[4][3] =
            {  { 1 },
               { 4 },
               { 7 } };
```

sets the first element of the first row of `matrix` to 1, the first element of the second row to 4, and the first element of the third row to 7. All remaining elements will be set to 0 by default.

4.3.2 Structures

General Format

```
struct name
{
      member_declaration
      member_declaration
           . . .
}  variable_list;
```

The structure *name* is defined to contain the members as specified by each *member_declaration*. Each such declaration consists of a type specification followed by a list of one or more member names.

Variables may be declared at the time that the structure is defined simply by listing them before the terminating semicolon, or they may subsequently be declared using the format:

```
struct name variable_list;
```

This format obviously cannot be used if *name* is omitted when the structure is defined. If that were the case, all variables of that structure type would have to be declared with the definition.

Most compilers only allow nonautomatic structure variables to be assigned initial values. The format of the initialization is similar to that for arrays. Therefore, the declaration

```
struct   entry
{
    char   *word;
    char   *definition;
} dictionary[1000] =
    { { "a",          "first letter of the alphabet" },
      { "aardvark",   "a burrowing African mammal"   },
      { "aback",      "to startle"                   } };
```

declares `dictionary` to contain 1000 `entry` structures, with the first three elements initialized to the specified character string pointers.

A *member_declaration* that has the format

type field_name : n

defines a *field* that is *n* bits wide inside the structure, where *n* is an integer value. Fields may not go across word boundaries and may be packed inside a word from left to right on some machines and right to left on others. If *field_name* is omitted, the specified number of bits are reserved, but cannot be referenced. If *field_name* is omitted and *n* is zero, the field that follows is aligned on the next word boundary. The type of a field is normally `unsigned int`, although some compilers may support other types as well (beware that compilers that seemingly support `int` fields may actually treat them as `unsigned`). The address operator (`&`) cannot be applied to a field, and arrays of fields cannot be defined.

4.3.3 Unions

General Format

```
union name
{
    member_declaration
    member_declaration
        . . .
}   variable_list;
```

This defines a union called *name* with members as specified by each *member_declaration*. Each member of the union shares overlapping storage space, and the compiler takes care of ensuring that enough space is reserved to contain the largest member of the union.

Variables can be declared at the time that the union is defined, or they may be subsequently declared using the notation

    union   *name variable_list;*

provided the union was given a name when it was defined.

It is the programmer's responsibility to ensure that the value retrieved from a union is consistent with the last value that was stored inside the union. A union variable cannot be initialized.

4.3.4 Pointers

The basic format for declaring a pointer variable is as follows:

    type *name;

The identifier *name* is declared to be of type "pointer to *type*," which can be a basic C data type, or a derived data type. For example,

    int   *ip;

declares `ip` to be a pointer to an `int`, and the declaration

    struct   entry   *ep;

declares `ep` to be a pointer to an `entry` structure.

Pointers that will point to elements in an array are declared to point to the type of element contained in the array. For example, the declaration of `ip` above would also be used to declare a pointer into an array of integers.

More advanced forms of pointer declarations are also permitted. For example, the declaration

    char *tp[100];

declares `tp` to be an array of 100 character pointers, and the declaration

    struct entry (*fn_pointer) ();

declares `fn_pointer` to be a pointer to a function that returns an `entry` structure.

The C language guarantees that no object will have a pointer value of 0. Therefore, by convention, a pointer value of 0 is used to represent the *null* pointer.

Some programmers have the bad habit of interchangeably using pointers and `ints`. For example, they frequently omit the declaration for a function that returns a pointer. The manner in which pointers are converted to integers, and integers are converted to pointers, is machine dependent, as is the size of the integer required to hold a pointer. However, the language does guarantee that a pointer can be converted to an integer (of the appropriate size) and then back to the same pointer.

4.4 Enumerated Data Types

General Format

enum   *name* { *enum_1, enum_2, ...*   } *variable_list;*

The enumerated type *name* is defined with enumerated values *enum_1, enum_2,* ..., each of which is an identifier or an identifier followed by an equals sign and a constant expression. *variable_list* is an optional list of variables (with optional initial values) declared to be of type enum *name*.

The compiler assigns sequential integers to the enumeration identifiers starting at 0. If an identifier is followed by = and a constant expression, the value of that expression is assigned to the identifier. Subsequent identifiers are assigned values beginning with that constant expression plus one. Enumeration identifiers are treated as constant values.

If it is desired to declare variables to be of a previously defined (and named) enumeration type, then the construct

enum   *name variable_list;*

is used.

A variable declared to be of a particular enumerated typed can only be assigned a value of the same data type, although many compilers do not strictly enforce this rule.

Even though most compilers treat enumerated types as integers, they should still be treated as though they are unique types by the program.

4.5 typedef

The typedef statement is used to assign a new name to a basic or derived data type. The typedef does not define a new type but simply a new name for an existing type. Therefore, variables declared to be of the newly named type are treated by the compiler exactly as if they were declared to be of the type associated with the new name.

In forming a typedef definition, proceed as though a normal variable declaration were being made. Then, place the new type name where the variable name would normally appear. Finally, in front of everything, place the keyword typedef.

As an example,

```
typedef struct
        {
               float  x;
               float  y;
        }  POINT;
```

associates the name POINT with a structure containing two floating point members called x and y. Variables can subsequently be declared to be of type POINT, as in

```
static POINT  origin = { 0.0, 0.0 };
```

◆ 5.0 Expressions ◆

Variable names, function names, array names, constants, function calls, array references, and structure references are all considered expressions. Applying a unary operator (where appropriate) to one of these expressions is also an expression, as is combining two or more of these expressions with a binary or ternary operator. Finally, an expression enclosed within parentheses is also an expression.

An expression that may be assigned a value is known as an *lvalue*.

An lvalue expression is required in certain places: The expression on the left-hand side of an assignment operator must be an lvalue. Furthermore, the increment and decrement operators can only be applied to lvalues, as can the unary address operator &. An lvalue is also required to the left of the structure member operator '.'.

5.1 Summary of C Operators

Table A-3 summarizes the various operators in the C language. These operators are listed in order of decreasing precedence. Operators grouped together have the same precedence.

As an example of how to use Table A-3, consider the expression

```
b | c & d * e
```

The multiplication operator has higher precedence than both the bitwise OR and bitwise AND operators, since it appears above both of these in Table A-3. Similarly, the bitwise AND operator has higher precedence than the bitwise OR operator since the former appears above the latter in the table. Therefore, this

TABLE A-3. Summary of C operators

Operator	Description	Associativity
() [] -> .	Function call Array element reference Pointer to structure member reference Structure member reference	Left to right
− ++ -- ! ~ * & sizeof (type)	Unary minus Increment Decrement Logical negation Ones complement Pointer reference (indirection) Address Size of an object Type cast (conversion)	Right to left
* / %	Multiplication Division Modulus	Left to right
+ −	Addition Subtraction	Left to right
<< >>	Left shift Right shift	Left to right
< <= > >=	Less than Less than or equal to Greater than Greater than or equal to	Left to right
== !=	Equality Inequality	Left to right
&	Bitwise AND	Left to right
^	Bitwise XOR	Left to right
|	Bitwise OR	Left to right
&&	Logical AND	Left to right
||	Logical OR	Left to right
?:	Conditional	Right to left
= *= /= %= += -= &= ^= |= <<= >>=	Assignment operators	Right to left
,	Comma operator	Right to left

expression would be evaluated as

```
b | ( c & ( d * e ) )
```

Now consider the following expression:

```
b % c * d
```

Since the modulus and multiplication operator appear in the same grouping in Table A-3, they have the same precedence. The associativity listed for these operators is left to right, indicating that the expression would be evaluated as

```
( b % c ) * d
```

As another example, the expression

```
++a->b
```

would be evaluated as

```
++(a->b)
```

since the -> operator has higher precedence than the ++ operator.

Finally, since the assignment operators group from right to left, the statement

```
a = b = 0;
```

would be evaluated as

```
a = (b = 0);
```

which would have the net result of setting the values of a and b to zero.

In an expression that uses the same associative and commutative operator (like +), the compiler can regroup the expression if desired. For example, in the expression

```
a + b + c
```

it is not defined whether a or b will be added first, or b and c. Furthermore, the compiler can even add a and c, and then add the result with b. Parentheses *do not* change this. So even if you write

```
(a + b) + c
```

the compiler can evaluate it as

```
(a + b) + c
```

or as

```
a + (b + c)
```

or even as

```
(a + c) + b
```

In the case of the expression

```
x[i] + ++i
```

it is not defined whether the compiler will evaluate the left side of the plus operator or the right side. Here, the way that it's done will effect the result, since the value of i may be incremented before x[i] is evaluated.

Another case in which the order of evaluation is not defined is in the expression

```
x[i] = ++i
```

In this situation, it is not defined whether the value of i will be incremented before or after its value is used to index into x.

The order of evaluation of function arguments is also undefined. Therefore, in the function call

```
f (i, ++i);
```

i may be incremented first, thereby causing the same value to be sent as the two arguments to the function.

The C language guarantees that the && and || operators will be evaluted from left to right. Furthermore, in the case of &&, it is guaranteed that the second operand will not be evaluated if the first is zero; and in the case of || it is guaranteed that the second operand will not be evaluated if the first is nonzero. This fact is worth bearing in mind when forming expressions such as

```
if ( data_flag || check_data () )
    ...
```

since, in this case, check_data will only be called if the value of data_flag is zero. To take another example, if the array a is declared to contain n elements, then the statement that begins

```
if ( index >= 0  &&  index < n  &&  a[index] == 0 )
    ...
```

will reference the element contained in `a[index]` only if `index` is a valid subscript into the array.

5.2 Constant Expressions

A constant expression is an expression in which each of the terms is a constant value. Constant expressions are *required* in the following situations: (1) as the value after a case in a `switch` statement, (2) for specifying the size of an array, (3) for assigning a value to an enumeration identifier, (4) for specifying the bit field size in a structure definition, (5) for assigning initial values to external or `static` variables, and (6) as the expression following the `#if` in a `#if` Preprocessor statement.

In the first four cases, the constant expression must consist of integer constants, character constants, enumeration constants, and `sizeof` expressions. The only operators that can be used are the arithmetic operators, the bitwise operators, the relational operators, the conditional expression operator, and the type cast operator.

In the fifth case, in addition to the rules cited earlier, the address operator can be used. However, it can only be applied to external or static variables. So, for example, the expression

```
&x + 10
```

would be a valid constant expression, provided that `x` is an external or static variable. Furthermore, the expression

```
&a[10] - 5
```

is a valid constant expression if `a` is an external or static array. Finally, since `&a[0]` is equivalent to the expression `a`,

```
a + sizeof (char) * 100
```

is also a valid constant expression.

For the last situation that requires a constant expression (after the `#if`), the rules are the same as for the first four cases, except the `sizeof` operator and enumeration constants cannot be used. However, the special `defined` operator is permitted.

5.3 Arithmetic Operators

Given that

    `a, b`   are expressions of any basic data type except `void`;

    `i, j`   are expressions of any integer data type;

then the expression

    `-a`   Negates the value of `a` (is equivalent to `0 - a`);

    `a + b`   adds `a` with `b`;

    `a - b`   subtracts `b` from `a`;

    `a * b`   multiplies `a` by `b`;

    `a / b`   divides `a` by `b`;

    `i % j`   gives the remainder of `i` divided by `j`;

In each expression, the usual arithmetic conversions are performed on the operands (see Section 5.16). If two integral values are divided, then the result is truncated. If either operand is negative, then the direction of the truncation is not defined (i.e., -3 / 2 may produce -1 on some machines and -2 on others); otherwise, truncation is always towards zero (3 / 2 will always produce 1). See Section 5.15 for a summary of arithmetic operations with pointers.

5.4 Logical Operators

Given that

    `a, b`   are expressions of any basic data type except `void`, or are both pointers;

then the expression

    `a && b`   has the value 1 if both `a` and `b` are nonzero, and 0 otherwise (and `b` is evaluated only if `a` is nonzero);

    `a || b`   has the value 1 if either `a` or `b` is nonzero, and 0 otherwise (and `b` is evaluated only if `a` is zero);

    `! a`   has the value 1 if `a` is zero, and 0 otherwise.

The usual arithmetic conversions are applied to `a` and `b` (see Section 5.16). The type of the result in all cases is `int`.

5.5 Relational Operators

Given that

a, b   are expressions of any basic data type except void, or are both pointers;

then the expression

a < b   has the value 1 if a is less than b, and 0 otherwise;

a <= b   has the value 1 if a is less than or equal to b, and 0 otherwise;

a > b   has the value 1 if a is greater than b, and 0 otherwise;

a >= b   has the value 1 if a is greater than or equal to b, and 0 otherwise;

a == b   has the value 1 if a is equal to b, and 0 otherwise;

a != b   has the value 1 if a is not equal to b, and 0 otherwise.

The usual arithmetic conversions are performed on a and b (see Section 5.16). The first four relational tests are only meaningful for pointers if they both point into the same array. The type of the result in each case is int.

5.6 Bitwise Operators

Given that

i, j, n   are expressions of any integer data type;

then the expression

i & j   performs a bitwise AND of i and j;

i | j   performs a bitwise OR of i and j;

i ^ j   performs a bitwise XOR of i and j;

~i   takes the ones complement of i;

i << n   shifts i to the left n bits;

i >> n   shifts i to the right n bits;

The usual arithmetic conversions are performed on the operands. If the shift count is negative, or is greater than or equal to the number of bits contained in the object being shifted, the result of the shift is undefined. On some machines, a right shift is arithmetic (sign fill) and on others logical (zero fill).

5.7 Increment and Decrement Operators

Given that

l   is an lvalue expression;

then the expression

     ++l   increments l and then uses its value as the value of the expression;

     l++   uses l as the value of the expression and then increments l;

     --l   decrements l and then uses its value as the value of the expression;

     l--   uses l as the value of the expression and then decrements l;

Section 5.15 describes these operations on pointers.

5.8 Assignment Operators

Given that

l   is an lvalue expression;

op   is any operator that can be used as an assignment operator (see Table A-3);

a   is an expression;

then the expression

     l = a   stores the value of a into l;

     l *op*= a   applies *op* to l and a, storing the result into l.

In the first expression, if a is one of the basic data types (except void), then it is converted to match the type of l. If l is a pointer, then a should be a pointer to the same type as l, or the *null* pointer. The second expression is treated as if it were written l = l *op* (a), except l is only evaluated once (consider x[i++] += 10).

5.9 Conditional Expression Operator

Given that

    `a, b, c`   are expressions;

then the expression

    `a ? b : c`   has as its value `b` if `a` is nonzero, and `c` otherwise.

Expressions `b` and `c` must be of the same data type. (If one is a pointer and the other is zero, then the latter is taken as a null pointer of the same type as the former.) If they are not, but are both basic data types, then the usual arithmetic conversions are applied to make their types the same. Only expression `b` or `c` is evaluated.

5.10 Type Cast Operator

Given that

    type   is the name of a basic data type, an enumerated data type (preceded by the keyword `enum`), a `typedef`-defined type, or is a derived data type;

    `a`   is an expression;

then the expression

    (*type*) `a`   converts `a` to the specified type.

5.11 `sizeof` Operator

Given that

    type   is as described above;

    `a`   is an expression;

then the expression

    `sizeof` (*type*)   has as its value the number of bytes needed to contain a value of the specified type;

    `sizeof a`   has as its value the number of bytes required to hold the result of the evaluation of `a`.

If a is the name of an array that has been dimensioned (either explictly or implictly through initialization) and is not a formal parameter or extern array, then sizeof a gives the number of bytes required to store the elements in a. Since the sizeof operator is evaluated at compile time, it can be used in constant expressions (see Section 5.2).

5.12 Comma Operator

Given that

a, b   are expressions;

then the expression

a, b   causes a to be evaluated, and then b to be evaluated. The type
            and value of the expression is that of b.

5.13 Basic Operations with Arrays

Given that

a   is declared as an array of *n* elements;

i   is an expression of any integer data type;

v   is an expression

then the expression

a[0]   references the first element of a;

a[n - 1]   references the last element of a;

a[i]   references element number i of a;

a[i] = v   stores the value of v into a[i].

In each case, the type of the result is the type of the elements contained in a. See Section 5.15 for a summary of operations with pointers and arrays.

5.14 Basic Operations with Structures[†]

Given that

x	is an lvalue expression of type struct s.
y	is an expression of type struct s.
m	is the name of one of the members of the structure s;
v	is an expression;

then the expression

x	references the entire structure, and is of type struct s;
y.m	references the member m of the structure y, and is of the type declared for the member m;
x.m = v	assigns v to the member m of x, and is of the type declared for the member m;
x = y	assigns y to x, and is of type struct s;
f (y)	calls the function f, passing the structure y as the argument. Inside f, the formal parameter must be declared to be of type struct s;
return (y)	returns the structure y. The return type declared for the function must be struct s;

5.15 Basic Operations with Pointers

Given that

x	is an lvalue expression of type t;
pt	is an lvalue expression of type "pointer to t";
v	is an expression;

then the expression:

&x	produces a pointer to x and has type "pointer to t";
pt = &x	sets pt pointing to x, and has type "pointer to t";
pt = (t *) 0	assigns the null pointer to pt;

---

† Also applies to unions.

*pt	references the value pointed to by pt, and has type *t*;
*pt = v	stores the value of v into the location pointed to by pt, and has type *t*;

Pointers to Arrays

Given that

a	is an array of elements of type *t*;
pal, pa2	are lvalue expressions of type "pointer to *t*" that point to elements in a;
v	is an expression;
n	is an expression of an integer data type;

then the expression:

a	produces a pointer to the first element of a, and has type "pointer to *t*";
&a[0]	also produces a pointer to the first element of a, and has type "pointer to *t*";
&a[n]	produces a pointer to element number n of a, and has type "pointer to *t*";
*pal	references the element of a that pal points to, and has type *t*;
*pal = v	stores the value of v into the element pointed to by pal, and has type *t*;
++pal	sets pal pointing to the next element of a, no matter what type of elements are contained in a, and has type "pointer to *t*";
--pal	sets pal pointing to the previous element of a, no matter what type of elements are contained in a, and has type "pointer to *t*";
*++pal	increments pal and then references the value in a that pal points to, and has type *t*;
*pal++	references the value in a that pal points to before incrementing pal, and has type *t*;
pal + n	produces a pointer that points n elements further into a than pal and has type "pointer to *t*";

`pa1 - n`	produces a pointer to a that points n elements previous to that pointed to by `pa1`, and has type "pointer to *t*";
`*(pa1 + n) = v`	stores the value of v into the element pointed to by `pa1 + n`, and has type *t*;
`pa1 < pa2`	tests if `pa1` is pointing to an earlier element in a than is `pa2`, and has type `int` (any relational operators can be used to compare two pointers);
`pa2 - pa1`	produces the number of elements in a contained between the pointers `pa2` and `pa1` (assuming that `pa2` points to an element further in a than `pa1`), and has type `int`;
`a + n`	produces a pointer to element number n of a, has type "pointer to t," and is in all ways equivalent to the expression `&a[n]`;
`*(a + n)`	references element number n of a, has type *t*, and is in all ways equivalent to the expression `a[n]`.

Pointers to Structures[†]

Given that

x	is an lvalue expression of type `struct s`;
ps	is an lvalue expression of type "pointer to `struct s`";
m	is the name of a member of the structure s and is of type *t*;
v	is an expression;

then the expression

`&x`	produces a pointer to x, and is of type "pointer to `struct s`";
`ps = &x`	sets `ps` pointing to x, and is of type "pointer to `struct s`";
`ps->m`	references member m of the structure pointed to by `ps`, and is of type *t*;
`(*ps).m`	also references this member and is in all ways equivalent to the expression `ps->m`;
`ps->m = v`	stores the value of v into the member m of the structure pointed to by `ps`, and is of type *t*;

---

† Also applies to unions.

5.16 Conversion of Basic Data Types

The C language converts operands in an arithmetic expression in the following order:

1. If either operand is of type `float`, then it is converted to type `double`. If either is of type `char` or of type `short`, then it is converted to type `int`.

2. If either operand is of type `double`, then the other is converted to type `double`, and that is the type of the result.

3. If either operand is of type `long int`, then the other is converted to type `long int`, and that is the type of the result.

4. If either operand is of type `unsigned`, then the other is converted to `unsigned`, and that is the type of the result.

5. If this step is reached, then both operands are of type `int`, and that is the type of the result.

Note that the conversion of all `float` operands to `double` implies that all floating point operations are performed in double precision. This is implemented by virtually all existing compilers. However, recent changes to the language grant the ability to perform single-precision floating operations. In such a case, the automatic conversion of all `float`s to `double`s would not be performed.

Conversion of operands is well behaved in most situations, although the following points should be noted:

1. Conversion of a `char` to an `int` may involve sign extension on some machines, unless the `char` is declared as `unsigned`.

2. Conversion of a signed integer to a longer integer results in extension of the sign to the left; conversion of an unsigned integer to a longer integer results in zero fill to the left.

3. Conversion of a longer integer to a shorter integer results in truncation of the integer on the left.

4. Conversion of a floating point value to an integer results in truncation of the decimal portion of the value. If the value is negative, then truncation may be towards zero on some machines and away from zero on others (i.e., some machines may convert -5.7 to -5 and others to -6). If the integer is not large enough to contain the converted floating point value, then the result will be undefined.

5. Conversion of a `double` to a `float` results in rounding of the `double` value before the truncation occurs.

◆ 6.0 Storage Classes and Scope ◆

The term *storage class* refers to the manner in which memory is allocated by the compiler in the case of variables, and to the scope of a particular function definition in the case of functions. Storage classes are `auto`, `static`, `extern`, and `register`. A storage class can be omitted in a function or variable declaration and a default storage class will be assigned, as discussed below.

The term *scope* refers to the extent of the meaning of a particular identifier within a program. An identifier defined outside a function can be referenced anywhere subsequent in the file. Identifiers defined within a function or block are local to the function or block, and can locally redefine an identifier defined outside the function or block. Label names are known throughout the function, as are formal parameter names. Labels, structure and structure member names, union and union member names, and enumerated type names do not have to be distinct from each other or from variable or function names. However, enumeration identifiers *do* have to be distinct from variable names and from other enumeration identifers defined within the same scope.

TABLE A-4. Variables: summary of storage classes, scope, and initialization

If Storage Class is	And Variable is declared	Then it can be referenced	And can be initialized with	Comments
`static`	Outside a function	Anywhere within the file	Constant expressions only	Variables are initialized only once at the start of program execution; values are retained through function calls; default initial value is zero
	Inside a function/block	Within the function/block		
`extern`	Outside a function	Anywhere within the file	Variable reference only cannot be initialized	Variable must be defined in exactly one place without the `extern` declaration
	Inside a function/block	Within the function/block		
`auto`	Inside a function/block	Within the function/block	Any valid expression	Most compilers don't allow arrays and structures to be initialized; variable is initialized each time the function/block is entered; no default value
`register`	Inside a function/block	Within the function/block	Any valid expression	Assignment to a register not guaranteed; varying restrictions on types of variables that can be declared; cannot take the address of a register variable; initialized each time function/block is entered; no default value
omitted	Outside a function	Anywhere within the file or by other files that contain appropriate declarations	Constant expressions only	This declaration can appear in only one place; variable is initialized at the start of program execution; default value is zero
	Inside a function/block	(*See* `auto`)	(*See* `auto`)	Defaults to `auto`

6.1 Functions

If a storage class is specified when a function is defined, then it must be either `static` or `extern`. Functions that are declared `static` can only be referenced from within the same file that contains the function. Functions that are specified as `extern` (or that have no class specified) may be called by functions from other files.

6.2 Variables

Table A-4 summarizes the various storage classes that may be used in declaring variables as well as their scope and methods of initialization.

♦ 7.0 Functions ♦

7.1 Function Definition

General Format

return_type   name (param1, param2, ...)
param_declarations
{
      variable_declarations

      program_statement
      program_statement
      . . .
      `return` *expression;*
}

The function called *name* is defined, which returns a value of type *return_type* and has formal parameters *param1, param2,...* .

If the function does not return a value, then *return_type* is not specified or is `void`. If the function returns an `int` value, then *return_type* may be omitted, although specifying an `int` as the return type is a better programming practice.

If no formal parameters are specified, the function takes no arguments; otherwise each formal parameter must be declared with an appropriate declaration before the opening brace of the function body (exception: formal parameters that are `int`s don't have to be declared). Declarations for single-dimensional arrays do not have to specify the number of elements contained in the array. For multidimensional arrays, the size of each dimension but the first must be specified.

See Section 8.9 for a discussion of the `return` statement.

7.2 Function Call

General Format

name (arg1, arg2, ...)

The function called *name* is called and the values *arg1, arg2, ...* are passed as arguments to the function. If the function takes no arguments, just the open and closed parentheses are specified (as in `initialize ()`). The type of each argument must agree with the type declared for the corresponding formal parameter in the function definition. Arguments of type `float` are automatically converted to type `double`, and arguments of type `char` or `short int` are automatically converted to type `int` before being passed to the function.

If the function is not defined before the call appears in the program or is not declared otherwise, the compiler assumes that the function returns a value of type `int`.

A function declared as `void` will cause the compiler to flag any calls to that function that try to make use of a returned value.

All arguments to a function are passed by value; therefore, their values cannot be changed by the function. If a pointer is passed to a function, the function *can* change values referenced by the pointer, but still cannot change the value of the pointer itself.

A function name, without a following set of parentheses, produces a pointer to that function.

◆ 8.0 Statements ◆

A program statement is any valid expression (usually an assignment or function call) that is immediately followed by a semicolon, or it is one of the special statements described below. A *label* may optionally precede any statement, and consists of an identifier followed immediately by a colon (see the `goto` statement).

8.1 Compound Statements

Program statements that are contained within a pair of braces are known collectively as a *compound* statement or *block*, and can appear anywhere in the program that a single statement is permitted. A block can have its own set of variable declarations. The scope of such local variables is the block in which they are defined.

8.2 The break Statement

General Format

```
break;
```

Execution of a break statement from within a for, while, do, or switch statement causes execution of that statement to be immediately terminated. Execution continues with the statement that immediately follows the loop or switch.

8.3 The continue Statement

General Format

```
continue;
```

Execution of the continue statement from within a loop causes any statements that follow the continue in the loop to be skipped. Execution of the loop otherwise continues as normal.

8.4 The do Statement

General Format

```
do
    program_statement
while ( expression );
```

program_statement is executed as long as the result of the evaluation of *expression* is nonzero. Note that, since *expression* is evaluated each time *after* the execution of *program_statement*, it is guaranteed that *program_statement* will be executed at least once.

8.5 The for Statement

General Format

```
for ( expression_1; expression_2; expression_3 )
    program_statement
```

expression_1 is evaluated once when execution of the loop begins. Next, *expression_2* is evaluated. If its value is nonzero, *program_statement* is executed and then *expression_3* is evaluated. Execution of *program_statement* and the subsequent evaluation of *expression_3* continues as long as the value of *expression_2* is nonzero. Note that, since *expression_2* is evaluated each time before *program_statement* is executed, *program_statement* may never be executed if the value of *expression_2* is zero when the loop is first entered.

8.6 The goto Statement

General Format

goto *identifier;*

Execution of the goto statement causes control to be sent directly to the statement labeled *identifier*. The labeled statement must be within the same function as the goto.

8.7 The if Statement

Format 1

if (*expression*)
    program_statement

If the value of *expression* is nonzero, then *program_statement* is executed; otherwise, it is skipped.

Format 2

if (*expression*)
    program_statement_1
else
    program_statement_2

If the value of *expression* is nonzero then *program_statement_1* is executed; otherwise, *program_statement_2* is executed. If *program_statement_2* is another if statement, then an if-else if chain is effected:

if (*expression_1*)
    program_statement_1
else if (*expression_2*)
    program_statement_2
    . . .
else
    program_statement_n

An else clause is always associated with the last if statement that does not contain an else. Braces can be used to change this association if necessary.

8.8 The Null Statement

General Format

```
;
```

Execution of a null statement has no effect and is used primarily to satisfy the requirement of a program statement in a for, do, or while loop. For example, in the following statement, which copies a character string pointed to by from to one pointed to by to

```
while ( *to++ = *from++ )
    ;
```

the null statement is used to satisfy the requirement that a program statement appear after the looping expression of the while.

8.9 The return Statement

Format 1

```
return;
```

Execution of the return statement causes program execution to be immediately returned to the calling function. This format can only be used to return from a function that does not return a value.

If execution proceeds to the end of a function and a return statement is not encountered, the function returns as if a return statement of this form had been executed. Therefore, in such a case, no value is returned.

Format 2

```
return    expression;
```

The value of *expression* is returned to the calling function. If the type of *expression* does not agree with the return type declared in the function declaration, its value will be automatically converted to the declared type before it is returned. By convention, *expression* is usually enclosed in parentheses.

8.10 The `switch` Statement

General Format

```
switch ( expression )
{
    case constant_1:
        program_statement
        program_statement
            . . .
        break;
    case constant_2:
        program_statement
        program_statement
            . . .
        break;
    . . .
    case constant_n:
        program_statement
        program_statement
            . . .
        break;
    default:
        program_statement
        program_statement
            . . .
        break;
}
```

expression is evaluated and compared against the constant expression values *constant_1, constant_2, ..., constant_n*. If the value of *expression* matches one of these case values, the program statements that immediately follow are executed. If no case value matches the value of *expression*, the `default` case, if included, is executed. If the `default` case is not included, then no statements contained in the `switch` are executed.

The result of the evaluation of *expression* must be of integral type and no two cases can have the same value. Omitting the `break` statement from a particular case causes execution to continue into the next case.

8.11 The `while` Statement

General Format

```
while ( expression )
    program_statement
```

program_statement is executed as long as the value of *expression* is nonzero. Note that, since *expression* is evaluated each time *before* the execution of *program_statement*, *program_statement* may never be executed.

♦ 9.0 Preprocessor Statements ♦

All preprocessor statements begin with the character #, which must be the first character on the line.

9.1 The #define Statement

Format 1

```
#define name text
```

This defines the identifier *name* to the preprocessor and associates with it whatever *text* appears after the first blank space after *name* to the end of the line. Subsequent use of *name* in the program causes *text* to be substituted directly into the program at that point.

Format 2

```
#define name (param_1, param_2, ..., param_n)    text
```

The macro *name* is defined to take arguments as specified by *param_1, param_2, ..., param_n*, each of which is an identifier. Subsequent use of *name* in the program with an argument list causes *text* to be substituted directly into the program at that point, with the arguments of the macro call replacing all occurrences of the corresponding parameters inside *text*.

If a definition in either format requires more than one line, then each line to be continued must be ended with a backslash character. Once a name has been defined, it can be used subsequently anywhere in the file.

9.2 The #if Statement

Format 1

```
#if constant_expression
   ...
#endif
```

The value of *constant_expression* is evaluated. If the result is nonzero, then all program lines up until the #endif statement are processed; otherwise, they are automatically skipped and are not processed by the preprocessor or by the compiler.

Format 2

```
#if constant_expression_1
   . . .
#elif constant_expression_2
   . . .
#elif constant_expression_n
   . . .
#else
   . . .
#endif
```

If *constant_expression_2* is nonzero, all program lines up until the #elif are processed. Otherwise, if *constant_expression_2* is nonzero, all program lines up until the next #elif are processed. If none of the constant expressions evaluates to nonzero, the lines after the #else (if included) are processed.

The special operator defined(*identifier*) can be used as part of the constant expression, so

```
#if defined(DEBUG)
   . . .
#endif
```

causes the code between the #if and #endif to be processed if the identifier DEBUG has been previously defined (see also #ifdef in Section 9.3).

9.3 The #ifdef Statement

General Format

```
#ifdef identifier
   . . .
#endif
```

If the value of *identifier* has been previously defined (either through a #define or with the -D command-line option when the program was compiled), then all program lines up until the #endif are processed; otherwise, they are skipped. As with the #if statement, #elif and #else statements can be used with a #ifdef statement.

9.4 The `#ifndef` Statement

General Format

```
#ifndef identifier
    . . .
#endif
```

If the value of *identifier* has not been previously defined, then all program lines up until the `#endif` are processed; otherwise, they are skipped. As with the `#if` statement, `#elif` and `#else` statements can be used with a `#ifndef` statement.

9.5 The `#include` Statement

Format 1

```
#include "file_name"
```

The directory that contains the source file is searched first for the file *file_name*. If it is not found there, than a sequence of standard places is searched. Once found, the contents of the file is included in the program at the precise point that the `#include` statement appears. Preprocessor statements contained within the `#include` file will be analyzed, and therefore an included file can itself contain another `#include` statement.

Format 2

```
#include <file_name>
```

The preprocessor searches for the specified file only in the standard places, and not in the same directory as the source file. The action taken after the file is found is otherwise identical to that described above.

9.6 The `#line` Statement

General Format

```
#line   constant   "file_name"
```

This statement causes the compiler to treat subsequent lines in the program as if the name of the source file were *file_name*, and as if the line number of all subsequent lines began at *constant*. If *file_name* is not specified, then the file name specified by the last #*line* statement, or the name of the source file (if no file name was previously specified), is used.

The #line statement is primarily used to control the file name and line number that are displayed whenever an error message is issued by the compiler. This statement is not described elsewhere in this book.

9.7 The #undef Statement

General Format

#undef *identifier*

The specified *identfier* becomes undefined to the preprocessor. Subsequent #ifdef or #ifndef statements will behave as if the identifier were never defined.

ANSI Standard C

This section summarizes the major *differences* between the American National Standards Institute (ANSI) definition of the C language and the language summary given in Appendix A.[†] It is not intended that this section be a complete definition of ANSI C.

Section numbers that follow refer to corresponding sections from Appendix A. In some instances, new sections are added.

◆ 1.0 Identifiers ◆

Identifiers are guaranteed to be significant to at least 31 characters, although some implementations may choose to treat more than 31 as significant. Only the first six characters of an external identifier are guaranteed to be significant. Furthermore, on some systems upper- and lowercase letters may not be distinguishable in an external name.

The keywords `asm` and `fortran` are no longer *reserved* identifiers, but the identifiers `const`, `signed`, and `volatile` now are.

1.1 Trigraph Sequences

To handle non-ASCII character sets, the following three-character sequences (called *trigraphs*) are recognized and treated special wherever they occur inside a program (even inside character strings):

[†] As of this writing, the ANSI Standard definition of C was not yet officially approved. Approval is slated for some time in 1988.

Trigraph	Meaning
??=	#
??(	[
??)	]
??<	{
??>	}
??/	\
??'	^
??!		
??-	~

◆ 3.0 Constants ◆

3.1 Integer Constants

If an octal or hexadecimal integer constant is too large to fit into a signed integer, then it is treated as an unsigned integer (if it can be stored into such). If it's too large to be stored into a signed integer, then it's treated as a long (signed) integer. Finally, if it's too large to be stored into a long integer, then it's treated as an unsigned long integer.

A decimal integer constant is taken as a unsigned long integer constant if it is a decimal integer constant that is too large to be stored in a signed long integer.

If the letter u or U immediately follows an integer constant, then the constant is treated as unsigned.

Both the letters u (U) and l (L) may follow an integer constant to specify an unsigned long integer, as in

```
0xff0055ul
```

3.2 Floating Point Constants

If a floating point constant is immediately followed by the letter f (or F), then the constant is treated as type float (and not as type double, which is the default).

If a floating point constant is immediately followed by the letter l (or L), then the constant is treated as type long double.

3.3 Character Constants

A character constant is defined to be one *or more* characters enclosed in single quotes. How two or more characters, when stored in a single-character constant, are internally represented is machine dependent.

An escape character can be specified as a \ followed by from one to three octal digits (as before), or as the characters \x followed by from one to three hexadecimal digits.

The escape characters \a (the *alert* character—produces an audible or visible alert) and \? (a question mark) were added to the ANSI definition for C.

3.4 Character String Constants

Two or more adjacent character strings are concatenated by the compiler. The strings may be separated by zero or more spaces, tabs, or newlines. So writing the three strings

```
"a" " character "
"string"
```

is equivalent to writing the single string

```
"a character string"
```

Character string constants cannot be modified by the program.

◆ 4.0 Data Types and Declarations ◆

4.2 Basic Data Types

The keyword signed, when used before the types char, short, int, or long, explicitly declares the corresponding type as a signed value. For the cases of short, int, and long, the keyword signed may be omitted, since it is the default. However, signed char explicitly declares a signed character type, which may not be the default representation of characters on the machine (they may be represented as unsigned by default).

The type long double represents an extended double-precision value, and has at least as much precision as a double value.

4.3 Derived Data Types

4.3.1 Arrays

Single-Dimensional Arrays

When initializing a character array with a set of characters in double quotes, the terminating null is placed at the end of array only if there's room to hold it. As before, the declaration

```
char today[] = "Monday";
```

declares today as an array of characters and initializes it to the *seven* characters 'M', 'o', 'n', 'd', 'a', 'y', and '\0', respectively. The declaration

```
char today[6] = "Monday";
```

also declares today as an array of characters. Since there's no room here to contain the terminating null, today will be initialized to the *six* characters 'M', 'o', 'n', 'd', 'a', and 'y'.

Automatic arrays can be initialized.

4.3.2 Structures

Automatic structure variables can be initialized.

Bit fields may have types int, signed int, or unsigned int. For the first type, int, the implementation can define whether the field is signed or unsigned.

4.3.3 Unions

A union variable can be initialized. The initial value is assigned to the first member of the union. So, for example,

```
union mixed
{
    int    i;
    long   l;
    float  f;
} u1 = { 100 };
```

defines a union called mixed and declares u1 to be of this union type. The member i of u1 is assigned an initial value of 100.

4.3.4 Pointers

The type "pointer to `void`" was added as a generic pointer. The declaration

```
void  *xptr;
```

declares `xptr` to be of this pointer type.

A pointer to `void` can be converted to any other pointer type. A pointer to any type can be converted to a pointer to `void` and then back again. The result will be the original pointer.

A constant expression whose value is zero and which is optionally type cast to a pointer represents a *constant null* pointer. The implementation may choose to internally represent a null pointer with a value other than zero. However, a comparison between such an internally represented null pointer and a constant null pointer must prove equal.

It is not guaranteed that a pointer can be converted to an integer and then back again to the same pointer. The result of converting an integer value (other than zero) to a pointer, and vice versa, is machine dependent.

4.6 Type Modifiers `const` and `volatile`

The keyword `const` may be placed before a type declaration to tell the compiler that the value cannot be modified. So the declaration

```
const int x5 = 100;
```

declares `x5` to be a constant integer (that is, it won't be set to anything else during the program's execution). The compiler can then specify that `x5` be stored in read-only memory, if desired.

The compiler is *not* required to flag attempts to change the value of a `const` variable.

The `volatile` modifier explicitly tells the compiler that the value changes (usually dynamically). When a `volatile` variable is used in an expression, its value will be accessed each place it appears. For example, writing the statements

```
volatile char *port17 = (char *) 0x17755;

while ( *port17 == 0 ) {
    ...
}
```

tells the compiler that the expression `*port17` must be recalculated each time through the `while` loop, since we told the compiler that `port17` is of type "pointer to volatile `char`". (To declare `port17` to be of type "volatile pointer to `char`"—a different declaration—you would write `char *volatile port17`.) Without making the `volatile` declaration, some compilers might calculate `*port17` only once when the loop began (as an optimization) if `*port17` was never changed inside the loop. But if the memory address pointed to by `port17` is being changed by someone else (say, by an I/O driver), then the expression needs to be calculated each time through the loop.

♦ 5.0 Expressions ♦

A unary plus operator (+) is now provided. So the expression

```
a + +b - +100.5;
```

is valid. The compiler is no longer permitted to regroup expressions involving the same associative and commutative operator if the regrouping could produce a different result. Previously, the compiler was allowed to evaluate an expression like

```
a + b + c
```

in any order. Now it can only do so if the result is guaranteed to be the same as if it were evaluated using the normal associativity rules.

5.3 Arithmetic Operators

The expression

```
+a
```
gives the value of `a`;

5.6 Bitwise Operators

The type of the shift count has no bearing on the type of the result (so shifting an `int` by a `long` gives an `int`).

5.11 `sizeof` Operator

The expression `sizeof (char)` is defined to have the value 1, no matter how many bits are required to represent a character. Thus the term "byte" (as defined to be the storage unit given by `sizeof`) is defined as the amount of storage needed to store a character.

5.16 Conversion of Basic Data Types

The C language converts operands in an arithmetic expression in the following order:

1. If either operand is of type `long double`, the other is converted to `long double`, and that is the type of the result.

2. If either operand is of type `double`, the other is converted to `double`, and that is the type of the result.

3. If either operand is of type `float`, the other is converted to `float`, and that is the type of the result.

4. If either operand is of type `char`, `short int`, `int` bit field, or of an enumerated data type, it is converted to `int`, if an `int` can fully represent its range of values; otherwise it is converted to `unsigned int`.

5. If either operand is of type `unsigned long int`, the other is converted to `unsigned long int`, and that is the type of the result.

6. If one operand is of type `long int` and the other is of type `unsigned int`, the `unsigned int` is converted to `long int` if a `long int` can represent all values of an `unsigned int`. In such a case, the type of the result will be `long int`. If a `long int` cannot represent all values of an `unsigned int`, both operands are converted to `unsigned long int`, and that is the type of the result.

7. If either operand is of type `long int`, the other is converted to `long int`, and that is the type of the result.

8. If either operand is of type `unsigned int`, the other operand is converted to type `unsigned int`, and that is the type of the result.

9. If this step is reached, both operands are of type `int`, and that is the type of the result.

1. Conversion of a floating point value to an integer results in truncation of the decimal portion. If the value is negative, truncation is defined to be towards zero (i.e., -5.7 is converted to -5).

2. Conversion of a `double` to a `float` does not require that the `double` value be rounded before the truncation occurs.

◆ 6.0 Storage Classes and Scope ◆

6.2 Variables

An external variable must have storage allocated for it (i.e., it must be *defined*) in exactly one place. All source files that reference the external variable do so by placing the keyword `extern` in front of the declaration. In precisely one place, the variable must be declared outside of any function without the keyword `extern`, or outside of any function with the keyword `extern` and with an initial value. This constitutes a definition of the variable.

If the following lines were in the file `foo1.c`:

```
extern int i1 = 0;
extern int i2;
    . . .
```

and these were in `foo2.c`:

```
extern int i1;
int i2;
    . . .
```

then `foo1.c` would define the variable `i1` (`extern` declared variable with an initial value), and `foo2.c` would define the variable `i2` (variable with no `extern` keyword), which could also be assigned an initial value if desired.

◆ 7.0 Functions ◆

7.1 Function Definition

Prototype Format

return_type name (type1 param1, type2 param2, ...)
```
{
        variable_declarations

        program_statement
        program_statement
        . . .
        return expression;
}
```

The function called *name* is defined, which returns a value of type *return_type* and has formal parameters *param1, param2,...* . *param1* is declared to be of type *type1*, *param2* of type *type2*, and so on. This declaration of the argument types inside the formal parameter list is known as a *prototype* declaration.

When the compiler encounters a call to a function that has been previously defined or declared using the prototype format, the compiler will ensure that the correct number of arguments and types are passed to the function. If necessary, it will convert arguments (where feasible) so that they match the expected types. The usual conversion of argument types (float to double, and char and short int to int) is not done for calls to functions that have been previously defined or declared using the prototype format.

Using the prototype format, the function add

```
int add (int a, int b)
{
    return (a + b);
}
```

is defined to take two arguments, a and b, both of type int. Subsequently calling add with

```
add (10, 12.5)
```

will cause the integer 10 to be passed as the first argument, and the floating value 12.5 will be *automatically converted to an integer* and passed as the second argument.

If a function takes no arguments, the keyword void is used in the prototype declaration, as in

```
int print_message (void)
{
    ...
}
```

If the function takes a variable number of arguments, you must write a prototype declaration, using three dots (ellipsis) to indicate that an unspecified number of arguments may follow:

```
int myprintf ( char *fmt, ...)
{
    ...
}
```

Here, the first argument to myprintf is specified as a char pointer. It can be followed by any number of arguments of any type (and the compiler will convert them when passed in the usual way). Several functions in the standard library enable you to process a variable number of arguments in a portable way.

A prototype declaration for a function called `power` that takes `float` and `int` arguments and that returns a `long double` value looks like this:

```
long double power (float, int);
```

If desired, arbitrary names can be used inside the prototype declaration:

```
long double power (float x, int n);
```

The names are ignored by the compiler.

7.3 Function Pointers

The address operator `&` can be applied to a function name to produce a pointer to it, as can simply writing the function name (in both cases, the function name is not followed by the function call operator `()`).

If `fp` is a pointer to a function that takes no arguments, the corresponding function can be called either by writing `(*fp) ()` or `fp ()`.

Pointers to functions are distinguished not just by their return types but by the number of arguments and their types as well. For example,

```
long  (*fp) (int, int);
```

declares `fp` as a pointer to a function that returns a `long` and that takes two `int` arguments, whereas

```
long  (*fp2) (int, float);
```

declare `fp2` as a pointer to a function that returns a `long` and the takes an `int` and a `float` argument. `fp` and `fp2` are *different* pointer types.

◆ 9.0 Preprocessor Statements ◆

9.1 The #define Statement

The `#` operator is permitted in `#define` statements that take arguments. It is followed by the name of an argument to the macro. The preprocessor puts double quotes around the actual value passed to the macro when it's invoked. That is, it turns it into a character string. For example, consider this definition:

```
#define  printint(x)  printf (# x " = %d\n", x)
```

If you have an integer variable called `count`, then the call

```
printint (count);
```

will be expanded by the preprocessor into

```
printf ("count" " = %d\n", count);
```

or, equivalently,

```
printf ("count = %d\n", count);
```

The `##` operator is also allowed in `#define` statements that take arguments. It is preceded (or followed) by the name of an argument to the macro. The preprocessor takes the value that is passed when the macro is invoked and creates a single token from the argument to the macro and the token that follows (or precedes) it. For example, the macro definition

```
#define printx(n)  printf ("%d\n", x ## n );
```

with the call

```
printx (5)
```

produces

```
printf ("%d\n", x5);
```

The definition

```
#define printx(n) printf ("x" # n " = %d\n", x ## n );
```

with the call

```
printx(10)
```

produces

```
printf ("x10 = %d\n", x10);
```

after substitution and concatenation of the character strings.

Spaces are not required around the `#` and `##` operators.

Common Programming
Mistakes

The following list summarizes some of the more common programming mistakes made in C. They are not arranged in any particular order. Knowledge of these mistakes will hopefully help prevent you from making them in your own programs.

1. *Misplacing a semicolon.*

    Example

    ```
    if ( j == 100 );
        j = 0;
    ```

    In the above statements, the value of j will always be set to 0 due to the misplaced semicolon after the closed parenthesis. Remember, this semicolon is syntactically valid (it represents the null statement) and therefore no error is produced by the compiler. This same type of mistake is frequently made in while and for loops.

2. *Confusing the operator = with the operator ==.*

    This mistake is usually made inside an if, while, or do statement.

    Example

    ```
    if ( a = 2 )
        printf ("Your turn.\n");
    ```

    The above statement is perfectly valid, and has the effect of assigning 2 to a and then executing the printf call. The printf function will *always* be called since the value of the expression contained in the `if` statement will always be nonzero (its value will be 2).

3. *Omitting return type declarations.*

   Example

   ```
   result = square_root (value);
   ```

   If `square_root` is defined later in the program, or in another file, and is not explicitly declared otherwise, then the compiler will assume that this function returns a value of type `int`.

4. *Passing the wrong argument type to a function.*

   Example

   ```
   result = square_root (2);
   ```

   If the `square_root` function is expecting a floating point argument, then the above statement will produce erroneous results, since an integer value is being passed. Remember that the type cast operator can be used to explicitly force conversion of a value that is passed to a function.

5. *Confusing the precedences of the various operators.*

   Examples

   ```
   while ( c = getchar ()   !=   EOF )
       . . .


   if ( x & 0xF   ==   y )
       . . .
   ```

   In the first example, the value returned by `getchar` will be compared against the value `EOF` first. This is because the inequality test has higher precedence than the assignment operator. The value that will therefore be assigned to `c` will be the TRUE/FALSE result of the test: 1 if the value returned by `getchar` is not equal to `EOF`, and 0 otherwise.

   In the second example, the integer constant `0xF` will be compared against y first, since the equality test has higher precedence than any of the bitwise operators. The result of this test (0 or 1) will then be ANDed with the value of `x`.

6.   *Confusing a character constant and a character string.*

In the statement

```
text = 'a';
```

a single character is assigned to `text`. In the statement

```
text = "a";
```

a pointer to the character string `"a"` is assigned to `text`. Whereas, in the first case, `text` is normally declared to be a `char` variable, in the second case, it should be declared to be of type "pointer to `char`."

7.   *Using the wrong bounds for an array.*

Example

```
int  a[100], i, sum = 0;
    . . .
for ( i = 1;  i <= 100;  ++i )
    sum += a[i];
```

Valid subscripts of an array range from 0 through the number of elements minus one. Therefore, the above loop is incorrect since the last valid subscript of a is 99 and not 100. The writer of this statement also probably intended to start with the first element of the array; therefore, i should have been initially set to 0.

8.   *Forgetting to reserve an extra location in an array for the terminating null character of a string.*

Remember to declare character arrays so that they are large enough to contain the terminating null character. For example, the character string `"hello"` would require six locations in a character array.

9.   *Confusing the operator -> with the operator . when referencing structure members.*

Remember, the operator . is used for structure variables, while the operator -> is used for structure *pointer* variables. So, if x is a structure variable, then the notation x.m is used to reference the member m of x. On the other hand, if x is a pointer to a structure, then the notation x->m is used to reference the member m of the structure pointed to by x.

10. *Omitting the ampersand before nonpointer variables in a* scanf *call.*

    Example

    ```
    int   number;
          . . .
    scanf ("%d", number);
    ```

    Remember that all arguments appearing after the format string in a scanf call must be pointers.

11. *Using a pointer variable before it's initialized.*

    Example

    ```
    char  *char_pointer;

    *char_pointer = 'X';
    ```

    You can only apply the indirection operator to a pointer variable *after* you have set the variable to pointing somewhere. In this example, char_pointer is never set pointing to anything, so the assignment is not meaningful.

12. *Omitting the* break *statement at the end of a case in a* switch *statement.*

    Remember that if a break is not included at the end of a case, then execution will continue into the next case.

13. *Inserting a semicolon at the end of a preprocessor definition.*

    This usually happens because it becomes a matter of habit to end all statements with semicolons. Remember that everything appearing to the right of the defined name in the #define statement gets directly substituted into the program. So the definition

    ```
    #define   END_OF_DATA   999;
    ```

    would lead to a syntax error if used in an expression such as

    ```
    if ( value == END_OF_DATA )
         . . .
    ```

14. *Omitting parentheses around arguments in macro definitions.*

    Example

    ```
    #define    reciprocal(x)    1 / x
        . . .
    w = reciprocal (a + b);
    ```

    The preceding assignment statement would be incorrectly evaluated as:

    ```
    w = 1 / a + b;
    ```

15. *Leaving a blank space between the name of a macro and its argument list in the* *#define statement.*

    Example

    ```
    #define MIN (a,b)   ( ( (a) < (b) ) ? (a) : (b) )
    ```

    This definition is incorrect, as the preprocessor considers the first blank space after the defined name as the start of the definition for that name.

16. *Using an expression that has side effects in a macro call.*

    Example

    ```
    #define    SQUARE(x)    (x) * (x)
        . . .
    w = SQUARE (++v);
    ```

    The invocation of the SQUARE macro will cause v to be incremented *twice,* since this statement will be expanded by the preprocessor to

    ```
    w = (++v)  *  (++v);
    ```

The Standard C Library

The UNIX operating system provides the user with a vast selection of functions that may be called from a C program. This section does not list all of these functions, but rather some of the more commonly used ones that are available from the standard UNIX C library, as of System V Release 2. For a more thorough description of these routines, consult *Topics in C Programming* (Kochan & Wood, Hayden Books, 1987).

UNIX also offers a wide selection of math functions that are available from the math library `libm`.

If you're not using UNIX, you should find that most, if not all, of the functions described here are available.

◆ String Functions ◆

The following functions perform operations on null-terminated character strings. In the description of these routines, *s*, *s1*, and *s2* represent pointers to such character strings, *c* represents a single character, and *n* represents an integer.

```
char *strcat (s1, s2)
```
Concatenates the character string *s2* to the end of *s1*, placing a null character at the end of the final string. The function returns *s1*.

```
char *strchr (s, c)
```
Searches the string *s* for the first occurrence of the character *c*. If it is found, then a pointer to the character is returned; otherwise, the null pointer is returned.

```
int strcmp (s1, s2)
```
Compares strings *s1* and *s2* and returns a value less than zero if *s1* is lexicographically less than *s2*, equal to zero if *s1* is equal to *s2*, and greater than zero if *s1* is lexicographically greater than *s2*.

```
char *strcpy (s1, s2)
```
   Copies the string *s2* to *s1*, returning *s1*.

```
int strlen (s)
```
   Returns the number of characters in *s*, excluding the null character.

```
char *strncat (s1, s2, n)
```
   Concatenates *s2* to the end of *s1* until either the null character is reached or *n* characters have been concatenated, whichever occurs first. Returns *s1*.

```
int strncmp (s1, s2, n)
```
   Performs the same function as `strcmp`, except that, at most, *n* characters from the strings are compared.

```
char *strncpy (s1, s2)
```
   Copies *s2* to *s1* until either the null character is reached or *n* characters have been copied, whichever occurs first. Returns *s1*.

```
char *strrchr (s, c)
```
   Searches the string *s* for the last occurrence of the character *c*. If it is found, then a pointer to the character in *s* is returned; otherwise, the null pointer is returned.

◆ Character Functions ◆

The following functions deal with single characters. These are all implemented as macro definitions in the file `ctype.h`, which must be included in your program with the `#include` statement

```
#include <ctype.h>
```

Each of the macros that follow takes a single character *c* as an argument and returns a TRUE value (nonzero) if the test is satisfied, and a FALSE (zero) value otherwise. The specific octal values, as listed, are for an ASCII character set.

Name	*Test*
isalnum	Is *c* an alphanumeric character?
isalpha	Is *c* an alphabetic character?
isascii	Is *c* an ASCII character (octal 0-0177)?
iscntrl	Is *c* a control character (octal 0-037 or 0177)?
isdigit	Is *c* a digit character?
isgraph	Is *c* a graphics character (octal 041-0176)?
islower	Is *c* a lowercase letter?

isprint	Is c a printable character (including spaces)?
ispunct	Is c a punctuation character?
isspace	Is c a white space character (blank, newline, horizontal or vertical tab, or form-feed)?
isupper	Is c an uppercase letter?
isxdigit	Is c a hexadecimal digit character?

The following two functions are provided for performing character translation.

    int tolower (*c*)
        Returns the lowercase equivalent of the character c. If c is not an uppercase character, then c itself is returned.

    int toupper (*c*)
        Returns the uppercase equivalent of the character c. If c is not a lowercase letter, then c itself is returned.

◆ I/O Functions ◆

The following describes some of the more commonly used I/O functions from the C library. You should include the header file stdio.h at the front of any program that uses one of these functions, using the include statement

    #include <stdio.h>

Included in this file are definitions for many of the character functions and for the names EOF, NULL, stdin, stdout, stderr (all constant values), and FILE.

    In the descriptions that follow, *file_name*, *access_mode*, and *format* are pointers to null-terminated strings, *buffer* is a pointer to a character array, *file_pointer* is a pointer to a FILE structure, *n* and *size* are positive integer values, and *c* is a character.

    int fclose (*file_pointer*)
        Closes the file identified by *file_pointer*, and returns zero if the close is successful, EOF if an error occurs.

    int feof (*file_pointer*)
        Returns nonzero if the identified file has reached the end of the file and zero otherwise.

    int ferror (*file_pointer*)
        Checks for an error condition on the indicated file and returns zero if an error exists, and nonzero otherwise. (There is a related function clearerr, which can be used to reset an error condition on a file.)

int fflush (*file_pointer*)
Flushes (writes) any data from internal buffers to the indicated file, returning zero on success and the value EOF if an error occurs.

int fgetc (*file_pointer*)
Returns the next character from the file identified by *file_pointer*, or the value EOF if an end of file condition occurs (remember that this function returns an int).

char *fgets (*buffer, n, file_pointer*)
Reads characters from the indicated file, until either *n* - 1 character are read or until a newline character is read, whichever occurs first. Characters that are read are stored into the character array pointed to by *buffer*. If a newline character is read, then it *will* be stored in the array. If an end of file is reached or an error occurs, then the value NULL is returned; otherwise, *buffer* is returned.

FILE *fopen (*file_name, access_mode*)
Opens the specified file with the indicated access mode. Valid modes are "r" for reading, "w" for writing, "a" for appending to the end of an existing file, "r+" for read/write access starting at the beginning of an existing file, "w+" for read/write access (and the previous contents of the file, if it exists, are lost), and "a+" for read/write access with all writes going to the end of the file. If the file to be opened does not exist, then it will be created if the *access_mode* is write ("w", "w+"), or append ("a", "a+"). If a file is opened in append mode ("a" or "a+"), then it is not possible to overwrite existing data in the file. If the fopen call is successful, then a FILE pointer will be returned to be used to identify the file in subsequent I/O operations; otherwise, the value NULL is returned.

int fprintf (*file_pointer, format, arg1, arg2, ..., argn*)
Writes the specified arguments to the file identified by *file_pointer*, according to the format specified by the character string *format*. Format characters are the same as for the printf function (see Chapter 16). The number of characters written is returned.

int fputc (*c, file_pointer*)
Writes the character *c* to the file identified by *file_pointer*, returning *c* if the write is successful, and the value EOF otherwise.

int fputs (*buffer, file_pointer*)
Writes the characters in the array pointed to by *buffer* to the indicated file until the terminating null character in *buffer* is reached. A newline character is *not* automatically written to the file by this function. On failure, the value EOF is returned.

int fread (*buffer, size, n, file_pointer*)
Reads *n* items of data from the identified file into *buffer*. Each item of data is *size* bytes in length. For example, the call

```
fread (text, sizeof (char), 80, in_file)
```

reads 80 characters from the file identified by `in_file`, and stores them into the array pointed to by `text`. The function returns the number of characters that are successfully read.

`FILE *freopen` (*file_name, access_mode, file_pointer*)
Closes the file associated with *file_pointer*, and opens the file *file_name* with the specified *access_mode* (see the `fopen` function). The file that is opened is subsequently associated with *file_pointer*. If the `freopen` call is successful, then *file_pointer* will be returned; otherwise, the value `NULL` will be returned. The `freopen` function is frequently used to reassign `stdin`, `stdout`, or `stderr` in the program. For example, the call

```
freopen ("input_data", "r", stdin)
```

will have the effect of reassigning `stdin` to the file `input_data`, which will be opened in read access mode. Subsequent I/O operations performed with `stdin` will be performed with the file `input_data`, as if `stdin` had been redirected to this file when the program was executed.

`int fscanf` (*file_pointer, format, arg1, arg2, ..., argn*)
Data items are read from the file identified by *file_pointer*, according to the format specified by the character string *format*. The values that are read are stored into the arguments specified after *format*, each of which must be a pointer. The *format* characters that are allowed in *format* are the same as those for the `scanf` function (see Chapter 16). The `fscanf` function returns the number of items successfully read and assigned or the value `EOF` if end of file is reached before the first item is read.

`int fseek` (*file_pointer, offset, mode*)
Positions the indicated file to a point that is *offset* (a `long` integer) bytes from the beginning of the file, from the current position in the file, or from the end of the file, depending upon the value of *mode* (an integer). If *mode* equals 0, then positioning is relative to the beginning of the file. If *mode* equals 1, then positioning is relative to the current position in the file. If *mode* equals 2, then positioning is relative to the end of the file. If the `fseek` call is successful, then a nonzero value is returned; otherwise, zero is returned.

`long ftell` (*file_pointer*)
Returns the relative offset in bytes of the current position in the file identified by *file_pointer*, or -1 on error.

`int fwrite` *(buffer, size, n, file_pointer)*
Writes *n* items of data from *buffer* into the specified file. Each item of data is *size* bytes in length. Returns the number of items successfully written.

`int getc` *(file_pointer)*
Reads and returns the next character from the indicated file. The value `EOF` is returned if an error occurs or if the end of the file is reached.

`int getchar ()`
Reads and returns the next character from `stdin`. The value `EOF` is returned upon error or end of file.

`char *gets` *(buffer)*
Reads characters from `stdin` into *buffer* until a newline character is read. The newline character is *not* stored in *buffer*, and the character string is terminated with a null character. If an error occurs in performing the read, or if no characters are read, then the value `NULL` is returned; otherwise, *buffer* is returned.

`int printf` *(format, arg1, arg2, ..., argn)*
Writes the specified arguments to `stdout`, according to the format specified by the character string *format* (see Chapter 16). Returns the number of characters written.

`int putc` *(c, file_pointer)*
Writes the character *c* to the indicated file. On success, *c* is returned; otherwise, `EOF` is returned.

`int putchar` *(c)*
Writes the character *c* to `stdout`, returning *c* on success and the value `EOF` on failure.

`int puts` *(buffer)*
Writes the characters contained in *buffer* to `stdout` until a null character is encountered. A newline character is automatically written as the last character (unlike the `fputs` function). On error, the value `EOF` is returned.

`void rewind` *(file_pointer)*
Resets the indicated file back to the beginning of the file.

`int scanf` *(format, arg1, arg2, ..., argn)*
Reads items from `stdin` according to the format specified by the string *format* (see Chapter 16). The arguments that follow *format* must all be pointers. The number of items successfully read and assigned is returned by the function. The value `EOF` is returned if an end of file is encountered before any items have been read.

```
FILE *tmpfile ()
```
Creates and opens a temporary file in write update mode, returning a `FILE` pointer identifying the file, or `NULL` if an error occurs. The temporary file is automatically removed when the program terminates. (Functions called `tmpnam` and `tempnam` are also available for creating temporary file names.)

```
int ungetc (c, file_pointer)
```
Effectively "puts back" a character to the indicated file. The character is not actually written to the file but is placed in a buffer associated with the file. The next call to `getc` will return this character. The `ungetc` function can only be called to "put back" one character to a file at a time; that is, a read operation must be performed on the file before another call to `ungetc` can be made. The function returns *c* if the character is successfully "put back," or the value `EOF` otherwise.

♦ In-Memory Format Conversion Functions ♦

The functions `sprintf` and `sscanf` are provided for performing data conversion in memory. These functions are analogous to the `fprintf` and `fscanf` functions except a character string replaces the `FILE` pointer as the first argument.

```
int sprintf (buffer, format, arg1, arg2, ..., argn)
```
The specified arguments are converted according to the format specified by the character string *format* (see Chapter 16), and are placed into the character array pointed to by *buffer*. A null character is automatically placed at the end of the string inside *buffer*. The number of characters placed into *buffer* is returned, excluding the terminating null. As an example, the call

```
sprintf (text, "%d + %d", 20, 50)
```

will place the character string `"20 + 50"` into `text`.

```
int sscanf (buffer, format, arg1, arg2, ..., argn)
```
The values as specified by the character string *format* are "read" from buffer and stored into the corresponding pointer arguments that follow *format* (see Chapter 16). The number of items successfully assigned is returned by this function. As an example, the call

```
sscanf ("July 16", "%s%d", month, &day)
```

will store the string `"July"` inside `month` (assumed to be a character array) and will assign the integer value 16 to day (assumed to be an integer). As a more practical example, the code

```
if ( sscanf (argv[1], "%f", &fval) != 1 )
{
    fprintf (stderr, "Bad number: %s\n", argv[1]);
    exit (1);
}
```

will convert the first command line argument (pointed to by argv[1]) to a floating point number, and will check the value returned by sscanf to see if a number was successfully "read" from argv[1].

◆ Dynamic Memory Allocation Functions ◆

The following functions are available for allocating and freeing memory dynamically. For each of these functions, *n* and *size* represent unsigned integers, and *pointer* represents a character pointer.

char *calloc (*n, size*)

Allocates contiguous space for *n* items of data, where each item is *size* bytes in length. The allocated space is initially set to all zeroes. On success, a pointer to the allocated space is returned; on failure, the null pointer is returned.

void free (*pointer*)

Returns a block of memory pointed to by *pointer* that was previously allocated by a calloc, malloc, or realloc call.

char *malloc (*size*)

Allocates contiguous space of *size* bytes, returning a pointer to the beginning of the allocated block if successful, and, the null pointer otherwise.

char *realloc (*pointer, size*)

Changes the size of a previously allocated block to *size* bytes, returning a pointer to the new block (which may have moved if an increase of space was requested), or a null pointer if an error occurs.

Compiling Programs Under UNIX

This section summarizes many of the options that may be specified to the cc command when compiling programs under UNIX. For a description of other options that are available, consult your local UNIX documentation.

The general format of the cc command is:

cc   [*options*]   *file1 file2 file3 ...*

Each of the files listed on the cc command line can be a C source program, an assembler program, or a previously compiled C program (object program). A file name that end with the characters .c is treated as a source program by the compiler. The resulting object code for that program will be placed into a file having the same name as the source file, with the last two characters .o instead of .c. If a single file is compiled and linked with the cc command, then this .o file will be automatically deleted after linking is completed; otherwise, it will be retained.

A file name ending with the characters .o is treated as an object program and is therefore not compiled by the C compiler, but is automatically linked with other files specified to the cc command.

Finally, a file name that ends with .s is taken as an assembler source program and is automatically assembled. The resulting object program is placed into the corresponding .o file.

If a function from the Standard Library libc is referenced by any of the specified files, then it will automatically be linked with the program. If a function from another library is referenced, then the -l option must be specified with the name of the library to be searched (see the following options list).

If an executable object program is desired (the default), then in one of the files specified to the cc command, there must exist a function called main, which is where program execution will begin. The resulting executable object will be placed into the file a.out by default.

The following is a list of the some of the commonly used options:

-c   Specifies that the programs that are compiled are not to be linked, and also forces creation of a '.o' file, even if only one program is compiled.

-f   If your machine does not contain floating point hardware, then this option is required. (Program examples shown in this book that used types `float` or `double` require this option if your machine does not have floating point hardware.)

-o *file*   Specifies that the executable object program be placed in the file *file*, as opposed to `a.out`, which is the default.

-l *x*   This is actually an option that gets passed to the linker. The string *x* is an abbreviation for a library that is to be searched. If you want to use a function from a library other than the Standard Library `libc`, then you must include this option. For example, to use a function from the math library `libm`, the correct option would be `-lm`.

-I *dir*   Specifies that if an include file is not found in the same directory as the `.c` file, then the directory *dir* is to be searched. (This does not apply to the case where a full directory path name is specified in the `#include` statement.)

-D *name=def*
-D *name*   Defines the indicated *name* to the preprocessor, with the indicated definition. If *def* is not supplied, then *name* is defined as 1.

-O   Causes a special optimization program to be executed to improve the efficiency of the object program. It is generally a good idea to use this option when compiling a final version of the program.

Examples

```
cc x.c
```

This is the simplest form of the `cc` command. The C source program contained in `x.c` is compiled, and the resulting executable object program placed into the file `a.out`.

```
cc main.c mod2.o mod3.o -o search
```

This command causes the source program contained in the file `main.c` to be compiled and subsequently linked with the object programs contained in `mod2.o` and `mod3.o`. The executable object file will be named `search`, which can be executed simply by typing `search`.

```
cc -D MACHINE=2 x.c
```

This specifies that the source program contained in `x.c` is to be compiled, and that the name `MACHINE` is to have a defined value of 2 (see Chapter 13 for more details).

```
cc stats.c -lm
```

This causes the program `stats.c` to be compiled and linked with the UNIX math library. It is important that the `-lm` option be placed *after* the file name `stats.c`. This is because the linker only searches a library for those functions referenced by files appearing before the `-l` option on the `cc` command line.

The Program *lint*

The UNIX operating system provides a program called `lint` that can be used to help uncover bugs in a C program. `lint` can analyze a program contained in a single file, or a program contained in multiple files. In the latter case, `lint` will ensure that variables and functions are used consistently across the files. Since the features and options that are available under `lint` have changed over the past several years, you should check with your local UNIX documentation to find out the precise options that are available at your facility.

The following describes `lint` as of UNIX System V. For a more detailed discussion of `lint`, refer to the document, "LINT: a C Program Checker," *System V Programmer's Manual* (AT&T Bell Laboratories), and to *Topics in C Programming* (Kochan & Wood, Hayden Books).

The `lint` program may be executed simply by typing the command `lint`, followed by a single source file or a list of source files that you would like `lint` to check.

> lint *file1 file2 ...*

`lint` will analyze the specified file(s) and will issue a message if any of several conditions are detected. It will also automatically check your program against the Standard C Library (`libc`) to ensure that your arguments agree in number and in type to any routine used from the Library. `lint` will also make sure that if you're using a routine from the library that doesn't return an `int`, that it has been declared as such.

If you put the `-lm` option at the end of your `lint` command line, then `lint` will also check your program against the Math Library.

Among the conditions that `lint` checks for, `lint` will issue a message if it finds any of the following.

- Declared variables that are never used, arguments to functions that are not used by the function, or automatic variables that are used before being assigned a value.

- Program statements that cannot be reached, such as statements that immediately follow a `goto`, `break`, `continue`, or `return` and do not contain a label.

- Calls to a function in which the returned value is not used, and calls to a function in which a returned value is used yet no value is returned by the function. (If the function is defined or declared as `void` in the same file in which the function call appears, then the compiler will catch this one; otherwise, you need `lint`.)

- Function arguments that do not agree in type or in number with the arguments expected by the function (in this case, `floats` and `doubles` are considered interchangeable, as are `chars`, `shorts`, and `ints`— either signed or unsigned).

- Functions that return a value whose type is inconsistent with the (explictly or implicitly) declared return type for the function.

- Expressions in which the precedence of the various operators may have been confused.

- Expressions whose use may not be portable.

G

The ASCII Character Set

The following table lists the characters in the ASCII character set and their octal and hexadecimal equivalents.

Char	Oct	Hex	Char	Oct	Hex	Char	Oct	Hex	Char	Oct	Hex
nul	0	0	sp	40	20	@	100	40	`	140	60
soh	1	1	!	41	21	A	101	41	a	141	61
stx	2	2	"	42	22	B	102	42	b	142	62
etx	3	3	#	43	23	C	103	43	c	143	63
eot	4	4	$	44	24	D	104	44	d	144	64
enq	5	5	%	45	25	E	105	45	e	145	65
ack	6	6	&	46	26	F	106	46	f	146	66
bel	7	7	'	47	27	G	107	47	g	147	67
bs	10	8	(	50	28	H	110	48	h	150	68
ht	11	9	)	51	29	I	111	49	i	151	69
nl	12	A	*	52	2A	J	112	4A	j	152	6A
vt	13	B	+	53	2B	K	113	4B	k	153	6B
np	14	C	,	54	2C	L	114	4C	l	154	6C
cr	15	D	-	55	2D	M	115	4D	m	155	6D
so	16	E	.	56	2E	N	116	4E	n	156	6E
si	17	F	/	57	2F	O	117	4F	o	157	6F
dle	20	10	0	60	30	P	120	50	p	160	70
dc1	21	11	1	61	31	Q	121	51	q	161	71
dc2	22	12	2	62	32	R	122	52	r	162	72
dc3	23	13	3	63	33	S	123	53	s	163	73
dc4	24	14	4	64	34	T	124	54	t	164	74
nak	25	15	5	65	35	U	125	55	u	165	75
syn	26	16	6	66	36	V	126	56	v	166	76
etb	27	17	7	67	37	W	127	57	w	167	77
can	30	18	8	70	38	X	130	58	x	170	78
em	31	19	9	71	39	Y	131	59	y	171	79
sub	32	1A	:	72	3A	Z	132	5A	z	172	7A
esc	33	1B	;	73	3B	[	133	5B	{	173	7B
fs	34	1C	<	74	3C	\	134	5C	|	174	7C
gs	35	1D	=	75	3D	]	135	5D	}	175	7D
rs	36	1E	>	76	3E	^	136	5E	~	176	7E
us	37	1F	?	77	3F	_	137	5F	del	177	7F

Index

Topics in C Programming
Kochan and Wood

This advanced-level book for C programmers provides detailed coverage of structures and pointers—the most difficult concepts in the C language—and explores both the standard C library and the standard I/O library.

Experienced C programmers can examine the UNIX System Interface through discussions on controlling processes, pipes, and terminal I/O.

Topics covered include:

- Structures and Pointers
- The Standard C Library
- The Standard I/O Library
- UNIX System Interface
- Writing Terminal-Independent Programs with the "Curses" Library
- Debug and Performance Analysis of C Programs
- Generating Program Systems with "make"

400 Pages, 7½ x 9¾, Softbound
ISBN: 0-672-46290-7
No. 46290, $24.95

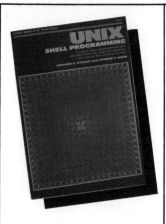

UNIX® Shell Programming
Kochan and Wood

Here's a complete, easy-to-understand introduction to UNIX shell programming. The book covers all the features of the standard shell, including the System V, Release 2 shell and the newer Korn shell. Many complete, practical programs are included, and the exercises provide reinforcement for each new shell application.

Topics covered include:

- A Review of the UNIX System
- What the Shell Is and What It Does
- Shell Programming Tools
- Writing Your Own Commands and Shell Variables
- Writing Shell Programs
- How to Set Up Program Loops
- Reading Data
- Your Environment
- Parameters
- The Rolo Program
- The Korn Shell
- The C Shell

432 Pages, 7 x 9¾, Softbound
ISBN: 0-8104-6309-1
No. 46309, $24.95

UNIX® System Security
Wood and Kochan

This practical guide to system security describes and provides programs for administrating passwords, security auditing, checking file permissions, securing terminals, DES data encryption, and setting up a restricted environment. Sources for the programs described are included.

If you're a UNIX user, administrator, or potential UNIX buyer, this excellent reference contains everything you need to know to make your system secure and keep it that way.

Topics covered include:

- A Perspective on Security
- Security for Users
- Security for Administrators
- Network Security
- Appendices Include:
  References, Security Commands and Functions, Permissions, Security Auditing Program, File Permission Program, Password Administration Program, Password Expiration Program, Terminal Security Program, SUID/SGID Shell Execution Program, Restricted Environment Program, DES Encryption Program, and SUID Patent

300 Pages, 7¼ x 10, Hardbound
ISBN: 0-8104-6267-2
No. 46267, $34.95

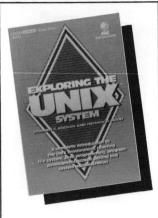

UNIX® Text Processing
Dale Dougherty and Tim O'Reilly

This practical, in-depth reference presents a range of useful UNIX tools that facilitate such word processing functions as format design, printing, and editing. It introduces the tools and illustrates how they can work together to create large writing projects such as technical manuals, reports, and proposals.

With the examples in this text you can put your knowledge to work immediately. It provides examples of integrating the text processing tools of the UNIX environment in document preparation. It also mentions other useful UNIX capabilities and suggests directions for future study.

Topics covered include:

- What's in the UNIX Toolbox for Writers
- Fundamental Concepts
- Coding and Formatting a Document
- Essential UNIX Commands
- Producing Tables and Mathematical Equations
- Shell Scripts
- Advanced NROFF/TROFF Operations
- Custom Macros for Document Formatting
- Building Documentation Tools
- Integrated UNIX

672 Pages, 7½ x 9¾, Softbound
ISBN: 0-672-46291-5
No. 46291, $26.95

Exploring the UNIX® System
Kochan and Wood

Everything you need to know to maximize the true potential of the UNIX operating system is covered in this book. It teaches you how to use the UNIX system, including the newer UNIX System V, Release 2 version. It provides a vast assortment of commands that perform small, well-defined functions along with the tools needed to combine these commands to perform more sophisticated functions.

Topics covered include:

- Introduction
- What Is an Operating System?
- The UNIX File System
- Getting Started
- Using the UNIX System
- The Old Shell Game
- Screen Editing with *vi*
- In the Office
- Program Development
- Security
- Communications
- Administrating Your System
- Appendices Include: For More Information, Overview of Commands, Complete Command Summary, Administrative Commands, Comparison of sh and csh, Adding New Users

380 Pages, 7 x 9¾, Softbound
ISBN: 0-8104-6268-0
No. 46268, $22.95

UNIX® System Administration
Fiedler and Hunter

This is an essential guide for everyone who runs a UNIX operating system—UNIX owners, operators, and administrators. It contains the tricks and shortcuts to making your system run easier.

The book begins with a system overview and then proceeds through setting up file systems, adding and removing users from the system, and improving system security. Troubleshooting charts and ready-to-run programs are included.

Topics covered include:

- The System Administrator's Overview of UNIX
- Bringing Up the System
- Checking the File System
- Where Everything Is and How to Find It
- Mounting and Unmounting File Systems
- Shutting Down the System
- Adding and Removing Users for the System
- Backups
- Security
- Terminals
- Printers on the UNIX System
- Modems and an Even Bigger World
- Shell Programming
- Assorted Administration Tips
- Appendices Include: Where to Learn More, Talking to the Outside World, A Typical UUCP Connection

336 Pages, 7 x 9¾, Softbound
ISBN: 0-8104-6289-3
No. 46289, $24.95

Advanced C Primer++
Stephen Prata, The Waite Group

Programmers, students, managers, and hackers alike, will learn to master the C programming language. Anyone who knows the basics of C will learn practical C tips never before published. This in-depth coverage gives you a rare and complete examination of video access ports, segmented memory, and registers.

Advanced C Primer++ takes the reader further than most C books on the market, showing how to manipulate the hardware of the IBM PC family of computers directly from C. Readers learn how to access routines in the Read Only Memory (ROM) of an IBM PC, how to use system calls in PC DOS from C and i/o ports, how to control the video screen, and to integrate assembly routines into C programs.

Topics covered include:

- Advanced C Programming
- Register and Bit Level System Control
- Hardware Operation for Beginners and Experienced Users
- Advanced Use of Pointers, Functions, Storage Classes, Arrays and Structures
- C Library Access
- Use of Assembly Language Modules
- Binary and Text File Input and Output

512 Pages, 7½ x 9¾, Softbound
ISBN: 0-672-22486-0
No. 22486, $23.95

C Primer Plus, Revised Edition

Mitchell Waite, Stephen Prata, and Donald Martin, The Waite Group

This revised and expanded edition of a best-seller presents everything you should know to begin programming in the exciting C language, now used by over 80 percent of the software community. The book is organized for quick learning and encourages problem solving through questions and exercises.

Topics covered include:

- Structure of a Simple C Program
- Variables, Constants, and Data Types
- Character Strings, *#define, print( ), and scanf( )*
- Operators, Expressions, and Statements
- Input/Output Functions and Redirection
- Choosing Alternatives: *if, else,* Relational and Conditional Operators
- Loops and Other Control Aids
- How to "Function" Properly
- Storage Classes and Program Development
- The C Preprocessor
- Arrays and Pointers
- Character Strings and String Functions
- Structures and Other Data Delights
- The C Library and File I/O
- Bit Fiddling, Keywords, Binary Numbers, IBM® PC Music, and More

576 Pages, 7½ x 9¾, Softbound
ISBN: 0-672-22582-4
No. 22582, $24.95

Microsoft® C Programming for the IBM®

Robert Lafore, The Waite Group

Programmers using the Microsoft C compiler can learn to write useful and marketable programs with this entry level book on Microsoft C programming.

This title is a tutorial geared specifically to the IBM PC family of computers. Unlike other introductory C titles, it is written for the Microsoft C compiler. It provides special coverage of IBM features such as sound, color graphics including CGA and EGA, keyboard, variable storage, and character graphics.

Topics covered include:

- Getting Started
- Building Blocks
- Loops
- Decisions
- Functions
- Arrays and Strings
- Pointers
- Keyboard and Cursor
- Structures, Unions, and ROM Bios
- Memory and the Monochrome Display
- CGA and EGA Color Graphics
- Files Preprocessor
- Serial Ports and Telecommunications
- Larger Programs
- Advanced Variables
- Appendices Include: Supplemental Programs, Hexadecimal Numbering, IBM Character Codes, and a Bibliography

640 Pages, 7½ x 9¾, Softbound
ISBN: 0-672-22515-8
No. 22515, $24.95

Turbo C® Programming for the IBM®

Robert Lafore, The Waite Group

This entry-level text teaches readers the C language while also helping them write useful and marketable programs for the IBM PC, XT, AT, and PC/2.

This tutorial is based on Borland's new Turbo C compiler with its powerful integrated environment that makes it easy to edit, compile, and run C programs. The author's proven hands-on intensive approach includes example programs, exercises, and questions and answers and covers CGA and EGA graphic modes.

Topics covered include:

- C Building Blocks
- Loops
- Decisions
- Functions
- Arrays and Strings
- Pointers
- Keyboard and Cursor
- Structures, Unions, and ROM BIOS
- Memory and the Character Display
- CGA and EGA Color Graphics
- Files
- Larger Programs
- Advanced Variables
- Appendices Include: References, Hexadecimal Numbering, Bibliography, ASCII Chart, and Answers to Questions and Exercises

608 Pages, 7½ x 9¾, Softbound
ISBN: 0-672-22614-6
No. 22614, $22.95

C Programmer's Guide to Serial Communications

Joe Campbell

Written for those with an understanding of assembly language and C programming this sequel to the best-selling *The RS-232 Solution* offers comprehensive coverage of C programming and serial and asynchronous communications. It stresses the generality of program design and the portability of C code across operating environments such as PC DOS™ and CP/M.®

Topics covered include:

- ASCII
- Fundamentals of Asynchronous Technology
- Flow Control and Transfer Protocols
- RS-232 and Modems
- The UART—A Conceptual Model
- Designing an SIO Library
- Portability Considerations
- Timer Functions
- Functions for Baud Rate and Data Format
- Functions for RS-232 Input and Output
- Miscellaneous I/O Functions
- Formatted Output and Input
- Smartmodem Programming
- Xmodem File Transfer
- Interrupts

672 Pages, 7½ x 9¾, Softbound
ISBN: 0-672-22584-0
No. 22584, $26.95

C with Excellence: Programming Proverbs
Henry Ledgard with John Tauer

C programmers will learn how to increase their programming skills and to write carefully constructed and readable programs with this handbook on C programming. Its clear and concise style provides both the novice and the expert programmer with guidelines or "proverbs" for writing high-quality, error-free software.

The reader familiar with the fundamentals of C, BASIC, or Pascal will be able to apply these principles to develop systems and application software as well as write C programs that can be easily ported from one microcomputer to another.

After introducing the 24 "proverbs" and their applications, this handbook focuses on the entire development process from conceptualizing to coding, documenting, testing, debugging, and maintaining and modifying programs.

Topics covered include:

■ Programming Proverbs
■ Structure Is Logic
■ Coding the Program
■ Global Variables, Selecting Names, Recursion, and Efficiency
■ Top-down Programming
■ Appendices Include: Summary of Program Standards and a Program for Kriegspiel Checkers

288 Pages, 7½ x 9¾, Softbound
ISBN: 0-672-46294-X
No. 46294, $18.95

Programming in ANSI C
Stephen G. Kochan

This comprehensive programming guide is the newest title in the Hayden Books C Library, written by the series editor Stephen G. Kochan. A tutorial in nature, the book teaches the beginner how to write, compile and execute programs even with no previous experience with C.

The book's clear, logical style provides a well-organized instruction to C with over 90 program examples covering all features of the language. It details such C essentials as program looping, decision making, arrays, functions, structures, character strings, bit operations, and enumerated data types. Examples are complete with step-by-step explanations of each procedure and routine involved as well as end-of-chapter exercises, making it ideally suited for classroom use.

Topics covered include:

■ Introduction to Fundamentals
■ Writing a Program in ANSI C
■ Variables, Data Types, and Arithmetic Expressions
■ Program Looping
■ Making Decisions
■ Arrays, Functions, Structures
■ Character Strings, Pointers
■ Operations on Bits
■ The Preprocessor
■ More on Data Types
■ Working with Larger Programs
■ Input and Output
■ Miscellaneous Features and Topics
■ Appendices: ANSI C Language Summary, The UNIX C Library, Compiling Programs Under UNIX, The Program LINT, The ASCII Character Set

450 Pages, 7½ x 9¾, Softbound
ISBN: 0-672-48408-0
No. 48408, $24.95

Advanced C: Tips and Techniques
Paul L. Anderson and Gail C. Anderson

If you have a working knowledge of the C language and want to enhance your programming skills, the examples and techniques found in this new book are just what you need. It is an in-depth look at the C programming language with special emphasis on portability, execution efficiency, and application techniques.

With entire chapters devoted to special areas of C such as debugging techniques, C's run-time environment, and a memory object allocator, the book contains detailed explanations and examples that will show you how to speed up your C programs. Techniques for creating and deciphering expressions, moving data, and coding expressions that execute predictably are included as well as end-of-chapter exercises that help you learn what has been explained.

Topics covered include:

■ C Refresher
■ The Run-Time Environment
■ Bits of C
■ There's No Such Thing as an Array
■ A Closer Look at C
■ C Debugging Techniques
■ A Memory Object Allocator
■ Appendices: Portable C Under UNIX System V, Microsoft C Under XENIX, Microsoft C Under DOS, Turbo C Under DOS

325 Pages, 7½ x 9¾, Softbound
ISBN: 0-672-48417-X
No. 48417, $24.95

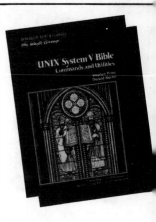

UNIX® System V Bible
Stephen Prata and Donald Martin, The Waite Group

You'll never have to open the UNIX manual again! This is a comprehensive reference to UNIX commands and utilities, focusing on the basic and advanced command groups found in standard UNIX System V manuals.

Commands are listed alphabetically and explained in down-to-earth language. Each entry states the purpose of a command, what it does, and how it is used. A graduated set of example programs goes far beyond the UNIX manuals, showing you each command in several different situations.

Features of this unique resource include:

■ Detailed Table of Contents for Quick Reference
■ Cross-Referencing of Commands and Features
■ Friendly Format for Beginning and Advanced Users
■ Coverage of All Major UNIX Features
■ Guidance to UNIX Command Idiosyncracies

640 Pages, 7½ x 9¾, Softbound
ISBN: 0-672-22562-X
No. 22562, $24.95